Stanley Nemeth

ESSAYS AND INTRODUCTIONS

W. B. YEATS

By John Butler Yeats the Elder
Courtesy of the National Gallery of Ireland

W. B. YEATS

Essays
and
Introductions

NEW YORK

THE MACMILLAN COMPANY

1961

CONTENTS

Contents

INTRODUCTION

Wᴇɴ I ᴡᴀs ᴛʜɪʀᴛʏ I thought the best of modern pictures were four or five portraits by Watts (I disliked his allegorical pictures—had not allegory spoiled Edmund Spenser?); four or five pictures by Madox Brown; four or five early Millais; four or five Rossettis where there are several figures engaged in some dramatic action; and an indefinite number of engravings by William Blake who was my particular study. When I was thirty-five or so a woman of genius asked me to defend her against a German connoisseur. She had made her beautiful house a shrine for certain late Burne-Jones's.

> The Burne-Jones Cartoons
> Have preserved her eyes.

When I arrived he had firmly planted on a drawing-room chair a picture by Renoir or perhaps an imitator, of a fat, naked woman lying on a Turkey carpet and had begun to call Burne-Jones empty and obsolete. She took me to another room and reproached me for keeping silent, but excused me as I must be upset by the connoisseur's 'over-dressed wife.' I could not excuse myself because I admired that slight, elegant, pale lady.

A little later poets younger than myself, especially the one I knew best, began to curse that romantic subject-matter which English literature seemed to share

¹ Written for a complete edition of Yeats's works which was never produced.

with all great literature, those traditional metres which seemed to have grown up with the language, and still, though getting much angrier, I was silent. I was silent because I am a timid man except before a piece of paper or rioters at the Abbey Theatre, and even there my courage is limited to certain topics. Perhaps I am a better man than I think, perhaps some part of my timidity is a dread of speaking ill-chosen words, of reproving Mr. Wells, let us say, with the voice of Bulwer-Lytton; or perhaps there is some censorship like that of the psycho-analysts—yes, there must be a censorship. Now that I have all my critical prose before me, much seems an evasion, a deliberate turning away. Can I do better now that I am almost beyond caring?

I have never said clearly that I condemn all that is not tradition, that there is a subject-matter which has descended like that 'deposit' certain philosophers speak of. At the end of his essay upon 'Style' Pater says that a book written according to the principles he has laid down will be well written, but whether it is a great book or not depends upon subject-matter. This subject-matter is something I have received from the generations, part of that compact with my fellow men made in my name before I was born. I cannot break from it without breaking from some part of my own nature, and sometimes it has come to me in super-normal experience; I have met with ancient myths in my dreams, brightly lit; and I think it allied to the wisdom or instinct that guides a migratory bird.

A table of values, heroic joy always, intellectual curiosity and so on—and a public theme: in Japan the mountain scenery of China; in Greece its cyclic tales; in Europe the Christian mythology; this or that national theme. I speak of poets and imaginative writers; the great realistic novelists almost without exception describe familiar scenes and people; realism is always topical, it has for public theme the public itself. Flaubert excused the failure of the principal character in his *Salammbô* by the words 'I could not visit her.' I think of the German actress who said to a reporter, 'To know a man you must talk with him, eat with him, sleep with him. That is how I know Mr. Bernard Shaw.' Then too I would have all the arts draw together; recover their ancient association, the painter painting what the poet has written, the musician setting the poet's words to simple airs, that the horse-man and the engine-driver may sing them at their work. Nor am I for a changeless tradition. I would rejoice if a rich betrothed man asked Mr. T. S. Eliot and the dancer Ninette de Valois to pick a musician and compose a new marriage service, for such a service might restore a lost subject-matter to the imaginative arts and be good for the clergy. I admit other themes, even those that have no tradition; I have never blamed the brothers Caracci for painting the butcher's shop they came from, and why should not that fat, naked woman look like pork? But those themes we share and inherit, so long as they engage our emotions, come first.

When that is no longer possible we are broken off and separate, some sort of dry faggot, and the time has come to read criticism and talk of our point of view.

Introduction

I thought when I was young—Walt Whitman had
something to do with it—that the poet, painter, and
musician should do nothing but express themselves.
When the laboratories, pulpits, and newspapers had
imposed themselves in the place of tradition the thought
was our protection. It may be so still in the provinces,
but sometimes when the provinces are out of earshot
I may speak the truth. A poet is justified not by the
expression of himself, but by the public he finds or
creates; a public made by others ready to his hand if he
is a mere popular poet, but a new public, a new form of
life, if he is a man of genius. Somebody saw a woman
of exuberant beauty coming from a public-house with
a pot of beer and commended her to Rossetti; twenty
years later Mrs. Langtry called upon Watts and delighted him with her simplicity. Lady Gregory had the
story from Watts himself. Two painters created their
public; two types of beauty decided what strains of
blood would most prevail.

I say against all the faggots that it is our first business
to paint, or describe, desirable people, places, states of
mind. Rimbaud showed in a famous poem that the
picking of lice was a good lawful theme for the Silver
Age; the radical critics encourage our painters to decorate the walls with those cubes, triangles, ovoids, that
are all stiff under the touch, or with gods and goddesses,
distorted by Rubensesque exaggeration, dulled by hard
doll-like faces that they may chill desire. We have
arrived at that point where in every civilisation Caesar
is killed, Alexander catches some complaint and dies;
personality is exhausted, that conscious, desirous,

Introduction

shaping fate rules. But a relative of mine wears silver, many rings, and turns from gold with indifference; there are poetry societies that understand what I never could, books of prosody, and the art schools are more intelligent every day. (I have written of all these things in *A Vision*, but that book is intended, to use a phrase of Jacob Boehme's, for my 'schoolmates only.')

W. B. Y.

1937

I
IDEAS OF GOOD AND EVIL
1896–1903

WHAT IS 'POPULAR POETRY'?

I THINK IT WAS A YOUNG IRELAND SOCIETY that set my mind running on 'popular poetry.' We used to discuss everything that was known to us about Ireland, and especially Irish literature and Irish history. We had no Gaelic, but paid great honour to the Irish poets who wrote in English, and quoted them in our speeches. I could have told you at that time the dates of the birth and death, and quoted the chief poems, of men whose names you have not heard, and perhaps of some whose names I have forgotten. I knew in my heart that the most of them wrote badly, and yet such romance clung about them, such a desire for Irish poetry was in all our minds, that I kept on saying, not only to others but to myself, that most of them wrote well, or all but well. I had read Shelley and Spenser and had tried to mix their styles together in a pastoral play which I have now come to dislike much, and yet I do not think Shelley or Spenser ever moved me as did these poets. I thought one day—I can remember the very day when I thought it—'If somebody could make a style which would not be an English style and yet would be musical and full of colour, many others would catch fire from him, and we would have a really great school of ballad poetry in Ireland. If these poets, who have never ceased to fill the newspapers and the ballad-books with their verses, had a good tradition they would write beautifully and move everybody as they move me.' Then a little later on I thought, 'If they had something else to write about besides political opinions, if more of them would write about the beliefs of the people like Allingham, or about old legends like Ferguson, they would find it easier to get a style.' Then with a deliberateness that still surprises me, for in my heart of hearts I have never been quite certain that one should be more than an artist, that even patriotism is more than an impure desire in an artist, I set to work to find a style and things to write about that the ballad-writers might be the better.

They are no better, I think, and my desire to make them so was, it may be, one of the illusions Nature holds before one, because she knows that the gifts she has to give are not worth troubling about. It is for her sake that we must stir ourselves, but we would not trouble to get out of bed in the morning, or to leave our chairs once we are in them, if she had not her conjuring bag. She wanted a few verses from me, and because it would not have seemed worth while taking so much trouble to see my books lie on a few drawing-room tables, she filled my head with thoughts of making a whole literature, and plucked me out of the Dublin art schools where I should have stayed drawing from the round, and sent me into a library to read bad translations from the Irish, and at last down into Connacht to sit by turf fires. I wanted to write 'popular poetry' like those Irish poets, for I believed that all good literatures were popular, and even cherished the fancy that the Adelphi melodrama, which I had never seen, might be good literature, and I hated what I called the coteries. I thought that one must write without care, for that was of the coteries, but with a gusty energy that would put all straight if it came out of the right heart. I had a conviction, which indeed I have still, that one's verses should hold, as in a mirror, the colours of one's own climate and scenery in their right proportion; and, when I found my verses too full of the reds and yellows Shelley gathered in Italy, I thought for two days of setting things right, not as I should now by making my rhythms faint and nervous and filling my images with a certain coldness, a certain wintry wildness, but by eating little and sleeping upon a board. I felt indignant with Matthew Arnold because he complained that somebody, who had translated Homer into a ballad measure, had tried to write epic to the tune of 'Yankee Doodle.' It seemed to me that it did not matter what tune one wrote to, so long as that gusty energy came often enough and strongly enough. And I delighted in Victor Hugo's book upon Shakespeare, because he abused critics and coteries and thought that Shakespeare wrote without care or premeditation and to please everybody. I would indeed have had every illusion had I believed in that straightforward logic, as of newspaper articles, which so tickles an ignorant ear; but I always knew that the line of Nature is crooked, that, though we dig the canal-beds as straight as we can, the rivers run hither and thither in their wildness.

From that day to this I have been busy among the verses and stories that the people make for themselves, but I had been busy a very little while before I knew that what we call 'popular poetry' never came from the people at all. Longfellow, and Campbell, and Mrs.

Hemans, and Macaulay in his *Lays*, and Scott in his longer poems are the poets of a predominant portion of the middle class, of people who have unlearned the unwritten tradition which binds the unlettered, so long as they are masters of themselves, to the beginning of time and to the foundation of the world, and who have not learned the written tradition which has been established upon the unwritten. I became certain that Burns, whose greatness has been used to justify the littleness of others, was in part a poet of this portion of the middle class, because though the farmers he sprang from and lived among had been able to create a little tradition of their own, less a tradition of ideas than of speech, they had been divided by religious and political changes from the images and emotions which had once carried their memories backward thousands of years. Despite his expressive speech which sets him above all other popular poets, he has the triviality of emotion, the poverty of ideas, the imperfect sense of beauty of a poetry whose most typical expression is in Longfellow. Longfellow has his popularity, in the main, because he tells his story or his idea so that one needs nothing but his verses to understand it. No words of his borrow their beauty from those that used them before, and one can get all that there is in story and idea without seeing them as if moving before a half-faded curtain embroidered with kings and queens, their loves and battles and their days out hunting, or else with holy letters and images of so great antiquity that nobody can tell the god or goddess they would commend to an unfading memory. Poetry that is not

6

What is 'Popular Poetry'?

'popular poetry' presupposes, indeed, more than it says, though we, who cannot know what it is to be disinherited, only understand how much more, when we read it in its most typical expressions, in the *Epipsychidion* of Shelley, or in Spenser's description of the gardens of Adonis, or when we meet the misunderstandings of others. Go down into the street and read to your baker or your candlestick-maker any poem which is not 'popular poetry.' I have heard a baker, who was clever enough with his oven, deny that Tennyson could have known what he was writing when he wrote, 'Warming his five wits, the white owl in the belfry sits,' and once when I read out Omar Khayyám to one of the best of candlestick-makers, he said, 'What is the meaning of "I came like water and like wind I go"?' Or go down into the street with some thought whose bare meaning must be plain to everybody; take with you Ben Jonson's 'Beauty like sorrow dwelleth everywhere,' and find out how utterly its enchantment depends on an association of beauty with sorrow which written tradition has from the unwritten, which had it in its turn from ancient religion; or take with you these lines in whose bare meaning also there is nothing to stumble over, and find out what men lose who are not in love with Helen—

> Brightness falls from the air,
> Queens have died young and fair,
> Dust hath closed Helen's eye.

I pick my examples at random, for I am writing where I have no books to turn the pages of, but one

7

need not go east of the sun or west of the moon in so simple a matter.

On the other hand, when Walt Whitman writes in seeming defiance of tradition, he needs tradition for protection, for the butcher and the baker and the candlestick-maker grow merry over him when they meet his work by chance. Nature, being unable to endure emptiness, has made them gather conventions which cannot hide that they are low-born things though copies, as from far off, of the dress and manners of the well-bred and the well-born. The gatherers mock all expression that is wholly unlike their own, just as little boys in the street mock at strangely dressed people and at old men who talk to themselves.

There is only one kind of good poetry, for the poetry of the coteries, which presupposes the written tradition, does not differ in kind from the true poetry of the people, which presupposes the unwritten tradition. Both are alike strange and obscure, and unreal to all who have not understanding, and both, instead of that manifest logic, that clear rhetoric of the 'popular poetry,' glimmer with thoughts and images whose 'ancestors were stout and wise,' 'anigh to Paradise' 'ere yet men knew the gift of corn.' It may be that we know as little of their descent as men knew of 'the man born to be a king' when they found him in that cradle marked with the red lion crest, and yet we know somewhere in the heart that they have been sung in temples, in ladies' chambers, and quiver with a recognition our nerves have been shaped to by a thousand emotions. If men did not remember or half remember impossible things, and, it may be, if the worship of sun and moon had not left a faint reverence behind it, what Aran fisher-girl would sing:—

'It is late last night the dog was speaking of you; the snipe was speaking of you in her deep marsh. It is you are the lonely bird throughout the woods; and that you may be without a mate until you find me.

'You promised me and you said a lie to me, that you would be before me where the sheep are flocked. I gave a whistle and three hundred cries to you; and I found nothing there but a bleating lamb.

'You promised me a thing that was hard for you, a ship of gold under a silver mast; twelve towns and a market in all of them, and a fine white court by the side of the sea.

'You promised me a thing that is not possible; that you would give me gloves of the skin of a fish; that you would give me shoes of the skin of a bird, and a suit of the dearest silk in Ireland.

'My mother said to me not to be talking with you, to-day or to-morrow or on Sunday. It was a bad time she took for telling me that, it was shutting the door after the house was robbed. . . .

'You have taken the east from me, you have taken the west from me, you have taken what is before me and what is behind me; you have taken the moon, you have taken the sun from me, and my fear is great you have taken God from me.'

The Gael of the Scottish islands could not sing his beautiful song over a bride, had he not a memory of the belief that Christ was the only man who measured

9

six feet and not a little more or less, and was perfectly
shaped in all other ways, and if he did not remember
old symbolical observances:——

> I bathe thy palms
> In showers of wine,
> In the cleansing fire,
> In the juice of raspberries,
> In the milk of honey.
>
> .   .   .   .   .
>
> Thou art the joy of all joyous things,
> Thou art the light of the beam of the sun,
> Thou art the door of the chief of hospitality,
> Thou art the surpassing pilot star,
> Thou art the step of the deer of the hill,
> Thou art the step of the horse of the plain,
> Thou art the grace of the sun rising,
> Thou art the loveliness of all lovely desires.
>
> The lovely likeness of the Lord
> Is in thy pure face,
> The loveliest likeness that was upon earth.

I soon learned to cast away one other illusion of
'popular poetry.' I learned from the people themselves,
before I learned it from any book, that they cannot
separate the idea of an art or a craft from the idea of a
cult with ancient technicalities and mysteries. They can
hardly separate mere learning from witchcraft, and are
fond of words and verses that keep half their secret to
themselves. Indeed, it is certain that before the counting-house had created a new class and a new art without
breeding and without ancestry, and set this art and this
class between the hut and the castle, and between the

hut and the cloister, the art of the people was as closely mingled with the art of the coteries as was the speech of the people that delighted in rhythmical animation, in idiom, in images, in words full of far-off suggestion, with the unchanging speech of the poets.

Now I see a new generation in Ireland which discusses Irish literature and history in Young Ireland Societies, and societies with newer names, and there are far more than when I was a boy who would make verses for the people. They have the help, too, of a vigorous journalism, and this journalism sometimes urges them to desire the direct logic, the clear rhetoric of 'popular poetry.' It sees that Ireland has no cultivated minority, and it does not see, though it would cast out all English things, that its literary ideal belongs more to England than to other countries. I have hope that the new writers will not fall into its illusion, for they write in Irish, and for a people the counting-house has not made forgetful. Among the seven or eight hundred thousand who have had Irish from the cradle, there is, perhaps, nobody who has not enough of the unwritten tradition to know good verses from bad ones, if he have enough mother-wit. Among all that speak English in Australia, in America, in Great Britain, are there many more than the ten thousand the prophet saw who have enough of the written tradition education has set in room of the unwritten to know good verses from bad ones, even though their mother-wit has made them Ministers of the Crown or what you will? Nor can things be better till that ten thousand have gone hither and thither to preach their faith that 'the imagination

is the man himself,' and that the world as imagination
sees it is the durable world, and have won men as did
the disciples of Him who—

> His seventy disciples sent
> Against religion and government.

1901

Speaking to the Psaltery

SPEAKING TO THE PSALTERY

I

I HAVE ALWAYS KNOWN that there was something I disliked about singing, and I naturally dislike print and paper, but now at last I understand why, for I have found something better. I have just heard a poem spoken with so delicate a sense of its rhythm, with so perfect a respect for its meaning, that if I were a wise man and could persuade a few people to learn the art I would never open a book of verses again. A friend, who was here a few minutes ago, has sat with a beautiful stringed instrument upon her knee, her fingers passing over the strings, and has spoken to me some verses from Shelley's *Skylark* and Sir Ector's lamentations over the dead Launcelot out of the *Morte d'Arthur* and some of my own poems. Wherever the rhythm was most delicate, and wherever the emotion was most ecstatic, her art was most beautiful, and yet, although she sometimes spoke to a little tune, it was never singing, as we sing to-day, never anything but speech. A singing note, a word chanted as they chant in churches, would have spoiled everything; nor was it reciting, for she spoke to a notation as definite as that of song, using the instrument, which murmured sweetly and faintly, under the spoken sounds, to give her the changing notes. Another speaker could have repeated all her effects, except those which came from her own beautiful voice, a voice that would have given her fame if the only art that offers the speaking voice its perfect

opportunity were as well known among us as it was
known in the ancient world.

II

Since I was a boy I have always longed to hear
poems spoken to a harp, as I imagined Homer to have
spoken his, for it is not natural to enjoy an art only
when one is by oneself. Whenever one finds a fine verse
one wants to read it to somebody, and it would be
much less trouble and much pleasanter if we could all
listen, friend by friend, lover by beloved. Images used
to rise up before me, as I am sure they have arisen before
nearly everybody else who cares for poetry, of wild-
eyed men speaking harmoniously to murmuring wires
while audiences in many-coloured robes listened,
hushed and excited. Whenever I spoke of my desire to
anybody they said I should write for music, but when I
heard anything sung I did not hear the words, or if
I did their natural pronunciation was altered and their
natural music was altered, or it was drowned in another
music which I did not understand. What was the good
of writing a love-song if the singer pronounced love
'lo-o-o-o-o-ve,' or even if he said 'love,' but did not
give it its exact place and weight in the rhythm? Like
every other poet, I spoke verses in a kind of chant
when I was making them; and sometimes, when I was
alone on a country road, I would speak them in a loud
chanting voice, and feel that if I dared I would speak
them in that way to other people. One day I was walking through a Dublin street with Mr. George Russell

('A.E.'), and he began speaking his verses out aloud with the confidence of those who have the inner light. He did not mind that people stopped and looked after him even on the far side of the road, but went on through poem after poem. Like myself, he knew nothing of music, but was certain that he had written them to a manner of music, and he had once asked somebody who played on a wind instrument of some kind, and then a violinist, to write out the music and play it. The violinist had played it, or something like it, but had not written it down; but the man with the wind instrument said it could not be played because it contained quarter-tones and would be out of tune. We were not at all convinced by this, and one day, when we were staying with a Galway friend who is a learned musician, I asked him to listen to our verses, and to the way we spoke them. Mr. Russell found to his surprise that he did not make every poem to a different tune, and to the surprise of the musician that he did make them all to two quite definite tunes, which are, it seems, like very simple Arabic music. It was, perhaps, to some such music, I thought, that Blake sang his *Songs of Innocence* in Mrs. Williams' drawing-room, and perhaps he, too, spoke rather than sang. I, on the other hand, did not often compose to a tune, though I sometimes did, yet always to notes that could be written down and played on my friend's organ, or turned into something like a Gregorian hymn if one sang them in the ordinary way. I varied more than Mr. Russell, who never forgot his two tunes, one for long and one for short lines, and I could not always speak a poem in the same way. When I got to London I gave the notation, as it had been played on the organ, to the friend who has just gone out, Miss Florence Farr, and she spoke it to me, giving my words a new quality by the beauty of her voice.

III

But she and I soon wandered into the wood of error; we tried speaking through music in the ordinary way, under I know not whose evil influence, until we got to hate the two competing tunes and rhythms that were so often at discord with one another, the tune and rhythm of the verse and the tune and rhythm of the music. Then we tried, persuaded by somebody who thought quarter-tones and less intervals the especial mark of speech as distinct from singing, to write out what we did in wavy lines. On finding something like these lines in Tibetan music, we became so confident that we covered a large piece of pasteboard, which now blows up my fire in the morning, with a notation in wavy lines as a demonstration for a lecture; but at last Mr. Dolmetsch put us back to our first thought. He made us a beautiful instrument, half psaltery, half lyre, which contains, I understand, all the chromatic intervals within the range of the speaking voice; and he taught us to regulate our speech by the ordinary musical notes.

Some of the notations he taught us—those in which there is no lilt, no recurring pattern of sounds—are like this notation for a song out of the first act of *The Countess Cathleen*.

It is written in the old C clef, which is, I am told, the most reasonable way to write it, for it would be 'below the stave on the treble clef or above it on the bass clef.' The central line of the stave 'corresponds to the middle C of the piano; the first note of the poem is therefore D.' The marks of long and short over the syllables are not marks of scansion, but show the syllables one makes the voice hurry or linger over.

One needs, of course, a far less complicated notation than a singer, and one is even permitted slight modifications of the fixed note when dramatic expression demands it and the instrument is not sounding. The notation, which regulates the general form of the sound, leaves it free to add a complexity of dramatic expression from its own incommunicable genius which compensates the lover of speech for the lack of complex musical expression. Ordinary speech is formless, and its variety is like the variety which separates bad prose from the regulated speech of Milton, or anything that is formless and void from anything that has form and beauty. The orator, the speaker who has some little of the great tradition of his craft, differs from the debater very largely because he understands how to assume that subtle monotony of voice which runs through the nerves like fire.

Even when one is speaking to a single note sounded faintly on the psaltery, if one is sufficiently practised to speak on it without thinking about it one can get an endless variety of expression. All art is, indeed, a monotony in external things for the sake of an interior variety, a sacrifice of gross effects to subtle effects, an asceticism of the imagination. But this new art, new in modern life, I mean, will have to train its hearers as well as its speakers, for it takes time to surrender gladly the gross effects one is accustomed to, and one may well find mere monotony at first where one soon learns to find a variety as incalculable as in the outline of faces or in the expression of eyes. Modern acting and recitation have taught us to fix our attention on the gross effects till we have come to think gesture, and the intonation that copies the accidental surface of life, more important than the rhythm; and yet we understand theoretically that it is precisely this rhythm that separates good writing from bad, that is the glimmer, the fragrance, the spirit of all intense literature. I do not say that we should speak our plays to musical notes, for dramatic verse will need its own method, and I have hitherto experimented with short lyric poems alone; but I am certain that, if people would listen for a while

to lyrical verse spoken to notes, they would soon find
it impossible to listen without indignation to verse as
it is spoken in our leading theatres. They would get a
subtlety of hearing that would demand new effects from
actors and even from public speakers, and they might,
it may be, begin even to notice one another's voices till
poetry and rhythm had come nearer to common life.

I cannot tell what changes this new art is to go
through, or to what greatness or littleness of fortune;
but I can imagine little stories in prose with their dialogues in metre going pleasantly to the strings. I am
not certain that I shall not see some Order naming
itself from the Golden Violet of the Troubadours or
the like, and having among its members none but well-
taught and well-mannered speakers who will keep the
new art from disrepute. They will know how to keep
from singing notes and from prosaic lifeless intonations, and they will always understand, however far
they push their experiments, that poetry and not music
is their object; and they will have by heart, like the
Irish *File*, so many poems and notations that they will
never have to bend their heads over the book, to the
ruin of dramatic expression and of that wild air the
bard had always about him in my boyish imagination.
They will go here and there speaking their verses and
their little stories wherever they can find a score or
two of poetical-minded people in a big room, or a
couple of poetical-minded friends sitting by the hearth,
and poets will write them poems and little stories to
the confounding of print and paper. I, at any rate, from
this out mean to write all my longer poems for the

stage, and all my shorter ones for the psaltery, if only some strong angel keep me to my good resolutions.

1902

IV. POEMS FOR THE PSALTERY

The relation between formal music and speech will yet become the subject of science, not less than the occasion of artistic discovery. I suggest that we will discover in this relation a very early stage in the development of music, with its own great beauty, and that those who love lyric poetry but cannot tell one tune from another repeat a state of mind which created music and yet was incapable of the emotional abstraction which delights in patterns of sound separated from words. To it the music was an unconscious creation, the words a conscious, for no beginnings are in the intellect, and no living thing remembers its own birth.

Three of the following settings are by Miss Farr, and she accompanies the words upon her psaltery for the most part. I give after Miss Farr's three settings two taken down by Mr. Arnold Dolmetsch from myself, and one from Mr. A. H. Bullen, a fine scholar in poetry, who hates all music but that of poetry, and knows of no instrument that does not fill him with rage and misery. I do not mean that there is only one way of reciting a poem that is correct, for different tunes will fit different speakers or different moods of the same speaker, but as a rule the more the music of the verse becomes a movement of the stanza as a whole, at the same time detaching itself from the sense as in much of Mr. Swinburne's poetry, the less does the poet vary in his recitation. I mean in the way he recites when alone, or unconscious of an audience, for before an audience he will remember the imperfection of his ear in note and tune, and cling to daily speech, or something like it.

Sometimes one composes to a remembered air. I wrote and I still speak the verses that begin 'Autumn is over the long leaves that love us' to some traditional air, though I could not tell that air or any other on another's lips, and *The Ballad of Father Gilligan* to a modification of the air *A Fine Old English Gentleman*. When, however, the rhythm is more personal than it is in these simple verses, the tune will always be original and personal, alike in the poet and in the reader who has the right ear; and these tunes will now and again have great beauty.

1907

V. NOTE BY FLORENCE FARR UPON HER SETTINGS

I made an interesting discovery after I had been elaborating the art of speaking to the psaltery for some time. I had tried to make it more beautiful than the speaking by priests at High Mass, the singing of recitative in opera and the speaking through music of actors in melodrama. My discovery was that those who had invented these arts had all said about them exactly what Mr. Arnold Dolmetsch and Mr. W. B. Yeats said about my art. Any one can prove this for himself who will go to a library and read the authorities that describe how early liturgical chant, plain-song and jubilations or melismata were adapted from the ancient traditional music; or if they read the history of the beginning of

21

opera and the 'nuove musiche' by Caccini, or study the music of Monteverdi and Carissimi, who flourished at the beginning of the seventeenth century, they will find these masters speak of doing all they can to give an added beauty to the words of the poet, often using simple vowel sounds when a purely vocal effect was to be made whether of joy or sorrow. There is no more beautiful sound than the alternation of carolling or keening and a voice speaking in regulated declamation. The very act of alternation has a peculiar charm.

Now to read these records of music of the eighth and seventeenth centuries one would think that the Church and the opera were united in the desire to make beautiful speech more beautiful, but I need not say if we put such a hope to the test we discover it is groundless. There is no ecstasy in the delivery of ritual, and recitative is certainly not treated by opera-singers in a way that makes us wish to imitate them.

When beginners attempt to speak to musical notes they fall naturally into the intoning as heard throughout our lands in our various religious rituals. It is not until they have been forced to use their imaginations and express the inmost meaning of the words, not until their thought imposes itself upon all listeners and each word invokes a special mode of beauty, that the method rises once more from the dead and becomes a living art.

It is the belief in the power of words and the delight in the purity of sound that will make the arts of plain-chant and recitative the great arts they are described as being by those who first practised them.

F. F., 1907

Speaking to the Psaltery

THE WIND BLOWS OUT OF THE GATES OF THE DAY [1]

FLORENCE FARR.

The wind blows out of the gates of the day, The wind blows

over the lonely of heart, And the lonely of heart is withered

away, While the faeries dance in a place apart, Shaking their

milk-white feet in a ring, Tossing their milk-white arms in the

air. For they hear the wind laugh and murmur and sing Of

a land where even the old are fair, And even the wise are

merry of tongue; But I heard a reed of Coolaney say,

'When the wind has laughed and murmured and sung, The

lonely of heart must wither away.'

[1] The music as written suits my speaking voice if played an octave lower than the notation.—F. F.

Ideas of Good and Evil

THE HAPPY TOWNLAND [1]

FLORENCE FARR.

O, Death's old bony finger Will never find us there   In the high

hollow townland Where love's to give and to spare;   Where

boughs have fruit and blossom At all times of the year;   Where

rivers are running over With red beer and brown beer. An old

man plays the bagpipes In a golden and silver wood;   Queens,

their eyes   blue like the ice, Are dancing in a crowd.

CHORUS.

The little fox he murmured,   'O, what of the world's   bane?'

The sun was laughing   sweetly, The moon plucked at my rein;

But the little red fox murmured,   'O, do not pluck at his rein,

He is riding to the townland That is the world's bane.'

[1] The music as written suits my speaking voice if played an octave lower than the notation.—F. F.

24

Speaking to the Psaltery

I HAVE DRUNK ALE FROM THE COUNTRY OF THE YOUNG [1]

FLORENCE FARR.

I have drunk ale from the Country of the Young And weep

because I know all things now: I have been a hazel - tree, and

they hung The Pilot Star and the Crooked Plough Among my

leaves in times out of mind: I became a rush that horses tread:

I became a man, a hater of the wind, Knowing one, out of all

things, alone, that his head May not lie on the breast nor his

lips on the hair Of the woman that he loves, until he dies;

Although the rushes and the fowl of the air Cry of his love

with their piti - ful cries.

[1] To be spoken an octave lower than it would be sung.—F. F.

25

Ideas of Good and Evil

THE SONG OF WANDERING AENGUS

W. B. Y.

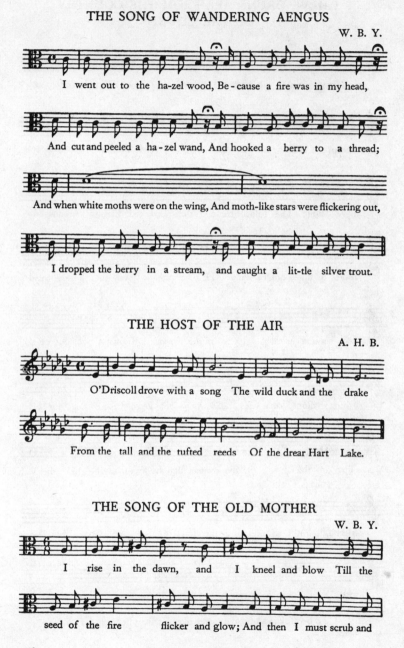

I went out to the ha-zel wood, Be-cause a fire was in my head,

And cut and peeled a ha-zel wand, And hooked a berry to a thread;

And when white moths were on the wing, And moth-like stars were flickering out,

I dropped the berry in a stream, and caught a lit-tle silver trout.

THE HOST OF THE AIR

A. H. B.

O'Driscoll drove with a song The wild duck and the drake

From the tall and the tufted reeds Of the drear Hart Lake.

THE SONG OF THE OLD MOTHER

W. B. Y.

I rise in the dawn, and I kneel and blow Till the

seed of the fire flicker and glow; And then I must scrub and

Speaking to the Psaltery

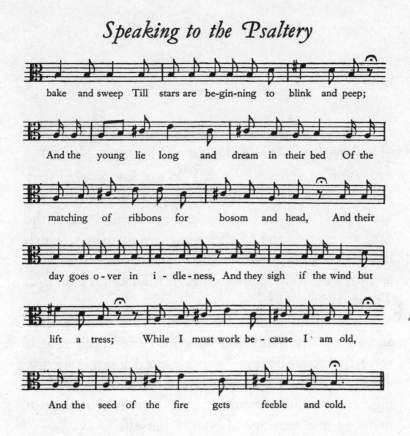

bake and sweep Till stars are be-gin-ning to blink and peep;

And the young lie long and dream in their bed Of the

matching of ribbons for bosom and head, And their

day goes o-ver in i-dle-ness, And they sigh if the wind but

lift a tress; While I must work be-cause I am old,

And the seed of the fire gets feeble and cold.

Ideas of Good and Evil

MAGIC

I

I BELIEVE IN THE PRACTICE and philosophy of what we have agreed to call magic, in what I must call the evocation of spirits, though I do not know what they are, in the power of creating magical illusions, in the visions of truth in the depths of the mind when the eyes are closed; and I believe in three doctrines, which have, as I think, been handed down from early times, and been the foundations of nearly all magical practices. These doctrines are:—

(1) That the borders of our mind are ever shifting, and that many minds can flow into one another, as it were, and create or reveal a single mind, a single energy.

(2) That the borders of our memories are as shifting, and that our memories are a part of one great memory, the memory of Nature herself.

(3) That this great mind and great memory can be evoked by symbols.

I often think I would put this belief in magic from me if I could, for I have come to see or to imagine, in men and women, in houses, in handicrafts, in nearly all sights and sounds, a certain evil, a certain ugliness, that comes from the slow perishing through the centuries of a quality of mind that made this belief and its evidences common over the world.

II

Some ten or twelve years ago, a man with whom I have since quarrelled for sound reasons, a very singular man who had given his life to studies other men despised, asked me and an acquaintance, who is now dead, to witness a magical work. He lived a little way from London, and on the way my acquaintance told me that he did not believe in magic, but that a novel of Bulwer Lytton's had taken such a hold upon his imagination that he was going to give much of his time and all his thought to magic. He longed to believe in it, and had studied, though not learnedly, geomancy, astrology, chiromancy, and much cabbalistic symbolism, and yet doubted if the soul outlived the body. He awaited the magical work full of scepticism. He expected nothing more than an air of romance, an illusion as of the stage, that might capture the consenting imagination for an hour. The evoker of spirits and his beautiful wife received us in a little house, on the edge of some kind of garden or park belonging to an eccentric rich man, whose curiosities he arranged and dusted, and he made his evocation in a long room that had a raised place on the floor at one end, a kind of dais, but was furnished meagrely and cheaply. I sat with my acquaintance in the middle of the room, and the evoker of spirits on the dais, and his wife between us and him. He held a wooden mace in his hand, and turning to a tablet of many-coloured squares, with a number on each of the squares, that stood near him on a chair, he repeated a form of words. Almost at once my imagination began to move of itself and to bring before me vivid images that, though never too vivid to be imagination, as I had always understood it, had yet a motion of their own, a life I could not change or shape. I remember seeing a number of white figures, and wondering whether their mitred heads had been suggested by the mitred head of the mace, and then, of a sudden, the image of my acquaintance in the midst of them. I told what I had seen, and the evoker of spirits cried in a deep voice, 'Let him be blotted out,' and as he said it the image of my acquaintance vanished, and the evoker of spirits or his wife saw a man dressed in black with a curious square cap standing among the white figures. It was my acquaintance, the seeress said, as he had been in a past life, the life that had moulded his present, and that life would now unfold before us. I too seemed to see the man with a strange vividness. The story unfolded itself chiefly before the mind's eye of the seeress, but sometimes I saw what she described before I heard her description. She thought the man in black was perhaps a Fleming of the sixteenth century, and I could see him pass along narrow streets till he came to a narrow door with some rusty ironwork above it. He went in, and wishing to find out how far we had one vision among us, I kept silent when I saw a dead body lying upon the table within the door. The seeress described him going down a long hall and up into what she called a pulpit, and beginning to speak. She said, 'He is a clergyman, I can hear his words. They sound like Low Dutch.' Then after a little silence, 'No, I am wrong. I can see the listeners; he is a doctor lecturing among his pupils.' I said, 'Do you see anything near the door?' and she said, 'Yes, I see a subject for dissection.' Then we saw him go out again into the narrow streets, I following the story of the seeress, sometimes merely

following her words, but sometimes seeing for myself.
My acquaintance saw nothing; I think he was forbidden
to see, it being his own life, and I think could not in
any case. His imagination had no will of its own.
Presently the man in black went into a house with two
gables facing the road, and up some stairs into a room
where a hump-backed woman gave him a key; and
then along a corridor, and down some stairs into a large
cellar full of retorts and strange vessels of all kinds.
Here he seemed to stay a long while, and one saw him
eating bread that he took down from a shelf. The
evoker of spirits and the seeress began to speculate
about the man's character and habits, and decided, from
a visionary impression, that his mind was absorbed in
naturalism, but that his imagination had been excited
by stories of the marvels wrought by magic in past
times, and that he was trying to copy them by naturalistic means. Presently one of them saw him go to a
vessel that stood over a slow fire, and take out of the
vessel a thing wrapped up in numberless cloths, which
he partly unwrapped, showing at length what looked
like the image of a man made by somebody who could
not model. The evoker of spirits said that the man in
black was trying to make flesh by chemical means, and
though he had not succeeded, his brooding had drawn
so many evil spirits about him that the image was
partly alive. He could see it moving a little where it lay
upon a table. At that moment I heard something like
little squeals, but kept silent, as when I saw the dead
body. In a moment more the seeress said, 'I hear little
squeals.' Then the evoker of spirits heard them, but

said, 'They are not squeals; he is pouring a red liquid out of a retort through a slit in the cloth; the slit is over the mouth of the image and the liquid is gurgling in rather a curious way.' Weeks seemed to pass by hurriedly, and somebody saw the man still busy in his cellar. Then more weeks seemed to pass, and now we saw him lying sick in a room upstairs, and a man in a conical cap standing beside him. We could see the image too. It was in the cellar, but now it could move feebly about the floor. I saw fainter images of the image passing continually from where it crawled to the man in his bed, and I asked the evoker of spirits what they were. He said, 'They are the images of his terror.' Presently the man in the conical cap began to speak, but who heard him I cannot remember. He made the sick man get out of bed and walk, leaning upon him, and in much terror till they came to the cellar. There the man in the conical cap made some symbol over the image, which fell back as if asleep, and putting a knife into the other's hand he said, 'I have taken from it the magical life, but you must take from it the life you gave.' Somebody saw the sick man stoop and sever the head of the image from its body, and then fall as if he had given himself a mortal wound, for he had filled it with his own life. And then the vision changed and fluttered, and he was lying sick again in the room upstairs. He seemed to lie there a long time with the man in the conical cap watching beside him, then, I cannot remember how, the evoker of spirits discovered that though he would in part recover, he would never be well, and that the story had got abroad in the town and shattered his good name. His pupils had left him and men avoided him. He was accursed. He was a magician.

The story was finished, and I looked at my acquaintance. He was white and awestruck. He said, as nearly as I can remember, 'All my life I have seen myself in dreams making a man by some means like that. When I was a child I was always thinking out contrivances for galvanising a corpse into life.' Presently he said, 'Perhaps my bad health in this life comes from that experiment.' I asked if he had read *Frankenstein*, and he answered that he had. He was the only one of us who had, and he had taken no part in the vision.

III

Then I asked to have some past life of mine revealed, and a new evocation was made before the tablet full of little squares. I cannot remember so well who saw this or that detail, for now I was interested in little but the vision itself. I had come to a conclusion about the method. I knew that the vision may be in part common to several people.

A man in chain armour passed through a castle door, and the seeress noticed with surprise the bareness and rudeness of castle rooms. There was nothing of the magnificence or the pageantry she had expected. The man came to a large hall and to a little chapel opening out of it, where a ceremony was taking place. There were six girls dressed in white, who took from the altar some yellow object—I thought it was gold, for though, like my acquaintance, I was told not to see, I could not help seeing. Somebody else thought that it was yellow flowers, and I think the girls, though I cannot remember clearly, laid it between the man's hands. He went out for a time, and as he passed through the great hall one of us, I forget who, noticed that he passed over two gravestones. Then the vision became broken, but presently he stood in a monk's habit among men-at-arms in the middle of a village reading from a parchment. He was calling villagers about him, and presently he and they and the men-at-arms took ship for some long voyage. The vision became broken again, and when we could see clearly they had come to what seemed the Holy Land. They had begun some kind of sacred labour among palm-trees. The common men among them stood idle, but the gentlemen carried large stones, bringing them from certain directions, from the cardinal points, I think, with a ceremonious formality. The evoker of spirits said they must be making some Masonic house. His mind, like the minds of so many students of these hidden things, was always running on Masonry and discovering it in strange places.

We broke the vision that we might have supper, breaking it with some form of words which I forget. When supper had ended the seeress cried out that while we had been eating they had been building, and that they had built not a Masonic house but a great stone cross. And now they had all gone away but the man who had been in chain armour and two monks we had not noticed before. He was standing against the cross, his feet upon two stone rests a little above the ground, and his arms spread out. He seemed to stand there all day, but when night came he went to a little cell, that was beside two other cells. I think they were like the cells I have seen in the Aran Islands, but I cannot be certain. Many days seemed to pass, and all day every day he stood upon the cross, and we never saw anybody there but him and the two monks. Many years seemed to pass, making the vision flutter like a drift of leaves before our eyes, and he grew old and white-haired, and we saw the two monks, old and white-haired, holding him upon the cross. I asked the evoker of spirits why the man stood there, and before he had time to answer I saw two people, a man and a woman, rising like a dream within a dream before the eyes of the man upon the cross. The evoker of spirits saw them too, and said that one of them held up his arms and they were without hands. I thought of the two gravestones the man in chain mail had passed over in the great hall when he came out of the chapel, and asked the evoker of spirits if the knight was undergoing a penance for violence, and while I was asking him, and he was saying that it might be so but he did not know, the vision, having completed its circle, vanished.

It had not, so far as I could see, the personal significance of the other vision, but it was certainly strange and beautiful, though I alone seemed to see its beauty. Who was it that made the story, if it were but a story? I did not, and the seeress did not, and the evoker of spirits did not and could not. It arose in three minds, for I cannot remember my acquaintance taking any part, and it rose without confusion, and without labour, except the labour of keeping the mind's eye awake, and more swiftly than any pen could have written it out. It may be, as Blake said of one of his poems, that the author was in eternity. In coming years I was to see and hear of many such visions, and though I was not to be convinced, though half convinced once or twice, that they were old lives, in an ordinary sense of the word life, I was to learn that they have almost always some quite definite relation to dominant moods and moulding events in this life. They are, perhaps, in most cases, though the vision I have but just described was not, it seems, among the cases, symbolical histories of these moods and events, or rather symbolical shadows of the impulses that have made them, messages as it were out of the ancestral being of the questioner.

At the time these two visions meant little more to me, if I can remember my feeling at the time, than a proof of the supremacy of imagination, of the power of many minds to become one, overpowering one another by spoken words and by unspoken thought till they have become a single, intense, unhesitating energy. One mind was doubtless the master, I thought, but all the minds gave a little, creating or revealing for a moment what I must call a supernatural artist.

IV

Some years afterwards I was staying with some friends in Paris. I had got up before breakfast and gone out to buy a newspaper. I had noticed the servant, a girl who had come from the country some years before, laying the table for breakfast. As I had passed her I had been telling myself one of those long foolish tales which one tells only to oneself. If something had happened that had not happened, I would have hurt my arm, I thought. I saw myself with my arm in a sling in the middle of some childish adventures. I returned with the newspaper and met my host and hostess in the door. The moment they saw me they cried out, 'Why, the *bonne* has just told us you had your arm in a sling. We thought something must have happened to you last night, that you had been run over maybe'—or some such words. I had been dining out at the other end of Paris, and had come in after everybody had gone to bed. I had cast my imagination so strongly upon the servant that she had seen it, and with what had appeared to be more than the mind's eye.

One afternoon, about the same time, I was thinking very intently of a certain fellow-student for whom I had a message, which I hesitated about writing. In a couple of days I got a letter from a place some hundreds of miles away where that student was. On the afternoon when I had been thinking so intently I had suddenly appeared there amid a crowd of people in a hotel and as seeming solid as if in the flesh. My fellow-student had seen me, but no one else, and had asked me to come again when the people had gone. I had vanished, but had come again in the middle of the night and given the message. I myself had no knowledge of either apparition.

I could tell of stranger images, of stranger enchantments, of stranger imaginations, cast consciously or unconsciously over as great distances by friends or by myself, were it not that the greater energies of the mind seldom break forth but when the deeps are loosened. They break forth amid events too private or too sacred for public speech, or seem themselves, I know not why, to belong to hidden things. I have written of these breakings forth, these loosenings of the deep, with some care and some detail, but I shall keep my record shut. After all, one can but bear witness less to convince him who won't believe than to protect him who does, as Blake puts it, enduring unbelief and misbelief and ridicule as best one may. I shall be content to show that past times have believed as I do, by quoting Joseph Glanvil's description of the Scholar-Gipsy. Joseph Glanvil is dead, and will not mind unbelief and misbelief and ridicule.

The Scholar-Gipsy, too, is dead, unless indeed perfectly wise magicians can live till it please them to die, and he is wandering somewhere, even if one cannot see him, as Arnold imagined, 'at some lone alehouse in the Berkshire moors, on the warm ingle-bench,' or 'crossing the stripling Thames at Bablock Hithe,' or trailing his fingers in the cool stream, or giving 'store of flowers—the frail-leaf'd white anemone, dark bluebells drenched with dews of summer eves,' to the girls 'who from the distant hamlets come to dance around the Fyfield elm in May,' or 'sitting upon the river bank o'ergrown,' living on through time 'with a free, onward impulse.' This is Joseph Glanvil's story:—

'There was very lately a lad in the University of Oxford who, being of very pregnant and ready parts and yet wanting the encouragement of preferment, was

by his poverty forced to leave his studies there, and to
cast himself upon the wide world for a livelihood.
Now his necessities growing daily on him, and wanting
the help of friends to relieve him, he was at last forced
to join himself to a company of vagabond gipsies,
whom occasionally he met with, and to follow their
trade for a maintenance. . . . After he had been a pretty
while exercised in the trade, there chanced to ride by
a couple of scholars, who had formerly been of his
acquaintance. The scholars quickly spied out their
old friend among the gipsies, and their amazement to
see him among such society had wellnigh discovered
him; but by a sign he prevented them owning him before that crew, and taking one of them aside privately,
desired him with his friend to go to an inn, not
far distant, promising there to come to them. They
accordingly went thither and he follows: after their
first salutation his friends inquire how he came to lead so
odd a life as that was, and so joined himself into such
a beggarly company. The scholar-gipsy having given
them an account of the necessity which drove him to
that kind of life, told them that the people he went with
were not such impostors as they were taken for, but
that they had a traditional kind of learning among them
and could do wonders by the power of imagination,
and that himself had learned much of their art and im-
proved it further than themselves could. And to evince
the truth of what he told them, he said he'd remove
into another room, leaving them to discourse together;
and upon his return tell them the sense of what they
had talked of; which accordingly he performed, giving

them a full account of what had passed between them in his absence. The scholars being amazed at so unexpected a discovery, earnestly desired him to unriddle the mystery. In which he gave them satisfaction, by telling them that what he did was by the power of imagination, his phantasy leading theirs; and that himself had dictated to them the discourse they had held together while he was from them; that there were warrantable ways of heightening the imagination to that pitch as to bend another's, and that when he had compassed the whole secret, some parts of which he was yet ignorant of, he intended to leave their company and give the whole world an account of what he had learned.'

If all who have described events like this have not dreamed, we should rewrite our histories, for all men, certainly all imaginative men, must be for ever casting forth enchantments, glamours, illusions; and all men, especially tranquil men who have no powerful egotistic life, must be continually passing under their power. Our most elaborate thoughts, elaborate purposes, precise emotions, are often, as I think, not really ours, but have on a sudden come up, as it were, out of Hell or down out of Heaven. The historian should remember, should he not? angels and devils not less than kings and soldiers, and plotters and thinkers. What matter if the angel or devil, as indeed certain old writers believed, first wrapped itself with an organised shape in some man's imagination? what matter 'if God Himself only acts or is in existing beings or men,' as Blake believed? we must none the less admit that invisible beings, far-wandering influences, shapes that may have floated from a hermit of the wilderness, brood over council-chambers and studies and battle-fields. We should never be certain that it was not some woman treading in the wine-press who began that subtle change in men's minds, that powerful movement of thought and imagination about which so many Germans have written; or that the passion, because of which so many countries were given to the sword, did not begin in the mind of some shepherd boy, lighting up his eyes for a moment before it ran upon its way.

v

We cannot doubt that barbaric people receive such influences more visibly and obviously, and in all likeli-hood more easily and fully than we do, for our life in cities, which deafens or kills the passive meditative life, and our education that enlarges the separated, self-moving mind, have made our souls less sensitive. Our souls that were once naked to the winds of heaven are now thickly clad, and have learned to build a house and light a fire upon its hearth, and shut-to the doors and windows. The winds can, indeed, make us draw near to the fire, or can even lift the carpet and whistle under the door, but they could do worse out on the plains long ago. A certain learned man, quoted by Mr. Lang in his *Making of Religion*, contends that the memories of primitive man and his thoughts of distant places must have had the intensity of hallucination, because there was nothing in his mind to draw his attention away from them—an explanation that does not seem to me complete—and Mr. Lang goes on to quote certain travellers to prove that savages live always on the edges of vision. One Laplander who wished to become a Christian, and thought visions but heathenish, confessed to a traveller, to whom he had given a minute account of many distant events, read doubtless in that traveller's mind, 'that he knew not how to make use of his eyes, since things altogether distant were present to them.' I myself could find in one district in Galway but one man who had not seen what I can but call spirits, and he was in his dotage. 'There is no man mowing a meadow but sees them at one time or another,' said a man in a different district.

If I can unintentionally cast a glamour, an enchantment, over persons of our own time who have lived for years in great cities, there is no reason to doubt that men could cast intentionally a far stronger enchantment, a far stronger glamour, over the more sensitive people of ancient times, or that men can still do so where the old order of life remains unbroken. Why should not the Scholar-Gipsy cast his spell over his friends? Why should not Saint Patrick, or he of whom the story was first told, pass his enemies, he and all his clerics, as a herd of deer? Why should not enchanters like him in the *Morte d'Arthur* make troops of horse seem but grey stones? Why should not the Roman soldiers, though they came of a civilisation which was ceasing to be sensitive to these things, have trembled for a moment before the enchantments of the Druids

42

of Mona? Why should not the Jesuit father, or the Count Saint-Germain, or whoever the tale was first told of, have really seemed to leave the city in a coach and four and by all the Twelve Gates at once? Why should not Moses and the enchanters of Pharaoh have made their staffs, as the medicine-men of many primitive peoples make their pieces of old rope, seem like devouring serpents? Why should not that mediaeval enchanter have made summer and all its blossoms seem to break forth in middle winter?

May we not learn some day to rewrite our histories, when they touch upon these things?

Men who are imaginative writers to-day may well have preferred to influence the imagination of others more directly in past times. Instead of learning their craft with paper and a pen they may have sat for hours imagining themselves to be stocks and stones and beasts of the wood, till the images were so vivid that the passers-by became but a part of the imagination of the dreamer, and wept or laughed or ran away as he would have them. Have not poetry and music arisen, as it seems, out of the sounds the enchanters made to help their imagination to enchant, to charm, to bind with a spell themselves and the passers-by? These very words, a chief part of all praises of music or poetry, still cry to us their origin. And just as the musician or the poet enchants and charms and binds with a spell his own mind when he would enchant the mind of others, so did the enchanter create or reveal for himself as well as for others the supernatural artist or genius, the seeming transitory mind made out of many minds, whose work I saw, or thought I saw, in that suburban house. He kept the doors, too, as it seems, of those less transitory minds, the genius of the family, the genius of the tribe, or it may be, when he was mighty-souled enough, the genius of the world. Our history speaks of opinions and discoveries, but in ancient times when, as I think, men had their eyes ever upon those doors, history spoke of commandments and revelations. They looked as carefully and as patiently towards Sinai and its thunders as we look towards parliaments and laboratories. We are always praising men in whom the individual life has come to perfection, but they were always praising the one mind, their foundation of all perfection.

VI

I once saw a young Irishwoman, fresh from a convent school, cast into a profound trance, though not by a method known to any hypnotist. In her waking state she thought the apple of Eve was the kind of apple you can buy at the greengrocer's, but in her trance she saw the Tree of Life with ever-sighing souls moving in its branches instead of sap, and among its leaves all the fowls of the air, and on its highest bough one white fowl wearing a crown. When I went home I took from the shelf a translation of *The Book of Concealed Mystery*,[1] an old Jewish book, and cutting the pages came upon this passage, which I cannot think I had ever read: 'The Tree, . . . is the Tree of the Knowledge of Good and Evil . . . in its branches the birds

[1] Translated by Mathers in *The Kabbalah Unveiled*.

44

lodge and build their nests, the souls and the angels have their place.'

I once saw a young Church of Ireland man, a bank-clerk in the West of Ireland, thrown in a like trance. I have no doubt that he, too, was quite certain that the apple of Eve was a greengrocer's apple, and yet he saw the tree and heard the souls sighing through its branches, and saw apples with human faces, and laying his ear to an apple heard a sound as of fighting hosts within. Presently he strayed from the tree and came to the edge of Eden, and there he found himself not by the wilderness he had learned of at the Sunday-school, but upon the summit of a great mountain, of a mountain 'two miles high.' The whole summit, in contradiction to all that would have seemed probable to his waking mind, was a great walled garden. Some years afterwards I found a mediaeval diagram, which pictured Eden as a walled garden upon a high mountain.

Where did these intricate symbols come from? Neither I nor the one or two people present nor the seers had ever seen, I am convinced, the description in *The Book of Concealed Mystery*, or the mediaeval diagram. Remember that the images appeared in a moment perfect in all their complexity. If one can imagine that the seers or that I myself or another had indeed read of these images and forgotten it, that the supernatural artist's knowledge of what was in our buried memories accounted for these visions, there are numberless other visions to account for. One cannot go on believing in improbable knowledge for ever. For instance, I find

in my diary that on December 27, 1897, a seer, to
whom I had given a certain old Irish symbol, saw
Brigid, the goddess, holding out 'a glittering and wrig-
gling serpent,' and yet I feel certain that neither I nor
he knew anything of her association with the serpent
until *Carmina Gaedelica* was published a few months
ago. And an old Irishwoman who can neither read nor
write has described to me a woman dressed like Dian,
with helmet, and short skirt and sandals, and what
seemed to be buskins. Why, too, among all the countless stories of visions that I have gathered in Ireland,
or that a friend has gathered for me, are there none that
mix the dress of different periods? The seers when they
are but speaking from tradition will mix everything
together, and speak of Finn mac Cumhal going to the
Assizes at Cork. Almost every one who has ever busied
himself with such matters has come, in trance or dream,
upon some new and strange symbol or event, which he
has afterwards found in some work he had never read
or heard of. Examples like this are as yet too little classified, too little analysed, to convince the stranger, but
some of them are proof enough for those they have
happened to, proof that there is a memory of Nature
that reveals events and symbols of distant centuries.
Mystics of many countries and many centuries have
spoken of this memory; and the honest men and char-
latans, who keep the magical traditions which will some
day be studied as a part of folk-lore, base most that is
of importance in their claims upon this memory. I have
read of it in *Paracelsus* and in some Indian book that
describes the people of past days as still living within

46

it, 'thinking the thought and doing the deed.' And I
have found it in the 'Prophetic Books' of William Blake,
who calls its images 'the bright sculptures of Los's
Hall'; and says that all events, 'all love stories,' renew
themselves from those images. It is perhaps well that
so few believe in it, for if many did many would go out
of parliaments and universities and libraries and run
into the wilderness to so waste the body, and to so hush
the unquiet mind that, still living, they might pass the
doors the dead pass daily; for who among the wise
would trouble himself with making laws or in writing
history or in weighing the earth if the things of eternity
seemed ready to hand?

VII

I find in my diary of magical events for 1899 that I
awoke at 3 A.M. out of a nightmare, and imagined one
symbol to prevent its recurrence, and imagined another,
a simple geometrical form, which calls up dreams of
luxuriant vegetable life, that I might have pleasant
dreams. I imagined it faintly, being very sleepy, and
went to sleep. I had confused dreams which seemed to
have no relation with the symbol. I awoke about eight,
having for the time forgotten both nightmare and
symbol. Presently I dozed off again and began half to
dream and half to see, as one does between sleep and
waking, enormous flowers and grapes. I awoke and
recognised that what I had dreamed or seen was the
kind of thing appropriate to the symbol before I remembered having used it. I find another record, though
made some time after the event, of having imagined

over the head of a person, who was a little of a seer, a combined symbol of elemental air and elemental water. This person, who did not know what symbol I was using, saw a pigeon flying with a lobster in his bill. I find that on December 13, 1898, I used a certain star-shaped symbol with a seeress, getting her to look at it intently before she began seeing. She saw a rough stone house, and in the middle of the house the skull of a horse. I find that I had used the same symbol a few days before with a seer, and that he had seen a rough stone house, and in the middle of the house something under a cloth marked with the Hammer of Thor. He had lifted the cloth and discovered a skeleton of gold with teeth of diamonds, and eyes of some unknown dim precious stones. I had made a note to this last vision, pointing out that we had been using a Solar symbol a little earlier. Solar symbols often call up visions of gold and precious stones. I do not give these examples to prove my arguments, but to illustrate them. I know that my examples will awaken in all who have not met the like, or who are not on other grounds inclined towards my arguments, a most natural in-credulity. It was long before I myself would admit an inherent power in symbols, for it long seemed to me that one could account for everything by the power of one imagination over another, or by telepathy, as the Society for Psychical Research would say. The symbol seemed powerful, I thought, merely because we thought it powerful, and we would do just as well without it. In those days I used symbols made with some ingenuity instead of merely imagining them. I used to give them

to the person I was experimenting with, and tell him
to hold them to his forehead without looking at them;
and sometimes I made a mistake. I learned from these
mistakes that if I did not myself imagine the symbol,
in which case he would have a mixed vision, it was the
symbol I gave by mistake [1] that produced the vision.
Then I met with a seer who could say to me, 'I have a
vision of a square pond, but I can see your thought,
and you expect me to see an oblong pond,' or, 'The
symbol you are imagining has made me see a woman
holding a crystal, but it was a moonlight sea I should
have seen.' I discovered that the symbol hardly ever
failed to call up its typical scene, its typical event, its
typical person, but that I could practically never call up,
no matter how vividly I imagined it, the particular
scene, the particular event, the particular person I had
in my own mind, and that when I could, the two visions
rose side by side.

I cannot now think symbols less than the greatest
of all powers whether they are used consciously by the
masters of magic, or half unconsciously by their successors, the poet, the musician and the artist. At first
I tried to distinguish between symbols and symbols,
between what I called inherent symbols and arbitrary
symbols, but the distinction has come to mean little or
nothing. Whether their power has arisen out of them-

[1] I forgot that my 'subconsciousness' would know clairvoyantly
what symbol I had really given and would respond to the associations of that symbol. I am, however, certain that the main symbols
(symbolic roots, as it were) draw upon associations which are beyond the reach of the individual 'subconsciousness'.   1924.

selves, or whether it has an arbitrary origin, matters little, for they act, as I believe, because the Great Memory associates them with certain events and moods and persons. Whatever the passions of man have gathered about, becomes a symbol in the Great Memory, and in the hands of him who has the secret it is a worker of wonders, a caller-up of angels or of devils. The symbols are of all kinds, for everything in heaven or earth has its association, momentous or trivial, in the Great Memory, and one never knows what forgotten events may have plunged it, like the toadstool and the ragweed, into the great passions. Knowledgeable men and women in Ireland sometimes distinguish between the simples that work cures by some medical property in the herb, and those that do their work by magic. Such magical simples as the husk of the flax, water out of the fork of an elm-tree, do their work, as I think, by awaking in the depths of the mind where it mingles with the Great Mind, and is enlarged by the Great Memory, some curative energy, some hypnotic command. They are not what we call faith cures, for they have been much used and successfully, the traditions of all lands affirm, over children and over animals, and to me they seem the only medicine that could have been committed safely to ancient hands. To pluck the wrong leaf would have been to go uncured, but, if one had eaten it, one might have been poisoned.

VIII

I have now described that belief in magic which has set me all but unwilling among those lean and fierce minds who are at war with their time, who cannot accept the days as they pass, simply and gladly; and I look at what I have written with some alarm, for I have told more of the ancient secret than many among my fellow-students think it right to tell. I have come to believe so many strange things because of experience, that I see little reason to doubt the truth of many things that are beyond my experience; and it may be that there are beings who watch over that ancient secret, as all tradition affirms, and resent, and perhaps avenge, too fluent speech. They say in the Aran Islands that if you speak over-much of the things of Faery your tongue becomes like a stone, and it seems to me, though doubtless naturalistic reason would call it auto-suggestion or the like, that I have often felt my tongue become just so heavy and clumsy. More than once, too, as I wrote this very essay I have become uneasy, and have torn up some paragraph, not for any literary reason, but because some incident or some symbol that would perhaps have meant nothing to the reader, seemed, I know not why, to belong to hidden things. Yet I must write or be of no account to any cause, good or evil; I must commit what merchandise of wisdom I have to this ship of written speech, and after all, I have many a time watched it put out to sea with not less alarm when all the speech was rhyme. We who write, we who bear witness, must often hear our hearts cry out against us, complaining because of their hidden things, and I know not but he who speaks of wisdom may sometimes, in the change that is coming upon the world, have to fear the anger of the people of Faery, whose country is the heart of the world — 'The Land of the Living Heart.' Who can keep always to the little pathway between speech and silence, where one meets none but discreet revelations? And surely, at whatever risk, we must cry out that imagination is always seeking to remake the world according to the impulses and the patterns in that Great Mind, and that Great Memory? Can there be anything so important as to cry out that what we call romance, poetry, intellectual beauty, is the only signal that the supreme Enchanter, or some one in His councils, is speaking of what has been, and shall be again, in the consummation of time?

1901

The Happiest of the Poets

THE HAPPIEST OF THE POETS

I

ROSSETTI IN ONE OF HIS LETTERS numbers his favourite colours in the order of his favour, and throughout his work one feels that he loved form and colour for themselves and apart from what they represent. One feels sometimes that he desired a world of essences, of unmixed powers, of impossible purities. It is as though the Last Judgment had already begun in his mind and that the essences and powers, which the Divine Hand had mixed into one another to make the loam of life, fell asunder at his touch. If he painted a flame or a blue distance, he painted as though he had seen the flame out of whose heart all flames had been taken, or the blue of the abyss that was before all life; and if he painted a woman's face he painted it in some moment of intensity when the ecstasy of the lover and of the saint are alike, and desire becomes wisdom without ceasing to be desire. He listens to the cry of the flesh till it becomes proud and passes beyond the world where some immense desire that the intellect cannot understand mixes with the desire for a body's warmth and softness. His genius like Shelley's can hardly stir but to the rejection of Nature, whose delight is profusion, but never intensity, and like Shelley's it follows the Star of the Magi, the Morning and Evening Star, the mother of impossible hope, although it follows through deep woods, where the Star glimmers among dew-drenched boughs, and not through 'a wind-swept valley of the Apennine.' Men like him cannot be happy as we understand happiness, for to be happy one must delight like Nature in mere profusion, in mere abundance, in making and doing things, and if one sets an image of the perfect before one it must be the image that draws her perpetually, the image of a perfect fullness of natural life, of an Earthly Paradise. That is to say, one must not be among those that would have prayed in old times in some chapel of the Star, but among those who would have prayed under the shadow of the Green Tree, and on the wet stones of the Well, among the worshippers of natural abundance.

II

I do not think it was accident, so subtle are the threads that lead the soul, that made William Morris, who seems to me the one perfectly happy and fortunate poet of modern times, celebrate the Green Tree and the goddess Habundia, and wells and enchanted waters in so many books. In *The Well at the World's End* green trees and enchanted waters are shown to us as they were understood by old writers, who thought that the generation of all things was through water; for when the water that gives a long and a fortunate life, and that can be found by none but such a one as all women love, is found at last, the Dry Tree, the image of the ruined land, becomes green. To him indeed as to older writers Well and Tree are all but images of the one thing, of an 'energy' that is not the less 'eternal delight' because it is half of the body. He never wrote, and could not have written, of a man or woman who was not of the kin of Well or Tree. Long before he had named either he had made his 'Wanderers' follow a dream indeed, but a dream of natural happiness, and all the people of all his poems and stories, from the confused beginning of his art in *The Hollow Land* to its end in *The Sundering Flood*, are full of the heavy sweetness of this dream. He wrote indeed of nothing but of the quest of the Grail, but it was the Heathen Grail that gave every man his chosen food, and not the Grail of Malory or Wagner; and he came at last to praise, as other men have praised the martyrs of religion or of passion, men with lucky eyes and men whom all women love.

We know so little of man and of the world that we cannot be certain that the same invisible hands that gave him an imagination preoccupied with good fortune, gave him also health and wealth, and the power to create beautiful things without labour, that he might honour the Green Tree. It pleases me to imagine the copper mine which brought, as Mr. Mackail has told, so much unforeseen wealth and in so astonishing a way, as no less miraculous than the three arrows in *The Sundering Flood*. No mighty poet in his misery dead could have himself delighted or made us delight in men 'who knew no vain desire of foolish fame,' but who thought the dance upon 'the stubble field' and 'the battle with the earth' better than 'the bitter war' 'where right and wrong are mixed together.' 'Oh, the trees, the trees!' he wrote in one of his early letters, and it was his work to make us, who had been taught to sympathise with the unhappy till we had grown morbid, to sympathise with men and women who turned everything into happiness because they had in them something of the abundance of the beechen boughs or of the bursting wheat-ear. He alone, I think, has told the story of Alcestis with perfect sympathy for Admetus, with so perfect a sympathy that he cannot persuade himself that one so happy died at all; and he, unlike all other poets, has delighted to tell us that the men after his own heart, the men of his *News from Nowhere*, sorrowed but a little while over unhappy love. He cannot even think of nobility and happiness apart, for all his people are like his men of Burg Dale who lived 'in much plenty and ease of life, though not delicately or desiring things out of measure. They wrought with their hands and wearied themselves; and they rested from their toil and feasted and were merry; to-morrow was not a burden to them, nor yesterday a thing which they would fain forget; life shamed them not nor did death make them afraid. As for the Dale wherein they dwelt, it was indeed most fair and lovely and they deemed it the Blessing of the earth, and they trod the flowery grass beside its rippled stream amidst the green tree-boughs proudly and joyfully with goodly bodies and merry hearts.'

III

I think of his men as with broad brows and golden beards and mild eyes and tranquil speech, and of his good women as like 'The Bride' in whose face Rossetti saw and painted for once the abundance of earth and not the half-hidden light of his star. They are not in love with love for its own sake, with a love that is apart from the world or at enmity with it, as Swinburne imagines Mary Stuart and as all men have imagined Helen. They do not seek in love that ecstasy which Shelley's nightingale called death, that extremity of life in which life seems to pass away like the phoenix in flame of its own lighting, but rather a gentle self-surrender that would lose more than half its sweetness if it lost the savour of coming days. They are good housewives; they sit often at the embroidery frame, and they have wisdom in flocks and herds and they are before all fruitful mothers. It seems at times as if their love was less a passion for one man out of the world than submission to the hazard of destiny, and the hope of motherhood and the innocent desire of the body. They accept changes and chances of life as gladly as they accept spring and summer and autumn and winter, and because they have sat under the shadow of the Green Tree and drunk the Waters of Abundance out of their hollow hands, the barren blossoms do not seem to them the most beautiful. When Habundia takes the shape of Birdalone she comes first as a young naked girl standing among great trees, and then as an old carline, Birdalone in stately old age. And when she praises Birdalone's naked body, and speaks of the desire it shall awaken, praise and desire are innocent because they would not break the links that chain the days to one another. The desire seems not other than the desire of the bird for its mate in the heart of the wood, and we listen to that joyous praise as though a bird watching its plumage in still water had begun to sing in its joy, or as if we heard hawk praising hawk in the middle air, and because it is the praise of one made for all noble life and not for pleasure only, it seems, though it is the praise of the body, that it is the noblest praise.

Birdalone has never seen her image but in 'a broad latten-dish,' so the wood-woman must tell her of her body and praise it.

'Thus it is with thee; thou standest before me a tall and slim maiden, somewhat thin as befitteth thy seventeen summers; where thy flesh is bare of wont, as thy throat and thine arms and thy legs from the middle down, it is tanned a beauteous colour, but otherwhere it is even as fair a white, wholesome and clean as if the golden sunlight which fulfilleth the promise of the earth were playing therein. . . . Delicate and clear-made is the little trench that goeth from thy nose to thy lips, and sweet it is, and there is more might in it than in sweet words spoken. Thy lips they are of the finest fashion, yet rather thin than full; and some would not have it so; but I would, whereas I see therein a sign of thy valiancy and friendliness. Surely he who did thy carven chin had a mind to a master-work and did no less. Great was the deftness of thine imaginer, and he would have all folk who see thee wonder at thy deep thinking and thy carefulness and thy kindness. Ah maiden! is it so that thy thoughts are ever deep and solemn? Yet at least I know it of thee that they be hale and true and sweet.

'My friend, when thou hast a mirror, some of all this thou shalt see, but not all; and when thou hast a lover some deal wilt thou hear, but not all. But now thy she-friend may tell it thee all, if she have eyes to see it, as have I; whereas no man could say so much of thee before the mere love should overtake him, and turn his speech into the folly of love and the madness of desire.'

All his good women, whether it is Danaë in her tower, or that woman in *The Wood beyond the World* who can make the withered flowers in her girdle grow young again by the touch of her hand, are of the kin of the wood-woman. All his bad women too and his half-bad women are of her kin. The evils their enchantments make are a disordered abundance like that of weedy places, and they are cruel as wild creatures are cruel and they have unbridled desires. One finds these evils in their typical shape in that isle of the Wondrous Isles, where the wicked witch has her pleasure-house and her prison, and in that 'isle of the old and the young,' where until her enchantment is broken second childhood watches over children who never grow old and who seem to the bystander who knows their story 'like images' or like 'the rabbits on the grass.' It is as though Nature spoke through him at all times in the mood that is upon her when she is opening the apple-blossom or reddening the apple or thickening the shadow of the boughs, and that the men and women of his verse and of his stories are all the ministers of her mood.

IV

When I was a child I often heard my elders talking of an old turreted house where an old great-uncle of mine lived, and of its gardens and its long pond where

there was an island with tame eagles; and one day somebody read me some verses and said they made him think
of that old house where he had been very happy. The
verses ran in my head for years and became to me the
best description of happiness in the world, and I am not
certain that I know a better even now. They were those
first dozen verses of *Golden Wings* that begin:—

> Midways of a walled garden,
>   In the happy poplar land,
>   Did an ancient castle stand,
> With an old knight for a warden.
>
> Many scarlet bricks there were
>   In its walls, and old grey stone;
>   Over which red apples shone
> At the right time of the year.
>
> On the bricks the green moss grew,
>   Yellow lichen on the stone,
>   Over which red apples shone;
> Little war that castle knew.

When William Morris describes a house of any kind,
and makes his description poetical, it is always, I think,
some house that he would have liked to have lived
in, and I remember him saying about the time when
he was writing of that great house of the Wolfings, 'I
decorate modern houses for people, but the house that
would please me would be some great room where one
talked to one's friends in one corner and ate in another
and slept in another and worked in another.' Indeed all
he writes seems to me like the make-believe of a child
who is remaking the world, not always in the same

way, but always after its own heart; and so, unlike all other modern writers, he makes his poetry out of unending pictures of a happiness that is often what a child might imagine, and always a happiness that sets mind and body at ease. Now it is a picture of some great room full of merriment, now of the wine-press, now of the golden threshing-floor, now of an old mill among apple-trees, now of cool water after the heat of the sun, now of some well-sheltered, well-tilled place among woods or mountains, where men and women live happily, knowing of nothing that is too far off or too great for the affections. He has but one story to tell us, how some man or woman lost and found again the happiness that is always half of the body; and even when they are wandering from it, leaves must fall over them, and flowers make fragrances about them, and warm winds fan them, and birds sing to them, for being of Habundia's kin they must not forget the shadow of her Green Tree even for a moment, and the waters of her Well must be always wet upon their sandals. His poetry often wearies us as the unbroken green of July wearies us, for there is something in us, some bitterness because of the Fall, it may be, that takes a little from the sweetness of Eve's apple after the first mouthful; but he who did all things gladly and easily, who never knew the curse of labour, found it always as sweet as it was in Eve's mouth. All kinds of associations have gathered about the pleasant things of the world and half taken the pleasure out of them for the greater number of men, but he saw them as when they came from the Divine Hand. I often see him in my mind as I saw him once at Hammersmith holding up a glass of claret towards the light and saying, 'Why do people say it is prosaic to get inspiration out of wine? Is it not the sunlight and the sap in the leaves? Are not grapes made by the sunlight and the sap?'

V

In one of his little Socialist pamphlets he tells how he sat under an elm-tree and watched the starlings and thought of an old horse and an old labourer that had passed him by, and of the men and women he had seen in towns; and he wondered how all these had come to be as they were. He saw that the starlings were beautiful and merry, and that men and the old horse they had subdued to their service were ugly and miserable, and yet the starlings, he thought, were of one kind whether there or in the South of England, and the ugly men and women were of one kind with those whose nobility and beauty had moved the ancient sculptors and poets to imagine the gods and the heroes after the images of men. Then, he began, he tells us, to meditate how this great difference might be ended and a new life, which would permit men to have beauty in common among them as the starlings have, be built on the wrecks of the old life. In other words, his mind was illuminated from within and lifted into prophecy in the full right sense of the word, and he saw the natural things he was alone gifted to see in their perfect form; and having that faith which is alone worth having, for it includes all others, a sure knowledge established in the constitution of his mind that perfect things are final things, he announced that all he had seen would come to pass. I do not think he troubled to understand books of economics, and Mr. Mackail says, I think, that they vexed him and wearied him. He found it enough to hold up, as it were, life as it is to-day beside his visions, and to show how faded its colours were and how sapless it was. And if we had not enough artistic feeling, enough feeling for the perfect, that is, to admit the authority of the vision; or enough faith to understand that all that is imperfect passes away, he would not, as I think, have argued with us in a serious spirit. Though I think that he never used the kinds of words I use in writing of him, though I think he would even have disliked a word like faith with its theological associations, I am certain that he understood thoroughly, as all artists understand a little, that the important things, the things we must believe in or perish, are beyond argument. We can no more reason about them than can the pigeon, come but lately from the egg, about the hawk whose shadow makes it cower among the grass. His vision is true because it is poetical, because we are a little happier when we are looking at it; and he knew as Shelley knew, by an act of faith, that the economists should take their measurements not from life as it is, but from the vision of men like him, from the vision of the world made perfect that is buried under all minds. The early Christians were of the kin of the Wilderness and of the Dry Tree, and they saw an unearthly Paradise, but he was of the kin of the Well and of the Green Tree and he saw an Earthly Paradise.

He obeyed his vision when he tried to make first his own house, for he was in this matter also like a child playing with the world, and then houses of other people, places where one could live happily; and he obeyed it when he wrote essays about the nature of happy work, and when he spoke at street-corners about the coming changes.

He knew clearly what he was doing towards the end, for he lived at a time when poets and artists have begun again to carry the burdens that priests and theologians took from them angrily some few hundred years ago. His art was not more essentially religious than Rossetti's art, but it was different, for Rossetti, drunken with natural beauty, saw the supernatural beauty, the impossible beauty, in his frenzy, while he being less intense and more tranquil would show us a beauty that would wither if it did not set us at peace with natural things, and if we did not believe that it existed always a little, and would some day exist in its fullness. He may not have been, indeed he was not, among the very greatest of the poets, but he was among the greatest of those who prepare the last reconciliation when the Cross shall blossom with roses.

1902

THE PHILOSOPHY OF SHELLEY'S POETRY

I. HIS RULING IDEAS

WHEN I WAS A BOY IN DUBLIN I was one of a group who rented a room in a mean street to discuss philosophy. My fellow-students got more and more interested in certain modern schools of mystical belief, and I never found anybody to share my one unshakable belief. I thought that whatever of philosophy has been made poetry is alone permanent, and that one should begin to arrange it in some regular order, rejecting nothing as the make-believe of the poets. I thought, so far as I can recollect my thoughts after so many years, that if a powerful and benevolent spirit has shaped the destiny of this world, we can better discover that destiny from the words that have gathered up the heart's desire of the world, than from historical records, or from speculation, wherein the heart withers. Since then I have observed dreams and visions very carefully, and am now certain that the imagination has some way of lighting on the truth that the reason has not, and that its commandments, delivered when the body is still and the reason silent, are the most binding we can ever know. I have re-read *Prometheus Unbound*, which I had hoped my fellow-students would have studied as a sacred book, and it seems to me to have an even more certain place than I had thought among the sacred books of the world. I remember going to a learned scholar to ask about its deep meanings, which I felt more than understood, and his telling me that it was

Godwin's *Political Justice* put into rhyme, and that
Shelley was a crude revolutionist, and believed that the
overturning of kings and priests would regenerate mankind. I quoted the lines which tell how the halcyons
ceased to prey on fish, and how poisonous leaves became good for food, to show that he foresaw more than
any political regeneration, but was too timid to push
the argument. I still believe that one cannot help believing him, as this scholar I know believes him, a
vague thinker, who mixed occasional great poetry with
a fantastic rhetoric, unless one compares such passages, and above all such passages as describe the
liberty he praised, till one has discovered the system
of belief that lay behind them. It should seem natural
to find his thought full of subtlety, for Mrs. Shelley
has told how he hesitated whether he should be a metaphysician or a poet, and has spoken of his 'huntings
after the obscure' with regret, and said of that *Prometheus Unbound*, which so many for three generations
have thought *Political Justice* put into rhyme, 'It requires a mind as subtle and penetrating as his own to
understand the mystic meanings scattered throughout
the poem. They elude the ordinary reader by their abstraction and delicacy of distinction, but they are far
from vague. It was his design to write prose metaphysical essays on the nature of Man, which would
have served to explain much of what is obscure in his
poetry; a few scattered fragments of observations and
remarks alone remain. He considered these philosophical views of Mind and Nature to be instinct with
the intensest spirit of poetry.' From these scattered

fragments and observations, and from many passages read in their light, one soon comes to understand that his liberty was so much more than the liberty of *Political Justice* that it was one with Intellectual Beauty, and that the regeneration he foresaw was so much more than the regeneration many political dreamers have foreseen, that it could not come in its perfection till the Hours bore 'Time to his tomb in eternity.' In *A Defence of Poetry*, he will have it that the poet and the lawgiver hold their station by the right of the same faculty, the one uttering in words and the other in the forms of society his vision of the divine order, the Intellectual Beauty. 'Poets, according to the circumstances of the age and nation in which they appeared, were called in the earliest epoch of the world legislators or prophets, and a poet essentially comprises and unites both these characters. For he not only beholds intensely the present as it is, and discovers those laws according to which present things are to be ordained, but he beholds the future in the present, and his thoughts are the germs of the flowers and the fruit of latest time.' 'Language, colour, form, and religious and civil habits of action are all the instruments and materials of poetry.' Poetry is 'the creation of actions according to the unchangeable process of human nature as existing in the mind of the creator, which is itself the image of all other minds.' 'Poets have been challenged to resign the civic crown to reasoners and merchants. . . . It is admitted that the exercise of the imagination is the most delightful, but it is alleged that that of reason is the more useful. . . . Whilst the mechanist abridges and the

political economist combines labour, let them be sure
that their speculations, for want of correspondence
with those first principles which belong to the imagination, do not tend, as they have in modern England, to
exasperate at once the extremes of luxury and want.
. . . The rich have become richer, the poor have become
poorer, . . . such are the effects which must ever flow
from an unmitigated exercise of the calculating faculty.'
The speaker of these things might almost be Blake,
who held that the Reason not only created Ugliness,
but all other evils. The books of all wisdom are hidden
in the cave of the Witch of Atlas, who is one of his
personifications of beauty, and when she moves over
the enchanted river that is an image of all life, the priests
cast aside their deceits, and the king crowns an ape to
mock his own sovereignty, and the soldiers gather
about the anvils to beat their swords to ploughshares,
and lovers cast away their timidity, and friends are
united; while the power which, in *Laon and Cythna*,
awakens the mind of the reformer to contend, and itself contends, against the tyrannies of the world, is first
seen as the star of love or beauty. And at the end of
the *Ode to Naples*, he cries out to 'the spirit of beauty'
to overturn the tyrannies of the world, or to fill them
with its 'harmonising ardours.' He calls the spirit of
beauty liberty, because despotism, and perhaps, as 'the
man of virtuous soul commands not, nor obeys,' all
authority, pluck virtue from her path towards beauty,
and because it leads us by that love whose service is
perfect freedom. It leads all things by love, for he cries
again and again that love is the perception of beauty in

thought and things, and it orders all things by love, for it is love that impels the soul to its expressions in thought and in action, by making us 'seek to awaken in all things that are, a community with what we experience within ourselves.' 'We are born into the world, and there is something within us which, from the instant that we live, more and more thirsts after its likeness.' We have 'a soul within our soul that describes a circle around its proper paradise which pain and sorrow and evil dare not overleap,' and we labour to see this soul in many mirrors, that we may possess it the more abundantly. He would hardly seek the progress of the world by any less gentle labour, and would hardly have us resist evil itself. He bids the reformers in the *Philosophical Review of Reform* receive 'the onset of the cavalry,' if it be sent to disperse their meetings, 'with folded arms,' and 'not because active resistance is not justifiable, but because temperance and courage would produce greater advantages than the most decisive victory'; and he gives them like advice in *The Masque of Anarchy*, for liberty, the poem cries, 'is love,' and can make the rich man kiss its feet, and, like those who followed Christ, give away his goods and follow it throughout the world.

He does not believe that the reformation of society can bring this beauty, this divine order, among men without the regeneration of the hearts of men. Even in *Queen Mab*, which was written before he had found his deepest thought, or rather perhaps before he had found words to utter it, for I do not think men change much in their deepest thought, he is less anxious to change men's beliefs, as I think, than to cry out against that serpent more subtle than any beast of the field, 'the cause and the effect of tyranny.' He affirms again and again that the virtuous, those who have 'pure desire and universal love,' are happy in the midst of tyranny, and he foresees a day when the 'Spirit of Nature,' the Spirit of Beauty of his later poems, who has her 'throne of power unappealable' in every human heart, shall have made men so virtuous that 'kingly glare will lose its power to dazzle,' and 'silently pass by,' and, as it seems, commerce, 'the venal interchange of all that human art or nature yield; which wealth should purchase not,' come as silently to an end.

He was always, indeed in chief, a witness for that 'power unappealable.' Maddalo, in *Julian and Maddalo*, says that the soul is powerless, and can only, like a 'dreary bell hung in a heaven-illumined tower, toll our thoughts and our desires to meet below round the rent heart and pray'; but Julian, who is Shelley himself, replies, as the makers of all religions have replied:—

> Where is the love, beauty, and truth we seek
> But in our mind? And if we were not weak,
> Should we be less in deed than in desire?

while *Mont Blanc* is an intricate analogy to affirm that the soul has its sources in 'the secret strength of things which governs thought, and to the infinite dome of heaven is as a law.' He even thought that men might be immortal were they sinless, and his Cythna bids the sailors be without remorse, for all that live are stained as they are. It is thus, she says, that time marks men and their thoughts for the tomb. And the 'Red Comet,' the image of evil in *Laon and Cythna*, when it began its war with the star of beauty, brought not only 'Fear, Hatred, Fraud and Tyranny,' but 'Death, Decay, Earthquake, and Blight and Madness pale.'

When the Red Comet is conquered, when Jupiter is overthrown by Demogorgon, when the prophecy of Queen Mab is fulfilled, visible Nature will put on perfection again. Shelley declares, in one of the notes to *Queen Mab*, that 'there is no great extravagance in presuming . . . that there should be a perfect identity between the moral and physical improvement of the human species,' and thinks it 'certain that wisdom is not compatible with disease, and that, in the present state of the climates of the earth, health, in the true and comprehensive sense of the word, is out of the reach of civilised man.' In *Prometheus Unbound* he sees, as in the ecstasy of a saint, the ships moving among the seas of the world without fear of danger—

> by the light
> Of wave-reflected flowers, and floating odours,
> And music soft,

and poison dying out of the green things, and cruelty out of all living things, and even the toads and efts becoming beautiful, and at last Time being borne 'to his tomb in eternity.'

This beauty, this divine order, whereof all things shall become a part in a kind of resurrection of the body, is already visible to the dead and to souls in ecstasy, for ecstasy is a kind of death. The dying Lionel hears the song of the nightingale, and cries:—

Heardst thou not sweet words among
That heaven-resounding minstrelsy?
Heardst thou not, that those who die
Awake in a world of ecstasy?
That love, when limbs are interwoven,
And sleep, when the night of life is cloven,
And thought, to the world's dim boundaries clinging,
And music, when one beloved is singing,
Is death? Let us drain right joyously
The cup which the sweet bird fills for me.

And in the most famous passage in all his poetry he sings of Death as of a mistress. 'Life, like a dome of many-coloured glass, stains the white radiance of Eternity.' 'Die, if thou wouldst be with that which thou dost seek'; and he sees his own soon-coming death in a rapture of prophecy, for 'the fire for which all thirst' beams upon him, 'consuming the last clouds of cold mortality.' When he is dead he will still influence the living, for though Adonais has fled 'to the burning fountain whence he came,' and 'is a portion of the Eternal which must glow through time and change, unquenchably the same,' and has 'awakened from the dream of life,' he has not gone from the 'young Dawn,' or the caverns and the forests, or the 'faint flowers and fountains.' He has been 'made one with Nature,' and his voice is 'heard in all her music,' and his presence is felt wherever 'that Power may move which has withdrawn his being to its own,' and he bears 'his part' when it is compelling mortal things to their appointed forms, and he overshadows men's minds at their supreme moments, for—

> when lofty thought
> Lifts a young heart above its mortal lair,
> And love and life contend in it for what
> Shall be its earthly doom, the dead live there,
> And move like winds of light on dark and stormy air.

'Of his speculations as to what will befall this inestimable spirit when we appear to die,' Mrs. Shelley has written, 'a mystic ideality tinged these speculations in Shelley's mind; certain stanzas in the poem of *The Sensitive Plant* express, in some degree, the almost inexpressible idea, not that we die into another state, when this state is no longer, from some reason, unapparent as well as apparent, accordant with our being —but that those who rise above the ordinary nature of man, fade from before our imperfect organs; they remain in their "love, beauty, and delight," in a world congenial to them, and we, clogged by "error, ignorance, and strife," see them not till we are fitted by purification and improvement to their higher state.' Not merely happy souls, but all beautiful places and movements and gestures and events, when we think they have ceased to be, have become portions of the Eternal.

> In this life
> Of error, ignorance and strife,
> Where nothing is, but all things seem,
> And we the shadows of the dream,
>
> It is a modest creed, and yet
> Pleasant, if one considers it,
> To own that death itself must be,
> Like all the rest, a mockery.

That garden sweet, that lady fair,
And all sweet shapes and odours there,
In truth have never past away;
'Tis we, 'tis ours, are changed, not they.

For love, and beauty, and delight
There is no death nor change; their might
Exceeds our organs, which endure
No light, being themselves obscure.

He seems in his speculations to have lit on that memory of Nature the visionaries claim for the foundation of their knowledge; but I do not know whether he thought, as they do, that all things good and evil remain for ever, 'thinking the thought and doing the deed,' though not, it may be, self-conscious; or only thought that 'love and beauty and delight' remain for ever. The passage where Queen Mab awakes 'all knowledge of the past,' and the good and evil 'events of old and wondrous times,' was no more doubtless than a part of the machinery of the poem, but all the machineries of poetry are parts of the convictions of antiquity, and readily become again convictions in minds that brood over them with visionary intensity.

Intellectual Beauty has not only the happy dead to do her will, but ministering spirits who correspond to the Devas of the East, and the Elemental Spirits of mediaeval Europe, and the Sidhe of ancient Ireland, and whose too constant presence, and perhaps Shelley's ignorance of their more traditional forms, give some of his poetry an air of rootless fantasy. They change continually in his poetry, as they do in the visions of the mystics everywhere and of the common people in

74

Ireland, and the forms of these changes display, in an especial sense, the flowing forms of his mind when freed from all impulse not out of itself or out of supersensual power. These are 'gleams of a remoter world which visit us in sleep,' spiritual essences whose shadows are the delights of all the senses, sounds 'folded in cells of crystal silence,' 'visions swift, and sweet, and quaint,' which lie waiting their moment 'each in its thin sheath, like a chrysalis,' 'odours' among 'ever-blooming Eden-trees,' 'liquors' that can give 'happy sleep,' or can make tears 'all wonder and delight'; 'the golden genii who spoke to the poets of Greece in dreams'; 'the phantoms' which become the forms of the arts when 'the mind, arising bright from the embrace of beauty,' 'casts on them the gathered rays which are reality'; 'the guardians' who move in 'the atmosphere of human thought,' as 'the birds within the wind, or the fish within the wave,' or man's thought itself through all things; and who join the throng of the happy Hours when Time is passing away—

> As the flying-fish leap
> From the Indian deep,
> And mix with the sea-birds half asleep.

It is these powers which lead Asia and Panthea, as they would lead all the affections of humanity, by words written upon leaves, by faint songs, by eddies of echoes that draw 'all spirits on that secret way,' by the 'dying odours' of flowers and by 'the sunlight of the spherèd dew,' beyond the gates of birth and death to awake Demogorgon, eternity, that 'the painted veil called life' may be 'torn aside.'

There are also ministers of ugliness and all evil, like those that came to Prometheus:—

> As from the rose which the pale priestess kneels
> To gather for her festal crown of flowers
> The aërial crimson falls, flushing her cheek,
> So from our victim's destined agony
> The shade which is our form invests us round;
> Else we are shapeless as our mother Night.

Or like those whose shapes the poet sees in *The Triumph of Life*, coming from the procession that follows the car of life, as 'hope' changes to 'desire,' shadows 'numerous as the dead leaves blown in autumn evening from a poplar-tree'; and resembling those they come from, until, if I understand an obscure phrase aright, they are 'wrapt' round 'all the busy phantoms that were there as the sun shapes the clouds.' Some to sit 'chattering like restless apes,' and some like 'old anatomies' 'hatching their bare broods under the shade of demon wings,' laughing 'to reassume the delegated power' they had given to the tyrants of the earth, and some 'like small gnats and flies' to throng 'about the brow of lawyers, statesmen, priest and theorist,' and some 'like discoloured flakes of snow' to fall 'on fairest bosoms and the sunniest hair,' to be 'melted by the youthful glow which they extinguished,' and many to 'fling shadows of shadows, yet unlike themselves,' shadows that are shaped into new forms by that 'creative ray' in which all move like motes.

These ministers of beauty and ugliness were certainly more than metaphors or picturesque phrases to

one who believed the 'thoughts which are called real
or external objects' differed but in regularity of recurrence from 'hallucinations, dreams, and the ideas of
madness,' and lessened this difference by telling how
he had dreamed 'three several times, between intervals
of two or more years, the same precise dream,' and
who had seen images with the mind's eye that left his
nerves shaken for days together. Shadows that were—

> as when there hovers
> A flock of vampire-bats before the glare
> Of the tropic sun, bringing, ere evening,
> Strange night upon some Indian isle,

could not but have had more than a metaphorical and
picturesque being to one who had spoken in terror with
an image of himself, and who had fainted at the apparition of a woman with eyes in her breasts, and who had
tried to burn down a wood, if we can trust Mrs.
Williams' account, because he believed a devil, who had
first tried to kill him, had sought refuge there.

It seems to me, indeed, that Shelley had reawakened
in himself the age of faith, though there were times
when he would doubt, as even the saints have doubted,
and that he was a revolutionist, because he had heard
the commandment, 'If ye know these things, happy are
ye if ye do them.' I have re-read his *Prometheus Unbound* for the first time for many years, in the woods of
Drim-na-Rod, among the Echtge hills, and sometimes I
have looked towards Slieve ná nOg where the country people say the last battle of the world shall be
fought till the third day, when a priest shall lift a
chalice, and the thousand years of peace begin. And I

think this mysterious song utters a faith as simple and as ancient as the faith of those country people, in a form suited to a new age, that will understand with Blake that the Holy Spirit is 'an intellectual fountain,' and that the kinds and degrees of beauty are the images of its authority.

II. HIS RULING SYMBOLS

At a comparatively early time Shelley made his imprisoned Cythna become wise in all human wisdom through the contemplation of her own mind, and write out this wisdom upon the sands in 'signs' that were 'clear elemental shapes, whose smallest change' made 'a subtler language within language,' and were 'the key of truths which once were dimly taught in old Crotona.' His early romances and much throughout his poetry show how strong a fascination the traditions of magic and of the magical philosophy had cast over his mind, and one can hardly suppose that he had not brooded over their doctrine of symbols or signatures, though I do not find anything to show that he gave it any deep study. One finds in his poetry, besides innumerable images that have not the definiteness of symbols, many images that are certainly symbols, and as the years went by he began to use these with a more and more deliberately symbolic purpose. I imagine that when he wrote his earlier poems he allowed the subconscious life to lay its hands so firmly upon the rudder of his imagination that he was little conscious of the abstract meaning of the images that rose in what seemed the idleness of his mind. Any one who has any experi-

ence of any mystical state of the soul knows how there
float up in the mind profound symbols,[1] whose meaning, if indeed they do not delude one into the dream
that they are meaningless, one does not perhaps understand for years. Nor I think has any one, who has
known that experience with any constancy, failed to
find some day, in some old book or on some old monu-
ment, a strange or intricate image that had floated up
before him, and to grow perhaps dizzy with the sudden
conviction that our little memories are but a part of
some great Memory that renews the world and men's
thoughts age after age, and that our thoughts are not,
as we suppose, the deep, but a little foam upon the deep.
Shelley understood this, as is proved by what he says
of the eternity of beautiful things and of the influence
of the dead, but whether he understood that the great
Memory is also a dwelling-house of symbols, of images
that are living souls, I cannot tell. He had certainly experience of all but the most profound of the mystical
states, and had known that union with created things
which assuredly must precede the soul's union with the
uncreated spirit. He says, in his fragment of an essay 'On
Life', mistaking a unique experience for the common
experience of all: 'Let us recollect our sensations as
children . . . we less habitually distinguished all that we
saw and felt from ourselves. They seemed as it were to
constitute one mass. There are some persons who in
this respect are always children. Those who are subject
to the state called reverie, feel as if their nature were

---

[1] *Marianne's Dream* was certainly copied from a real dream of
somebody's, but like images come to the mystic in his waking state.

resolved into the surrounding universe or as if the surrounding universe were resolved into their being,' and
he must have expected to receive thoughts and images
from beyond his own mind, just in so far as that mind
transcended its preoccupation with particular time and
place, for he believed inspiration a kind of death; and
he could hardly have helped perceiving that an image
that has transcended particular time and place becomes
a symbol, passes beyond death, as it were, and becomes
a living soul.

When Shelley went to the Continent with Godwin's
daughter in 1814 they sailed down certain great rivers
in an open boat, and when he summed up in his preface
to *Laon and Cythna* the things that helped to make
him a poet, he spoke of these voyages: 'I have sailed
down mighty rivers, and seen the sun rise and set, and
the stars come forth, whilst I have sailed night and day
down a rapid stream among mountains.'

He may have seen some cave that was the bed of a
rivulet by some river-side, or have followed some
mountain stream to its source in a cave, for from his
return to England rivers and streams and wells, flowing
through caves or rising in them, came into every poem
of his that was of any length, and always with the precision of symbols. Alastor passed in his boat along a
river in a cave; and when for the last time he felt the
presence of the spirit he loved and followed, it was
when he watched his image in a silent well; and when
he died it was where a river fell into 'an abysmal
chasm'; and the Witch of Atlas in her gladness, as he
in his sadness, passed in her boat along a river in a cave,

and it was where it bubbled out of a cave that she was born; and when Rousseau, the typical poet of *The Triumph of Life*, awoke to the vision that was life, it was where a rivulet bubbled out of a cave; and the poet of *Epipsychidion* met the evil beauty 'by a well, under blue nightshade bowers'; and Cythna bore her child imprisoned in a great cave beside 'a fountain round and vast, in which the wave, imprisoned, boiled and leaped perpetually'; and her lover Laon was brought to his prison in a high column through a cave where there was 'a putrid pool,' and when he went to see the con- quered city he dismounted beside a polluted fountain in the market-place, foreshadowing thereby that spirit who at the end of *Prometheus Unbound* gazes at a re- generated city from 'within a fountain in the public square'; and when Laon and Cythna are dead they awake beside a fountain and drift into Paradise along a river; and at the end of things Prometheus and Asia are to live amid a happy world in a cave where a foun- tain 'leaps with an awakening sound'; and it was by a fountain, the meeting-place of certain unhappy lovers, that Rosalind and Helen told their unhappiness to one another; and it was under a willow by a fountain that the enchantress and her lover began their unhappy love; while his lesser poems and his prose fragments use caves and rivers and wells and fountains continually as metaphors. It may be that his subconscious life seized upon some passing scene, and moulded it into an ancient symbol without help from anything but that great Memory; but so good a Platonist as Shelley could hardly have thought of any cave as a symbol, without

thinking of Plato's cave that was the world; and so
good a scholar may well have had Porphyry on 'the
Cave of the Nymphs' in his mind. When I compare
Porphyry's description of the cave where the Phaeacian
boat left Odysseus, with Shelley's description of the
cave of the Witch of Atlas, to name but one of many,
I find it hard to think otherwise. I quote Taylor's translation, only putting Mr. Lang's prose for Taylor's bad
verse. 'What does Homer obscurely signify by the cave
in Ithaca which he describes in the following verses?
"Now at the harbour's head is a long-leaved olive-tree,
and hard by is a pleasant cave and shadowy, sacred to
the nymphs, that are called Naiads. And therein are
mixing-bowls and jars of stone, and there moreover do
bees hive. And there are great looms of stone, whereon
the nymphs weave raiment of purple stain, a marvel to
behold; and there are waters welling evermore. Two
gates there are to the cave, the one set towards the
North wind, whereby men may go down, but the
portals towards the South pertain rather to the gods,
whereby men may not enter: it is the way of the im-
mortals." ' He goes on to argue that the cave was a
temple before Homer wrote, and that 'the ancients did
not establish temples without fabulous symbols,' and
then begins to interpret Homer's description in all its
detail. The ancients, he says, 'consecrated a cave to the
world' and held 'the flowing waters' and the 'obscurity
of the cavern' 'apt symbols of what the world contains,' and he calls to witness Zoroaster's cave with
fountains; and often caves are, he says, symbols of 'all
invisible power; because as caves are obscure and dark,

so the essence of all these powers is occult,' and quotes a lost hymn to Apollo to prove that nymphs living in caves fed men 'from intellectual fountains'; and he contends that fountains and rivers symbolise generation, and that the word nymph 'is commonly applied to all souls descending into generation,' and that the two gates of Homer's cave are the gate of generation and the gate of ascent through death to the gods, the gate of cold and moisture, and the gate of heat and fire. Cold, he says, causes life in the world, and heat causes life among the gods, and the constellation of the Cup is set in the heavens near the sign Cancer, because it is there that the souls descending from the Milky Way receive their draught of the intoxicating cold drink of generation. 'The mixing-bowls and jars of stone' are consecrated to the Naiads, and are also, as it seems, symbolical of Bacchus, and are of stone because of the rocky beds of the rivers. And 'the looms of stone' are the symbols of the 'souls that descend into generation.' 'For the formation of the flesh is on or about the bones, which in the bodies of animals resemble stones,' and also because 'the body is a garment' not only about the soul, but about all essences that become visible, for 'the heavens are called by the ancients a veil, in consequence of being as it were the vestments of the celestial gods.' The bees hive in the mixing-bowls and jars of stone, for so Porphyry understands the passage, because honey was the symbol adopted by the ancients for 'pleasure arising from generation.' The ancients, he says, called souls not only Naiads but bees, 'as the efficient cause of sweetness'; but not all souls 'proceeding into generation'

are called bees, 'but those who will live in it justly and
who after having performed such things as are acceptable to the gods will again return (to their kindred stars).
For this insect loves to return to the place from whence
it came and is eminently just and sober.' I find all these
details in the cave of the Witch of Atlas, the most
elaborately described of Shelley's caves, except the two
gates, and these have a far-off echo in her summer
journeys on her cavern river and in her winter sleep in
'an inextinguishable well of crimson fire.' We have for
the mixing-bowls, and jars of stone full of honey, those
delights of the senses, 'sounds of air' 'folded in cells of
crystal silence,' 'liquors clear and sweet' 'in crystal
vials,' and for the bees, visions 'each in its thin sheath
like a chrysalis,' and for 'the looms of stone' and 'raiment of purple stain' the Witch's spinning and em-
broidering; and the Witch herself is a Naiad, and was
born from one of the Atlantides, who lay in a 'chamber
of grey rock' until she was changed by the sun's embrace into a cloud.

When one turns to Shelley for an explanation of the
cave and fountain one finds how close his thought was
to Porphyry's. He looked upon thought as a condition
of life in generation and believed that the reality beyond was something other than thought. He wrote in
his fragment *On Life*: 'That the basis of all things
cannot be, as the popular philosophy alleges, mind, is
sufficiently evident. Mind, as far as we have any experience of its properties, and beyond that experience
how vain is argument, cannot create, it can only perceive'; and in another passage he defines mind as exist-

ence. Water is his great symbol of existence, and he continually meditates over its mysterious source. In his prose he tells how 'thought can with difficulty visit the intricate and winding chambers which it inhabits. It is like a river, whose rapid and perpetual stream flows outward. . . . The caverns of the mind are obscure and shadowy; or pervaded with a lustre, beautiful and bright indeed, but shining not beyond their portals.' When the Witch has passed in her boat from the caverned river, that is doubtless her own destiny, she passes along the Nile 'by Moeris and the Mareotid lakes,' and sees all human life shadowed upon its waters in shadows that 'never are erased but tremble ever'; and in 'many a dark and subterranean street under the Nile'—new caverns—and along the bank of the Nile; and as she bends over the unhappy, she compares unhappiness to the strife that 'stirs the liquid surface of man's life'; and because she can see the reality of things she is described as journeying 'in the calm depths' of 'the wide lake' we journey over unpiloted. Alastor calls the river that he follows an image of his mind, and thinks that it will be as hard to say where his thought will be when he is dead as where its waters will be in ocean or cloud in a little while. In *Mont Blanc*, a poem so overladen with descriptions in parentheses that one loses sight of its logic, Shelley compares the flowing through our mind of 'the universe of things,' which are, he has explained elsewhere, but thoughts, to the flowing of the Arve through the ravine, and compares the unknown sources of our thoughts, in some 'remoter world' whose 'gleams' 'visit the soul in sleep,' to Arve's sources among the glaciers on the mountain heights. Cythna, in the passage where she speaks of making signs 'a subtler language within language' on the sand by the 'fountain' of sea water in the cave where she is imprisoned, speaks of the 'cave' of her mind which gave its secrets to her, and of 'one mind, the type of all' which is a 'moveless wave' reflecting 'all moving things that are'; and then passing more completely under the power of the symbol, she speaks of growing wise through contemplation of the images that rise out of the fountain at the call of her will. Again and again one finds some passing allusion to the cave of man's mind, or to the caves of his youth, or to the cave of mysteries we enter at death, for to Shelley as to Porphyry it is more than an image of life in the world. It may mean any enclosed life, as when it is the dwelling-place of Asia and Prometheus, or when it is 'the still cave of poetry,' and it may have all meanings at once, or it may have as little meaning as some ancient religious symbol enwoven from the habit of centuries with the patterns of a carpet or a tapestry.

As Shelley sailed along those great rivers and saw or imagined the cave that associated itself with rivers in his mind, he saw half-ruined towers upon the hilltops, and once at any rate a tower is used to symbolise a meaning that is the contrary to the meaning symbolised by caves. Cythna's lover is brought through the cave where there is a polluted fountain to a high tower, for being man's far-seeing mind, when the world has cast him out he must to the 'towers of thought's crowned powers'; nor is it possible for Shelley to have forgotten this first imprisonment when he made men imprison Lionel in a tower for a like offence; and because I know how hard it is to forget a symbolical meaning, once one has found it, I believe Shelley had more than a romantic scene in his mind when he made Prince Athanase follow his mysterious studies in a lighted tower above the sea, and when he made the old hermit watch over Laon in his sickness in a half-ruined tower, wherein the sea, here doubtless, as to Cythna, 'the one mind,' threw 'spangled sands' and 'rarest sea shells.' The tower, important in Maeterlinck, as in Shelley, is, like the sea, and rivers, and caves with fountains, a very ancient symbol, and would perhaps, as years went by, have grown more important in his poetry. The contrast between it and the cave in *Laon and Cythna* suggests a contrast between the mind looking outward upon men and things and the mind looking inward upon itself, which may or may not have been in Shelley's mind, but certainly helps, with one knows not how many other dim meanings, to give the poem mystery and shadow. It is only by ancient symbols, by symbols that have numberless meanings besides the one or two the writer lays an emphasis upon, or the half-score he knows of, that any highly subjective art can escape from the barrenness and shallowness of a too conscious arrangement, into the abundance and depth of Nature. The poet of essences and pure ideas must seek in the half-lights that glimmer from symbol to symbol as if to the ends of the earth, all that the epic and dramatic poet finds of mystery and shadow in the accidental circumstances of life.

The most important, the most precise of all Shelley's symbols, the one he uses with the fullest knowledge of its meaning, is the Morning and Evening Star. It rises and sets for ever over the towers and rivers, and is the throne of his genius. Personified as a woman it leads Rousseau, the typical poet of *The Triumph of Life*, under the power of the destroying hunger of life, under the power of the sun that we shall find presently as a symbol of life, and it is the Morning Star that wars against the principle of evil in *Laon and Cythna*, at first as a star with a red comet, here a symbol of all evil as it is of disorder in *Epipsychidion*, and then as a serpent with an eagle—symbols in Blake too and in the Alchemists; and it is the Morning Star that appears as a winged youth to a woman, who typifies humanity amid its sorrows, in the first canto of *Laon and Cythna*; and it is invoked by the wailing women of *Hellas*, who call it 'lamp of the free' and 'beacon of love' and would go where it hides flying from the deepening night among those 'kingless continents sinless as Eden,' and 'mountains and islands' 'prankt on the sapphire sea' that are but the opposing hemispheres to the senses, but, as I think, the ideal world, the world of the dead, to the imagination; and in the *Ode to Liberty*, Liberty is bid lead wisdom out of the inmost cave of man's mind as the Morning Star leads the sun out of the waves. We know too that had *Prince Athanase* been finished it would have described the finding of Pandemos, the Star's lower genius, and the growing weary of her, and the coming of its true genius Urania at the coming of death, as the day finds the Star at evening. There is hardly indeed a poem of any length in which one does not find it as a symbol of love, or liberty, or wisdom, or beauty, or of some other expression of that Intellectual Beauty which was to Shelley's mind the central power of the world; and to its faint and fleeting light he offers up all desires, that are as—

> The desire of the moth for the star,
>   Of the night for the morrow,
> The devotion to something afar
>   From the sphere of our sorrow.

When its genius comes to Rousseau, shedding dew with one hand, and treading out the stars with her feet, for she is also the genius of the dawn, she brings him a cup full of oblivion and love. He drinks and his mind becomes like sand 'on desert Labrador' marked by the feet of deer and a wolf. And then the new vision, life, the cold light of day moves before him, and the first vision becomes an invisible presence. The same image was in his mind too when he wrote:—

> Hesperus flies from awakening night
> And pants in its beauty and speed with light,
> Fast fleeting, soft and bright.

Though I do not think that Shelley needed to go to Porphyry's account of the cold intoxicating cup, given to the souls in the constellation of the Cup near the constellation Cancer, for so obvious a symbol as the cup, or that he could not have found the wolf and the deer and the continual flight of his Star in his own mind, his poetry becomes the richer, the more emotional, and loses something of its appearance of idle fantasy when I remember that these are ancient symbols, and still

come to visionaries in their dreams. Because the wolf
is but a more violent symbol of longing and desire
than the hound, his wolf and deer remind me of the
hound and deer that Oisin saw in the Gaelic poem
chasing one another on the water before he saw the
young man following the woman with the golden apple;
and of a Galway tale that tells how Niamh, whose name
means brightness or beauty, came to Oisin as a deer;
and of a vision that a friend of mine saw when gazing
at a dark-blue curtain. I was with a number of Herme-
tists, and one of them said to another, 'Do you see
something in the curtain?' The other gazed at the curtain for a while and saw presently a man led through a
wood by a black hound, and then the hound lay dead
at a place the seer knew was called, without knowing
why, 'the Meeting of the Suns,' and the man followed
a red hound, and then the red hound was pierced by a
spear. A white fawn watched the man out of the wood,
but he did not look at it, for a white hound came and
he followed it trembling, but the seer knew that he
would follow the fawn at last, and that it would lead
him among the gods. The most learned of the Herme-
tists said, 'I cannot tell the meaning of the hounds or
where the Meeting of the Suns is, but I think the fawn
is the Morning and Evening Star.' I have little doubt
that when the man saw the white fawn he was coming
out of the darkness and passion of the world into some
day of partial regeneration, and that it was the Morning
Star and would be the Evening Star at its second coming. I have little doubt that it was but the story of
Prince Athanase and what may have been the story of

Rousseau in *The Triumph of Life*, thrown outward once again from that great Memory, which is still the mother of the Muses, though men no longer believe in it.

It may have been this memory, or it may have been some impulse of his nature too subtle for his mind to follow, that made Keats, with his love of embodied things, of precision of form and colouring, of emotions made sleepy by the flesh, see Intellectual Beauty in the Moon; and Blake, who lived in that energy he called eternal delight, see it in the Sun, where his personification of poetic genius labours at a furnace. I think there was certainly some reason why these men took so deep a pleasure in lights that Shelley thought of with weariness and trouble. The Moon is the most changeable of symbols, and not merely because it is the symbol of change. As mistress of the waters she governs the life of instinct and the generation of things, for, as Porphyry says, even 'the apparition of images' in the 'imagination' is through 'an excess of moisture'; and, as a cold and changeable fire set in the bare heavens, she governs alike chastity and the joyless idle drifting hither and thither of generated things. She may give God a body and have Gabriel to bear her messages, or she may come to men in their happy moments as she came to Endymion, or she may deny life and shoot her arrows; but because she only becomes beautiful in giving herself, and is no flying ideal, she is not loved by the children of desire.

Shelley could not help but see her with unfriendly eyes. He is believed to have described Mary Shelley at a time when she had come to seem cold in his eyes, in that passage of *Epipsychidion* which tells how a woman like the Moon led him to her cave and made 'frost' creep over the sea of his mind, and so bewitched Life and Death with 'her silver voice' that they ran from him crying, 'Away, he is not of our crew.' When he describes the Moon as part of some beautiful scene he can call her beautiful, but when he personifies, when his words come under the influence of that great Memory or of some mysterious tide in the depth of our being, he grows unfriendly or not truly friendly or at the most pitiful. The Moon's lips 'are pale and waning,' it is 'the cold Moon,' or 'the frozen and inconstant Moon,' or it is 'forgotten' and 'waning,' or it 'wanders' and is 'weary,' or it is 'pale and grey,' or it is 'pale for weariness,' and 'wandering companionless' and 'ever changing,' and finding 'no object worth' its 'constancy,' or it is like a 'dying lady' who 'totters' 'out of her chamber led by the insane and feeble wanderings of her fading brain,' and even when it is no more than a star, it casts an evil influence that makes the lips of lovers 'lurid' or pale. It only becomes a thing of delight when Time is being borne to his tomb in eternity, for then the spirit of the Earth, man's procreant mind, fills it with his own joyousness. He describes the spirit of the Earth and of the Moon, moving above the rivulet of their lives, in a passage which reads like a half-understood vision. Man has become 'one harmonious soul of many a soul' and 'all things flow to all' and 'familiar acts are beautiful through love,' and an 'animation of delight' at this change flows from spirit to spirit till the snow 'is loosened' from the Moon's 'lifeless mountains.'

Some old magical writer, I forget who, says if you wish to be melancholy hold in your left hand an image of the Moon made out of silver, and if you wish to be happy hold in your right hand an image of the Sun made out of gold.[1] The Sun is the symbol of sensitive life, and of belief and joy and pride and energy, of indeed the whole life of the will, and of that beauty which neither lures from far off, nor becomes beautiful in giving itself, but makes all glad because it is beauty. Taylor quotes Proclus as calling it 'the Demiurgos of everything sensible.' It was therefore natural that Blake, who was always praising energy, and all exalted over-flowing of oneself, and who thought art an impassioned labour to keep men from doubt and despondency, and woman's love an evil, when it would trammel man's will, should see the poetic genius not in a woman star but in the Sun, and should rejoice throughout his poetry in 'the Sun in his strength.' Shelley, however, except when he uses it to describe the peculiar beauty of Emilia Viviani, who was like 'an incarnation of the Sun when light is changed to love,' saw it with less friendly eyes. He seems to have seen it with perfect happiness only when veiled in mist, or glimmering upon water, or when faint enough to do no more than veil the brightness of his own Star; and in *The Triumph of Life*, the one poem in which it is part of the avowed symbolism, its power is the being and the source of all

[1] Wilde told me that he had read this somewhere. He had suggested it to Burne-Jones as a subject for a picture. 1924.

93

tyrannies. When the woman personifying the Morning Star has faded from before his eyes, Rousseau sees a 'new vision' in 'a cold bright car' with a rainbow hovering over her, and as she comes the shadow passes from 'leaf and stone' and the souls she has enslaved seem 'in that light, like atomies to dance within a sunbeam,' or they dance among the flowers that grow up newly in 'the grassy vesture of the desert,' unmindful of the misery that is to come upon them. These are 'the great, the unforgotten,' all who have worn 'mitres and helms and crowns, or wreaths of light,' and yet have not known themselves. Even 'great Plato' is there, because he knew joy and sorrow, because life that could not subdue him by gold or pain, by 'age, or sloth, or slavery,' subdued him by love. All who have ever lived are there except Christ and Socrates and the 'sacred few' who put away all life could give, being doubtless followers throughout their lives of the forms borne by the flying ideal, or who, 'as soon as they had touched the world with living flame, fled back like eagles to their native noon.'

In ancient times, it seems to me that Blake, who for all his protest was glad to be alive, and ever spoke of his gladness, would have worshipped in some chapel of the Sun, but that Shelley, who hated life because he sought 'more in life than any understood,' would have wandered, lost in a ceaseless reverie, in some chapel of the Star of infinite desire.

I think too that as he knelt before an altar where a thin flame burnt in a lamp made of green agate, a single vision would have come to him again and again, a vision of a boat drifting down a broad river between high hills where there were caves and towers, and following the light of one Star; and that voices would have told him how there is for every man some one scene, some one adventure, some one picture that is the image of his secret life, for wisdom first speaks in images, and that this one image, if he would but brood over it his life long, would lead his soul, disentangled from unmeaning circumstance and the ebb and flow of the world, into that far household where the undying gods await all whose souls have become simple as flame, whose bodies have become quiet as an agate lamp.

But he was born in a day when the old wisdom had vanished and was content merely to write verses, and often with little thought of more than verses.

1900

Ideas of Good and Evil

AT STRATFORD-ON-AVON

I

I HAVE BEEN HEARING SHAKESPEARE as the traveller in *News from Nowhere* might have heard him, had he not been hurried back into our noisy time. One passes through quiet streets, where gabled and red-tiled houses remember the Middle Ages, to a theatre that has been made not to make money, but for the pleasure of making it, like the market-houses that set the traveller chuckling; nor does one find it among hurrying cabs and ringing pavements, but in a green garden by a river-side. Inside I have to be content for a while with a chair, for I am unexpected, and there is not an empty seat but this; and yet there is no one who has come merely because one must go somewhere after dinner. All day, too, one does not hear or see an incongruous or noisy thing, but spends the hours reading the plays, and the wise and foolish things men have said of them, in the library of the theatre, with its oak-panelled walls and leaded windows of tinted glass; or one rows by reedy banks and by old farm-houses, and by old churches among great trees. It is certainly one's fault if one opens a newspaper, for Mr. Benson offers a new play every night, and there is no need to talk of anything but the play in the inn-parlour, under oak beams blackened by time, showing the mark of the adze that shaped them. I have seen this week *King John*, *Richard II*, the second part of *Henry IV*, *Henry V*, the second part of *Henry VI*, and *Richard III* played in their right order, with all the links that bind play to play unbroken; and partly because of a spirit in the place, and partly because of the way play supports play, the theatre has moved me as it has never done before. That strange procession of kings and queens, of warring nobles, of insurgent crowds, of courtiers, and of people of the gutter, has been to me almost too visible, too audible, too full of an unearthly energy. I have felt as I have sometimes felt on grey days on the Galway shore, when a faint mist has hung over the grey sea and the grey stones, as if the world might suddenly vanish and leave nothing behind, not even a little dust under one's feet. The people my mind's eye has seen have too much of the extravagance of dreams, like all the inventions of art before our crowded life had brought moderation and compromise, to seem more than a dream, and yet all else has grown dim before them.

In London the first man you meet puts any high dream out of your head, for he will talk of something at once vapid and exciting, the moment's choice among those subjects of discourse that build up our social unity. But here he gives back one's dream like a mirror. If we do not talk of the plays, we talk of the theatre, and how many more people may be got to come, and our isolation from common things makes the future become grandiose and important. One man tells how the theatre and the library were at their foundation but part of a scheme the future is to fulfil. To them will be added a school where speech, and gesture, and fencing, and all else that an actor needs will be taught, and the council, which will have enlarged its Festivals to some

six weeks, will engage all the chief players of Shakespeare, and perhaps of other great dramatists in this
and other countries.   These chief players will need to
bring but few of their supporters, for the school will
be able to fill all the lesser parts with players who are
slowly recovering the lost tradition of musical speech.
Another man is certain that the Festival, even without
the school, which would require a new endowment,
will grow in importance year by year, and that it may
become with favouring chance the supreme dramatic
event of the world; and when I suggest that it may
help to break the evil prestige of London he becomes
enthusiastic.

Surely a bitter hatred of London is becoming a mark
of those that love the arts, and all that have this hatred
should help anything that looks like a beginning of a
centre of art elsewhere. The easiness of travel, which
is always growing, began by emptying the country,
but it may end by filling it: for adventures like this of
Stratford-on-Avon show that people are ready to journey from all parts of England and Scotland and Ireland,
and even from America, to live with their favourite art
as shut away from the world as though they were in
'retreat,' as Catholics say. Nobody but an impressionist
painter, who hides it in light and mist, even pretends
to love a street for its own sake; and could we meet our
friends and hear music and poetry in the country, none
of us that are not captive would ever leave the thrushes.
In London, we hear something that we like some twice
or thrice in a winter, and among people who are thinking the while of a music-hall singer or of a member of

Parliament, but there we would hear it and see it among people who liked it well enough to have travelled some few hours to find it; and because those who care for the arts have few near friendships among those who do not, we would hear and see it among near friends. We would escape, too, from those artificial tastes and interests we cultivate, that we may have something to talk about among people we meet for a few minutes and not again, and the arts would grow serious as the Ten Commandments.

II

I do not think there is anything I disliked in Stratford, besides certain new houses, but the shape of the theatre; and as a larger theatre must be built sooner or later, that would be no great matter if one could put a wiser shape into somebody's head. I cannot think there is any excuse for a half-round theatre, where land is not expensive, or no very great audience to be seated within earshot of the stage; or that it was adopted for a better reason than because it has come down to us, though from a time when the art of the stage was a different art. The Elizabethan theatre was a half-round, because the players were content to speak their lines on a platform, as if they were speakers at a public meeting, and we go on building in the same shape, although our art of the stage is the art of making a succession of pictures. Were our theatres of the shape of a half-closed fan, like Wagner's theatre, where the audience sit on seats that rise towards the broad end while the play is played at the narrow end, their pictures could be

composed for eyes at a small number of points of view,
instead of for eyes at many points of view, above and
below and at the sides, and what is no better than a
trade might become an art. With the eyes watching
from the sides of a half-round, on the floor and in the
boxes and galleries, would go the solid-built houses and
the flat trees that shake with every breath of air; and
we could make our pictures with robes that contrasted
with great masses of colour in the back-cloth and such
severe or decorative forms of hills and trees and houses
as would not overwhelm, as our naturalistic scenery
does, the idealistic art of the poet, and all at a little price.
Naturalistic scene-painting is not an art, but a trade,
because it is, at best, an attempt to copy the more
obvious effects of Nature by the methods of the ordinary
landscape-painter, and by his methods made coarse and
summary. It is but flashy landscape-painting and lowers
the taste it appeals to, for the taste it appeals to has been
formed by a more delicate art. Decorative scene-painting would be, on the other hand, as inseparable from
the movements as from the robes of the players and
from the falling of the light; and being in itself a grave
and quiet thing it would mingle with the tones of the
voices and with the sentiment of the play, without overwhelming them under an alien interest. It would be a
new and legitimate art appealing to a taste formed by
itself and copying but itself. Mr. Gordon Craig used
scenery of this kind at the Purcell Society performance
the other day, and despite some marring of his effects
by the half-round shape of the theatre, it was the first
beautiful scenery our stage has seen. He created an ideal

country where everything was possible, even speaking in verse, or speaking to music, or the expression of the whole of life in a dance, and I would like to see Stratford-on-Avon decorate its Shakespeare with like scenery. As we cannot, it seems, go back to the platform and the curtain, and the argument for doing so is not without weight, we can only get rid of the sense of unreality, which most of us feel when we listen to the conventional speech of Shakespeare, by making scenery as conventional. Time after time his people use at some moment of deep emotion an elaborate or deliberate metaphor, or do some improbable thing which breaks an emotion of reality we have imposed upon him by an art that is not his, nor in the spirit of his. It also is an essential part of his method to give slight or obscure motives of many actions that our attention may dwell on what is of chief importance, and we set these cloudy actions among solid-looking houses, and what we hope are solid-looking trees, and illusion comes to an end, slain by our desire to increase it. In his art, as in all the older art of the world, there was much make-believe, and our scenery, too, should remember the time when, as my nurse used to tell me, herons built their nests in old men's beards! Mr. Benson did not venture to play the scene in *Richard III* where the ghosts walk as Shakespeare wrote it, but had his scenery been as simple as Mr. Gordon Craig's purple back-cloth that made Dido and Aeneas seem wandering on the edge of eternity, he would have found nothing absurd in pitching the tents of Richard and Richmond side by side. Goethe has said, 'Art is art, because it is not nature!'

It brings us near to the archetypal ideas themselves, and away from nature, which is but their looking-glass.

III

In *La Peau de chagrin* Balzac spends many pages in describing a coquette, who seems the image of heart-lessness, and then invents an improbable incident that her chief victim may discover how beautifully she can sing. Nobody had ever heard her sing, and yet in her singing, and in her chatter with her maid, Balzac tells us, was her true self. He would have us understand that behind the momentary self, which acts and lives in the world, and is subject to the judgment of the world, there is that which cannot be called before any mortal judgment seat, even though a great poet, or novelist, or philosopher be sitting upon it. Great literature has always been written in a like spirit, and is, indeed, the Forgiveness of Sin, and when we find it becoming the Accusation of Sin, as in George Eliot, who plucks her Tito in pieces with as much assurance as if he had been clockwork, literature has begun to change into something else. George Eliot had a fierceness hardly to be found but in a woman turned argumentative, but the habit of mind her fierceness gave its life to was characteristic of her century, and is the habit of mind of the Shakespearian critics. They and she grew up in a century of utilitarianism, when nothing about a man seemed important except his utility to the State, and nothing so useful to the State as the actions whose effect can be weighed by reason. The deeds of Coriolanus, Hamlet, Timon, Richard II had no obvious use, were, indeed, no more than the expression of their personalities, and so it was thought Shakespeare was accusing them, and telling us to be careful lest we deserve the like accusations. It did not occur to the critics that you cannot know a man from his actions because you cannot watch him in every kind of circumstance, and that men are made useless to the State as often by abundance as by emptiness, and that a man's business may at times be revelation, and not reformation. Fortinbras was, it is likely enough, a better king than Hamlet would have been, Aufidius was a more reasonable man than Coriolanus, Henry V was a better man-at-arms than Richard II, but, after all, were not those others who changed nothing for the better and many things for the worse greater in the Divine Hierarchies? Blake has said that 'the roaring of lions, the howling of wolves, the raging of the stormy sea, and the destructive sword are portions of Eternity, too great for the eye of man,' but Blake belonged by right to the ages of Faith, and thought the State of less moment than the Divine Hierarchies. Because reason can only discover completely the use of those obvious actions which everybody admires, and because every character was to be judged by efficiency in action, Shakespearian criticism became a vulgar worshipper of success. I have turned over many books in the library at Stratford-on-Avon, and I have found in nearly all an antithesis, which grew in clearness and violence as the century grew older, between two types, whose representatives were Richard II, 'sentimental,' 'weak,' 'selfish,' 'insincere,' and Henry V, 'Shakespeare's only hero.' These books took the same delight in abasing Richard II that schoolboys do in persecuting some boy of fine temperament, who has weak muscles and a distaste for school games. And they had the admiration for Henry V that schoolboys have for the sailor or soldier hero of a romance in some boys' paper. I cannot claim any minute knowledge of these books, but I think that these emotions began among the German critics, who perhaps saw something French and Latin in Richard II, and I know that Professor Dowden, whose book I once read carefully, first made these emotions eloquent and plausible. He lived in Ireland, where everything has failed, and he meditated frequently upon the perfection of character which had, he thought, made England successful, for, as we say, 'cows beyond the water have long horns.' He forgot that England, as Gordon has said, was made by her adventurers, by her people of wildness and imagination and eccentricity; and thought that Henry V, who only seemed to be these things because he had some commonplace vices, was not only the typical Anglo-Saxon, but the model Shakespeare held up before England; and he even thought it worth while pointing out that Shakespeare himself was making a large fortune while he was writing about Henry's victories. In Professor Dowden's successors this apotheosis went further; and it reached its height at a moment of imperialistic enthusiasm, of ever-deepening conviction that the commonplace shall inherit the earth, when somebody of reputation, whose name I cannot remember, wrote that Shakespeare admired this one character alone out of all his characters. The Accusation of Sin produced its necessary fruit, hatred of all that was abundant, extravagant, exuberant, of all that sets a sail for shipwreck, and flattery of the commonplace emotions and conventional ideals of the mob, the chief Paymaster of accusation.

IV

I cannot believe that Shakespeare looked on his Richard II with any but sympathetic eyes, understanding indeed how ill-fitted he was to be king, at a certain moment of history, but understanding that he was lovable and full of capricious fancy, 'a wild creature' as Pater has called him. The man on whom Shakespeare modelled him had been full of French elegances as he knew from Holinshed, and had given life a new luxury, a new splendour, and been 'too friendly' to his friends, 'too favourable' to his enemies. And certainly Shakespeare had these things in his head when he made his king fail, a little because he lacked some qualities that were doubtless common among his scullions, but more because he had certain qualities that are uncommon in all ages. To suppose that Shakespeare preferred the men who deposed his king is to suppose that Shakespeare judged men with the eyes of a Municipal Councillor weighing the merits of a Town Clerk; and that had he been by when Verlaine cried out from his bed, 'Sir, you have been made by the stroke of a pen, but I have been made by the breath of God,' he would have thought the Hospital Superintendent the better man.

He saw indeed, as I think, in Richard II the defeat that awaits all, whether they be artist or saint, who find themselves where men ask of them a rough energy and have nothing to give but some contemplative virtue, whether lyrical fantasy, or sweetness of temper, or dreamy dignity, or love of God, or love of His creatures. He saw that such a man through sheer bewilderment and impatience can become as unjust or as violent as any common man, any Bolingbroke or Prince John, and yet remain 'that sweet lovely rose.' The courtly and saintly ideals of the Middle Ages were fading, and the practical ideals of the modern age had begun to threaten the unuseful dome of the sky; Merry England was fading, and yet it was not so faded that the poets could not watch the procession of the world with that untroubled sympathy for men as they are, as apart from all they do and seem, which is the substance of tragic irony.

Shakespeare cared little for the State, the source of all our judgments, apart from its shows and splendours, its turmoils and battles, its flamings-out of the uncivilised heart. He did indeed think it wrong to overturn a king, and thereby to swamp peace in civil war, and the historical plays from *Henry IV* to *Richard III*, that monstrous birth and last sign of the wrath of Heaven, are a fulfilment of the prophecy of the Bishop of Carlisle, who was 'raised up by God' to make it; but he had no nice sense of utilities, no ready balance to measure deeds, like that fine instrument, with all the latest improvements, Gervinus and Professor Dowden handle so skilfully. He meditated as Solomon, not as Bentham meditated, upon blind ambitions, untoward acci-

dents, and capricious passions, and the world was almost
as empty in his eyes as it must be in the eyes of God.

> Tired with all these, for restful death I cry;—
>   As, to behold desert a beggar born,
> And needy nothing trimm'd in jollity,
>   And purest faith unhappily forsworn,
>   And gilded honour shamefully misplaced,
>   And maiden virtue rudely strumpeted,
>   And right perfection wrongfully disgraced,
>   And strength by limping sway disabled,
> And art made tongue-tied by authority,
>   And folly, doctor-like, controlling skill,
> And simple truth miscall'd simplicity,
>   And captive good attending captain ill:
> Tired with all these, from these would I be gone,
> Save that, to die, I leave my love alone.

V

The Greeks, a certain scholar has told me, considered
that myths are the activities of the Daimons, and that
the Daimons shape our characters and our lives. I have
often had the fancy that there is some one myth for
every man, which, if we but knew it, would make us
understand all he did and thought. Shakespeare's myth,
it may be, describes a wise man who was blind from
very wisdom, and an empty man who thrust him from
his place, and saw all that could be seen from very
emptiness. It is in the story of Hamlet, who saw too
great issues everywhere to play the trivial game of life,
and of Fortinbras, who came from fighting battles
about 'a little patch of ground' so poor that one of his
captains would not give 'six ducats' to 'farm it,' and

who was yet acclaimed by Hamlet and by all as the only befitting king. And it is in the story of Richard II, that unripened Hamlet, and of Henry V, that ripened Fortinbras. To pose character against character was an element in Shakespeare's art, and scarcely a play is lacking in characters that are the complement of one another, and so, having made the vessel of porcelain, Richard II, he had to make the vessel of clay, Henry V. He makes him the reverse of all that Richard was. He has the gross vices, the coarse nerves, of one who is to rule among violent people, and he is so little 'too friendly' to his friends that he bundles them out of doors when their time is over. He is as remorseless and undistinguished as some natural force, and the finest thing in his play is the way his old companions fall out of it broken-hearted or on their way to the gallows; and instead of that lyricism which rose out of Richard's mind like the jet of a fountain to fall again where it had risen, instead of that fantasy too enfolded in its own sincerity to make any thought the hour had need of, Shakespeare has given him a resounding rhetoric that moves men as a leading article does to-day. His purposes are so intelligible to everybody that everybody talks of him as if he succeeded, although he fails in the end, as all men great and little fail in Shakespeare. His conquests abroad are made nothing by a woman turned warrior. That boy he and Katharine were to 'compound,' 'half French, half English,' 'that' was to 'go to Constantinople and take the Turk by the beard,' turns out a saint and loses all his father had built up at home and his own life.

Shakespeare watched Henry V not indeed as he watched the greater souls in the visionary procession, but cheerfully, as one watches some handsome spirited horse, and he spoke his tale, as he spoke all tales, with tragic irony.

VI

The six plays, that are but one play, have, when played one after another, something extravagant and superhuman, something almost mythological. These nobles with their indifference to death and their immense energy seem at times no nearer the common stature of men than do the gods and the heroes of Greek plays. Had there been no Renaissance and no Italian influence to bring in the stories of other lands, English history would, it may be, have become as important to the English imagination as the Greek myths to the Greek imagination; and many plays by many poets would have woven it into a single story whose contours, vast as those of Greek myth, would have made living men and women seem like swallows building their nests under the architrave of some Temple of the Giants. English literature, because it would have grown out of itself, might have had the simplicity and unity of Greek literature, for I can never get out of my head that no man, even though he be Shakespeare, can write perfectly when his web is woven of threads that have been spun in many lands. And yet, could those foreign tales have come in if the great famine, the sinking down of popular imagination, the dying out of traditional fantasy, the ebbing out of the energy of race, had not made them necessary? The metaphors and language of Euphuism, compounded of the natural history and mythology of the classics, were doubtless a necessity also that something might be poured into the emptiness. Yet how they injured the simplicity and unity of the speech! Shakespeare wrote at a time when solitary great men were gathering to themselves the fire that had once flowed hither and thither among all men, when individualism in work and thought and emotion was breaking up the old rhythms of life, when the common people, sustained no longer by the myths of Christianity and of still older faiths, were sinking into the earth.

The people of Stratford-on-Avon have remembered little about him, and invented no legend to his glory. They have remembered a drinking-bout of his, and invented some bad verses for him, and that is about all. Had he been some hard-drinking, hard-living, hard-riding, loud-blaspheming squire they would have enlarged his fame by a legend of his dealings with the Devil; but in his day the glory of a poet, like that of all other imaginative powers, had ceased, or almost ceased, outside a narrow class. The poor Gaelic rhymer leaves a nobler memory among his neighbours, who will talk of angels standing like flames about his death-bed, and of voices speaking out of bramble-bushes that he may have the wisdom of the world. The Puritanism that drove the theatres into Surrey was but part of an inexplicable movement that was trampling out the minds of all but some few thousands born to cultivated ease.

May 1901

William Blake and the Imagination

WILLIAM BLAKE AND THE IMAGINATION

THERE HAVE BEEN MEN who loved the future like a mistress, and the future mixed her breath into their breath and shook her hair about them, and hid them from the understanding of their times. William Blake was one of these men, and if he spoke confusedly and obscurely it was because he spoke of things for whose speaking he could find no models in the world he knew. He announced the religion of art, of which no man dreamed in the world he knew; and he understood it more perfectly than the thousands of subtle spirits who have received its baptism in the world we know, because in the beginning of important things—in the beginning of love, in the beginning of the day, in the beginning of any work—there is a moment when we understand more perfectly than we understand again until all is finished. In his time educated people believed that they amused themselves with books of imagination, but that they 'made their souls' by listening to sermons and by doing or by not doing certain things. When they had to explain why serious people like themselves honoured the great poets greatly they were hard put to it for lack of good reasons. In our time we are agreed that we 'make our souls' out of some one of the great poets of ancient times, or out of Shelley or Wordsworth, or Goethe or Balzac, or Flaubert, or Count Tolstoy, in the books he wrote before he became a prophet and fell into a lesser order, or out of Mr. Whistler's pictures, while we amuse ourselves, or, at

best, make a poorer sort of soul, by listening to sermons
or by doing or by not doing certain things. We write
of great writers, even of writers whose beauty would
once have seemed an unholy beauty, with rapt sentences like those our fathers kept for the beatitudes and
mysteries of the Church; and no matter what we believe with our lips, we believe with our hearts that
beautiful things, as Browning said in his one prose essay
that was not in verse, have 'lain burningly on the
Divine hand,' and that when time has begun to wither,
the Divine hand will fall heavily on bad taste and
vulgarity. When no man believed these things William
Blake believed them, and began that preaching against
the Philistines which is as the preaching of the Middle
Ages against the Saracen.

He had learned from Jacob Boehme and from old
alchemist writers that imagination was the first emana-
tion of divinity, 'the body of God,' 'the Divine members,' and he drew the deduction, which they did not
draw, that the imaginative arts were therefore the
greatest of Divine revelations, and that the sympathy
with all living things, sinful and righteous alike, which
the imaginative arts awaken, is that forgiveness of sins
commanded by Christ. The reason, and by the reason
he meant deductions from the observations of the
senses, binds us to mortality because it binds us to the
senses, and divides us from each other by showing us
our clashing interests; but imagination divides us from
mortality by the immortality of beauty, and binds us
to each other by opening the secret doors of all hearts.
He cried again and again that everything that lives is

holy, and that nothing is unholy except things that do not live—lethargies, and cruelties, and timidities, and that denial of imagination which is the root they grew from in old times. Passions, because most living, are most holy—and this was a scandalous paradox in his time—and man shall enter eternity borne upon their wings.

And he understood this so literally that certain drawings to *Vala*, had he carried them beyond the first faint pencillings, the first faint washes of colour, would have been a pretty scandal to his time and to our time. The sensations of this 'foolish body,' this 'phantom of the earth and water,' were in themselves but half-living things, 'vegetative' things, but passion, that 'eternal glory,' made them a part of the body of God.

This philosophy kept him more simply a poet than any poet of his time, for it made him content to express every beautiful feeling that came into his head without troubling about its utility or chaining it to any utility. Sometimes one feels, even when one is reading poets of a better time—Tennyson or Wordsworth, let us say—that they have troubled the energy and simplicity of their imaginative passions by asking whether they were for the helping or for the hindrance of the world, instead of believing that all beautiful things have 'lain burningly on the Divine hand.' But when one reads Blake, it is as though the spray of an inexhaustible fountain of beauty was blown into our faces, and not merely when one reads the *Songs of Innocence*, or the lyrics he wished to call 'Ideas of Good and Evil,' but when one reads those 'Prophetic Books' in which he spoke confusedly and obscurely because he spoke of things for whose speaking he could find no models in the world about him. He was a symbolist who had to invent his symbols; and his counties of England, with their correspondence to tribes of Israel, and his mountains and rivers, with their correspondence to parts of a man's body, are arbitrary as some of the symbolism in the *Axël* of the symbolist Villiers de l'Isle-Adam is arbitrary, while they mix incongruous things as *Axël* does not. He was a man crying out for a mythology, and trying to make one because he could not find one to his hand. Had he been a Catholic of Dante's time he would have been well content with Mary and the angels; or had he been a scholar of our time he would have taken his symbols where Wagner took his, from Norse mythology; or have followed, with the help of Professor Rhys, that pathway into Welsh mythology which he found in *Jerusalem*; or have gone to Ireland and chosen for his symbols the sacred mountains, along whose sides the peasant still sees enchanted fires, and the divinities which have not faded from the belief, if they have faded from the prayers, of simple hearts; and have spoken without mixing incongruous things because he spoke of things that had been long steeped in emotion; and have been less obscure because a traditional mythology stood on the threshold of his meaning and on the margin of his sacred darkness. If Enitharmon had been named Freia, or Gwydeon, or Dana, and made live in Ancient Norway, or Ancient Wales, or Ancient Ireland, we would have forgotten that her maker was a mystic; and the hymn of her harping, that is in *Vala,* would but have reminded us of many ancient hymns.

> The joy of woman is the death of her most best beloved,
> Who dies for love of her,
> In torments of fierce jealousy and pangs of adoration.
> The lovers' night bears on my song,
> And the nine spheres rejoice beneath my powerful control.
>
> They sing unceasing to the notes of my immortal hand.
> The solemn, silent moon
> Reverberates the living harmony upon my limbs.
> The birds and beasts rejoice and play,
> And every one seeks for his mate to prove his inmost joy.
>
> Furious and terrible they sport and red the nether deep.
> The deep lifts up his rugged head,
> And lost in infinite humming wings vanishes with a cry.
> The fading cry is ever dying,
> The living voice is ever living in its inmost joy.

1897

WILLIAM BLAKE AND HIS ILLUSTRATIONS TO THE *DIVINE COMEDY*

I. HIS OPINIONS UPON ART

WILLIAM BLAKE WAS THE FIRST WRITER of modern times to preach the indissoluble marriage of all great art with symbol. There had been allegorists and teachers of allegory in plenty, but the symbolic imagination, or, as Blake preferred to call it, 'vision,' is not allegory, being 'a representation of what actually exists really and unchangeably.' A symbol is indeed the only possible expression of some invisible essence, a transparent lamp about a spiritual flame; while allegory is one of many possible representations of an embodied thing, or familiar principle, and belongs to fancy and not to imagination: the one is a revelation, the other an amusement. It is happily no part of my purpose to expound in detail the relations he believed to exist between symbol and mind, for in doing so I should come upon not a few doctrines which, though they have not been difficult to many simple persons, ascetics wrapped in skins, women who had cast away all common knowledge, peasants dreaming by their sheepfolds upon the hills, are full of obscurity to the man of modern culture; but it is necessary to just touch upon these relations, because in them was the fountain of much of the practice and of all the precept of his artistic life.

If a man would enter into 'Noah's rainbow,' he has written, and 'make a friend' of one of 'the images of wonder' which dwell there, and which always entreat him 'to leave mortal things,' 'then would he arise from the grave and meet the Lord in the air'; and by this rainbow, this sign of a covenant granted to him who is with Shem and Japhet, 'painting, poetry and music,' 'the three powers in man of conversing with Paradise which the flood "of time and space" did not sweep away,' Blake represented the shapes of beauty haunting our moments of inspiration: shapes held by most for the frailest of ephemera, but by him for a people older than the world, citizens of eternity, appearing and re-appearing in the minds of artists and of poets, creating all we touch and see by casting distorted images of themselves upon 'the vegetable glass of nature'; and because beings, none the less symbols, blossoms, as it were, growing from invisible immortal roots, hands, as it were, pointing the way into some divine labyrinth. If 'the world of imagination' was 'the world of eternity,' as this doctrine implied, it was of less importance to know men and nature than to distinguish the beings and substances of imagination from those of a more perishable kind, created by the fantasy, in uninspired moments, out of memory and whim; and this could best be done by purifying one's mind, as with a flame, in study of the works of the great masters, who were great because they had been granted by divine favour a vision of the unfallen world from which others are kept apart by the flaming sword that turns every way; and by flying from the painters who studied 'the vege-table glass' for its own sake, and not to discover there the shadows of imperishable beings and substances, and who entered into their own minds, not to make the unfallen world a test of all they heard and saw and felt with the senses, but to cover the naked spirit with 'the rotten rags of memory' of older sensations. The struggle of the first part of his life had been to distinguish between these two schools, and to cleave always to the Florentine, and so to escape the fascination of those who seemed to him to offer the sleep of nature to a spirit weary with the labours of inspiration; but it was only after his return to London from Felpham in 1804 that he finally escaped from 'temptations and perturbations' which sought to destroy 'the imaginative power' at 'the hands of Venetian and Flemish Demons.' 'The spirit of Titian'—and one must always remember that he had only seen poor engravings, and what his disciple, Palmer, has called 'picture-dealers' Titians'—'was particularly active in raising doubts concerning the possibility of executing without a model; and when once he had raised the doubt it became easy for him to snatch away the vision time after time'; and Blake's imagination 'weakened' and 'darkened' until a 'memory of nature and of pictures of various schools possessed his mind, instead of appropriate execution' flowing from the vision itself. But now he wrote, 'O glory, and O delight! I have entirely reduced that spectrous fiend to his station'—he had overcome the merely reasoning and sensual portion of the mind—'whose annoyance has been the ruin of my labours for the last passed twenty years of my life. . . . I speak with perfect confidence and certainty of the fact which has passed upon me. Nebuchadnezzar had seven times passed over

him, I have had twenty; thank God I was not altogether
a beast as he was. . . . Suddenly, on the day after visiting
the Truchsessian Gallery of pictures'—this was a gallery
containing pictures by Albert Dürer and by the great
Florentines—'I was again enlightened with the light I
enjoyed in my youth, and which has for exactly twenty
years been closed from me, as by a door and by window-
shutters. . . . Excuse my enthusiasm, or rather madness,
for I am really drunk with intellectual vision whenever
I take a pencil or graver into my hand, even as I used
to be in my youth.'

This letter may have been the expression of a moment's enthusiasm, but was more probably rooted in
one of those intuitions of coming technical power
which every creator feels, and learns to rely upon; for
all his greatest work was done, and the principles of his
art were formulated, after this date. Except a word here
and there, his writings hitherto had not dealt with the
principles of art except remotely and by implication;
but now he wrote much upon them, and not in obscure
symbolic verse, but in emphatic prose, and explicit if
not very poetical rhyme. He explained spiritual art, and
. praised the painters of Florence and their influence and
cursed all that has come of Venice and Holland in his
Descriptive Catalogue, in the *Address to the Public*, in
the notes on Sir Joshua Reynolds, in *The Book of
Moonlight*—of which some not very dignified rhymes
alone remain—in beautiful detached passages of his
MS. Book. The limitation of his view was from the
very intensity of his vision; he was a too literal realist
of imagination, as others are of nature; and because he

believed that the figures seen by the mind's eye, when exalted by inspiration, were 'eternal existences,' symbols of divine essences, he hated every grace of style that might obscure their lineaments. To wrap them about in reflected lights was to do this, and to dwell over-fondly upon any softness of hair or flesh was to dwell upon that which was least permanent and least characteristic, for 'The great and golden rule of art, as well as of life, is this: that the more distinct, sharp and wiry the bounding line, the more perfect the work of art; and the less keen and sharp, the greater is the evidence of weak imitation, plagiarism and bungling.' Inspiration was to see the permanent and characteristic in all forms, and if you had it not, you must needs imitate with a languid mind the things you saw or remembered, and so sink into the sleep of nature where all is soft and melting. 'Great inventors in all ages knew this. Protogenes and Apelles knew each other by this line. Raphael and Michelangelo and Albert Dürer are known by this and this alone. . . How do we distinguish the oak from the beech, the horse from the ox, but by the bounding outline? How do we distinguish one face or countenance from another, but by the bounding outline and its infinite inflections and movements? What is it that builds a house and plants a garden, but the definite and determinate? What is it that distinguishes honesty from knavery, but the hard and wiry line of rectitude and certainty in the actions and intentions? Leave out this line and you leave out life itself; all is chaos again, and the line of the Almighty must be drawn out upon it before man or beast can exist.' He even insisted that 'colouring does not depend upon where the colours are put, but upon where the lights and darks are put, and all depends on form or outline'—meaning, I suppose, that a colour gets its brilliance or its depth from being in light or in shadow. He does not mean by outline the bounding line dividing a form from its background, as one of his commentators has thought, but the line that divides it from surrounding space, and unless you have an overmastering sense of this you cannot draw true beauty at all, but only 'the beauty that is appended to folly,' a beauty of mere voluptuous softness, 'a lamentable accident of the mortal and perishing life,' for 'the beauty proper for sublime art is lineaments, or forms and features that are capable of being the receptacles of intellect,' and 'the face or limbs that alter least from infancy to old age are the face and limbs of greatest beauty and perfection.' His praise of a severe art had been beyond price had his age rested a moment to listen, in the midst of its enthusiasm for Correggio and the later Renaissance, for Bartolozzi and for Stothard. What matter if in his visionary realism, in his enthusiasm for what, after all, is perhaps the greatest art, he refused to admit that he who wraps the vision in lights and shadows, in iridescent or glowing colour, until form be half lost in pattern, may, as did Titian in his *Bacchus and Ariadne*, create a talisman as powerfully charged with intellectual virtue as though it were a jewel-studded door of the city seen on Patmos?

To cover the imperishable lineaments of beauty with shadows and reflected lights was to fall into the power of his 'Vala,' the indolent fascination of Nature, the woman divinity who is so often described in the 'Prophetic Books' as 'sweet pestilence,' and whose children weave webs to take the souls of men; but there was a yet more lamentable chance, for Nature has also a 'masculine portion' or 'spectre' which kills instead of taking prisoner, and is continually at war with inspiration. To 'generalise' forms and shadows, to 'smooth out' spaces and lines in obedience to 'laws of composition,' and of painting; founded not upon imagination, which always thirsts for variety and delights in freedom, but upon reasoning from sensation, which is always seeking to reduce everything to a lifeless and slavish uniformity; as the popular art of Blake's day had done, and as he understood Sir Joshua Reynolds to advise, was to fall into 'Entuthon Benithon,' or 'the Lake of Udan Adan,' or some other of those regions where the imagination and the flesh are alike dead, that he names by so many resonant fantastical names. 'General knowledge is remote knowledge,' he wrote; 'it is in particulars that wisdom consists, and happiness too. Both in art and life general masses are as much art as a pasteboard man is human. Every man has eyes, nose and mouth; this every idiot knows. But he who enters into and discriminates most minutely the manners and intentions, the characters in all their branches, is the alone wise or sensible man, and on this discrimination all art is founded. . . . As poetry admits not a letter that is insignificant, so painting admits not a grain of sand or a blade of grass insignificant, much less an insignificant blot or blur.'

Against another desire of his time, derivative also from what he has called 'corporeal reason,' the desire for 'a tepid moderation,' for a lifeless 'sanity in both art and life,' he had protested years before with a paradoxical violence. 'The roadway of excess leads to the palace of wisdom,' and we must only 'bring out weight and measure in time of dearth.' This protest, carried, in the notes on Sir Joshua Reynolds, to the point of dwelling with pleasure on the thought that 'The *Lives of the Painters* say that Raphael died of dissipation,' because dissipation is better than emotional penury, seemed as important to his old age as to his youth. He taught it to his disciples, and one finds it in its purely artistic shape in a diary written by Samuel Palmer, in 1824: 'Excess is the essential vivifying spirit, vital spark, embalming spice of the finest art. There are many mediums in the *means*—none, oh, not a jot, not a shadow of a jot, in the *end* of great art. In a picture whose merit is to be excessively brilliant, it can't be too brilliant, but individual tints may be too brilliant. . . . We must not begin with medium, but think always on excess and only use medium to make excess more abundantly excessive.'

These three primary commands, to seek a determinate outline, to avoid a generalised treatment, and to desire always abundance and exuberance, were insisted upon with vehement anger, and their opponents called again and again 'demons' and 'villains,' 'hired' by the wealthy and the idle; but in private, Palmer has told us, he could find 'sources of delight throughout the whole range of art,' and was ever ready to praise excellence in any school, finding, doubtless, among friends, no need for the emphasis of exaggeration. There is a beautiful passage in *Jerusalem* in which the merely mortal part of the mind, 'the spectre,' creates 'pyramids of pride,' and 'pillars in the deepest hell to reach the heavenly arches,' and seeks to discover wisdom in 'the spaces between the stars,' not 'in the stars,' where it is, but the immortal part makes all his labours vain, and turns his pyramids to 'grains of sand,' his 'pillars' to 'dust on the fly's wing,' and makes of 'his starry heavens a moth of gold and silver mocking his anxious grasp.' So when man's desire to rest from spiritual labour, and his thirst to fill his art with mere sensation and memory, seem upon the point of triumph, some miracle transforms them to a new inspiration; and here and there among the pictures born of sensation and memory is the murmuring of a new ritual, the glimmering of new talismans and symbols.

It was during and after the writing of these opinions that Blake did the various series of pictures which have brought him the bulk of his fame. He had already completed the illustrations to Young's *Night Thoughts*—in which the great sprawling figures, a little wearisome even with the luminous colours of the original water-colour, became nearly intolerable in plain black and white—and almost all the illustrations to the 'Prophetic Books,' which have an energy like that of the elements, but are rather rapid sketches taken while some phantasmic procession swept over him, than elaborate compositions, and in whose shadowy adventures one finds not merely, as did Dr. Garth Wilkinson, 'the hells of the ancient people, the Anakim, the Nephalim, and the Rephaim . . . gigantic petrifactions from which the fires of lust and intense selfish passion have long dissipated what was animal and vital'; not merely the shadows cast by the powers who had closed the light from him as 'with a door and window-shutters,' but the shadows of those who gave them battle. He did now, however, the many designs to Milton, of which I have only seen those to *Paradise Regained*; the reproductions of those to *Comus*, published, I think, by Mr. Quaritch; and the three or four to *Paradise Lost*, engraved by Bell Scott—a series of designs which one good judge considers his greatest work; the illustrations to Blair's *Grave*, whose gravity and passion struggled with the mechanical softness and trivial smoothness of Schiavonetti's engraving; the illustrations to Thornton's *Virgil*, whose influence is manifest in the work of the little group of landscape-painters who gathered about him in his old age and delighted to call him master. The member of the group whom I have already so often quoted has alone praised worthily these illustrations to the first Eclogue: 'There is in all such a misty and dreamy glimmer as penetrates and kindles the inmost soul and gives complete and unreserved delight, unlike the gaudy daylight of this world. They are like all this wonderful artist's work, the drawing aside of the fleshly curtain, and the glimpse which all the most holy, studious saints and sages have enjoyed, of the rest which remains to the people of God.' Now, too, he did the great series, the crowning work of his life, the illustrations to *The Book of Job* and the illustrations to the *Divine Comedy*. Hitherto he had protested against the mechanical 'dots and lozenges' and 'blots and blurs' of Woollett and Strange,[1] but had himself used both 'dot and lozenge,' 'blot and blur,' though always in subordination 'to a firm and determinate outline'; but in Marc Antonio, certain of whose engravings he was shown by Linnell, he found a style full of delicate lines, a style where all was living and energetic, strong and subtle. And almost his last words, a letter written upon his death-bed, attack the 'dots and lozenges' with even more than usually quaint symbolism, and praise expressive lines. 'I know too well that the majority of Englishmen are fond of the in-definite . . . a line is a line in its minutest subdivisions, straight or crooked. It is itself, not intermeasurable by anything else . . . but since the French Revolution'— since the reign of reason began, that is—'Englishmen are all intermeasurable by one another; certainly a happy state of agreement, in which I for one do not agree.' The Dante series occupied the last years of his life; even when too weak to get out of bed he worked on, propped up with the great drawing-book before him. He sketched a hundred designs, but left nearly all incomplete, some greatly so, and partly engraved seven plates, of which the 'Francesca and Paolo' is the most finished. It is not, I think, inferior to any but the finest in *Job*, if indeed to them, and shows in its perfection Blake's mastery

---

[1] Woollett and Strange had established names when Blake began to draw, and must have seemed to Blake in certain moods the types of all triumphant iniquity. Woollett used to fire a cannon from the roof of his house whenever he finished an important plate.

over elemental things, the swirl in which the lost spirits are hurried, 'a watery flame' he would have called it, the haunted waters and the huddling shapes. In the illustrations of Purgatory there is a serene beauty, and one finds his Dante and Virgil climbing among the rough rocks under a cloudy sun, and in their sleep upon the smooth steps towards the summit, a placid, marmoreal, tender, starry rapture.

All in this great series are in some measure powerful and moving, and not, as it is customary to say of the work of Blake, because a flaming imagination pierces through a cloudy and indecisive technique, but because they have the only excellence possible in any art, a mastery over artistic expression. The technique of Blake was imperfect, incomplete, as is the technique of wellnigh all artists who have striven to bring fires from remote summits; but where his imagination is perfect and complete, his technique has a like perfection, a like completeness. He strove to embody more subtle raptures, more elaborate intuitions than any before him; his imagination and technique are more broken and strained under a great burden than the imagination and technique of any other master. 'I am,' wrote Blake, 'like others, just equal in invention and execution.' And again, 'No man can improve an original invention; nor can an original invention exist without execution, organised, delineated and articulated either by God or man . . . I have heard people say, "Give me the ideas; it is no matter what words you put them into"; and others say, "Give me the design; it is no matter for the execution." . . . Ideas cannot be given but in their minutely appropriate words, nor can a design be made without its minutely appropriate execution.' Living in a time when technique and imagination are continually perfect and complete, because they no longer strive to bring fire from heaven, we forget how imperfect and incomplete they were in even the greatest masters, in Botticelli, in Orcagna, and in Giotto.

The errors in the handiwork of exalted spirits are as the more fantastical errors in their lives; as Coleridge's opium cloud; as Villiers de l'Isle-Adam's candidature for the throne of Greece; as Blake's anger against causes and purposes he but half understood; as that veritable madness an Eastern scripture thinks permissible among the saints; for he who half lives in eternity endures a rending of the structures of the mind, a crucifixion of the intellectual body.

II. HIS OPINIONS ON DANTE

As Blake sat bent over the great drawing-book, in which he made his designs to the *Divine Comedy*, he was very certain that he and Dante represented spiritual states which face one another in an eternal enmity. Dante, because a great poet, was 'inspired by the Holy Ghost'; but his inspiration was mingled with a certain philosophy, blown up out of his age, which Blake held for mortal and the enemy of immortal things, and which from the earliest times has sat in high places and ruled the world. This philosophy was the philosophy of soldiers, of men of the world, of priests busy with government, of all who, because of the absorption in active life, have been persuaded to judge and to punish, and partly also, he admitted, the philosophy of Christ, who in descending into the world had to take on the world; who, in being born of Mary, a symbol of the law in Blake's symbolic language, had to 'take after his mother,' and drive the money-changers out of the Temple. Opposed to this was another philosophy, not made by men of action, drudges of time and space, but by Christ when wrapped in the divine essence, and by artists and poets, who are taught by the nature of their craft to sympathise with all living things, and who, the more pure and fragrant is their lamp, pass the further from all limitations, to come at last to forget good and evil in an absorbing vision of the happy and the unhappy. The one philosophy was worldly, and established for the ordering of the body and the fallen will, and so long as it did not call its 'laws of prudence' 'the laws of God,' was a necessity, because 'you cannot have liberty in this world without what you call moral virtue'; the other was divine, and established for the peace of the imagination and the unfallen will, and, even when obeyed with a too literal reverence, could make men sin against no higher principality than prudence. He called the followers of the first philosophy pagans, no matter by what name they knew themselves, because the pagans, as he understood the word pagan, believed more in the outward life, and in what he called 'war, princedom, and victory,' than in the secret life of the spirit; and the followers of the second philosophy Christians, because only those whose sympathies had been enlarged and instructed by art and poetry could obey the Christian command of unlimited forgiveness. Blake had already found this 'pagan' philosophy in Swedenborg, in Milton, in Wordsworth, in Sir Joshua Reynolds, in many persons, and it had roused him so constantly and to such angry paradox that its overthrow became the signal passion of his life, and filled all he did and thought with the excitement of a supreme issue. Its kingdom was bound to grow weaker so soon as life began to lose a little in crude passion and naïve tumult, but Blake was the first to announce its successor, and he did this, as must needs be with revolutionists who have 'the law' for 'mother,' with a firm conviction that the things his opponents held white were indeed black, and the things they held black were white; with a strong persuasion that all busy with government are men of darkness and 'something other than human life.' One is reminded of Shelley, who was the next to take up the cry, though with a less abundant philosophic faculty, but still more of Nietzsche, whose thought flows always, though with an even more violent current, in the bed Blake's thought has worn.

The kingdom that was passing was, he held, the kingdom of the Tree of Knowledge; the kingdom that was coming was the kingdom of the Tree of Life: men who ate from the Tree of Knowledge wasted their days in anger against one another, and in taking one another captive in great nets; men who sought their food among the green leaves of the Tree of Life condemned none but the unimaginative and the idle, and those who forget that even love and death and old age are an imaginative art.

Blake's Illustrations to Dante

In these opposing kingdoms is the explanation of the petulant sayings he wrote on the margins of the great sketch-book, and of those others, still more petulant, which Crabb Robinson has recorded in his diary. The sayings about the forgiveness of sins have no need for further explanation, and are in contrast with the attitude of that excellent commentator, Herr Hettingen, who, though Dante swooned from pity at the tale of Francesca, will only 'sympathise' with her 'to a certain extent,' being taken in a theological net. 'It seems as if Dante,' Blake wrote, 'supposes God was something superior to the Father or Jesus; for if He gives rain to the evil and the good, and His sun to the just and the unjust, He can never have builded Dante's Hell, nor the Hell of the Bible, as our parsons explain it. It must have been framed by the dark spirit itself, and so I understand it.' And again, 'Whatever task is of vengeance and whatever is against forgiveness of sin is not of the Father, but of Satan, the accuser, the father of Hell.' And again, and this time to Crabb Robinson, 'Dante saw devils where I saw none. I see good only.' 'I have never known a very bad man who had not something very good about him.' This forgiveness was not the forgiveness of the theologian who has received a commandment from afar off, but of the poet and artist, who believes he has been taught, in a mystical vision, 'that the imagination is the man himself,' and believes he has discovered in the practice of his art that without a perfect sympathy there is no perfect imagination, and therefore no perfect life. At another moment he called Dante 'an atheist, a mere politician busied about this world, as Milton was, till, in his old age, he returned to God whom he had had in his child-hood.' 'Everything is atheism,' he had already explained, 'which assumes the reality of the natural and unspiritual world.' Dante, he held, assumed its reality when he made obedience to its laws a condition of man's happiness hereafter, and he set Swedenborg beside Dante in misbelief for calling Nature 'the ultimate of Heaven,' a lowest rung, as it were, of Jacob's ladder, instead of a net woven by Satan to entangle our wandering joys and bring our hearts into captivity. There are certain curious unfinished diagrams scattered here and there among the now separated pages of the sketch-book, and of these there is one which, had it had all its concentric rings filled with names, would have been a systematic exposition of his animosities and of their various intensity. It represents Paradise, and in the midst, where Dante emerges from the Earthly Paradise, is written 'Homer,' and in the next circle 'Swedenborg,' and on the margin these words: 'Everything in Dante's Paradise shows that he has made the earth the foundation of all, and its goddess Nature, memory,' memory of sensations, 'not the Holy Ghost. . . . Round Purgatory is Paradise, and round Paradise vacuum. Homer is the centre of all, I mean the poetry of the heathen.' The statement that round Paradise is vacuum is a proof of the persistence of his ideas, and of his curiously literal understanding of his own symbols; for it is but another form of the charge made against Milton many years before in *The Marriage of Heaven and Hell*. 'In Milton the Father is destiny, the Son a ratio of the five senses,'

Blake's Illustrations to Dante

Blake's definition of the reason which is the enemy of the imagination, 'and the Holy Ghost vacuum.' Dante, like other mediaeval mystics, symbolised the highest order of created beings by the fixed stars, and God by the darkness beyond them, the *Primum Mobile*. Blake, absorbed in his very different vision, in which God took always a human shape, believed that to think of God under a symbol drawn from the outer world was in itself idolatry, but that to imagine Him as an unpeopled immensity was to think of Him under the one symbol furthest from His essence—it being a creation of the ruining reason, 'generalising' away 'the minute particulars of life.' Instead of seeking God in the deserts of time and space, in exterior immensities, in what he called 'the abstract void,' he believed that the further he dropped behind him memory of time and space, reason builded upon sensation, morality founded for the ordering of the world; and the more he was absorbed in emotion; and, above all, in emotion escaped from the impulse of bodily longing and the restraints of bodily reason, in artistic emotion; the nearer did he come to Eden's 'breathing garden,' to use his beautiful phrase, and to the unveiled face of God. No worthy symbol of God existed but the inner world, the true humanity, to whose various aspects he gave many names, 'Jerusalem,' 'Liberty,' 'Eden,' 'The Divine Vision,' 'The Body of God,' 'The Human Form Divine,' 'The Divine Members,' and whose most intimate expression was art and poetry. He always sang of God under this symbol:—

For Mercy, Pity, Peace, and Love
  Is God our Father dear;
And Mercy, Pity, Peace, and Love
  Is Man, His child and care.

For Mercy has a human heart;
  Pity a human face;
And Love the human form divine;
  And Peace the human dress.

Then every man, of every clime,
  That prays in his distress,
Prays to the human form divine—
  Love, Mercy, Pity, Peace.

Whenever he gave this symbol a habitation in space he set it in the sun, the father of light and life; and set in the darkness beyond the stars, where light and life die away, Og and Anak and the giants that were of old, and the iron throne of Satan.

By thus contrasting Blake and Dante by the light of Blake's paradoxical wisdom, and as though there was no important truth hung from Dante's beam of the balance, I but seek to interpret a little-understood philosophy rather than one incorporate in the thought and habits of Christendom. Every philosophy has half its truth from times and generations; and to us one-half of the philosophy of Dante is less living than his poetry, while the truth Blake preached and sang and painted is the root of the cultivated life, of the fragile perfect blossom of the world born in ages of leisure and peace, and never yet to last more than a little season; the life those Phaeacians, who told Odysseus that they had set their hearts in nothing but in 'the dance and changes of raiment, and love and sleep,' lived before Poseidon heaped a mountain above them; the lives of all who, having eaten of the Tree of Life, love, more than did the barbarous ages when none had time to live, 'the minute particulars of life,' the little fragments of space and time, which are wholly flooded by beautiful emotion because they are so little they are hardly of time and space at all. 'Every space smaller than a globule of man's blood,' he wrote, 'opens into eternity of which this vegetable earth is but a shadow.' And again, 'Every time less than a pulsation of the artery is equal' in its tenor and value 'to six thousand years, for in this period the poet's work is done, and all the great events of time start forth, and are conceived in such a period, within a moment, a pulsation of the artery.' Dante, indeed, taught, in the *Purgatorio*, that sin and virtue are alike from love, and that love is from God; but this love he would restrain by a complex external law, a complex external Church. Blake upon the other hand cried scorn upon the whole spectacle of external things, a vision to pass away in a moment, and preached the cultivated life, the internal Church which has no laws but beauty, rapture and labour. 'I know of no other Christianity, and of no other gospel, than the liberty, both of body and mind, to exercise the divine arts of imagination, the real and eternal world of which this vegetable universe is but a faint shadow, and in which we shall live in our eternal or imaginative bodies when these vegetable mortal bodies are no more. The Apostles knew of no other gospel. What were all their

spiritual gifts? What is the divine spirit? Is the Holy
Ghost any other than an intellectual fountain? What
is the harvest of the Gospel and its labours? What is
the talent which it is a curse to hide? What are the
treasures of heaven which we are to lay up for ourselves? Are they any other than mental studies and performances? What are all the gifts of the Gospel, are
they not all mental gifts? Is God a spirit who must be
worshipped in spirit and truth? Are not the gifts of the
spirit everything to man? O ye religious! discounten-
ance every one among you who shall pretend to despise art and science. I call upon you in the name of
Jesus! What is the life of man but art and science? Is it
meat and drink? Is not the body more than raiment?
What is mortality but the things relating to the body
which dies? What is immortality but the things relating
to the spirit which lives immortally? What is the joy
of Heaven but improvement in the things of the spirit?
What are the pains of Hell but ignorance, idleness,
bodily lust, and the devastation of the things of the
spirit? Answer this for yourselves, and expel from
amongst you those who pretend to despise the labours
of art and science, which alone are the labours of the
Gospel. Is not this plain and manifest to the thought?
Can you think at all, and not pronounce heartily that
to labour in knowledge is to build Jerusalem, and to
despise knowledge is to despise Jerusalem and her
builders? And remember, he who despises and mocks
a mental gift in another, calling it pride, and selfishness,
and sin, mocks Jesus, the giver of every mental gift,
which always appear to the ignorance-loving hypo-

crite as sins. But that which is a Sin in the sight of cruel
Man is not so in the sight of our kind God. Let every
Christian, as much as in him lies, engage himself openly
and publicly before all the World in some Mental pursuit for the Building up of Jerusalem.' I have given the
whole of this long passage because, though the very
keystone of his thought, it is little known, being sunk,
like nearly all of his most profound thoughts, in the
mysterious 'Prophetic Books'. Obscure about much
else, they are always lucid on this one point, and return
to it again and again. 'I care not whether a man is good
or bad,' are the words they put into the mouth of God,
'all I care is whether he is a wise man or a fool. Go put
off holiness and put on intellect.' This cultivated life,
which seems to us so artificial a thing, is really, according to them, the laborious rediscovery of the Golden
Age, of the primeval simplicity, of the simple world in
which Christ taught and lived, and its lawlessness is
the lawlessness of Him 'who being all virtue, acted
from impulse and not from rules,' and—

> His seventy disciples sent
> Against religion and government.

The historical Christ was indeed no more than the
supreme symbol of the artistic imagination, in which,
with every passion wrought to perfect beauty by art
and poetry, we shall live, when the body has passed
away for the last time; but before that hour man must
labour through many lives and many deaths. 'Men are
admitted into Heaven not because they have curbed and
governed their passions, but because they have culti-

vated their understandings. The treasures of Heaven are
not negations of passion, but realities of intellect, from
which the passions emanate uncurbed in their eternal
glory. The fool shall not enter into Heaven, let him be
ever so holy. Holiness is not the price of entering into
Heaven. Those who are cast out are all those who,
having no passions of their own, because no intellect,
have spent their lives in curbing and governing other
people's by the various arts of poverty and cruelty of
all kinds. . . . The modern Church crucifies Christ with
the head downwards. Woe, woe, woe to you hypo-
crites!' After a time man has 'to return to the dark
valley whence he came and begin his labours anew,'
but before that return he dwells in the freedom of imagination, in the peace of the 'divine image,' 'the divine
vision,' in the peace that passes understanding and is the
peace of art. 'I have been very near the gates of death,'
Blake wrote in one of his last letters, 'and have returned very weak and an old man, feeble and tottering,
but not in spirit and life, not in the real man, the imagination, which liveth for ever. In that I am stronger
and stronger as this foolish body decays. . . . Flaxman
is gone, and we must all soon follow, every one to his
own eternal house, leaving the delusive goddess Nature
and her laws, to get into freedom from all law of the
Members,' the multiplicity of nature, 'into the mind
in which every one is king and priest in his own house.'
The phrase about the king and priest is a memory of
the crown and mitre set upon Dante's head before he
entered Paradise. Our imaginations are but fragments
of the universal imagination, portions of the universal

body of God, and as we enlarge our imagination by imaginative sympathy, and transform with the beauty and peace of art the sorrows and joys of the world, we put off the limited mortal man more and more and put on the unlimited 'immortal man.' 'As the seed waits eagerly watching for its flower and fruit, anxious its little soul looks out into the clear expanse to see if hungry winds are abroad with their invisible array, so man looks out in tree, and herb, and fish, and bird, and beast, collecting up the fragments of his immortal body into the elemental forms of everything that grows. . . . In pain he sighs, in pain he labours in his universe, sorrowing in birds over the deep, or howling in the wolf over the slain, and moaning in the cattle, and in the winds.' Mere sympathy for living things is not enough, because we must learn to separate their 'infected' from their eternal, their satanic from their divine part; and this can only be done by desiring always beauty, the one mask through which can be seen the unveiled eyes of eternity. We must then be artists in all things, and understand that love and old age and death are first among the arts. In this sense he insists that 'Christ's apostles were artists,' that 'Christianity is Art,' and that 'the whole business of man is the arts.' Dante, who deified law, selected its antagonist, passion, as the most important of sins, and made the regions where it was punished the largest. Blake, who deified imaginative freedom, held 'corporeal reason' for the most accursed of things, because it makes the imagination revolt from the sovereignty of beauty and pass under the sovereignty of corporeal law, and this is 'the captivity in Egypt.' True art is expressive and symbolic, and makes every form, every sound, every colour, every gesture, a signature of some unanalysable imaginative essence. False art is not expressive, but mimetic, not from experience but from observation, and is the mother of all evil, persuading us to save our bodies alive at no matter what cost of rapine and fraud. True art is the flame of the Last Day, which begins for every man when he is first moved by beauty, and which seeks to burn all things until they become 'infinite and holy.'

III. THE ILLUSTRATORS OF DANTE

The late Mr. John Addington Symonds wrote—in a preface to certain Dante illustrations by Stradanus, a sixteenth-century artist of no great excellence, published in phototype by Mr. Unwin in 1892—that the illustrations of Gustave Doré, 'in spite of glaring artistic defects, must, I think, be reckoned first among numerous attempts to translate Dante's conceptions into terms of plastic art.' One can only account for this praise of a noisy and demagogic art by supposing that a temperament, strong enough to explore with unfailing alertness the countless schools and influences of the Renaissance in Italy, is of necessity a little lacking in delicacy of judgment and in the finer substances of emotion. It is more difficult to account for so admirable a scholar not only preferring these illustrations to the work of what he called 'the graceful and affected Botticelli,'—although 'Doré was fitted for his task, not by dramatic vigour, by feeling for beauty, or by anything sterling in sympathy with the supreme poet's soul, but by a very effective sense of luminosity and gloom'— but preferring them because 'he created a fanciful world, which makes the movement of Dante's *dramatis personae* conceivable, introducing the ordinary intelligence into those vast regions thronged with destinies of souls and creeds and empires.' When the ordinary student finds this intelligence in an illustrator, he thinks, because it is his own intelligence, that it is an accurate interpretation of the text, while work of the extraordinary intelligences is merely an expression of their own ideas and feelings. Doré and Stradanus, he will tell you, have given us something of the world of Dante, but Blake and Botticelli have builded worlds of their own and called them Dante's—as if Dante's world were more than a mass of symbols of colour and form and sound which put on humanity, when they arouse some mind to an intense and romantic life that is not theirs; as if it was not one's own sorrows and angers and regrets and terrors and hopes that awaken to condemnation or repentance while Dante treads his eternal pilgrimage; as if any poet or painter or musician could be other than an enchanter calling, with a persuasive or compelling ritual, creatures, noble or ignoble, divine or demonic, covered with scales or in shining raiment, that he never imagined, out of the bottomless deeps of imaginations he never foresaw; as if the noblest achievement of art was not when the artist enfolds himself in darkness, while he casts over his readers a light as of a wild and terrible dawn.

Let us therefore put away the designs to the *Divine*

Comedy in which there is 'an ordinary intelligence,' and consider only the designs in which the magical ritual has called up extraordinary shapes, the magical light glimmered upon a world different from the Dantesque world of our own intelligence in its ordinary and daily moods, upon a difficult and distinguished world. Most of the series of designs to Dante, and there are a good number, need not busy any one for a moment. Genelli has done a copious series, which is very able in the 'formal' 'generalised' way which Blake hated, and which is spiritually ridiculous. Genelli has transformed the *Inferno* into a vulgar Walpurgis Night, and a certain Schuler, whom I do not find in the biographical dictionaries, but who was apparently a German, has prefaced certain flaccid designs with some excellent charts, while Stradanus has made a series for the *Inferno*, which has so many of the more material and unessential powers of art, and is so extremely undistinguished in conception, that one supposes him to have touched in the sixteenth century the same public Doré has touched in the nineteenth.

Though with many doubts, I am tempted to value Flaxman's designs to the *Inferno*, the *Purgatorio*, and the *Paradiso*, only a little above the best of these, because he does not seem to have ever been really moved by Dante, and so to have sunk into a formal manner, which is a reflection of the vital manner of his Homer and Hesiod. His designs to the *Divine Comedy* will be laid, one imagines, with some ceremony in that immortal wastepaper-basket in which Time carries with many sighs the failures of great men. I am perhaps wrong, however, because Flaxman even at his best has not yet touched me very deeply, and I hardly ever hope to escape this limitation of my ruling stars. That Signorelli does not seem greatly more interesting except here and there, as in the drawing of *The Angel*, full of innocence and energy, coming from the boat which has carried so many souls to the foot of the mountain of purgation, can only be because one knows him through poor reproductions from frescoes half mouldered away with damp. A little-known series, drawn by Adolph Stürler, an artist of German extraction, who was settled in Florence in the first half of this century, are very poor in drawing, very pathetic and powerful in invention, and full of most interesting Pre-Raphaelitic detail. There are admirable and moving figures, who, having set love above reason, listen in the last abandonment of despair to the judgment of Minos, or walk with a poignant melancholy to the foot of his throne through a land where owls and strange beasts move hither and thither with the sterile content of the evil that neither loves nor hates, and a Cerberus full of patient cruelty. All Stürler's designs have, however, the languor of a mind that does its work by a succession of laborious critical perceptions rather than the decision and energy of true creation, and are more a curious contribution to artistic methods than an imaginative force.

The only designs that compete with Blake's are those of Botticelli and Giulio Clovio, and these contrast rather than compete; for Blake did not live to carry his *Paradiso* beyond the first faint pencillings, the first thin washes of colour, while Botticelli only, as I think,

became supremely imaginative in his *Paradiso*, and
Clovio never attempted the *Inferno* and *Purgatorio* at all.
The imaginations of Botticelli and Clovio were over-
shadowed by the cloister, and it was only when they
passed beyond the world or into some noble peace,
which is not the world's peace, that they won a perfect
freedom. Blake had not such mastery over figure and
drapery as had Botticelli, but he could sympathise with
the persons and delight in the scenery of the *Inferno* and
the *Purgatorio* as Botticelli could not, and could fill
them with a mysterious and spiritual significance born
perhaps of mystical pantheism. The flames of Botticelli
give one no emotion, and his car of Beatrice is no symbolic chariot of the Church led by the gryphon, half
eagle, half lion, of Christ's dual nature, but is a fragment
of some mediaeval pageant pictured with a merely technical inspiration. Clovio, the illuminator of missals, has
tried to create with that too easy hand of his a Paradise
of serene air reflected in a little mirror, a Heaven of
sociability and humility and prettiness, a Heaven of
women and of monks; but one cannot imagine him
deeply moved, as the modern world is moved, by the
symbolism of bird and beast, of tree and mountain, of
flame and darkness. It was a profound understanding
of all creatures and things, a profound sympathy with
passionate and lost souls, made possible in their extreme intensity by his revolt against corporeal law, and
corporeal reason, which made Blake the one perfectly
fit illustrator for the *Inferno* and the *Purgatorio*; in the
serene and rapturous emptiness of Dante's Paradise he
would find no symbols but a few abstract emblems,

and he had no love for the abstract, while with the drapery and the gestures of Beatrice and Virgil, he would have prospered less than Botticelli or even Clovio.

1897

P.S.—Some seven or eight years ago I asked my friend Mr. Ezra Pound to point out everything in the language of my poems that he thought an abstraction, and I learned from him how much further the movement against abstraction had gone than my generation had thought possible. Now, in reading these essays, I am ashamed when I come upon such words as 'corporeal reason,' 'corporeal law,' and think how I must have wasted the keenness of my youthful senses. I would like to believe that there was no help for it, that we were compelled to protect ourselves by such means against people and things we should never have heard of.

1924

SYMBOLISM IN PAINTING

IN ENGLAND, which has made great Symbolic Art, most people dislike an art if they are told it is symbolic, for they confuse symbol and allegory. Even Johnson's Dictionary sees no great difference, for it calls a symbol 'That which comprehends in its figure a representation of something else'; and an allegory 'A figurative discourse, in which something other is intended than is contained in the words literally taken.' It is only a very modern Dictionary that calls a symbol 'the sign or representation of any moral thing by the images or properties of natural things,' which, though an imperfect definition, is not unlike 'The things below are as the things above' of the Emerald Tablet of Hermes! *The Faerie Queene* and *The Pilgrim's Progress* have been so important in England that Allegory has overtopped Symbolism, and for a time has overwhelmed it in its own downfall. William Blake was perhaps the first modern to insist on a difference; and the other day, when I sat for my portrait to a German symbolist in Paris, whose talk was all of his love for symbolism and his hatred for allegory, his definitions were the same as William Blake's, of whom he knew nothing. William Blake has written, 'Vision or imagination'—meaning symbolism by these words—'is a representation of what actually exists, really or unchangeably. Fable or Allegory is formed by the daughters of Memory.' The German insisted with many determined gestures that symbolism said things which could not be said so perfectly in any other way, and needed but a right instinct for its understanding; while allegory said things which could be said as well, or better, in another way, and needed a right knowledge for its understanding. The one thing gave dumb things voices, and bodiless things bodies; while the other read a meaning—which had never lacked its voice or its body—into something heard or seen, and loved less for the meaning than for its own sake. The only symbols he cared for were the shapes and motions of the body; ears hidden by the hair, to make one think of a mind busy with inner voices; and a head so bent that back and neck made the one curve, as in Blake's *Vision of Blood-thirstiness*, to call up an emotion of bodily strength; and he would not put even a lily, or a rose, or a poppy into a picture to express purity, or love, or sleep, because he thought such emblems were allegorical, and had their meaning by a traditional and not by a natural right. I said that the rose, and the lily, and the poppy were so married, by their colour and their odour and their use, to love and purity and sleep, or to other symbols of love and purity and sleep, and had been so long a part of the imagination of the world, that a symbolist might use them to help out his meaning without becoming an allegorist. I think I quoted the lily in the hand of the angel in Rossetti's *Annunciation*, and the lily in the jar in his *Girlhood of Mary, Virgin*, and thought they made the more important symbols, the women's bodies, and the angels' bodies, and the clear morning light, take that place, in the great procession of Christian symbols, where they can alone have all their meaning and all their beauty.

It is hard to say where allegory and symbolism melt into one another, but it is not hard to say where either comes to its perfection; and though one may doubt whether allegory or symbolism is the greater in the horns of Michelangelo's *Moses*, one need not doubt that its symbolism has helped to awaken the modern imagination; while Tintoretto's *Origin of the Milky Way*, which is allegory without any symbolism, is, apart from its fine painting, but a moment's amusement for our fancy. A hundred generations might write out what seemed the meaning of the one, and they would write different meanings, for no symbol tells all its meaning to any generation; but when you have said, 'That woman there is Juno, and the milk out of her breast is making the Milky Way,' you have told the meaning of the other, and the fine painting, which has added so much irrelevant beauty, has not told it better.

All art that is not mere story-telling, or mere portraiture, is symbolic, and has the purpose of those symbolic talismans which mediaeval magicians made with complex colours and forms, and bade their patients ponder over daily, and guard with holy secrecy; for it entangles, in complex colours and forms, a part of the Divine Essence. A person or a landscape that is a part of a story or a portrait, evokes but so much emotion as the story or the portrait can permit without loosening the bonds that make it a story or a portrait; but if you liberate a person or a landscape from the bonds of motives and their actions, causes and their effects, and from all bonds but the bonds of your love, it will change under your eyes, and become a symbol of an infinite emotion, a perfected emotion, a part of the Divine Essence; for we love nothing but the perfect, and our dreams make all things perfect, that we may love them. Religious and visionary people, monks and nuns, and medicine-men and opium-eaters, see symbols in their trances; for religious and visionary thought is thought about perfection and the way to perfection; and symbols are the only things free enough from all bonds to speak of perfection.

Wagner's dramas, Keats' odes, Blake's pictures and poems, Calvert's pictures, Rossetti's pictures, Villiers de l'Isle-Adam's plays, and the black-and-white art of Mr. Beardsley and Mr. Ricketts, and the lithographs of Mr. Shannon, and the pictures of Mr. Whistler, and the plays of M. Maeterlinck, and the poetry of Verlaine, in our own day, but differ from the religious art of Giotto and his disciples in having accepted all symbolisms, the symbolism of the ancient shepherds and star-gazers, that symbolism of bodily beauty which seemed a wicked thing to Fra Angelico, the symbolism in day and night, and winter and summer, spring and autumn, once so great a part of an older religion than Christianity; and in having accepted all the Divine Intellect, its anger and its pity, its waking and its sleep, its love and its lust, for the substance of their art. A Keats or a Calvert is as much a symbolist as a Blake or a Wagner; but he is a fragmentary symbolist, for while he evokes in his persons and his landscapes an infinite emotion, a perfected emotion, a part of the Divine Essence, he does not set his symbols in the great procession as Blake would have him, 'in a certain order, suited' to his 'imaginative energy.' If you paint a beautiful woman and fill her face, as Rossetti filled so many faces, with an infinite love, a perfected love, 'one's eyes meet no mortal thing when they meet the light of her peaceful eyes,' as Michelangelo said of Vittoria Colonna; but one's thoughts stray to mortal things, and ask, maybe, 'Has her lover gone from her, or is he coming?' or 'What predestinated unhappiness has made the shadow in her eyes?' If you paint the same face, and set a winged rose or a rose of gold somewhere about her, one's thoughts are of her immortal sisters, Piety and Jealousy, and of her mother, Ancestral Beauty, and of her high kinsmen, the Holy Orders, whose swords make a continual music before her face. The systematic mystic is not the greatest of artists, because his imagination is too great to be bounded by a picture or a song, and because only imperfection in a mirror of perfection, or perfection in a mirror of imperfection, delights our frailty. There is indeed a systematic mystic in every poet or painter who, like Rossetti, delights in a traditional symbolism, or, like Wagner, delights in a personal symbolism; and such men often fall into trances, or have waking dreams. Their thought wanders from the woman who is Love herself, to her sisters and her forebears, and to all the great procession; and so august a beauty moves before the mind that they forget the things which move before the eyes. William Blake, who was the chanticleer of the new dawn, has written: 'If the spectator could enter into one of these images of his imagination, approaching them on the fiery chariot of his contemplative thought, if . . . he could make a friend and companion of one of these images of wonder, which always entreat him to leave mortal things (as he must know), then would he arise from the grave, then would he meet the Lord in the air, and then he would be happy.' And again, 'The world of imagination is the world of Eternity. It is the Divine bosom into which we shall all go after the death of the vegetated body. The world of imagination is infinite and eternal, whereas the world of generation or vegetation is finite and temporal. There exist in that eternal world the eternal realities of everything which we see reflected in the vegetable glass of Nature.'

Every visionary knows that the mind's eye soon comes to see a capricious and variable world, which the will cannot shape or change, though it can call it up and banish it again. I closed my eyes a moment ago, and a company of people in blue robes swept by me in a blinding light, and had gone before I had done more than see little roses embroidered on the hems of their robes, and confused, blossoming apple-boughs some-where beyond them, and recognised one of the company by his square, black, curling beard.[1] I have often seen him; and one night a year ago I asked him questions which he answered by showing me flowers and precious stones, of whose meaning I had no knowledge,

[1] I did not mean that this particular vision had the intensity either of a dream or of those pictures that pass before us between sleep and waking. I had learned, and my fellow-students had learned, as described in *The Trembling of the Veil*, to set free imagination when we would, that it might follow its own law and impulse.

1924.

and he seemed too perfected a soul for any knowledge that cannot be spoken in symbol or metaphor.

Are he and his blue-robed companions, and their like, 'the eternal realities' of which we are the reflection 'in the vegetable glass of Nature,' or a momentary dream? To answer is to take sides in the only controversy in which it is greatly worth taking sides, and in the only controversy which may never be decided.

1898

THE SYMBOLISM OF POETRY

I

SYMBOLISM, as seen in the writers of our day, would have no value if it were not seen also, under one 'disguise or another, in every great imaginative writer,' writes Mr. Arthur Symons in *The Symbolist Movement in Literature*, a subtle book which I cannot praise as I would, because it has been dedicated to me; and he goes on to show how many profound writers have in the last few years sought for a philosophy of poetry in the doctrine of symbolism, and how even in countries where it is almost scandalous to seek for any philosophy of poetry, new writers are following them in their search. We do not know what the writers of ancient times talked of among themselves, and one bull is all that remains of Shakespeare's talk, who was on the edge of modern times; and the journalist is convinced, it seems, that they talked of wine and women and politics, but never about their art, or never quite seriously about their art. He is certain that no one who had a philosophy of his art, or a theory of how he should write, has ever made a work of art, that people have no imagination who do not write without forethought and afterthought as he writes his own articles. He says this with enthusiasm, because he has heard it at so many comfortable dinner-tables, where some one had mentioned through carelessness, or foolish zeal, a book whose difficulty had offended indolence, or a man who had not forgotten that beauty is an accusation. Those

153

formulas and generalisations, in which a hidden sergeant
has drilled the ideas of journalists and through them
the ideas of all but all the modern world, have created
in their turn a forgetfulness like that of soldiers in
battle, so that journalists and their readers have forgotten, among many like events, that Wagner spent
seven years arranging and explaining his ideas before
he began his most characteristic music; that opera, and
with it modern music, arose from certain talks at the
house of one Giovanni Bardi of Florence; and that the
Pléiade laid the foundations of modern French literature with a pamphlet. Goethe has said, 'a poet needs
all philosophy, but he must keep it out of his work,'
though that is not always necessary; and almost certainly no great art, outside England, where journalists
are more powerful and ideas less plentiful than elsewhere, has arisen without a great criticism, for its
herald or its interpreter and protector, and it may be for
this reason that great art, now that vulgarity has armed
itself and multiplied itself, is perhaps dead in England.

All writers, all artists of any kind, in so far as they
have had any philosophical or critical power, perhaps
just in so far as they have been deliberate artists at all,
have had some philosophy, some criticism of their art;
and it has often been this philosophy, or this criticism,
that has evoked their most startling inspiration, calling
into outer life some portion of the divine life, or of the
buried reality, which could alone extinguish in the
emotions what their philosophy or their criticism would
extinguish in the intellect. They have sought for no
new thing, it may be, but only to understand and to

copy the pure inspiration of early times, but because the divine life wars upon our outer life, and must needs change its weapons and its movements as we change ours, inspiration has come to them in beautiful startling shapes. The scientific movement brought with it a literature which was always tending to lose itself in externalities of all kinds, in opinion, in declamation, in picturesque writing, in word-painting, or in what Mr. Symons has called an attempt 'to build in brick and mortar inside the covers of a book'; and now writers have begun to dwell upon the element of evocation, of suggestion, upon what we call the symbolism in great writers.

II

In 'Symbolism in Painting,' I tried to describe the element of symbolism that is in pictures and sculpture, and described a little the symbolism in poetry, but did not describe at all the continuous indefinable symbolism which is the substance of all style.

There are no lines with more melancholy beauty than these by Burns:—

> The white moon is setting behind the white wave,[1]
> And Time is setting with me, O!

and these lines are perfectly symbolical. Take from them the whiteness of the moon and of the wave, whose relation to the setting of Time is too subtle for the intellect, and you take from them their beauty. But,

[1] [Burns actually wrote:—
　　'The wan moon is setting ayont the white wave,'
but Yeats's version has been retained for the sake of his comments.]

when all are together, moon and wave and whiteness and setting Time and the last melancholy cry, they evoke an emotion which cannot be evoked by any other arrangement of colours and sounds and forms. We may call this metaphorical writing, but it is better to call it symbolical writing, because metaphors are not profound enough to be moving, when they are not symbols, and when they are symbols they are the most perfect of all, because the most subtle, outside of pure sound, and through them one can best find out what symbols are. If one begins the reverie with any beautiful lines that one can remember, one finds they are like those by Burns. Begin with this line by Blake:—

The gay fishes on the wave when the moon sucks up the dew;

or these lines by Nash:—

> Brightness falls from the air,
> Queens have died young and fair,
> Dust hath closed Helen's eye;

or these lines by Shakespeare:—

> Timon hath made his everlasting mansion
> Upon the beached verge of the salt flood;
> Who once a day with his embossed froth
> The turbulent surge shall cover;

or take some line that is quite simple, that gets its beauty from its place in a story, and see how it flickers with the light of the many symbols that have given the story its beauty, as a sword-blade may flicker with the light of burning towers.

All sounds, all colours, all forms, either because of their preordained energies or because of long association, evoke indefinable and yet precise emotions, or, as I prefer to think, call down among us certain disembodied powers, whose footsteps over our hearts we call emotions; and when sound, and colour, and form are in a musical relation, a beautiful relation to one another, they become, as it were, one sound, one colour, one form, and evoke an emotion that is made out of their distinct evocations and yet is one emotion. The same relation exists between all portions of every work of art, whether it be an epic or a song, and the more perfect it is, and the more various and numerous the elements that have flowed into its perfection, the more powerful will be the emotion, the power, the god it calls among us. Because an emotion does not exist, or does not become perceptible and active among us, till it has found its expression, in colour or in sound or in form, or in all of these, and because no two modulations or arrangements of these evoke the same emotion, poets and painters and musicians, and in a less degree because their effects are momentary, day and night and cloud and shadow, are continually making and unmaking mankind. It is indeed only those things which seem useless or very feeble that have any power, and all those things that seem useful or strong, armies, moving wheels, modes of architecture, modes of government, speculations of the reason, would have been a little different if some mind long ago had not given itself to some emotion, as a woman gives herself to her lover, and shaped sounds or colours or forms, or all of these, into a musical relation, that their emotion might live in other minds. A little lyric evokes an emotion, and this emotion gathers others about it and melts into their being in the making of some great epic; and at last, needing an always less delicate body, or symbol, as it grows more powerful, it flows out, with all it has gathered, among the blind instincts of daily life, where it moves a power within powers, as one sees ring within ring in the stem of an old tree. This is maybe what Arthur O'Shaughnessy meant when he made his poets say they had built Nineveh with their sighing; and I am certainly never sure, when I hear of some war, or of some religious excitement, or of some new manufacture, or of anything else that fills the ear of the world, that it has not all happened because of something that a boy piped in Thessaly. I remember once telling a seeress to ask one among the gods who, as she believed, were standing about her in their symbolic bodies, what would come of a charming but seeming trivial labour of a friend, and the form answering, 'the devastation of peoples and the overwhelming of cities.' I doubt indeed if the crude circumstance of the world, which seems to create all our emotions, does more than reflect, as in multiplying mirrors, the emotions that have come to solitary men in moments of poetical contemplation; or that love itself would be more than an animal hunger but for the poet and his shadow the priest, for unless we believe that outer things are the reality, we must believe that the gross is the shadow of the subtle, that things are wise before they become foolish, and secret before they cry out in the market-place. Solitary men in moments of contemplation receive, as I think, the creative impulse from the lowest of the Nine Hierarchies, and so make and unmake mankind, and even the world itself, for does not 'the eye altering alter all'?

> Our towns are copied fragments from our breast;
> And all man's Babylons strive but to impart
> The grandeurs of his Babylonian heart.

III

The purpose of rhythm, it has always seemed to me, is to prolong the moment of contemplation, the moment when we are both asleep and awake, which is the one moment of creation, by hushing us with an alluring monotony, while it holds us waking by variety, to keep us in that state of perhaps real trance, in which the mind liberated from the pressure of the will is unfolded in symbols. If certain sensitive persons listen persistently to the ticking of a watch, or gaze persistently on the monotonous flashing of a light, they fall into the hypnotic trance; and rhythm is but the ticking of a watch made softer, that one must needs listen, and various, that one may not be swept beyond memory or grow weary of listening; while the patterns of the artist are but the monotonous flash woven to take the eyes in a subtler enchantment. I have heard in meditation voices that were forgotten the moment they had spoken; and I have been swept, when in more profound meditation, beyond all memory but of those things that came from beyond the threshold of waking life. I was writing once at a very symbolical and abstract poem, when my pen fell on the ground; and as I stooped to pick it up, I remembered some fantastic adventure that yet did not seem fantastic, and then another like adventure, and

when I asked myself when these things had happened,
I found that I was remembering my dreams for many
nights. I tried to remember what I had done the day
before, and then what I had done that morning; but all
my waking life had perished from me, and it was only
after a struggle that I came to remember it again, and
as I did so that more powerful and startling life perished
in its turn. Had my pen not fallen on the ground and
so made me turn from the images that I was weaving
into verse, I would never have known that meditation
had become trance, for I would have been like one who
does not know that he is passing through a wood because his eyes are on the pathway. So I think that in
the making and in the understanding of a work of art,
and the more easily if it is full of patterns and symbols
and music, we are lured to the threshold of sleep, and
it may be far beyond it, without knowing that we have
ever set our feet upon the steps of horn or of ivory.

IV

Besides emotional symbols, symbols that evoke
emotions alone,—and in this sense all alluring or hateful things are symbols, although their relations with
one another are too subtle to delight us fully, away
from rhythm and pattern,—there are intellectual symbols, symbols that evoke ideas alone, or ideas mingled
with emotions; and outside the very definite traditions
of mysticism and the less definite criticism of certain
modern poets, these alone are called symbols. Most
things belong to one or another kind, according to the

way we speak of them and the companions we give them, for symbols, associated with ideas that are more than fragments of the shadows thrown upon the intellect by the emotions they evoke, are the playthings of the allegorist or the pedant, and soon pass away. If I say 'white' or 'purple' in an ordinary line of poetry, they evoke emotions so exclusively that I cannot say why they move me; but if I bring them into the same sentence with such obvious intellectual symbols as a cross or a crown of thorns, I think of purity and sovereignty. Furthermore, innumerable meanings, which are held to 'white' or to 'purple' by bonds of subtle suggestion, and alike in the emotions and in the intellect, move visibly through my mind, and move invisibly beyond the threshold of sleep, casting lights and shadows of an indefinable wisdom on what had seemed before, it may be, but sterility and noisy violence. It is the intellect that decides where the reader shall ponder over the procession of the symbols, and if the symbols are merely emotional, he gazes from amid the accidents and destinies of the world; but if the symbols are intellectual too, he becomes himself a part of pure intellect, and he is himself mingled with the procession. If I watch a rushy pool in the moonlight, my emotion at its beauty is mixed with memories of the man that I have seen ploughing by its margin, or of the lovers I saw there a night ago; but if I look at the moon herself and remember any of her ancient names and meanings, I move among divine people, and things that have shaken off our mortality, the tower of ivory, the queen of waters, the shining stag among enchanted woods, the white hare sitting upon the hilltop, the fool of Faery with his shining cup full of dreams, and it may be 'make a friend of one of these images of wonder,' and 'meet the Lord in the air.' So, too, if one is moved by Shakespeare, who is content with emotional symbols that he may come the nearer to our sympathy, one is mixed with the whole spectacle of the world; while if one is moved by Dante, or by the myth of Demeter, one is mixed into the shadow of God or of a goddess. So, too, one is furthest from symbols when one is busy doing this or that, but the soul moves among symbols and unfolds in symbols when trance, or madness, or deep meditation has withdrawn it from every impulse but its own. 'I then saw,' wrote Gérard de Nerval of his madness, 'vaguely drifting into form, plastic images of antiquity, which outlined themselves, became definite, and seemed to represent symbols of which I only seized the idea with difficulty.' In an earlier time he would have been of that multitude whose souls austerity withdrew, even more perfectly than madness could withdraw his soul, from hope and memory, from desire and regret, that they might reveal those processions of symbols that men bow to before altars, and woo with incense and offerings. But being of our time, he has been like Maeterlinck, like Villiers de l'Isle-Adam in *Axël*, like all who are preoccupied with intellectual symbols in our time, a foreshadower of the new sacred book, of which all the arts, as somebody has said, are beginning to dream. How can the arts overcome the slow dying of men's hearts that we call the progress of the world, and lay their hands upon men's heart-strings again, without becoming the garment of religion as in old times?

V

If people were to accept the theory that poetry moves us because of its symbolism, what change should one look for in the manner of our poetry? A return to the way of our fathers, a casting out of descriptions of nature for the sake of nature, of the moral law for the sake of the moral law, a casting out of all anecdotes and of that brooding over scientific opinion that so often extinguished the central flame in Tennyson, and of that vehemence that would make us do or not do certain things; or, in other words, we should come to understand that the beryl stone was enchanted by our fathers that it might unfold the pictures in its heart, and not to mirror our own excited faces, or the boughs waving outside the window. With this change of substance, this return to imagination, this understanding that the laws of art, which are the hidden laws of the world, can alone bind the imagination, would come a change of style, and we would cast out of serious poetry those energetic rhythms, as of a man running, which are the invention of the will with its eyes always on something to be done or undone; and we would seek out those wavering, meditative, organic rhythms, which are the embodiment of the imagination, that neither desires nor hates, because it has done with time, and only wishes to gaze upon some reality, some beauty; nor would it be any longer possible for anybody to deny the importance of form, in all its kinds, for although you can expound an opinion, or describe a thing, when your words are not quite well chosen, you cannot give a body to something that moves beyond the senses, unless your words are as subtle, as complex, as full of mysterious life, as the body of a flower or of a woman. The form of sincere poetry, unlike the form of the 'popular poetry,' may indeed be sometimes obscure, or ungrammatical as in some of the best of the *Songs of Innocence and Experience*, but it must have the perfections that escape analysis, the subtleties that have a new meaning every day, and it must have all this whether it be but a little song made out of a moment of dreamy indolence, or some great epic made out of the dreams of one poet and of a hundred generations whose hands were never weary of the sword.

1900

THE THEATRE

I

I REMEMBER, some years ago, advising a distinguished, though too little recognised, writer of
poetical plays to write a play as unlike ordinary plays
as possible, that it might be judged with a fresh mind,
and to put it on the stage in some little suburban hall,
where a little audience would pay its expenses. I said
that he should follow it the year after, at the same time
of the year, with another play, and so on from year to
year; and that the people who read books, and do not
go to the theatre, would gradually find out about him.
I suggested that he should begin with a pastoral play,
because nobody would expect from a pastoral play the
succession of nervous tremors which the plays of commerce, like the novels of commerce, have substituted
for the purification that comes with pity and terror to
the imagination and intellect. He followed my advice
in part, and had a small but perfect success, filling his
small theatre for twice the number of performances he
had announced; but instead of being content with the
praise of his equals, and waiting to win their praise
another year, he hired immediately a well-known
London theatre, and put his pastoral play and a new
play before a meagre and unintelligent audience. I still
remember his pastoral play with delight, because, if not
always of a high excellence, it was always poetical; but
I remember it at the small theatre, where my pleasure
was magnified by the pleasure of those about me, and

not at the big theatre, where it made me uncomfortable, as an unwelcome guest always makes one uncomfortable.

Why should we thrust our works, which we have written with imaginative sincerity and filled with spiritual desire, before those quite excellent people who think that Rossetti's women are 'guys,' that Rodin's women are 'ugly,' and that Ibsen is 'immoral,' and who only want to be left at peace to enjoy the works so many clever men have made especially to suit them? We must make a theatre for ourselves and our friends, and for a few simple people who understand from sheer simplicity what we understand from scholarship and thought. We have planned the Irish Literary Theatre with this hospitable emotion, and that the right people may find out about us, we hope to act a play or two in the spring of every year; and that the right people may escape the stupefying memory of the theatre of commerce which clings even to them, our plays will be for the most part remote, spiritual, and ideal.

A common opinion is that the poetic drama has come to an end, because modern poets have no dramatic power; and Mr. Binyon seems to accept this opinion when he says: 'It has been too often assumed that it is the manager who bars the way to poetic plays. But it is much more probable that the poets have failed the managers. If poets mean to serve the stage, their dramas must be dramatic.' I find it easier to believe that audiences, who have learned, as I think, from the life of crowded cities to live upon the surface of life, and actors and managers, who study to please them, have changed, than that imagination, which is the voice of what is eternal in man, has changed. The arts are but one Art; and why should all intense painting and all intense poetry have become not merely unintelligible but hateful to the greater number of men and women, and intense drama move them to pleasure? The audiences of Sophocles and of Shakespeare and of Calderón were not unlike the audiences I have heard listening in Irish cabins to songs in Gaelic about 'an old poet telling his sins,' and about 'the five young men who were drowned last year,' and about 'the lovers that were drowned going to America,' or to some tale of Oisin and his three hundred years in Tir ná nOg. Mr. Bridges' *Return of Ulysses*, one of the most beautiful and, as I think, dramatic of modern plays, might have some success in the Aran Islands, if the Gaelic League would translate it into Gaelic, but I am quite certain that it would have no success in the Strand.

Blake has said that all art is a labour to bring again the Golden Age, and all culture is certainly a labour to bring again the simplicity of the first ages, with knowledge of good and evil added to it. The drama has need of cities that it may find men in sufficient numbers, and cities destroy the emotions to which it appeals, and therefore the days of the drama are brief and come but seldom. It has one day when the emotions of cities still remember the emotions of sailors and husbandmen and shepherds and users of the spear and the bow; as the houses and furniture and earthen vessels of cities, before the coming of machinery, remember the rocks and the woods and the hillside; and it has another day, now beginning, when thought and scholarship discover their desire. In the first day, it is the art of the people; and in the second day, like the dramas acted of old times in the hidden places of temples, it is the preparation of a priesthood. It may be, though the world is not old enough to show us any example, that this priesthood will spread their religion everywhere, and make their Art the Art of the people.

When the first day of the drama had passed by, actors found that an always larger number of people were more easily moved through the eyes than through the ears. The emotion that comes with the music of words is exhausting, like all intellectual emotions, and few people like exhausting emotions; and therefore actors began to speak as if they were reading something out of the newspapers. They forgot the noble art of oratory, and gave all their thought to the poor art of acting, that is content with the sympathy of our nerves; until at last those who love poetry found it better to read alone in their rooms what they had once delighted to hear sitting friend by friend, lover by beloved. I once asked Mr. William Morris if he had thought of writing a play, and he answered that he had, but would not write one, because actors did not know how to speak poetry with the half-chant men spoke it with in old times. Mr. Swinburne's *Locrine* was acted a month ago, and it was not badly acted, but nobody could tell whether it was fit for the stage or not, for not one rhythm, not one cry of passion, was spoken with a musical emphasis, and verse spoken without a musical emphasis seems but an artificial and cumbersome way of saying what might be said naturally and simply in prose.

As audiences and actors changed, managers learned to substitute meretricious landscapes, painted upon wood and canvas, for the descriptions of poetry, until the painted scenery, which had in Greece been a charming explanation of what was least important in the story, became as important as the story. It needed some imagination, some gift for day-dreams, to see the horses and the fields and flowers of Colonus as one listened to the elders gathered about Oedipus, or to see 'the pendent bed and procreant cradle' of the 'martlet' as one listened to Banquo before the castle of Macbeth; but it needs no imagination to admire a painting of one of the more obvious effects of nature painted by somebody who understands how to show everything to the most hurried glance. At the same time the managers made the costumes of the actors more and more magnificent, that the mind might sleep in peace, while the eye took pleasure in the magnificence of velvet and silk and in the physical beauty of women. These changes gradually perfected the theatre of commerce, the masterpiece of that movement towards externality in life and thought and art against which the criticism of our day is learning to protest.

Even if poetry were spoken as poetry, it would still seem out of place in many of its highest moments upon a stage where the superficial appearances of nature are so closely copied; for poetry is founded upon convention, and becomes incredible the moment painting or gesture reminds us that people do not speak verse when they meet upon the highway. The theatre of art, when it comes to exist, must therefore discover grave and decorative gestures, such as delighted Rossetti and Madox Brown, and grave and decorative scenery that will be forgotten the moment an actor has said, 'It is dawn,' or 'It is raining,' or 'The wind is shaking the trees'; and dresses of so little irrelevant magnificence that the mortal actors and actresses may change without much labour into the immortal people of romance. The theatre began in ritual, and it cannot come to its greatness again without recalling words to their ancient sovereignty.

It will take a generation, and perhaps generations, to restore the theatre of art; for one must get one's actors, and perhaps one's scenery, from the theatre of commerce, until new actors and new painters have come to help one; and until many failures and imperfect successes have made a new tradition, and perfected in detail the ideal that is beginning to float before our eyes. If one could call one's painters and one's actors from where one would, how easy it would be! I know some painters,[1] who have never painted scenery, who could paint the scenery I want, but they have their own work to do; and in Ireland I have heard a red-haired orator[2] repeat some bad political verses with a voice that went through one like flame, and made them seem the most beautiful verses in the world; but he has no practical knowledge of the stage, and probably despises it.

May 1899

[1] I had Charles Ricketts in my mind (1924).
[2] J. F. Taylor.

170

The Theatre

II

Dionysius, the Areopagite, wrote that 'He has set the borders of the nations according to His angels.' It is these angels, each one the genius of some race about to be unfolded, that are the founders of intellectual traditions; and as lovers understand in their first glance all that is to befall them, and as poets and musicians see the whole work in its first impulse, so races prophesy at their awakening whatever the generations that are to prolong their traditions shall accomplish in detail. It is only at the awakening—as in ancient Greece, or in Elizabethan England, or in contemporary Scandinavia —that great numbers of men understand that a right understanding of life and of destiny is more important than amusement. In London, where all the intellectual traditions gather to die, men hate a play if they are told it is literature, for they will not endure a spiritual superiority; but in Athens, where so many intellectual traditions were born, Euripides once changed hostility to enthusiasm by asking his playgoers whether it was his business to teach them, or their business to teach him. New races understand instinctively, because the future cries in their ears, that the old revelations are insufficient, and that all life is revelation beginning in miracle and enthusiasm, and dying out as it unfolds itself in what we have mistaken for progress. It is one of our illusions, as I think, that education, the softening of manners, the perfecting of law—countless images of a fading light—can create nobleness and beauty, and that life moves slowly and evenly towards some

171

perfection. Progress is miracle, and it is sudden, because miracles are the work of an all-powerful energy, and Nature in herself has no power except to die and to forget. If one studies one's own mind, one comes to think with Blake that 'every time less than a pulsation of the artery is equal to six thousand years, for in this period the poet's work is done, and all the great events of time start forth, and are conceived in such a period, within a moment, a pulsation of the artery.'

February 1900

The Celtic Element in Literature

THE CELTIC ELEMENT IN LITERATURE

I

ERNEST RENAN described what he held to be Celtic characteristics in *The Poetry of the Celtic Races*. I must repeat the well-known sentences: 'No race communed so intimately as the Celtic race with the lower creation, or believed it to have so big a share of moral life.' The Celtic race had 'a realistic naturalism,' 'a love of Nature for herself, a vivid feeling for her magic, commingled with the melancholy a man knows when he is face to face with her, and thinks he hears her communing with him about his origin and his destiny.' 'It has worn itself out in mistaking dreams for realities,' and 'compared with the classical imagination the Celtic imagination is indeed the infinite contrasted with the finite.' 'Its history is one long lament, it still recalls its exiles, its flights across the seas.' 'If at times it seems to be cheerful, its tear is not slow to glisten behind the smile. Its songs of joy end as elegies; there is nothing to equal the delightful sadness of its national melodies.' Matthew Arnold, in *The Study of Celtic Literature*, has accepted this passion for Nature, this imaginativeness, this melancholy, as Celtic characteristics, but has described them more elaborately. The Celtic passion for Nature comes almost more from a sense of her 'mystery' than of her 'beauty,' and it adds 'charm and magic' to Nature, and the Celtic imaginativeness and melancholy are alike 'a passionate, turbulent, indomitable reaction against the despotism of fact.' The Celt is not melancholy, as Faust or Werther are melancholy, from 'a perfectly definite motive,' but because of something about him 'unaccountable, defiant and titanic.' How well one knows these sentences, better even than Renan's, and how well one knows the passages of prose and verse which he uses to prove that wherever English literature has the qualities these sentences describe, it has them from a Celtic source. Though I do not think any of us who write about Ireland have built any argument upon them, it is well to consider them a little, and see where they are helpful and where they are hurtful. If we do not, we may go mad some day, and the enemy root up our rose-garden and plant a cabbage-garden instead. Perhaps we must re-state a little Renan's and Arnold's argument.

II

Once every people in the world believed that trees were divine, and could take a human or grotesque shape and dance among the shadows; and that deer, and ravens and foxes, and wolves and bears, and clouds and pools, almost all things under the sun and moon, and the sun and moon, were not less divine and changeable. They saw in the rainbow the still bent bow of a god thrown down in his negligence; they heard in the thunder the sound of his beaten water-jar, or the tumult of his chariot wheels; and when a sudden flight of wild ducks, or of crows, passed over their heads, they thought they were gazing at the dead hastening to their rest; while they dreamed of so great a mystery in little things that they believed the waving of a hand, or of a sacred bough, enough to trouble far-off hearts, or hood the moon with darkness. All old literatures are full of these or of like imaginations, and all the poets of races who have not lost this way of looking at things could have said of themselves, as the poet of the *Kalevala* said of himself, 'I have learned my songs from the music of many birds, and from the music of many waters.' When a mother in the *Kalevala* weeps for a daughter, who was drowned flying from an old suitor, she weeps so greatly that her tears become three rivers, and cast up three rocks, on which grow three birch-trees, where three cuckoos sit and sing, the one 'love, love,' the one 'suitor, suitor,' the one 'consolation, consolation.' And the makers of the Sagas made the squirrel run up and down the sacred ash-tree carrying words of hatred from the eagle to the worm, and from the worm to the eagle; although they had less of the old way than the makers of the *Kalevala*, for they lived in a more crowded and complicated world, and were learning the abstract meditation which lures men from visible beauty, and were unlearning, it may be, the impassioned meditation which brings men beyond the edge of trance and makes trees, and beasts, and dead things talk with human voices.

The old Irish and the old Welsh, though they had less of the old way than the makers of the *Kalevala*, had more of it than the makers of the Sagas, and it is this that distinguishes the examples Matthew Arnold quotes of their 'natural magic,' of their sense of 'the mystery' more than of 'the beauty' of Nature. When

Matthew Arnold wrote, it was not easy to know as much
as we know now of folk-song and folk-belief, and I do
not think he understood that our 'natural magic' is but
the ancient religion of the world, the ancient worship
of Nature and that troubled ecstasy before her, that
certainty of all beautiful places being haunted, which
it brought into men's minds. The ancient religion is in
that passage of the *Mabinogion* about the making of
'Flower Aspect.' Gwydion and Math made her 'by
charms and illusions' 'out of flowers.' 'They took the
blossoms of the oak, and the blossoms of the broom,
and the blossoms of the meadow-sweet, and produced
from them a maiden the fairest and most graceful that
man ever saw; and they baptized her, and called her
Flower Aspect'; and one finds it in the not less beautiful passage about the burning tree, that has half its
beauty from calling up a fancy of leaves so living and
beautiful, they can be of no less living and beautiful a
thing than flame: 'They saw a tall tree by the side of
the river, one half of which was in flames from the root
to the top, and the other half was green and in full leaf.'
And one finds it very certainly in the quotations Arnold
makes from English poets to prove a Celtic influence
in English poetry; in Keats's 'magic casements opening
on the foam of perilous seas in faery lands forlorn'; in
his 'moving waters at their priestlike task of pure
ablution round earth's human shores'; in Shakespeare's
'floor of heaven,' 'inlaid with patens of bright gold';
and in his Dido standing 'upon the wild sea banks,' 'a
willow in her hand,' and waving it in the ritual of the
old worship of Nature and the spirits of Nature, to wave

'her love to come again to Carthage.' And his other examples have the delight and wonder of devout worshippers among the haunts of their divinities. Is there not such delight and wonder in the description of Olwen in the *Mabinogion*: 'More yellow was her hair than the flower of the broom, and her skin was whiter than the foam of the wave, and fairer were her hands and her fingers than the blossoms of the wood-anemone amidst the spray of the meadow fountains'? And is there not such delight and wonder in—

> Meet we on hill, in dale, forest, or mead,
> By paved fountain or by rushy brook,
> Or on the beached margent of the sea?

If men had never dreamed that fair women could be made out of flowers, or rise up out of meadow fountains and paved fountains, neither passage could have been written. Certainly the descriptions of nature made in what Matthew Arnold calls 'the faithful way,' or in what he calls 'the Greek way,' would have lost nothing if all the meadow fountains or paved fountains were but what they seemed. When Keats wrote, in the Greek way, which adds lightness and brightness to nature—

> What little town by river or sea-shore,
> Or mountain-built with quiet citadel,
> Is emptied of its folk, this pious morn?;

when Shakespeare wrote in the Greek way—

> I know a bank where the wild thyme blows,
> Where oxlips and the nodding violet grows;

when Virgil wrote in the Greek way—

> Muscosi fontes et somno mollior herba,

and

Ideas of Good and Evil

Pallentes violas et summa papavera carpens
Narcissum et florem jungit bene olentis anethi;

they looked at nature without ecstasy, but with the
affection a man feels for the garden where he has
walked daily and thought pleasant thoughts. They
looked at nature in the modern way, the way of people
who are poetical, but are more interested in one another
than in a nature which has faded to be but friendly and
pleasant, the way of people who have forgotten the
ancient religion.

III

Men who lived in a world where anything might
flow and change, and become any other thing; and
among great gods whose passions were in the flaming
sunset, and in the thunder and the thunder-shower, had
not our thoughts of weight and measure. They worshipped nature and the abundance of nature, and had
always, as it seems, for a supreme ritual that tumultuous dance among the hills or in the depths of the
woods, where unearthly ecstasy fell upon the dancers,
until they seemed the gods or the godlike beasts, and
felt their souls overtopping the moon; and, as some
think, imagined for the first time in the world the
blessed country of the gods and of the happy dead.
They had imaginative passions because they did not
live within our own strait limits, and were nearer to
ancient chaos, every man's desire, and had immortal
models about them. The hare that ran by among the
dew might have sat up on his haunches when the first

man was made, and the poor bunch of rushes under their feet might have been a goddess laughing among the stars; and with but a little magic, a little waving of the hands, a little murmuring of the lips, they too could become a hare or a bunch of rushes, and know immortal love and immortal hatred.

All folk literature, and all literature that keeps the folk tradition, delights in unbounded and immortal things. The *Kalevala* delights in the seven hundred years that Luonnotar wanders in the depths of the sea with Wäinämöinen in her womb, and the Mahomedan king in the *Song of Roland*, pondering upon the greatness of Charlemagne, repeats over and over, 'He is three hundred years old, when will he be weary of war?' Cuchulain in the Irish folk-tale had the passion of victory, and he overcame all men, and died warring upon the waves, because they alone had the strength to overcome him. The lover in the Irish folk-song bids his beloved come with him into the woods, and see the salmon leap in the rivers, and hear the cuckoo sing, because death will never find them in the heart of the woods. Oisin, new come from his three hundred years of faeryland, and of the love that is in faeryland, bids Saint Patrick cease his prayers a while and listen to the blackbird, because it is the blackbird of Derrycarn that Finn brought from Norway, three hundred years before, and set its nest upon the oak-tree with his own hands. Surely if one goes far enough into the woods, one will find there all that one is seeking? Who knows how many centuries the birds of the woods have been singing?

All folk literature has indeed a passion whose like is not in modern literature and music and art, except where it has come by some straight or crooked way out of ancient times. Love was held to be a fatal sickness in ancient Ireland, and there is a love-poem in the *Love Songs of Connacht* that is like a death-cry: 'My love, O she is my love, the woman who is most for destroying me, dearer is she for making me ill than the woman who would be for making me well. She is my treasure, O she is my treasure, the woman of the grey eyes . . . a woman who would not lay a hand under my head. . . . She is my love, O she is my love, the woman who left no strength in me; a woman who would not breathe a sigh after me, a woman who would not raise a stone at my tomb. . . . She is my secret love, O she is my secret love. A woman who tells me nothing, . . . a woman who does not remember me to be out. . . . She is my choice, O she is my choice, the woman who would not look back at me, the woman who would not make peace with me. . . . She is my desire, O she is my desire: a woman dearest to me under the sun, a woman who would not pay me heed, if I were to sit by her side. It is she ruined my heart and left a sigh for ever in me.' There is another song that ends, 'The Erne shall be in strong flood, the hills shall be torn down, and the sea shall have red waves, and blood shall be spilled, and every mountain valley and every moor shall be on high, before you shall perish, my little black rose.' Nor do the old Irish weigh and measure their hatred. The nurse of O'Sullivan Bere in the folk-song prays that the bed of his betrayer may be the red

hearth-stone of Hell for ever. And an Elizabethan Irish
poet cries: 'Three things are waiting for my death. The
Devil, who is waiting for my soul and cares nothing
for my body or my wealth; the worms, who are waiting
for my body but care nothing for my soul or my
wealth; my children, who are waiting for my wealth
and care nothing for my body or my soul. O Christ,
hang all three in the one noose.' Such love and hatred
seek no mortal thing but their own infinity, and such
love and hatred soon become love and hatred of the
idea. The lover who loves so passionately can soon
sing to his beloved like the lover in the poem by A.E.,
'A vast desire awakes and grows into forgetfulness of
thee.'

When an early Irish poet calls the Irishman famous
for much loving, and a proverb a friend[1] has heard in
the Highlands of Scotland talks of the lovelessness of
the Irishman, they may say but the same thing, for if
your passion is but great enough it leads you to a
country where there are many cloisters. The hater who
hates with too good a heart soon comes also to hate
the idea only; and from this idealism in love and hatred
comes, as I think, a certain power of saying and forgetting things, especially a power of saying and forgetting things in politics, which others do not say and
forget. The ancient farmers and herdsmen were full of
love and hatred, and made their friends gods, and their
enemies the enemies of gods, and those who keep
their tradition are not less mythological. From this

---

[1] William Sharp, who probably invented the proverb, but, invented or not, it remains true. 1924.

'mistaking dreams,' which are perhaps essences, for 'realities,' which are perhaps accidents, from this 'passionate, turbulent reaction against the despotism of fact,' comes, it may be, that melancholy which made all ancient peoples delight in tales that end in death and parting, as modern peoples delight in tales that end in marriage bells; and made all ancient peoples, who, like the old Irish, had a nature more lyrical than dramatic, delight in wild and beautiful lamentations. Life was so weighed down by the emptiness of the great forests and by the mystery of all things, and by the greatness of its own desires, and, as I think, by the loneliness of much beauty; and seemed so little and so fragile and so brief, that nothing could be more sweet in the memory than a tale that ended in death and parting, and than a wild and beautiful lamentation. Men did not mourn merely because their beloved was married to another, or because learning was bitter in the mouth, for such mourning believes that life might be happy were it different, and is therefore the less mourning, but because they had been born and must die with their great thirst unslaked. And so it is that all the august sorrowful persons of literature, Cassandra and Helen and Deirdre, and Lear and Tristan, have come out of legends and are indeed but the images of the primitive imagination mirrored in the little looking-glass of the modern and classic imagination. This is that 'melancholy a man knows when he is face to face' with Nature, and thinks 'he hears her communing with him about' the mournfulness of being born and of dying; and how can it do otherwise than call into his mind 'its exiles, its flights

across the seas,' that it may stir the ever-smouldering
ashes? No Gaelic poetry is so popular in Gaelic-speaking places as the lamentations of Oisin, old and miserable, remembering the companions and the loves of
his youth, and his three hundred years in faeryland,
and his faery love: all dreams withering in the winds
of time lament in his lamentations: 'The clouds are long
above me this night; last night was a long night to me;
although I find this day long, yesterday was still longer.
Every day that comes to me is long. . . . No one in this
great world is like me—a poor old man dragging
stones. The clouds are long above me this night. I am
the last man of the Fianna, the great Oisin, the son of
Finn, listening to the sound of bells. The clouds are
long above me this night.' Matthew Arnold quotes the
lamentation of Llywarch Hen as a type of the Celtic
melancholy, but I prefer to quote it as a type of the
primitive melancholy: 'O my crutch, is it not autumn
when the fern is red and the water-flag yellow? Have
I not hated that which I love? . . . Behold, old age,
which makes sport of me, from the hair of my head
and my teeth, to my eyes which women loved. The
four things I have all my life most hated fall upon me
together—coughing and old age, sickness and sorrow.
I am old, I am alone, shapeliness and warmth are gone
from me, the couch of honour shall be no more mine;
I am miserable, I am bent on my crutch. How evil was
the lot allotted to Llywarch, the night he was brought
forth! Sorrows without end and no deliverance from
his burden.' An Elizabethan writer describes extravagant sorrow by calling it 'to weep Irish'; and Oisin

and Llywarch Hen are, I think, a little nearer even to us modern Irish than they are to most people. That is why our poetry and much of our thought is melancholy. 'The same man,' writes Dr. Hyde in the beautiful prose which he first writes in Gaelic, 'who will to-day be dancing, sporting, drinking, and shouting, will be soliloquising by himself to-morrow, heavy and sick and sad in his own lonely little hut, making a croon over departed hopes, lost life, the vanity of this world, and the coming of death.'

IV

Matthew Arnold asks how much of the Celt must one imagine in the ideal man of genius. I prefer to say, how much of the ancient hunters and fishers and of the ecstatic dancers among hills and woods must one imagine in the ideal man of genius? Certainly a thirst for unbounded emotion and a wild melancholy are troublesome things in the world, and do not make its life more easy or orderly, but it may be the arts are founded on the life beyond the world, and that they must cry in the ears of our penury until the world has been consumed and become a vision. Certainly, as Samuel Palmer wrote, excess is the vivifying spirit of the finest art, and we must always seek to make excess more abundantly excessive. Matthew Arnold has said that if he were asked 'where English got its turn for melancholy and its turn for natural magic,' he 'would answer with little doubt that it got much of its melancholy from a Celtic source, with no doubt at all that from a Celtic source it got nearly all its natural magic.'

The Celtic Element in Literature

I will put this differently and say that literature dwindles to a mere chronicle of circumstance, or passionless fantasies, and passionless meditations, unless it is constantly flooded with the passions and beliefs of ancient times,[1] and that of all the fountains of the passions and beliefs of ancient times in Europe, the Slavonic, the Finnish, the Scandinavian, and the Celtic, the Celtic alone has been for centuries close to the main river of European literature. It has again and again brought 'the vivifying spirit' 'of excess' into the arts of Europe. Ernest Renan has told how the visions of Purgatory seen by pilgrims to Lough Derg—once visions of the pagan underworld, as the boat made out of a hollow tree that bore the pilgrim to the holy island were alone enough to prove—gave European thought new symbols of a more abundant penitence; and had so great an influence that he has written, 'It cannot be doubted for a moment that to the number of poetical themes Europe owes to the genius of the Celt is to be added the framework of the *Divine Comedy*.'

A little later the legends of Arthur and his Table, and of the Holy Grail, once, it seems, the cauldron of an Irish god, changed the literature of Europe, and, it may be, changed, as it were, the very roots of man's emotions by their influence on the spirit of chivalry and on the spirit of romance; and later still Shakespeare found his Mab, and probably his Puck, and one knows not how much else of his faery kingdom, in

[1] I should have added as an alternative that the supernatural may at any moment create new myths, but I was timid. 1924.

Celtic legend; while at the beginning of our own day
Sir Walter Scott gave Highland legends and Highland
excitability so great a mastery over all romance that
they seem romance itself.

In our own time Scandinavian tradition, because of
the imagination of Richard Wagner and of William
Morris and of the earlier and, as I think, greater Hen-
rik Ibsen, has created a new romance, and, through
the imagination of Richard Wagner, become all but
the most passionate element in the arts of the modern
world. There is indeed but one other element as
passionate, the still unfaded legends of Arthur and of
the Holy Grail; and now a new fountain of legends,
and, as I think, a more abundant fountain than any in
Europe, is being opened, the fountain of Gaelic legends:
the tale of Deirdre, who alone among women who
have set men mad had equal loveliness and wisdom;
the tale of the Sons of Tuireann, with its unintelligible
mysteries, an old Grail Quest as I think; the tale of the
four children changed into four swans, and lamenting
over many waters; the tale of the love of Cuchulain
for an immortal goddess, and his coming home to a
mortal woman in the end; the tale of his many battles
at the ford with that dear friend he kissed before the
battles, and over whose dead body he wept when he
had killed him; the tale of his death and of the lamentations of Emer; the tale of the flight of Grania with
Diarmuid, strangest of all tales of the fickleness of
woman, and the tale of the coming of Oisin out of
faeryland, and of his memories and lamentations. 'The
Celtic movement,' as I understand it, is principally the

opening of this fountain, and none can measure of how great importance it may be to coming times, for every new fountain of legends is a new intoxication for the imagination of the world. It comes at a time when the imagination of the world is as ready as it was at the coming of the tales of Arthur and of the Grail for a new intoxication. The reaction against the rationalism of the eighteenth century has mingled with a reaction against the materialism of the nineteenth century, and the symbolical movement, which has come to perfection in Germany in Wagner, in England in the Pre-Raphaelites, in France in Villiers de l'Isle-Adam, and Mallarmé, and in Belgium in Maeterlinck, and has stirred the imagination of Ibsen and D'Annunzio, is certainly the only movement that is saying new things. The arts by brooding upon their own intensity have become religious, and are seeking, as I think Verhaeren has said, to create a sacred book. They must, as religious thought has always done, utter themselves through legends; and the Slavonic and Finnish legends tell of strange woods and seas, and the Scandinavian legends are held by a great master, and tell also of strange woods and seas, and the Welsh legends are held by almost as many great masters as the Greek legends, while the Irish legends move among known woods and seas, and have so much of a new beauty that they may well give the opening century its most memorable symbols.

1897

I could have written this essay with much more precision and have much better illustrated my meaning

if I had waited until Lady Gregory had finished
her book of legends, *Cuchulain of Muirthemne*, a book
to set beside the *Morte d'Arthur* and the *Mabinogion*.

1902

The Autumn of the Body

THE AUTUMN OF THE BODY

OUR THOUGHTS AND EMOTIONS are often but spray flung up from hidden tides that follow a moon no eye can see. I remember that when I first began to write I desired to describe outward things as vividly as possible, and took pleasure, in which there was, perhaps, a little discontent, in picturesque and declamatory books. And then quite suddenly I lost the desire of describing outward things, and found that I took little pleasure in a book unless it was spiritual and unemphatic. I did not then understand that the change was from beyond my own mind, but I understand now that writers are struggling all over Europe, though not often with a philosophic understanding of their struggle, against that picturesque and declamatory way of writing, against that 'externality' which a time of scientific and political thought has brought into literature. This struggle has been going on for some years, but it has only just become strong enough to draw within itself the little inner world which alone seeks more than amusement in the arts. In France, where movements are more marked, because the people are pre-eminently logical, *The Temptation of Saint Anthony*, the last great dramatic invention of the old romanticism, contrasts very plainly with *Axël*, the first great dramatic invention of the new; and Maeterlinck has followed Count Villiers de l'Isle-Adam. Flaubert wrote unforgettable descriptions of grotesque, bizarre, and beautiful scenes and persons, as they show to the ear and to the eye, and crowded them with historical and ethnographical details; but Count Villiers de l'Isle-Adam swept together, by what seemed a sudden energy, words behind which glimmered a spiritual and passionate mood, as the flame glimmers behind the dusky blue and red glass in an Eastern lamp; and created persons from whom has fallen all even of personal characteristic except a thirst for that hour when all things shall pass away like a cloud, and a pride like that of the Magi following their star over many mountains; while Maeterlinck has plucked away even this thirst and this pride and set before us faint souls, naked and pathetic shadows already half vapour and sighing to one another upon the border of the last abyss. There has been, as I think, a like change in French painting, for one sees everywhere, instead of the dramatic stories and picturesque moments of an older school, frail and tremulous bodies unfitted for the labour of life, and landscape where subtle rhythms of colour and of form have overcome the clear outline of things as we see them in the labour of life.

There has been a like change in England, but it has come more gradually and is more mixed with lesser changes than in France. The poetry which found its expression in the poems of writers like Browning and Tennyson, and even of writers who are seldom classed with them, like Swinburne, and like Shelley in his earlier years, pushed its limits as far as possible, and tried to absorb into itself the science and politics, the philosophy and morality of its time; but a new poetry, which is always contracting its limits, has grown up under the shadow of the old. Rossetti began it, but was too much of a painter in his poetry to follow it with a perfect devotion; and it became a movement when Mr. Lang and Mr. Gosse and Mr. Dobson devoted themselves to the most condensed of lyric poems, and when Mr. Bridges, a more considerable poet, elaborated a rhythm too delicate for any but an almost bodiless emotion, and repeated over and over the most ancient notes of poetry, and none but these. The poets who followed have either, like Mr. Kipling, turned from serious poetry altogether, and so passed out of the processional order, or speak out of some personal or spiritual passion in words and types and metaphors that draw one's imagination as far as possible from the complexities of modern life and thought. The change has been more marked in English painting, which, when intense enough to belong to the processional order, began to cast out things, as they are seen by minds plunged in the labour of life, so much before French painting that ideal art is sometimes called English art upon the Continent.

I see, indeed, in the arts of every country those faint lights and faint colours and faint outlines and faint energies which many call 'the decadence,' and which I, because I believe that the arts lie dreaming of things to come, prefer to call the autumn of the body. An Irish poet whose rhythms are like the cry of a sea-bird in autumn twilight has told its meaning in the line, 'The very sunlight's weary, and it's time to quit the plough.' Its importance is the greater because it comes to us at the moment when we are beginning to be interested in many things which positive science, the interpreter of exterior law, has always denied: communion of mind with mind in thought and without words, foreknowledge in dreams and in visions, and the coming among us of the dead, and of much else. We are, it may be, at a crowning crisis of the world, at the moment when man is about to ascend, with the wealth he has been so long gathering upon his shoulders, the stairway he has been descending from the first days. The first poets, if one may find their images in the *Kalevala*, had not Homer's preoccupation with things, and he was not so full of their excitement as Virgil. Dante added to poetry a dialectic which, although he made it serve his laborious ecstasy, was the invention of minds trained by the labour of life, by a traffic among many things, and not a spontaneous expression of an interior life; while Shakespeare shattered the symmetry of verse and of drama that he might fill them with things and their accidental relations to one another.

Each of these writers had come further down the stairway than those who had lived before him, but it was only with the modern poets, with Goethe and Wordsworth and Browning, that poetry gave up the right to consider all things in the world as a dictionary of types and symbols and began to call itself a critic of life and an interpreter of things as they are. Painting, music, science, politics, and even religion, because they have felt a growing belief that we know nothing but the fading and flowering of the world, have changed in numberless elaborate ways. Man has wooed and won the world, and has fallen weary, and not, I think, for a time, but with a weariness that will not end until the last autumn, when the stars shall be blown away like withered leaves. He grew weary when he said, 'These things that I touch and see and hear are alone real,' for he saw them without illusion at last, and found them but air and dust and moisture. And now he must be philosophical above everything, even about the arts, for he can only return the way he came, and so escape from weariness, by philosophy. The arts are, I believe, about to take upon their shoulders the burdens that have fallen from the shoulders of priests, and to lead us back upon our journey by filling our thoughts with the essences of things, and not with things. We are about to substitute once more the distillation of alchemy for the analyses of chemistry and for some other sciences; and certain of us are looking everywhere for the perfect alembic that no silver or golden drop may escape. Mr. Symons has written lately on Mallarmé's method, and has quoted him as saying that we should 'abolish the pretension, aesthetically an error, despite its dominion over almost all the masterpieces, to enclose within the subtle paper other than—for example—the horror of the forest or the silent thunder in the leaves, not the intense dense wood of the trees,' and as desiring to substitute for 'the old lyric afflatus or the enthusiastic personal direction of the phrase' words 'that take light from mutual reflection, like an actual trail of fire over precious stones,' and 'to make an entire word hitherto unknown to the language' 'out of many vocables.' Mr. Symons understands these and other sentences to mean that poetry will henceforth be a poetry of essences, separated one from another in little and intense poems. I think there will be much poetry of this kind, because of an ever more arduous search for an almost disembodied ecstasy, but I think we will not cease to write long poems, but rather that we will write them more and more as our new belief makes the world plastic under our hands again. I think that we will learn again how to describe at great length an old man wandering among enchanted islands, his return home at last, his slow-gathering vengeance, a flitting shape of a goddess, and a flight of arrows, and yet to make all of these so different things 'take light from mutual reflection, like an actual trail of fire over precious stones,' and become 'an entire word,' the signature or symbol of a mood of the divine imagination as imponderable as 'the horror of the forest or the silent thunder in the leaves.'

1898

The Moods

THE MOODS

LITERATURE differs from explanatory and scientific writing in being wrought about a mood, or a community of moods, as the body is wrought about an invisible soul; and if it uses argument, theory, erudition, observation, and seems to grow hot in assertion or denial, it does so merely to make us partakers at the banquet of the moods. It seems to me that these moods are the labourers and messengers of the Ruler of All, the gods of ancient days still dwelling on their secret Olympus, the angels of more modern days ascending and descending upon their shining ladder; and that argument, theory, erudition, observation, are merely what Blake called 'little devils who fight for themselves,' illusions of our visible passing life, who must be made serve the moods, or we have no part in eternity. Everything that can be seen, touched, measured, explained, understood, argued over, is to the imaginative artist nothing more than a means, for he belongs to the invisible life, and delivers its ever new and ever ancient revelation. We hear much of his need for the restraints of reason, but the only restraint he can obey is the mysterious instinct that has made him an artist, and that teaches him to discover immortal moods in mortal desires, an undecaying hope in our trivial ambitions, a divine love in sexual passion.

1895

THE BODY OF THE FATHER
CHRISTIAN ROSENCRUX

THE FOLLOWERS of the Father Christian Rosencrux, says the old tradition, wrapped his imperishable body in noble raiment and laid it under the house of their Order, in a tomb containing the symbols of all things in heaven and earth, and in the waters under the earth, and set about him inextinguishable magical lamps, which burnt on generation after generation, until other students of the Order came upon the tomb by chance. It seems to me that the imagination has had no very different history during the last two hundred years, but has been laid in a great tomb of criticism, and had set over it inextinguishable magical lamps of wisdom and romance, and has been altogether so nobly housed and apparelled that we have forgotten that its wizard lips are closed, or but opened for the complaining of some melancholy and ghostly voice. The ancients and the Elizabethans abandoned themselves to imagination as a woman abandons herself to love, and created beings who made the people of this world seem but shadows, and great passions which made our loves and hatreds appear but ephemeral and trivial fantasies; but now it is not the great persons or the great passions we imagine which absorb us, for the persons and passions in our poems are mainly reflections our mirror has caught from older poems or from the life about us, but the wise comments we make upon them, the criticism of life we wring from their fortunes. Arthur and

196

his Court are nothing, but the many-coloured lights that play about them are as beautiful as the lights from cathedral windows; Pompilia and Guido are but little, while the ever-recurring meditations and expositions which climax in the mouth of the Pope are among the wisest of the Christian age. I cannot get it out of my mind that this age of criticism is about to pass, and an age of imagination, of emotion, of moods, of revelation, about to come in its place; for certainly belief in a supersensual world is at hand again; and when the notion that we are 'phantoms of the earth and water' has gone down the wind, we will trust our own being and all it desires to invent; and when the external world is no more the standard of reality, we will learn again that the great passions are angels of God, and that to embody them 'uncurbed in their eternal glory,' even in their labour for the ending of man's peace and prosperity, is more than to comment, however wisely, upon the tendencies of our time, or to express the socialistic, or humanitarian, or other forces of our time, or even 'to sum up' our time, as the phrase is; for art is a revelation, and not a criticism, and the life of the artist is in the old saying, 'The wind bloweth where it listeth, and thou hearest the sound thereof, but canst not tell whence it cometh and whither it goeth; so is every one that is born of the Spirit.'

1895

THE RETURN OF ULYSSES

I

M. MAETERLINCK, in his beautiful *Treasure of the Humble*, compares the dramas of our stage to the paintings of an obsolete taste; and the dramas of the stage for which he hopes, to the paintings of a taste that cannot become obsolete. 'The true artist,' he says, 'no longer chooses Marius triumphing over the Cimbrians, or the assassination of the Duke of Guise, as fit subjects for his art; for he is well aware that the psychology of victory or murder is but elementary and exceptional, and that the solemn voice of men and things, the voice that issues forth so timidly and hesitatingly, cannot be heard amidst the idle uproar of acts of violence. And therefore will he place on his canvas a house lost in the heart of the country, a door open at the end of a passage, a face or hands at rest.' I do not understand him to mean that our dramas should have no victories or murders, for he quotes for our example plays that have both, but only that their victories and murders shall not be to excite our nerves, but to illustrate the reveries of a wisdom which shall be as much a part of the daily life of the wise as a face or hands at rest. And certainly the greater plays of the past ages have been built after such a fashion. If this fashion is about to become our fashion also, and there are signs that it is, plays like some of Mr. Robert Bridges' will come out of that obscurity into which all poetry that is not lyrical poetry has fallen, and even popular criticism will begin to know something about them. Some day the few among us who care for poetry more than any temporal thing, and who believe that its delights cannot be perfect when we read it alone in our rooms and long for one to share its delights, but that they might be perfect in the theatre, when we share them friend with friend, lover with beloved, will persuade a few idealists to seek out the lost art of speaking, and seek out ourselves the lost art, that is perhaps nearest of all arts to eternity, the subtle art of listening. When that day comes we will talk much of Mr. Bridges; for did he not write scrupulous, passionate poetry to be sung and to be spoken, when there were few to sing and as yet none to speak? There is one play especially, *The Return of Ulysses*, which we will praise for perfect after its kind, the kind of our new drama of wisdom, for it moulds into dramatic shape, and with as much as possible of literal translation, those closing books of the *Odyssey* which are perhaps the most perfect poetry of the world, and compels that great tide of song to flow through delicate dramatic verse, with little abatement of its own leaping and clamorous speed. As I read, the gathering passion overwhelms me, as it did when Homer himself was the singer, and when I read at last the lines in which the maid describes to Penelope the battle with the suitors, at which she looks through the open door, I tremble with excitement.

PENELOPE
Alas! what cries! Say, is the prince still safe?

THE MAID
He shieldeth himself well, and striketh surely.

199

His foes fall down before him. Ah! now what can I see?
Who cometh? Lo! a dazzling helm, a spear
Of silver or electron; sharp and swift
The piercings. How they fall! Ha! shields are raised
In vain. I am blinded, or the beggar-man
Hath waxed in strength. He is changed, he is young. O
    strange!
He is all in golden armour. These are gods
That slay the suitors. (*Runs to* PENELOPE) O lady, forgive
    me.
'Tis Ares' self. I saw his crispèd beard;
I saw beneath his helm his curlèd locks.

The coming of Athene helmed in 'silver or electron' and her transformation of Ulysses are not, as the way is with the only modern dramas that popular criticism holds to be dramatic, the climax of an excitement of the nerves, but of that unearthly excitement which has wisdom for fruit, and is of like kind with the ecstasy of the seers, an altar flame, unshaken by the winds of the world, and burning every moment with whiter and purer brilliance.

Mr. Bridges has written it in what is practically the classical manner, as he has done in *Achilles in Scyros*— a placid and charming setting for many placid and charming lyrics:—

    And ever we keep a feast of delight,
    The betrothal of hearts, when spirits unite,
    Creating an offspring of joy, a treasure
        Unknown to the bad, for whom
        The gods foredoom
        The glitter of pleasure
        And a dark tomb.

The poet who writes best in the Shakespearian

manner is a poet with a circumstantial and instinctive mind, who delights to speak with strange voices and to see his mind in the mirror of nature; while Mr. Bridges, like most of us to-day, has a lyrical and meditative mind, and delights to speak with his own voice and to see nature in the mirror of his mind. In reading his plays in a Shakespearian manner, I find that he is constantly arranging his story in such-and-such a way because he has read that the persons he is writing of did such-and-such things, and not because his soul has passed into the soul of their world and understood its unchangeable destinies. His *Return of Ulysses* is admirable in beauty, because its classical gravity of speech, which does not, like Shakespeare's verse, desire the vivacity of common life, purifies and subdues all passion into lyrical and meditative ecstasies, and because the unity of place and time in the late acts compels a logical rather than instinctive procession of incidents; and if the Shakespearian *Nero: Second Part* approaches it in beauty and in dramatic power, it is because it eddies about Nero and Seneca, who had both, to a great extent, lyrical and meditative minds. Had Mr. Bridges been a true Shakespearian, the pomp and glory of the world would have drowned that subtle voice that speaks amid our heterogeneous lives of a life lived in obedience to a lonely and distinguished ideal.

II

The more a poet rids his verses of heterogeneous knowledge and irrelevant analysis, and purifies his mind with elaborate art, the more does the little ritual of his verse resemble the great ritual of Nature, and become mysterious and inscrutable. He becomes, as all the great mystics have believed, a vessel of the creative power of God; and whether he be a great poet or a small poet, we can praise the poems, which but seem to be his, with the extremity of praise that we give this great ritual which is but copied from the same eternal model. There is poetry that is like the white light of noon, and poetry that has the heaviness of woods, and poetry that has the golden light of dawn or of sunset; and I find in the poetry of Mr. Bridges in the plays, but still more in the lyrics, the pale colours, the delicate silence, the low murmurs of cloudy country days, when the plough is in the earth, and the clouds darkening towards sunset; and had I the great gift of praising, I would praise it as I would praise these things.

1896

IRELAND AND THE ARTS

THE ARTS HAVE FAILED; fewer people are interested in them every generation. The mere business of living, of making money, of amusing oneself, occupies people more and more, and makes them less and less capable of the difficult art of appreciation. When they buy a picture it generally shows a long-current idea, or some conventional form that can be admired in that lax mood one admires a fine carriage in or fine horses in; and when they buy a book it is so much in the manner of the picture that it is forgotten, when its moment is over, as a glass of wine is forgotten. We who care deeply about the arts find ourselves the priesthood of an almost forgotten faith, and we must, I think, if we would win the people again, take upon ourselves the method and the fervour of a priesthood. We must be half humble and half proud. We see the perfect more than others, it may be, but we must find the passions among the people. We must baptize as well as preach.

The makers of religions have established their cere-monies, their form of art, upon fear of death, upon the hope of the father in his child, upon the love of man and woman. They have even gathered into their cere-monies the ceremonies of more ancient faiths, for fear a grain of the dust turned into crystal in some past fire, a passion that had mingled with the religious idea, might perish if the ancient ceremony perished. They have re-named wells and images and given new mean-ings to ceremonies of spring and midsummer and

harvest. In very early days the arts were so possessed
by this method that they were almost inseparable from
religion, going side by side with it into all life. But,
to-day, they have grown, as I think, too proud, too
anxious to live alone with the perfect, and so one sees
them, as I think, like charioteers standing by deserted
chariots and holding broken reins in their hands, or
seeking to go upon their way drawn by that sexual
passion which alone remains to them out of the passions
of the world. We should not blame them, but rather a
mysterious tendency in things which will have its end
some day. In England, men like William Morris, seeing
about them passions so long separated from the perfect
that it seemed as if they could not be changed until
society had been changed, tried to unite the arts once
more to life by uniting them to use. They advised
painters to paint fewer pictures upon canvas, and to
burn more of them on plates; and they tried to persuade
sculptors that a candlestick might be as beautiful as a
statue. But here in Ireland, when the arts have grown
humble, they will find two passions ready to their
hands, love of the Unseen Life and love of country. I
would have a devout writer or painter often content
himself with subjects taken from his religious beliefs;
and if his religious beliefs are those of the majority, he
may at last move hearts in every cottage; while even
if his religious beliefs are those of some minority, he
will have a better welcome than if he wrote of the rape
of Persephone, or painted the burning of Shelley's
body. He will have founded his work on a passion
which will bring him to many besides those who have

been trained to care for beautiful things by a special education. If he is a painter or a sculptor he will find churches awaiting his hand everywhere, and if he follows the masters of his craft our other passion will come into his work also, for he will show his Holy Family winding among hills like those of Ireland, and his Bearer of the Cross among faces copied from the faces of his own town. Our art teachers should urge their pupils into this work, for I can remember, when I was myself a Dublin art student, how I used to despond, when youthful ardour burned low, at the general indifference of the town.

But I would rather speak to those who, while moved in other things than the arts by love of country, are beginning to write, as I was some sixteen years ago, without any decided impulse to one thing more than another, and especially to those who are convinced, as I was convinced, that art is tribeless, nationless, a blossom gathered in No Man's Land. The Greeks looked within their borders, and we, like them, have a history fuller than any modern history of imaginative events; and legends which surpass, as I think, all legends but theirs in wild beauty, and in our land, as in theirs, there is no river or mountain that is not associated in the memory with some event or legend; while political reasons have made love of country, as I think, even greater among us than among them. I would have our writers and craftsmen of many kinds master this history and these legends, and fix upon their memory the appearance of mountains and rivers and make it all visible again in their arts, so that Irishmen, even though they had gone thousands of miles away, would still be in their own country. Whether they chose for the subject the carrying off of the Brown Bull or the coming of Patrick, or the political struggle of later times, the other world comes so much into it all that their love of it would move in their hands also, and as much, it may be, as in the hands of the Greek craftsmen. In other words, I would have Ireland re-create the ancient arts, the arts as they were understood in Judaea, in India, in Scandinavia, in Greece and Rome, in every ancient land; as they were understood when they moved a whole people and not a few people who have grown up in a leisured class and made this understanding their business.

I think that my reader[1] will have agreed with most that I have said up till now, for we all hope for arts like these. I think indeed I first learned to hope for them myself in Young Ireland Societies, or in reading the essays of Davis. An Englishman, with his belief in progress, with his instinctive preference for the cosmopolitan literature of the last century, may think arts like these parochial, but they are the arts we have begun the making of.

I will not, however, have all my readers with me when I say that no writer, no artist, even though he choose Brian Borúmha or Saint Patrick for his subject, should try to make his work popular. Once he has chosen a subject he must think of nothing but giving it such an expression as will please himself. As Walt Whitman has written:—

---

[1] This essay was first published in the *United Irishman*, August 31, 1904.

Ireland and the Arts

The oration is to the orator, the acting is to the actor and
   actress, not to the audience:
And no man understands any greatness or goodness, but his
   own or the indication of his own.

He must make his work a part of his own journey
towards beauty and truth. He must picture saint or
hero, or hillside, as he sees them, not as he is expected
to see them, and he must comfort himself, when others
cry out against what he has seen, by remembering that
no two men are alike, and that there is no 'excellent
beauty without strangeness.' In this matter he must be
without humility. He may, indeed, doubt the reality
of his vision if men do not quarrel with him as they did
with the Apostles, for there is only one perfection and
only one search for perfection, and it sometimes has
the form of the religious life and sometimes of the
artistic life; and I do not think these lives differ in their
wages, for 'The end of art is peace,' and out of the one
as out of the other comes the cry: *Sero te amavi, Pul-
chritudo tam antiqua et tam nova! Sero te amavi!*
   The Catholic Church is not the less the Church of
the people because the Mass is spoken in Latin, and art
is not less the art of the people because it does not
always speak in the language they are used to. I once
heard my friend Mr. Ellis say, speaking at a celebration
in honour of a writer whose fame had not come till
long after his death, 'It is not the business of a poet to
make himself understood, but it is the business of the
people to understand him. That they are at last compelled to do so is the proof of his authority.' And certainly if you take from art its martyrdom, you will take

from it its glory. It might still reflect the passing modes of mankind, but it would cease to reflect the face of God.

If our craftsmen were to choose their subjects under what we may call, if we understand faith to mean that belief in a spiritual life which is not confined to one Church, the persuasion of their faith and their country, they would soon discover that although their choice seemed arbitrary at first, it had obeyed what was deepest in them. I could not now write of any other country but Ireland, for my style has been shaped by the subjects I have worked on, but there was a time when my imagination seemed unwilling, when I found myself writing of some Irish event in words that would have better fitted some Italian or Eastern event, for my style had been shaped in that general stream of European literature which has come from so many watersheds, and it was slowly, very slowly, that I made a new style. It was years before I could rid myself of Shelley's Italian light, but now I think my style is myself. I might have found more of Ireland if I had written in Irish, but I have found a little, and I have found all myself. I am persuaded that if the Irishmen who are painting conventional pictures or writing conventional books on alien subjects, which have been worn away like pebbles on the shore, would do the same, they, too, might find themselves. Even the landscape-painter, who paints a place that he loves, and that no other man has painted, soon discovers that no style learned in the studios is wholly fitted to his purpose. And I cannot but believe that if our painters of Highland cattle and moss-covered barns were to care enough for their country to care for what makes it different from other countries, they would discover, when struggling, it may be, to paint the exact grey of the bare Burren Hills,[1] and of a sudden, it may be, a new style, their very selves. And I admit, though in this I am moved by some touch of fanaticism, that even when I see an old subject written of or painted in a new way, I am yet jealous for Cuchulain, and for Baile and Aillinn, and for those grey mountains that still are lacking their celebration. I sometimes reproach myself because I cannot admire Mr. Hughes' beautiful, piteous *Orpheus and Eurydice* with an unquestioning mind. I say with my lips, 'The Spirit made it, for it is beautiful, and the Spirit bloweth where it listeth,' but I say in my heart, 'Aengus and Edain would have served his turn'; but one cannot, perhaps, love or believe at all if one does not love or believe a little too much.

And I do not think with unbroken pleasure of our scholars who write about German writers or about periods of Greek history. I always remember that they could give us a number of little books which would tell, each book for some one county, or some one parish, the verses, or the stories, or the events that would make every lake or mountain a man can see from his own door an excitement in his imagination. I would have some of them leave that work of theirs

[1] Robert Gregory painted the Burren Hills and thereby found what promised to grow into a great style, but he had hardly found it before he was killed. His few finished pictures, so full of austerity and sweetness, should find their way into Irish public galleries.

1924.

which will never lack hands, and begin to dig in Ireland the garden of the future, understanding that here in Ireland the spirit of man may be about to wed the soil of the world.

Art and scholarship like these I have described would give Ireland more than they received from her, for they would make love of the unseen more unshakable, more ready to plunge deep into the abyss, and they would make love of country more fruitful in the mind, more a part of daily life. One would know an Irishman into whose life they had come—and in a few generations they would come into the life of all, rich and poor—by something that set him apart among men. He himself would understand that more was expected of him than of others because he had greater possessions. The Irish race would have become a chosen race, one of the pillars that uphold the world.

1901

THE GALWAY PLAINS

Lady Gregory has just given me her beautiful *Poets and Dreamers*, and it has brought to mind a day two or three years ago when I stood on the side of Slieve Echtge, looking out over Galway. The Burren Hills were to my left, and though I forget whether I could see the cairn over Bald Conan of the Fianna, I could certainly see many places there that are in poems and stories. In front of me, over many miles of level Galway plains, I saw a low blue hill flooded with evening light. I asked a countryman who was with me what hill that was, and he told me it was Cruachmaa of the Sidhe. I had often heard of Cruachmaa of the Sidhe even as far north as Sligo, for the countrypeople have told me a great many stories of the great host of the Sidhe who live there, still fighting and holding festivals.

I asked the old countryman about it, and he told me of strange women who had come from it, and who would come into a house having the appearance of countrywomen, but would know all that happened in that house; and how they would always pay back with increase, though not by their own hands, whatever was given to them. And he had heard, too, of people who had been carried away into the hill, and how one man went to look for his wife there, and dug into the hill and all but got his wife again, but at the very moment she was coming out to him, the pick he was digging with struck her upon the head and killed her. I asked him if he had himself seen any of its enchantments, and he said, 'Sometimes when I look over to the hill, I see a mist lying on the top of it, that goes away after a while.'

A great part of the poems and stories in Lady Gregory's book were made or gathered between Burren and Cruachmaa. It was here that Raftery, the wandering country poet of ninety years ago, praised and blamed, chanting fine verses, and playing badly on his fiddle. It is here the ballads of meeting and parting have been sung, and some whose lamentations for defeat are still remembered may have passed through this plain flying from the battle of Aughrim.

'I will go up on the mountain alone; and I will come hither from it again. It is there I saw the camp of the Gael, the poor troop thinned, not keeping with one another; Och Ochone!' And here, if one can believe many devout people whose stories are in the book, Christ has walked upon the roads, bringing the needy to some warm fireside, and sending one of His saints to anoint the dying.

I do not think these country imaginations have changed much for centuries, for they are still busy with those two themes of the ancient Irish poets, the sternness of battle and the sadness of parting and death. The emotion that in other countries has made many love-songs has here been given, in a long wooing, to danger, that ghostly bride. It is not a difference in the substance of things that the lamentations that were sung after battles are now sung for men who have died upon the gallows.

The Galway Plains

The emotion has become not less, but more noble, by the change, for the man who goes to death with the thought—

It is with the people I was,
It is not with the law I was,

has behind him generations of poetry and poetical life.

The poets of to-day speak with the voice of the unknown priest who wrote, some two hundred years ago, that *Sorrowful Lament for Ireland* Lady Gregory has put into passionate and rhythmical prose:—

I do not know of anything under the sky
That is friendly or favourable to the Gael,
But only the sea that our need brings us to,
Or the wind that blows to the harbour
The ship that is bearing us away from Ireland;
And there is reason that these are reconciled with us,
For we increase the sea with our tears,
And the wandering wind with our sighs.

There is still in truth upon these great level plains a people, a community bound together by imaginative possessions, by stories and poems which have grown out of its own life, and by a past of great passions which can still waken the heart to imaginative action. One could still, if one had the genius, and had been born to Irish, write for these people plays and poems like those of Greece. Does not the greatest poetry always require a people to listen to it? England or any other country which takes its tunes from the great cities and gets its taste from schools and not from old custom may have a mob, but it cannot have a people. In England there are a few groups of men and women who have good taste, whether in cookery or in books; and the great multitudes but copy them or their copiers. The poet must always prefer the community where the perfected minds express the people, to a community that is vainly seeking to copy the perfected minds. To have even perfectly the thoughts that can be weighed, the knowledge that can be got from books, the precision that can be learned at school, to belong to any aristocracy, is to be a little pool that will soon dry up. A people alone are a great river; and that is why I am persuaded that where a people has died, a nation is about to die.

1903

EMOTION OF MULTITUDE

I HAVE BEEN THINKING a good deal about plays lately, and I have been wondering why I dislike the clear and logical construction which seems necessary if one is to succeed on the modern stage. It came into my head the other day that this construction, which all the world has learnt from France, has everything of high literature except the emotion of multitude. The Greek drama has got the emotion of multitude from its chorus, which called up famous sorrows, even all the gods and all heroes, to witness, as it were, some well-ordered fable, some action separated but for this from all but itself. The French play delights in the well-ordered fable, but by leaving out the chorus it has created an art where poetry and imagination, always the children of far-off multitudinous things, must of necessity grow less important than the mere will. This is why, I said to myself, French dramatic poetry is so often rhetorical, for what is rhetoric but the will trying to do the work of the imagination? The Shakespearian drama gets the emotion of multitude out of the sub-plot which copies the main plot, much as a shadow upon the wall copies one's body in the firelight. We think of *King Lear* less as the history of one man and his sorrows than as the history of a whole evil time. Lear's shadow is in Gloucester, who also has ungrateful children, and the mind goes on imagining other shadows, shadow beyond shadow, till it has pictured the world. In *Hamlet*, one hardly notices, so subtly is the web woven, that the murder of Hamlet's father and the sorrow of Hamlet are shadowed in the lives of Fortinbras and Ophelia and Laertes, whose fathers, too, have been killed. It is so in all the plays, or in all but all, and very commonly the sub-plot is the main plot working itself out in more ordinary men and women, and so doubly calling up before us the image of multitude. Ibsen and Maeterlinck have, on the other hand, created a new form, for they get multi-tude from the wild duck in the attic, or from the crown at the bottom of the fountain, vague symbols that set the mind wandering from idea to idea, emotion to emotion. Indeed all the great masters have understood that there cannot be great art without the little limited life of the fable, which is always the better the simpler it is, and the rich, far-wandering, many-imaged life of the half-seen world beyond it. There are some who understand that the simple unmysterious things living as in a clear noon light are of the nature of the sun, and that vague, many-imaged things have in them the strength of the moon. Did not the Egyptian carve it on emerald that all living things have the sun for father and the moon for mother, and has it not been said that a man of genius takes the most after his mother?

1903

THE END

THE CUTTING OF AN AGATE
1903–1915

PREFACE

I WROTE THE GREATER NUMBER of these essays during the ten years after 1902. During those years I wrote little verse and no prose that did not arise out of some need of the Irish players, or from some thought suggested by their work, or in the defence of some friend connected with that work, or with the movement of events that made it possible. I was busy with a single art, that of a small, unpopular theatre; and this art may well seem to practical men busy with some programme of industrial or political regeneration—and in Ireland we have many excellent programmes—of no more account than the shaping of an agate; and yet in the shaping of an agate, whether in the cutting or in the making of the design, one discovers, if one have a speculative mind, thoughts that seem important and principles that may be applied to life itself. Certainly if one does not believe so, one is but a poor cutter of so hard a stone.

W. B. YEATS

December 1918

P.S.—I have to thank Mr. T. C. and Mr. E. C. Jack of Edinburgh for leave to reprint the essay I wrote in their selection from Edmund Spenser before the ten years began, and while I had still time to give a couple of summers to *The Faerie Queene*.

CERTAIN NOBLE PLAYS OF JAPAN

I

I AM WRITING with my imagination stirred by a visit to the studio of Mr. Dulac, the distinguished illustrator of the *Arabian Nights*. I saw there the mask and head-dress to be worn in a play of mine by the player who will speak the part of Cuchulain, and who, wearing this noble, half-Greek, half-Asiatic face, will appear perhaps like an image seen in reverie by some Orphic worshipper. I hope to have attained the distance from life which can make credible strange events, elaborate words. I have written a little play that can be played in a room for so little money that forty or fifty readers of poetry can pay the price. There will be no scenery, for three musicians, whose seeming sunburned faces will, I hope, suggest that they have wandered from village to village in some country of our dreams, can describe place and weather, and at moments action and accompany it all by drum and gong or flute and dulcimer. Instead of the players working themselves into a violence of passion indecorous in our sitting-room, the music, the beauty of form and voice all come to climax in pantomimic dance.

In fact, with the help of Japanese plays 'translated by Ernest Fenollosa and finished by Ezra Pound,' I have invented a form of drama, distinguished, indirect, and symbolic, and having no need of mob or Press to pay its way—an aristocratic form. When this play and its performance run as smoothly as my skill can make them, I shall hope to write another of the same sort and so complete a dramatic celebration of the life of Cuchulain planned long ago. Then having given enough performances for, I hope, the pleasure of personal friends and a few score people of good taste, I shall record all discoveries of method and turn to something else. It is an advantage of this noble form that it need absorb no one's life, that its few properties can be packed up in a box or hung upon the walls where they will be fine ornaments.

II

And yet this simplification is not mere economy. For nearly three centuries invention has been making the human voice and the movements of the body seem always less expressive. I have long been puzzled why passages that are moving when read out or spoken during rehearsal seem muffled or dulled during performance. I have simplified scenery, having *The Hour-Glass*, for instance, played now before green curtains, now among those admirable ivory-coloured screens invented by Gordon Craig. With every simplification the voice has recovered something of its importance, and yet when verse has approached in temper to, let us say, *Kubla Khan*, or the *Ode to the West Wind*, the most typical modern verse, I have still felt as if the sound came to me from behind a veil. The stage-opening, the powerful light and shade, the number of feet between myself and the players have destroyed intimacy. I have found myself thinking of players who needed perhaps but to unroll a mat in some Eastern garden. Nor have I felt this only when I listened to speech, but even more when I have watched the movement of a player or heard singing in a play. I love all the arts that can still remind me of their origin among the common people, and my ears are only comfortable when the singer sings as if mere speech had taken fire, when he appears to have passed into song almost imperceptibly. I am bored and wretched, a limitation I greatly regret, when he seems no longer a human being but an invention of science. To explain him to myself I say that he has become a wind instrument and sings no longer like active men, sailor or camel-driver, because he has had to compete with an orchestra, where the loudest instrument has always survived. The human voice can only become louder by becoming less articulate, by discovering some new musical sort of roar or scream. As poetry can do neither, the voice must be freed from this competition and find itself among little instruments, only heard at their best perhaps when we are close about them. It should be again possible for a few poets to write as all did once, not for the printed page but to be sung. But movement also has grown less expressive, more declamatory, less intimate. When I called the other day upon a friend I found myself among some dozen people who were watching a group of Spanish boys and girls, professional dancers, dancing some national dance in the midst of a drawing-room. Doubtless their training had been long, laborious, and wearisome; but now one could not be deceived, their movement was full of joy. They were among friends, and it all seemed but the play of children; how powerful it seemed, how passionate, while an even more miraculous art, separated from us by the footlights, appeared in the comparison laborious and professional. It is well to be close enough to an artist to feel for him a personal liking, close enough perhaps to feel that our liking is returned.

My play is made possible by a Japanese dancer whom I have seen dance in a studio and in a drawing-room and on a very small stage lit by an excellent stage-light. In the studio and in the drawing-room alone, where the lighting was the light we are most accustomed to, did I see him as the tragic image that has stirred my imagination. There, where no studied lighting, no stage-picture made an artificial world, he was able, as he rose from the floor, where he had been sitting cross-legged, or as he threw out an arm, to recede from us into some more powerful life. Because that separation was achieved by human means alone, he receded but to inhabit as it were the deeps of the mind. One realised anew, at every separating strangeness, that the measure of all arts' greatness can be but in their intimacy.

III

All imaginative art remains at a distance and this distance, once chosen, must be firmly held against a pushing world. Verse, ritual, music, and dance in association with action require that gesture, costume, facial expression, stage arrangement must help in keeping the door. Our unimaginative arts are content to set a piece

224

of the world as we know it in a place by itself, to put
their photographs as it were in a plush or a plain frame,
but the arts which interest me, while seeming to separate from the world and us a group of figures, images,
symbols, enable us to pass for a few moments into a
deep of the mind that had hitherto been too subtle for
our habitation. As a deep of the mind can only be approached through what is most human, most delicate,
we should distrust bodily distance, mechanism, and
loud noise.

It may be well if we go to school in Asia, for the
distance from life in European art has come from little
but difficulty with material. In half-Asiatic Greece
Callimachus could still return to a stylistic manage-
ment of the falling folds of drapery, after the naturalistic drapery of Phidias, and in Egypt the same age that
saw the village Head-man carved in wood, for burial
in some tomb, with so complete a naturalism, saw set
up in public places statues full of an august formality
that implies traditional measurements, a philosophic
defence. The spiritual painting of the fourteenth century passed on into Tintoretto and that of Velasquez
into modern painting with no sense of loss to weigh
against the gain, while the painting of Japan, not having
our European moon to churn the wits, has understood
that no styles that ever delighted noble imaginations
have lost their importance, and chooses the style according to the subject. In literature also we have had
the illusion of change and progress, the art of Shakespeare passing into that of Dryden, and so into the
prose drama, by what has seemed when studied in its

details unbroken progress. Had we been Greeks, and so but half-European, an honourable mob would have martyred, though in vain, the first man who set up a painted scene, or who complained that soliloquies were unnatural, instead of repeating with a sigh, 'We cannot return to the arts of childhood however beautiful.' Only our lyric poetry has kept its Asiatic habit and renewed itself at its own youth, putting off perpetually what has been called its progress in a series of violent revolutions.

Therefore it is natural that I go to Asia for a stage convention, for more formal faces, for a chorus that has no part in the action, and perhaps for those movements of the body copied from the marionette shows of the fourteenth century. A mask will enable me to substitute for the face of some commonplace player, or for that face repainted to suit his own vulgar fancy, the fine invention of a sculptor, and to bring the audience close enough to the play to hear every inflection of the voice. A mask never seems but a dirty face, and no matter how close you go is yet a work of art; nor shall we lose by stilling the movement of the features, for deep feeling is expressed by a movement of the whole body. In poetical painting and in sculpture the face seems the nobler for lacking curiosity, alert attention, all that we sum up under the famous word of the realists, 'vitality.' It is even possible that being is only possessed completely by the dead, and that it is some knowledge of this that makes us gaze with so much emotion upon the face of the Sphinx or of Buddha. Who can forget the face of Chaliapine as the Mogul King in *Prince Igor*, when a mask covering its upper portion made him seem like a phoenix at the end of its thousand wise years, awaiting in condescension the burning nest, and what did it not gain from that immobility in dignity and in power?

IV

Realism is created for the common people and was always their peculiar delight, and it is the delight to-day of all those whose minds, educated alone by schoolmasters and newspapers, are without the memory of beauty and emotional subtlety. The occasional humorous realism that so much heightened the emotional effect of Elizabethan tragedy—Cleopatra's old man with an asp, let us say—carrying the tragic crisis by its contrast above the tide-mark of Corneille's courtly theatre, was made at the outset to please the common citizen standing on the rushes of the floor; but the great speeches were written by poets who remembered their patrons in the covered galleries. The fanatic Savonarola was but dead a century, and his lamentation, in the frenzy of his rhetoric, that every prince of the Church or State throughout Europe was wholly occupied with the fine arts, had still its moiety of truth. A poetical passage cannot be understood without a rich memory, and like the older school of painting appeals to a tradition, and that not merely when it speaks of 'Lethe wharf' or 'Dido on the wild sea banks' but in rhythm, in vocabulary; for the ear must notice slight variations upon old cadences and customary words, all that high breeding of poetical style where there is nothing ostentatious, nothing crude, no breath of parvenu or journalist.

Let us press the popular arts on to a more complete realism—that would be their honesty—for the commercial arts demoralise by their compromise, their incompleteness, their idealism without sincerity or elegance, their pretence that ignorance can understand beauty. In the studio and in the drawing-room we can found a true theatre of beauty. Poets from the time of Keats and Blake have derived their descent only through what is least declamatory, least popular in the art of Shakespeare, and in such a theatre they will find their habitual audience and keep their freedom. Europe is very old and has seen many arts run through the circle and has learned the fruit of every flower and known what this fruit sends up, and it is now time to copy the East and live deliberately.

V

Ye shall not, while ye tarry with me, taste
From unrinsed barrel the diluted wine
Of a low vineyard or a plant ill-pruned,
But such as anciently the Aegean Isles
Poured in libation at their solemn feasts:
And the same goblets shall ye grasp embost
With no vile figures of loose languid boors,
But such as Gods have lived with and have led.

The Noh theatre of Japan became popular at the close of the fourteenth century, gathering into itself dances performed at Shinto shrines in honour of spirits and gods, or by young nobles at the Court, and much old lyric poetry, and receiving its philosophy and its final shape perhaps from priests of a contemplative school of Buddhism. A small *daimio* or feudal lord of the ancient capital Nara, a contemporary of Chaucer, was the author, or perhaps only the stage-manager, of many plays. He brought them to the Court of the Shogun at Kioto. From that on the Shogun and his Court were as busy with dramatic poetry as the Mikado and his with lyric. When for the first time *Hamlet* was being played in London, Noh was made a necessary part of official ceremonies at Kioto, and young nobles and princes, forbidden to attend the popular theatre, in Japan as elsewhere a place of mimicry and naturalism, were encouraged to witness and to perform in spectacles where speech, music, song, and dance created an image of nobility and strange beauty. When the modern revolution came, Noh after a brief unpopularity was played for the first time in certain ceremonious public theatres, and in 1897 a battleship was named *Takasago*, after one of its most famous plays. Some of the old noble families are to-day very poor, their men, it may be, but servants and labourers, but they still frequent these theatres. 'Accomplishment' the word Noh means, and it is their accomplishment and that of a few cultivated people who understand the literary and mythological allusions and the ancient lyrics quoted in speech or chorus, their discipline, a part of their breeding. The players themselves, unlike the despised players of the popular theatre, have passed on proudly from father to son an elaborate art, and even now a player will publish his family tree to prove his skill. One player wrote in 1906 in a business circular—I am quoting from Mr. Pound's redaction of the Notes of Fenollosa—that after thirty generations of nobles a woman of his house dreamed that a mask was carried to her from Heaven, and soon after she bore a son who became a player and the father of players. His family, he declared, still possessed a letter from a fifteenth-century Mikado conferring upon them a theatre-curtain, white below and purple above.

There were five families of these players and, forbidden before the Revolution to perform in public, they had received grants of land or salaries from the State. The white and purple curtain was no doubt to hang upon a wall behind the players or over their entrance-door, for the Noh stage is a platform surrounded upon three sides by the audience. No 'naturalistic' effect is sought. The players wear masks and found their movements upon those of puppets: the most famous of all Japanese dramatists composed entirely for puppets. A swift or a slow movement and a long or a short stillness, and then another movement. They sing as much as they speak, and there is a chorus which describes the scene and interprets their thought and never becomes as in the Greek theatre a part of the action. At the climax, instead of the disordered passion of nature, there is a dance, a series of positions and movements which may represent a battle, or a marriage, or the pain of a ghost in the Buddhist Purgatory. I have lately studied certain of these dances, with Japanese players, and I notice that their ideal of beauty,

unlike that of Greece and like that of pictures from
Japan and China, makes them pause at moments of
muscular tension. The interest is not in the human form
but in the rhythm to which it moves, and the triumph
of their art is to express the rhythm in its intensity.
There are few swaying movements of arms or body
such as make the beauty of our dancing. They move
from the hip, keeping constantly the upper part of their
body still, and seem to associate with every gesture or
pose some definite thought. They cross the stage with
a sliding movement, and one gets the impression not of
undulation but of continuous straight lines.

The Print Room of the British Museum is now
closed as a war-economy, so I can only write from
memory of theatrical colour-prints, where a ship is
represented by a mere skeleton of willows or osiers
painted green, or a fruit-tree by a bush in a pot, and
where actors have tied on their masks with ribbons that
are gathered into a bunch behind the head. It is a child's
game become the most noble poetry, and there is no
observation of life, because the poet would set before
us all those things which we feel and imagine in silence.

Mr. Ezra Pound has found among the Fenollosa
manuscripts a story traditional among Japanese players.
A young man was following a stately old woman
through the streets of a Japanese town, and presently
she turned to him and spoke: 'Why do you follow
me?' 'Because you are so interesting.' 'That is not so,
I am too old to be interesting.' But he wished, he told
her, to become a player of old women on the Noh
stage. If he would become famous as a Noh player,

she said, he must not observe life, nor put on an old face and stint the music of his voice. He must know how to suggest an old woman and yet find it all in the heart.

VI

In the plays themselves I discover a beauty or a subtlety that I can trace perhaps to their threefold origin. The love-sorrows—the love of father and daughter, of mother and son, of boy and girl—may owe their nobility to a courtly life, but he to whom the adventures happen, a traveller commonly from some distant place, is most often a Buddhist priest; and the occasional intellectual subtlety is perhaps Buddhist. The adventure itself is often the meeting with ghost, god, or goddess at some holy place or much-legended tomb; and god, goddess, or ghost reminds me at times of our own Irish legends and beliefs, which once, it may be, differed little from those of the Shinto worshipper.

The feather mantle, for whose lack the moon goddess (or should we call her faery?) cannot return to the sky, is the red cap whose theft can keep our faeries of the sea upon dry land; and the ghost-lovers in *Nishikigi* remind me of the Aran boy and girl who in Lady Gregory's story come to the priest after death to be married. These Japanese poets, too, feel for tomb and wood the emotion, the sense of awe that our Gaelic-speaking countrypeople will sometimes show when you speak to them of Castle Hackett or of some holy well; and that is why perhaps it pleases them to begin so many plays by a traveller asking his way with many

questions, a convention agreeable to me, for when I
first began to write poetical plays for an Irish theatre I
had to put away an ambition of helping to bring again
to certain places their old sanctity or their romance. I
could lay the scene of a play on Baile's Strand, but
I found no pause in the hurried action for descriptions
of strand or sea or the great yew-tree that once stood
there; and I could not in *The King's Threshold* find
room, before I began the ancient story, to call up the
shallow river and the few trees and rocky fields of
modern Gort. But in the *Nishikigi* the tale of the lovers
would lose its pathos if we did not see that forgotten
tomb where 'the hiding fox' lives among 'the orchids
and the chrysanthemum flowers.' The men who created
this convention were more like ourselves than were the
Greeks and Romans, more like us even than are Shakespeare and Corneille. Their emotion was self-conscious
and reminiscent, always associating itself with pictures
and poems. They measured all that time had taken or
would take away and found their delight in remembering celebrated lovers in the scenery pale passion loves.
They travelled seeking for the strange and for the
picturesque: 'I go about with my heart set upon no
particular place, no more than a cloud. I wonder now
would the sea be that way, or the little place Kefu that
they say is stuck down against it.' When a traveller asks
his way of girls upon the roadside he is directed to find
it by certain pine-trees, which he will recognise because
many people have drawn them.

I wonder am I fanciful in discovering in the plays
themselves (few examples have as yet been translated

233

and I may be misled by accident or the idiosyncrasy of some poet) a playing upon a single metaphor, as deliberate as the echoing rhythm of line in Chinese and Japanese painting. In the *Nishikigi* the ghost of the girl-lover carries the cloth she went on weaving out of grass when she should have opened the chamber door to her lover, and woven grass returns again and again in metaphor and incident. The lovers, now that in an aëry body they must sorrow for unconsummated love, are 'tangled up as the grass patterns are tangled.' Again they are like an unfinished cloth: 'these bodies, having no weft, even now are not come together; truly a shameful story, a tale to bring shame on the gods.' Before they can bring the priest to the tomb they spend the day 'pushing aside the grass from the overgrown ways in Kefu,' and the countryman who directs them is 'cutting grass on the hill'; and when at last the prayer of the priest unites them in marriage the bride says that he has made 'a dream-bridge over wild grass, over the grass I dwell in'; and in the end bride and bridegroom show themselves for a moment 'from under the shadow of the love-grass.'

In *Hagoromo* the feather mantle of the faery woman creates also its rhythm of metaphor. In the beautiful day of opening spring 'the plumage of Heaven drops neither feather nor flame,' 'nor is the rock of earth over-much worn by the brushing of the feathery skirt of the stars.' One half remembers a thousand Japanese paintings, or whichever comes first into the memory: that screen painted by Korin, let us say, shown lately at the British Museum, where the same form is echoing

in wave and in cloud and in rock. In European poetry
I remember Shelley's continually repeated fountain and
cave, his broad stream and solitary star. In neglecting
character, which seems to us essential in drama, as do
their artists in neglecting relief and depth, whether in
their paintings or in arranging flowers in a vase in a
thin row, they have made possible a hundred lovely
intricacies.

VII

These plays arose in an age of continual war and
became a part of the education of soldiers. These
soldiers, whose natures had as much of Walter Pater
as of Achilles, combined with Buddhist priests and
women to elaborate life in a ceremony, the playing of
football, the drinking of tea, and all great events of
State, becoming a ritual. In the painting that decorated
their walls and in the poetry they recited one discovers
the only sign of a great age that cannot deceive us, the
most vivid and subtle discrimination of sense and
the invention of images more powerful than sense; the
continual presence of reality. It is still true that the
Deity gives us, according to His promise, not His
thoughts or His convictions but His flesh and blood,
and I believe that the elaborate technique of the arts,
seeming to create out of itself a superhuman life, has
taught more men to die than oratory or the Prayer
Book. We only believe in those thoughts which have
been conceived not in the brain but in the whole body.
The Minoan soldier who bore upon his arm the shield
ornamented with the dove in the Museum at Crete, or

had upon his head the helmet with the winged horse, knew his rôle in life. When Nobuzane painted the child Saint Kōbō Daishi kneeling full of sweet austerity upon the flower of the lotus, he set up before our eyes exquisite life and the acceptance of death.

I cannot imagine those young soldiers and the women they loved pleased with the ill-breeding and theatricality of Carlyle, nor, I think, with the magniloquence of Hugo. These things belong to an industrial age, a mechanical sequence of ideas; but when I remember that curious game which the Japanese called, with a confusion of the senses that had seemed typical of our own age, 'listening to incense,' I know that some among them would have understood the prose of Walter Pater, the painting of Puvis de Chavannes, the poetry of Mallarmé and Verlaine. When heroism returned to our age it bore with it as its first gift technical sincerity.

VIII

For some weeks now I have been elaborating my play in London where alone I can find the help I need, Mr. Dulac's mastery of design and Mr. Ito's genius of movement; yet it pleases me to think that I am working for my own country. Perhaps some day a play in the form I am adapting for European purposes may excite once more, whether in Gaelic or in English, under the slope of Slieve-na-mon or Croagh Patrick, ancient memories; for this form has no need of scenery that runs away with money nor of a theatre-building. Yet I know that I only amuse myself with a fancy; for my writings if they be seaworthy will put to sea, and I cannot tell where they may be carried by the wind. Are not the faery-stories of Oscar Wilde, which were written for Mr. Ricketts and Mr. Shannon and for a few ladies, very popular in Arabia?

April 1916

The Cutting of an Agate

THE TRAGIC THEATRE

I DID NOT FIND A WORD in the printed criticism of Synge's *Deirdre of the Sorrows* about the qualities that made certain moments seem to me the noblest tragedy, and the play was judged by what seemed to me but wheels and pulleys necessary to the effect, but in themselves nothing.

Upon the other hand, those who spoke to me of the play never spoke of these wheels and pulleys, but if they cared at all for the play, cared for the things I cared for. One's own world of painters, of poets, of good talkers, of ladies who delight in Ricard's portraits or Debussy's music, all those whose senses feel instantly every change in our mother the moon, saw the stage in one way; and those others who look at plays every night, who tell the general playgoer whether this play or that play is to his taste, saw it in a way so different that there is certainly some body of dogma—whether in the instincts or in the memory—pushing the ways apart. A printed criticism, for instance, found but one dramatic moment, that when Deirdre in the second act overhears her lover say that he may grow weary of her; and not one—if I remember rightly—chose for praise or explanation the third act which alone had satisfied the author, or contained in any abundance those sentences that were quoted at the fall of the curtain and for days after.

Deirdre and her lover, as Synge tells the tale, returned to Ireland, though it was nearly certain they

238

would die there, because death was better than broken love, and at the side of the open grave that had been dug for one and would serve for both, quarrelled, losing all they had given their life to keep. 'Is it not a hard thing that we should miss the safety of the grave and we trampling its edge?' That is Deirdre's cry at the outset of a reverie of passion that mounts and mounts till grief itself has carried her beyond grief into pure contemplation. Up to this the play had been a Master's unfinished work, monotonous and melancholy, ill-arranged, little more than a sketch of what it would have grown to, but now I listened breathless to sentences that may never pass away, and as they filled or dwindled in their civility of sorrow, the player, whose art had seemed clumsy and incomplete, like the writing itself, ascended into that tragic ecstasy which is the best that art—perhaps that life—can give. And at last when Deirdre, in the paroxysm before she took her life, touched with compassionate fingers him that had killed her lover, we knew that the player had become, if but for a moment, the creature of that noble mind which had gathered its art in waste islands, and we too were carried beyond time and persons to where passion, living through its thousand purgatorial years, as in the wink of an eye, becomes wisdom; and it was as though we too had touched and felt and seen a disembodied thing.

One dogma of the printed criticism is that if a play does not contain definite character, its constitution is not strong enough for the stage, and that the dramatic moment is always the contest of character with character.

In poetical drama there is, it is held, an antithesis between character and lyric poetry, for lyric poetry—however much it move you when read out of a book—can, as these critics think, but encumber the action. Yet when we go back a few centuries and enter the great periods of drama, character grows less and sometimes disappears, and there is much lyric feeling, and at times a lyric measure will be wrought into the dialogue, a flowing measure that had well befitted music, or that more lumbering one of the sonnet. Suddenly it strikes us that character is continuously present in comedy alone, and that there is much tragedy, that of Corneille, that of Racine, that of Greece and Rome, where its place is taken by passions and motives, one person being jealous, another full of love or remorse or pride or anger. In writers of tragi-comedy (and Shakespeare is always a writer of tragi-comedy) there is indeed character, but we notice that it is in the moments of comedy that character is defined, in Hamlet's gaiety, let us say; while amid the great moments, when Timon orders his tomb, when Hamlet cries to Horatio 'Absent thee from felicity awhile,' when Antony names 'Of many thousand kisses the poor last,' all is lyricism, unmixed passion, 'the integrity of fire.' Nor does character ever attain to complete definition in these lamps ready for the taper, no matter how circumstantial and gradual the opening of events, as it does in Falstaff, who has no passionate purpose to fulfil, or as it does in Henry V, whose poetry, never touched by lyric heat, is oratorical; nor when the tragic reverie is at its height do we say, 'How well that man is realised! I should know him were I to meet him in the street,' for it is always ourselves that we see upon the stage, and should it be a tragedy of love, we renew, it may be, some loyalty of our youth, and go from the theatre with our eyes dim for an old love's sake.

I think it was while rehearsing a translation of *Les Fourberies de Scapin* in Dublin, and noticing how passionless it all was, that I saw what should have been plain from the first line I had written, that tragedy must always be a drowning and breaking of the dykes that separate man from man, and that it is upon these dykes comedy keeps house. But I was not certain of the site of that house (one always hesitates when there is no testimony but one's own) till somebody told me of a certain letter of Congreve's. He describes the external and superficial expressions of 'humour' on which farce is founded and then defines 'humour' itself—the foundation of comedy—as a 'singular and unavoidable way of doing anything peculiar to one man only, by which his speech and actions are distinguished from all other men,' and adds to it that 'passions are too powerful in the sex to let humour have its course,' or, as I would rather put it, that you can find but little of what we call character in unspoiled youth, whatever be the sex, for, as he indeed shows in another sentence, it grows with time like the ash of a burning stick, and strengthens towards middle life till there is little else at seventy years.

Since then I have discovered an antagonism between all the old art and our new art of comedy and understand why I hated at nineteen years Thackeray's novels and the new French painting. A big picture of *cocottes* sitting at little tables outside a café, by some follower of Manet, was exhibited at the Royal Hibernian Academy while I was a student at a life class there, and I was miserable for days. I found no desirable place, no man I could have wished to be, no woman I could have loved, no Golden Age, no lure for secret hope, no adventure with myself for theme out of that endless tale I told myself all day long. Years after, I saw the *Olympia* of Manet at the Luxembourg and watched it without hostility indeed, but as I might some incomparable talker whose precision of gesture gave me pleasure, though I did not understand his language. I returned to it again and again at intervals of years, saying to myself, 'Some day I will understand'; and yet it was not until Sir Hugh Lane brought the *Eva Gonzales* to Dublin, and I had said to myself, 'How perfectly that woman is realised as distinct from all other women that have lived or shall live,' that I understood I was carrying on in my own mind that quarrel between a tragedian and a comedian which the Devil on Two Sticks in Le Sage showed to the young man who had climbed through the window.

There is an art of the flood, the art of Titian when his *Ariosto*, and his *Bacchus and Ariadne*, give new images to the dreams of youth, and of Shakespeare when he shows us Hamlet broken away from life by the passionate hesitations of his reverie. And we call this art poetical, because we must bring more to it than our daily mood if we would take our pleasure; and because it takes delight in the moment of exaltation, of excitement, of dreaming (or in the capacity for it, as in that still face of Ariosto's that is like some vessel soon to be full of wine). And there is an art that we call real, because character can only express itself perfectly in a real world, being that world's creature, and because we understand it best through a delicate discrimination of the senses which is but entire wakefulness, the daily mood grown cold and crystalline.

We may not find either mood in its purity, but in mainly tragic art one distinguishes devices to exclude or lessen character, to diminish the power of that daily mood, to cheat or blind its too clear perception. If the real world is not altogether rejected, it is but touched here and there, and into the places we have left empty we summon rhythm, balance, pattern, images that remind us of vast passions, the vagueness of past times, all the chimeras that haunt the edge of trance; and if we are painters, we shall express personal emotion through ideal form, a symbolism handled by the generations, a mask from whose eyes the disembodied looks, a style that remembers many masters that it may escape contemporary suggestion; or we shall leave out some element of reality as in Byzantine painting, where there is no mass, nothing in relief; and so it is that in the supreme moment of tragic art there comes upon one that strange sensation as though the hair of one's head stood up. And when we love, if it be in the excitement of youth, do we not also, that the flood may find no stone to convulse, no wall to narrow it, exclude character or the signs of it by choosing that beauty which seems unearthly because the individual woman is lost amid the labyrinth of its lines as though life were trembling into stillness and silence, or at last folding itself away? Some little irrelevance of line, some promise of character to come, may indeed put us at our ease, 'give more interest' as the humour of the old man with the basket does to Cleopatra's dying; but should it come, as we had dreamed in love's frenzy, to our dying for that woman's sake, we would find that the discord had its value from the tune. Nor have we chosen illusion in choosing the outward sign of that moral genius that lives among the subtlety of the passions, and can for her moment make her of the one mind with great artists and poets. In the studio we may indeed say to one another, 'Character is the only beauty,' but when we choose a wife, as when we go to the gymnasium to be shaped for woman's eyes, we remember academic form, even though we enlarge a little the point of interest and choose 'a painter's beauty,' finding it the more easy to believe in the fire because it has made ashes.

When we look at the faces of the old tragic paintings, whether it is in Titian or in some painter of mediaeval China, we find there sadness and gravity, a certain emptiness even, as of a mind that waited the supreme crisis (and indeed it seems at times as if the graphic art, unlike poetry which sings the crisis itself, were the celebration of waiting). Whereas in modern art, whether in Japan or Europe, 'vitality' (is not that the great word of the studios?), the energy, that is to say, which is under the command of our common moments, sings, laughs, chatters or looks its busy thoughts.

The Tragic Theatre

Certainly we have here the Tree of Life and that of the Knowledge of Good and Evil which is rooted in our interests, and if we have forgotten their differing virtues it is surely because we have taken delight in a confusion of crossing branches. Tragic art, passionate art, the drowner of dykes, the confounder of understanding, moves us by setting us to reverie, by alluring us almost to the intensity of trance. The persons upon the stage, let us say, greaten till they are humanity itself. We feel our minds expand convulsively or spread out slowly like some moon-brightened image-crowded sea. That which is before our eyes perpetually vanishes and returns again in the midst of the excitement it creates, and the more enthralling it is, the more do we forget it.

August 1910

The Cutting of an Agate

POETRY AND TRADITION

I

WHEN O'LEARY DIED I could not bring myself to go to his funeral, though I had been once his close fellow-worker, for I shrank from seeing about his grave so many whose Nationalism was different from anything he had taught or that I could share. He belonged, as did his friend John F. Taylor, to the romantic conception of Irish Nationality on which Lionel Johnson and myself founded, so far as it was founded on anything but literature, our art and our Irish criticism. Perhaps his spirit, if it can care for or can see old friends now, will accept this apology for an absence that has troubled me. I learned much from him and much from Taylor, who will always seem to me the greatest orator I have heard; and that ideal Ireland, perhaps from this out an imaginary Ireland, in whose service I labour, will always be in many essentials their Ireland. They were the last to speak an understanding of life and Nationality, built up by the generation of Grattan, which read Homer and Virgil, and by the generation of Davis, which had been pierced through by the idealism of Mazzini,[1] and of the European revolutionists of the mid-century.

O'Leary had joined the Fenian movement with no hope of success, as we know, but because he believed

[1] Rose Kavanagh, the poet, wrote to her religious adviser from, I think, Leitrim, where she lived, and asked him to get her the works of Mazzini. He replied, 'You must mean Manzoni.'

246

such a movement good for the moral character of the people; and had taken his long imprisonment without complaining. Even to the very end, while often speaking of his prison life, he would have thought it took from his Roman courage to describe its hardship. The worth of a man's acts in the moral memory, a continual height of mind in the doing of them, seemed more to him than their immediate result, if, indeed, the sight of many failures had not taken away the thought of success. A man was not to lie, or even to give up his dignity, on any patriotic plea, and I have heard him say, 'I have but one religion, the old Persian: to bend the bow and tell the truth,' and again, 'There are things a man must not do to save a nation,' and again, 'A man must not cry in public to save a nation,' and that we might not forget justice in the passion of controversy, 'There was never cause so bad that it has not been defended by good men for what seemed to them good reasons.' His friend had a burning and brooding imagination that divided men not according to their achievement but by their degrees of sincerity, and by their mastery over a straight and, to my thought, too obvious logic that seemed to him essential to sincerity. Neither man had an understanding of style or of literature in the right sense of the word, though both were great readers, but because their imagination could come to rest no place short of greatness, they hoped, John O'Leary especially, for an Irish literature of the greatest kind. When Lionel Johnson and Katharine Tynan (as she was then), and I, myself, began to reform Irish poetry, we thought to keep unbroken the thread running up to Grattan which John O'Leary had put into our hands, though it might be our business to explore new paths of the labyrinth. We sought to make a more subtle rhythm, a more organic form, than that of the older Irish poets who wrote in English, but always to remember certain ardent ideas and high attitudes of mind which were the nation itself, to our belief, so far as a nation can be summarised in the intellect. If you had asked an ancient Spartan what made Sparta Sparta, he would have answered, the Laws of Lycurgus, and many Englishmen look back to Bunyan and to Milton as we did to Grattan and to Mitchel. Lionel Johnson was able to take up into his art one portion of this tradition that I could not, for he had a gift of speaking political thought in fine verse that I have always lacked. I, on the other hand, was more preoccupied with Ireland (for he had other interests), and took from Allingham and Walsh their passion for country spiritism, and from Ferguson his pleasure in heroic legend, and while seeing all in the light of European literature found my symbols of expression in Ireland. One thought often possessed me very strongly. New from the influence, mainly the personal influence, of William Morris, I dreamed of enlarging Irish hate, till we had come to hate with a passion of patriotism what Morris and Ruskin hated. Mitchel had already all but poured some of that hate drawn from Carlyle, who had it of an earlier and, as I think, cruder sort, into the blood of Ireland, and were we not a poor nation with ancient courage, unblackened fields and a barbarous gift of self-sacrifice? Ruskin and Morris had spent themselves

in vain because they had found no passion to harness
to their thought, but here were unwasted passion and
precedents in the popular memory for every needed
thought and action. Perhaps, too, it would be possible
to find in that new philosophy of spiritism coming to
a seeming climax in the work of Frederic Myers, and
in the investigations of uncounted obscure persons,
what could change the country spiritism into a reasoned
belief that would put its might into all the rest. A new
belief seemed coming that could be so simple and de-
monstrable, and above all so mixed into the common
scenery of the world, that it would set the whole man
on fire and liberate him from a thousand obediences
and complexities. We were to forge in Ireland a new
sword on our old traditional anvil for that great battle
that must in the end re-establish the old, confident,
joyous world. All the while I worked with this idea,
founding societies that became quickly or slowly everything I despised, one part of me looked on, mischievous
and mocking, and the other part spoke words which
were more and more unreal, as the attitude of mind
became more and more strained and difficult. Miss Maud
Gonne could still gather great crowds out of the slums
by her beauty and sincerity, and speak to them of
'Mother Ireland with the crown of stars about her head';
but gradually the political movement she was associated
with, finding it hard to build up any fine lasting thing,
became content to attack little persons and little things.
All movements are held together more by what they
hate than by what they love, for love separates and
individualises and quiets, but the nobler movements,

the only movements on which literature can found itself, hate great and lasting things. All who have any old traditions have something of aristocracy, but we had opposing us from the first, though not strongly from the first, a type of mind which had been without influence in the generation of Grattan, and almost without it in that of Davis, and which has made a new nation out of Ireland, that was once old and full of memories.

I remember, when I was twenty years old, arguing, on my way home from a Young Ireland Society, that Ireland, with its hieratic Church, its readiness to accept leadership in intellectual things,—and John O'Leary spoke much of this readiness,[1]—its Latin hatred of middle paths and uncompleted arguments, could never create a democratic poet of the type of Burns, although it had tried to do so more than once, but that its genius would in the long run be distinguished and lonely. Whenever I had known some old countryman, I had heard stories and sayings that arose out of an imagination that would have understood Homer better than *The Cotter's Saturday Night* or *Highland Mary*, because it was an ancient imagination, where the sediment had found the time to settle, and I believe that the makers of deliberate literature could still take passion and theme, though but little thought, from such as he. On some such old and broken stem, I thought, have all the most beautiful roses been grafted.

[1] I have heard him say more than once, 'I will not say our people know good from bad, but I will say that they don't hate the good when it is pointed out to them, as a great many people do in England.'

Poetry and Tradition

Him who trembles before the flame and the flood,
And the winds that blow through the starry ways,
Let the starry winds and the flame and the flood
Cover over and hide, for he has no part
With the proud, majestical multitude.

Three types of men have made all beautiful things,
Aristocracies have made beautiful manners, because
their place in the world puts them above the fear of
life, and the countrymen have made beautiful stories
and beliefs, because they have nothing to lose and so
do not fear, and the artists have made all the rest, because Providence has filled them with recklessness. All
these look backward to a long tradition, for, being
without fear, they have held to whatever pleased them.
The others, being always anxious, have come to possess
little that is good in itself, and are always changing
from thing to thing, for whatever they do or have must
be a means to something else, and they have so little
belief that anything can be an end in itself that they
cannot understand you if you say, 'All the most valuable things are useless.' They prefer the stalk to the
flower, and believe that painting and poetry exist that
there may be instruction, and love that there may be
children, and theatres that busy men may rest, and
holidays that busy men may go on being busy. At all
times they fear and even hate the things that have worth
in themselves, for that worth may suddenly, as it were
a fire, consume their Book of Life, where the world is
represented by ciphers and symbols; and before all

else, they fear irreverent joy and unserviceable sorrow. It seems to them that those who have been freed by position, by poverty, or by the traditions of art, have something terrible about them, a light that is unendurable to eyesight. They complain much of that commandment that we can do almost what we will, if we do it gaily, and think that freedom is but a trifling with the world.

If we would find a company of our own way of thinking, we must go backward to turreted walls, to Courts, to high rocky places, to little walled towns, to jesters like that jester of Charles V who made mirth out of his own death; to the Duke Guidobaldo in his sickness, or Duke Frederick in his strength, to all those who understood that life is not lived, if not lived for contemplation or excitement.

Certainly we could not delight in that so courtly thing, the poetry of light love, if it were sad; for only when we are gay over a thing, and can play with it, do we show ourselves its master, and have minds clear enough for strength. The raging fire and the destructive sword are portions of eternity, too great for the eye of man, wrote Blake, and it is only before such things, before a love like that of Tristan and Iseult, before noble or ennobled death, that the free mind permits itself aught but brief sorrow. That we may be free from all the rest, sullen anger, solemn virtue, calculating anxiety, gloomy suspicion, prevaricating hope, we should be reborn in gaiety. Because there is submission in a pure sorrow, we should sorrow alone over what is greater than ourselves, nor too soon admit that greatness, but all that is less than we are should stir us to some joy, for pure joy masters and impregnates; and so to world end, strength shall laugh and wisdom mourn.

III

In life courtesy and self-possession, and in the arts style, are the sensible impressions of the free mind, for both arise out of a deliberate shaping of all things, and from never being swept away, whatever the emotion, into confusion or dullness. The Japanese have numbered with heroic things courtesy at all times whatsoever, and though a writer, who has to withdraw so much of his thought out of his life that he may learn his craft, may find many his betters in daily courtesy, he should never be without style, which is but high breeding in words and in argument. He is indeed the creator of the standards of manners in their subtlety, for he alone can know the ancient records and be like some mystic courtier who has stolen the keys from the girdle of Time, and can wander where it please him amid the splendours of ancient Courts.

Sometimes, it may be, he is permitted the licence of cap and bell, or even the madman's bunch of straws, but he never forgets or leaves at home the seal and the signature. He has at all times the freedom of the well-bred, and being bred to the tact of words can take what theme he pleases, unlike the linen-drapers, who are rightly compelled to be very strict in their conversation. Who should be free if he were not? for none other has a continual deliberate self-delighting happiness—

style, 'the only thing that is immortal in literature,' as Sainte-Beuve has said, a still unexpended energy, after all that the argument or the story needs, a still un-broken pleasure after the immediate end has been ac-complished—and builds this up into a most personal and wilful fire, transfiguring words and sounds and events. It is the playing of strength when the day's work is done, a secret between a craftsman and his craft, and is so inseparate in his nature that he has it most of all amid overwhelming emotion, and in the face of death. Shakespeare's persons, when the last darkness has gathered about them, speak out of an ecstasy that is one-half the self-surrender of sorrow, and one-half the last playing and mockery of the victori-ous sword before the defeated world.

It is in the arrangement of events as in the words, and in that touch of extravagance, of irony, of surprise, which is set there after the desire of logic has been satisfied and all that is merely necessary established, and that leaves one, not in the circling necessity, but caught up into the freedom of self-delight: it is, as it were, the foam upon the cup, the long pheasant's feather on the horse's head, the spread peacock over the pasty. If it be very conscious, very deliberate, as it may be in comedy, for comedy is more personal than tragedy, we call it fantasy, perhaps even mischievous fantasy, recognising how disturbing it is to all that drag a ball at the ankle. This joy, because it must be always making and mastering, remains in the hands and in the tongue of the artist, but with his eyes he enters upon a submissive, sorrowful contemplation of the great irremediable things, and he is known from other men by making all he handles like himself, and yet by the unlikeness to himself of all that comes before him in a pure contemplation. It may have been his enemy or his love or his cause that set him dreaming, and certainly the phoenix can but open her young wings in a flaming nest; but all hate and hope vanishes in the dream, and if his mistress brag of the song or his enemy fear it, it is not that either has its praise or blame, but that the twigs of the holy nest are not easily set afire. The verses may make his mistress famous as Helen or give a victory to his cause, not because he has been either's servant, but because men delight to honour and to remember all that have served contemplation. It had been easier to fight, to die even, for Charles's house with Marvell's poem in the memory, but there is no zeal of service that had not been an impurity in the pure soil where the marvel grew. Timon of Athens contemplates his own end, and orders his tomb by the beached verge of the salt flood, and Cleopatra sets the asp to her bosom, and their words move us because their sorrow is not their own at tomb or asp, but for all men's fate. That shaping joy has kept the sorrow pure, as it had kept it were the emotion love or hate, for the nobleness of the arts is in the mingling of contraries, the extremity of sorrow, the extremity of joy, perfection of personality, the perfection of its surrender, overflowing turbulent energy, and marmorean stillness; and its red rose opens at the meeting of the two beams of the cross, and at the trysting-place of mortal and immortal, time and eternity. No new man has ever plucked that rose,

255

or found that trysting-place, for he could but come to the understanding of himself, to the mastery of unlocking words, after long frequenting of the great Masters, hardly without ancestral memory of the like. Even knowledge is not enough, for the 'recklessness' Castiglione thought necessary in good manners is necessary in this likewise, and if a man has it not he will be gloomy, and had better to his marketing again.

IV

When I saw John O'Leary first, every young Catholic man who had intellectual ambition fed his imagination with the poetry of Young Ireland; and the verses of even the least known of its poets were expounded with a devout ardour at Young Ireland Societies and the like, and their birthdays celebrated. The school of writers I belonged to tried to found itself on much of the subject-matter of this poetry, and, what was almost more in our thoughts, to begin a more imaginative tradition in Irish literature, by a criticism at once remorseless and enthusiastic. It was our criticism, I think, that set Clarence Mangan at the head of the Young Ireland poets in the place of Davis, and put Sir Samuel Ferguson, who had died with but little fame as a poet, next in the succession. Our attacks, mine especially, on verse which owed its position to its moral or political worth, roused a resentment which even I find it hard to imagine to-day, and our verse was attacked in return, and not for anything peculiar to ourselves, but for all that it had in common with the accepted poetry of the world, and most of all for its lack of rhetoric, its refusal to preach a doctrine or to consider the seeming necessities of a cause. Now, after so many years, I can see how natural, how poetical even, an opposition was, that showed what large numbers could not call up certain high feelings without accustomed verses, or believe we had not wronged the feelings when we did but attack the verses. I have just read in a newspaper that Sir Charles Gavan Duffy recited upon his death-bed his favourite poem, one of the worst of the patriotic poems of Young Ireland, and it has brought all this to mind, for the opposition to our school claimed him as its leader. When I was at Siena, I noticed that the Byzantine style persisted in faces of Madonnas for several generations after it had given way to a more natural style in the less loved faces of saints and martyrs. Passion had grown accustomed to those narrow eyes, which are almost Japanese, and to those gaunt cheeks, and would have thought it sacrilege to change. We would not, it is likely, have found listeners if John O'Leary, the irreproachable patriot, had not supported us. It was as clear to him that a writer must not write badly, or ignore the examples of the great Masters in the fancied or real service of a cause, as it was that he must not lie for it or grow hysterical. I believed in those days that a new intellectual life would begin, like that of Young Ireland, but more profound and personal, and that could we but get a few plain principles accepted, new poets and writers of prose would make an immortal music. I think I was more blind than Johnson, though I judge this from his poems rather than anything I remember of his talk, for he never talked ideas, but, as was common with his generation in Oxford, facts and immediate impressions from life. With others this renunciation was but a pose, a superficial reaction from the disordered abundance of the middle century, but with him it was the radical life. He was in all a traditionalist, gathering out of the past phrases, moods, attitudes, and disliking ideas less for their uncertainty than because they made the mind itself changing and restless. He measured the Irish tradition by another greater than itself, and was quick to feel any falling asunder of the two, yet at many moments they seemed but one in his imagination. Ireland, all through his poem of that name, speaks to him with the voice of the great poets, and in *Ireland's Dead* she is still mother of perfect heroism, but there doubt comes too.

> Can it be, thou dost repent
> That they went, thy chivalry,
> Those sad ways magnificent?

And in *Ways of War*, dedicated to John O'Leary, he dismissed the belief in an heroic Ireland as but a dream.

> A dream! a dream! an ancient dream!
> Yet, ere peace come to Inisfail,
> Some weapons on some field must gleam,
> Some burning glory fire the Gael.
>
> That field may lie beneath the sun,
> Fair for the treading of an host:
> That field in realms of thought be won,
> And armed minds do their uttermost:

Poetry and Tradition

Some way, to faithful Inisfail,
Shall come the majesty and awe
Of martial truth, that must prevail
To lay on all the eternal law.

I do not think either of us saw that, as belief in the possibility of armed insurrection withered, the old romantic Nationalism would wither too, and that the young would become less ready to find pleasure in whatever they believed to be literature. Poetical tragedy, and indeed all the more intense forms of literature, had lost their hold on the general mass of men in other countries as life grew safe, and the sense of comedy which is the social bond in times of peace as tragic feeling is in times of war, had become the inspiration of popular art. I always knew this, but I believed that the memory of danger, and the reality of it seemed near enough sometimes, would last long enough to give Ireland her imaginative opportunity. I could not foresee that a new class, which had begun to rise into power under the shadow of Parnell, would change the nature of the Irish movement, which, needing no longer great sacrifices, nor bringing any great risk to individuals, could do without exceptional men, and those activities of the mind that are founded on the exceptional moment.[1] John O'Leary had spent much of his

[1] A small political organiser told me once that he and a certain friend got together somewhere in Tipperary a great meeting of farmers for O'Leary on his coming out of prison, and O'Leary had said at it: 'The landlords gave us some few leaders, and I like them for that, and the artisans have given us great numbers of good patriots, and so I like them best: but you I do not like at all, for you have never given us any one.'

thought in an unavailing war with the agrarian party, believing it the root of change, but the fox that crept into the badger's hole did not come from there. Power passed to small shopkeepers, to clerks, to that very class who had seemed to John O'Leary so ready to bend to the power of others, to men who had risen above the traditions of the countryman, without learning those of cultivated life or even educating themselves, and who because of their poverty, their ignorance, their superstitious piety, are much subject to all kinds of fear. Immediate victory, immediate utility, became everything, and the conviction, which is in all who have run great risks for a cause's sake, in the O'Learys and Mazzinis as in all rich natures, that life is greater than the cause, withered, and we artists, who are the servants not of any cause but of mere naked life, and above all of that life in its nobler forms, where joy and sorrow are one, Artificers of the Great Moment, became as elsewhere in Europe protesting individual voices. Ireland's great moment had passed, and she had filled no roomy vessels with strong sweet wine, where we have filled our porcelain jars against the coming winter.

August 1907

DISCOVERIES

PROPHET, PRIEST AND KING

THE LITTLE THEATRICAL COMPANY I write my plays for had come to a West of Ireland town, and was to give a performance in an old ball-room, for there was no other room big enough. I went there from a neighbouring country-house, and, arriving a little before the players, tried to open a window. My hands were black with dirt in a moment, and presently a pane of glass and a part of the window-frame came out in my hands. Everything in this room was half in ruins, the rotten boards cracked under my feet, and our new proscenium and the new boards of the platform looked out of place, and yet the room was not really old, in spite of the musicians' gallery over the stage. It had been built by some romantic or philanthropic landlord some three or four generations ago, and was a memory of we knew not what unfinished scheme.

From there I went to look for the players, and called for information on a young priest, who had invited them and taken upon himself the finding of an audience. He lived in a high house with other priests, and as I went in I noticed with a whimsical pleasure a broken pane of glass in the fanlight over the door, for he had once told me the story of an old woman who a good many years ago quarrelled with the bishop, got drunk and hurled a stone through the painted glass. He was a clever man who read Meredith and Ibsen, but some of his books had been packed in the fire-grate by his housekeeper, instead of the customary view of an Italian lake or the coloured tissue-paper. The players, who had been giving a performance in a neighbouring town, had not yet come, or were unpacking their costumes and properties at the hotel he had recommended them. We should have time, he said, to go through the half-ruined town and to visit the convent schools and the cathedral, where, owing to his influence, two of our young Irish sculptors had been set to carve an altar and the heads of pillars. I had only heard of this work, and I found its strangeness and simplicity—one of them had been Rodin's pupil—could not make me forget the meretriciousness of the architecture and the commercial commonplace of the inlaid pavement. The new movement had seized on the cathedral midway in its growth, and the worst of the old and the best of the new were side by side without any sign of transition. The convent school was, as other like places have been to me,—a long room in a workhouse hospital at Portumna, in particular,—a delight to the imagination and the eyes. A new floor had been put into some ecclesiastical building, and the light from a great mullioned window, cut off at the middle, fell aslant upon rows of clean and seemingly happy children. The nuns, who show in their own convents, where they can put what they like, a love of what is mean and pretty, make beautiful rooms where the regulations compel them to do all with a few colours and a few flowers. I think it was that day, but am not sure, that I had lunch at a convent and told faery-stories to a couple of nuns, and I hope it was not mere politeness that made them seem to have a child's interest in such things.

A good many of our audience, when the curtain went up in the old ball-room, were drunk, but all were attentive, for they had a great deal of respect for my friend, and there were other priests there. Presently the man at the door opposite to the stage strayed off somewhere and I took his place, and when boys came up offering two or three pence and asking to be let into the sixpenny seats, I let them join the melancholy crowd. The play professed to tell of the heroic life of ancient Ireland, but was really full of sedentary refinement and the spirituality of cities. Every emotion was made as dainty-footed and dainty-fingered as might be, and a love and pathos where passion had faded into sentiment, emotions of pensive and harmless people, drove shadowy young men through the shadows of death and battle. I watched it with growing rage. It was not my own work, but I have sometimes watched my own work with a rage made all the more salt in the mouth from being half despair. Why should we make so much noise about ourselves and yet have nothing to say that was not better said in that workhouse dormitory, where a few flowers and a few coloured counterpanes and the coloured walls had made a severe appropriate beauty? Presently the play was changed and our comedian began to act a little farce, and when I saw him struggle to wake into laughter an audience out of whom the life had run as if it were water, I rejoiced, as I had over that broken window-pane. Here was something secular, abounding, even a little vulgar, for he was gagging horribly, condescending to his audience, though not without contempt.

We had supper in the priest's house, and a Government official who had come down from Dublin, partly out of interest in this attempt 'to educate the people,' and partly because it was his holiday and it was necessary to go somewhere, entertained us with little jokes. Somebody, not, I think, a priest, talked of the spiritual destiny of our race and praised the night's work, for the play was refined and the people really very attentive, and he could not understand my discontent; but presently he was silenced by the patter of jokes.

I had my breakfast by myself the next morning, for the players had got up in the middle of the night and driven some ten miles to catch an early train to Dublin, and were already on their way to their shops and offices. I had brought the visitors' book of the hotel, to turn over its pages while waiting for my bacon and eggs, and found several pages full of obscenities, scrawled there some two or three weeks before, by Dublin visitors, it seemed, for a notorious Dublin street was mentioned. Nobody had thought it worth his while to tear out the page or blacken out the lines, and as I put the book away impressions that had been drifting through my mind for months rushed up into a single thought: 'If we poets are to move the people, we must reintegrate the human spirit in our imagination. The English have driven away the kings, and turned the prophets into demagogues, and you cannot have health among a people if you have not prophet, priest and king.'

Discoveries

My work in Ireland has continually set this thought before me: 'How can I make my work mean something to vigorous and simple men whose attention is not given to art but to a shop, or teaching in a National School, or dispensing medicine?' I had not wanted to 'elevate them' or 'educate them,' as these words are understood, but to make them understand my vision, and I had not wanted a large audience, certainly not what is called a national audience, but enough people for what is accidental and temporary to lose itself in the lump. In England, where there have been so many changing activities and so much systematic education, one only escapes from crudities and temporary interests among students, but here there is the right audience, could one but get its ears. I have always come to this certainty: what moves natural men in the arts is what moves them in life, and that is, intensity of personal life, intonations that show them, in a book or a play, the strength, the essential moment of a man who would be exciting in the market or at the dispensary door. They must go out of the theatre with the strength they live by strengthened from looking upon some passion that could, whatever its chosen way of life, strike down an enemy, fill a long stocking with money or move a girl's heart. They have not much to do with the speculations of science, though they have a little, or with the speculations of metaphysics, though they have a little. Their legs will tire on the road if there is nothing in their hearts but vague sentiment, and though

265

it is charming to have an affectionate feeling about flowers, that will not pull the cart out of the ditch. An exciting person, whether the hero of a play or the maker of poems, will display the greatest volume of personal energy, and this energy must seem to come out of the body as out of the mind. We must say to ourselves continually when we imagine a character: 'Have I given him the roots, as it were, of all faculties necessary for life?' And only when one is certain of that may one give him the one faculty that fills the imagination with joy. I even doubt if any play had ever a great popularity that did not use, or seem to use, the bodily energies of its principal actor to the full. Villon the robber could have delighted these Irishmen with plays and songs, if he and they had been born to the same traditions of word and symbol, but Shelley could not; and as men came to live in towns and to read printed books and to have many specialised activities, it has become more possible to produce Shelleys and less and less possible to produce Villons. The last Villon dwindled into Robert Burns because the highest faculties had faded, taking the sense of beauty with them, into some sort of vague heaven and left the lower to lumber where they best could. In literature, partly from the lack of that spoken word which knits us to normal man, we have lost in personality, in our delight in the whole man—blood, imagination, intellect, running together—but have found a new delight, in essences, in states of mind, in pure imagination, in all that comes to us most easily in elaborate music. There are two ways before literature—upward into ever-growing

266

subtlety, with Verhaeren, with Mallarmé, with Maeterlinck, until at last, it may be, a new agreement among refined and studious men gives birth to a new passion, and what seems literature becomes religion; or downward, taking the soul with us until all is simplified and solidified again. That is the choice of choices—the way of the bird until common eyes have lost us, or to the market carts; but we must see to it that the soul goes with us, for the bird's song is beautiful, and the traditions of modern imagination, growing always more musical, more lyrical, more melancholy, casting up now a Shelley, now a Swinburne, now a Wagner, are, it may be, the frenzy of those that are about to see what the magic hymn printed by the Abbé de Villars has called the Crown of Living and Melodious Diamonds. If the carts have hit our fancy we must have the soul tight within our bodies, for it has grown so fond of a beauty accumulated by subtle generations that it will for a long time be impatient with our thirst for mere force, mere personality, for the tumult of the blood. If it begin to slip away we must go after it, for Shelley's Chapel of the Morning Star is better than Burns's beerhouse—surely it was beer, not barleycorn—except at the day's weary end; and it is always better than that uncomfortable place where there is no beer, the machine-shop of the realists.

THE MUSICIAN AND THE ORATOR

Walter Pater says music is the type of all the arts, but somebody else, I forget now who, that oratory is their type. You will side with the one or the other according to the nature of your energy, and I in my present mood am all for the man who, with an average audience before him, uses all means of persuasion— stories, laughter, tears, and but so much music as he can discover on the wings of words. I would even avoid the conversation of the lovers of music, who would draw us into the impersonal land of sound and colour, and I would have no one write with a sonata in his memory. We may even speak a little evil of musicians, having admitted that they will see before we do that melodious crown. We may remind them that the housemaid does not respect the piano-tuner as she does the plumber, and of the enmity that they have aroused among all poets. Music is the most impersonal of things, and words the most personal, and that is why musicians do not like words. They masticate them for a long time, being afraid they would not be able to digest them, and when the words are so broken and softened and mixed with spittle that they are not words any longer, they swallow them.

A GUITAR PLAYER

A girl has been playing on the guitar. She is pretty, and if I had not listened to her I could have watched her, and if I had not watched her I could have listened. Her voice, the movements of her body, the expression of her face, all said the same thing. A player of a different temper and body would have made all different, and might have been delightful in some other way. A movement not of music only but of life came to its perfection. I was delighted and I did not know why until I thought, 'That is the way my people, the people I see in the mind's eye, play music, and I like it because it is all personal, as personal as Villon's poetry.' The little instrument is quite light, and the player can move freely and express a joy that is not of the fingers and the mind only but of the whole being; and all the while her movements call up into the mind, so erect and natural she is, whatever is most beautiful in her daily life. Nearly all the old instruments were like that; even the organ was once a little instrument, and when it grew big our wise forefathers gave it to God in the cathedrals, where it befits Him to be everything. But if you sit at the piano, it is the piano, the mechanism, that is the important thing, and nothing of you means anything but your fingers and your intellect.

THE LOOKING-GLASS

I have just been talking to a girl with a shrill monotonous voice and an abrupt way of moving. She is fresh from school, where they have taught her history and geography whereby 'a soul can be discerned,' but what is the value of an education, or even in the long run of a science, that does not begin with the personality, the habitual self, and illustrate all by that? Somebody should have taught her to speak for the most part on whatever note of her voice is most musical, and soften those harsh notes by speaking, not singing, to some stringed instrument, taking note after note and, as it were, caressing her words a little as if she loved the sound of them, and have taught her after this some beautiful pantomimic dance, till it had grown a habit to live for eye and ear. A wise theatre might make a training in strong and beautiful life the fashion, teaching before all else the heroic discipline of the looking-glass, for is not beauty, even as lasting love, one of the most difficult of the arts?

THE TREE OF LIFE

We artists have taken over-much to heart that old commandment about seeking after the Kingdom of Heaven. Verlaine told me that he had tried to translate *In Memoriam*, but could not because Tennyson was 'too noble, too *anglais*, and, when he should have been broken-hearted, had many reminiscences.' About that time I found in some English review an essay of his on Shakespeare. 'I had once a fine Shakespeare,' he wrote, or some such words, 'but I have it no longer. I write from memory.' One wondered in what vicissitude he had sold it, and for what money; and an image of the man rose in the imagination. To be his ordinary self as much as possible, not a scholar or even a reader, that was certainly his pose; and in the lecture he gave at Oxford he insisted that 'the poet should hide nothing of himself,' though he must speak it all with 'a care of that dignity which should manifest itself, if not in the perfection of form, at all events with an invisible, insensible, but effectual endeavour after this lofty and severe quality, I was about to say this virtue.' It was this feeling for his own personality, his delight in singing his own life, even more than that life itself, which made the generation I belong to compare him to Villon. It was not till after his death that I understood the meaning his words should have had for me, for while he lived I was interested in nothing but states of mind, lyrical moments, intellectual essences. I would not then have been as delighted as I am now by that guitar player, or as shocked as I am now by that girl whose movements have grown abrupt, and whose voice has grown harsh by the neglect of all but external activities. I had not learned what sweetness, what rhythmic movement, there is in those who have become the joy that is themselves. Without knowing it, I had come to care for nothing but impersonal beauty. I had set out on life with the thought of putting my very self into poetry, and had understood this as a representation of my own visions and an attempt to cut away the non-essential, but as I imagined the visions outside myself my imagination became full of decorative landscape and of still life. I thought of myself as something unmoving and silent living in the middle of my own mind and body, a grain of sand in Bloomsbury or in Connacht that Satan's watch-fiends cannot find. Then one day I understood quite suddenly, as the way is, that I was seeking something unchanging and unmixed and always outside myself, a Stone or an Elixir that was always out of reach, and that I myself was the fleeting thing that held out its hand. The more I tried to make my art deliberately beautiful, the more did I follow the opposite of myself, for deliberate beauty is like a woman always desiring man's desire. Presently I found that I entered into myself and pictured myself and not some essence when I was not seeking beauty at all, but merely to lighten the mind of some burden of love or bitterness thrown upon it by the events of life. We are only permitted to desire life, and all the rest should be our complaints or our praise of that exacting mistress who can awake our lips into song with her kisses. But we must not give her all, we must deceive her a little at times, for, as Le Sage says in *Le Diable boiteux*, the false lovers who do not become melancholy or jealous with honest passion have the happiest mistresses and are rewarded the soonest and by the most beautiful. Our deceit will give us style, mastery, that dignity, that lofty and severe quality Verlaine spoke of. To put it otherwise, we should ascend out of common interests, the thoughts of the newspapers, of the market-place, of men of science, but only so far as we can carry the normal, passionate, reasoning self, the personality as a whole. We must find some place upon the Tree of Life for the phoenix' nest, for the passion that is exaltation and the negation of the will, for the wings that are always upon fire, set high that the forked branches may keep it safe, yet low enough to be out of the little wind-tossed boughs, the quivering of the twigs.

THE PRAISE OF OLD WIVES' TALES

An art may become impersonal because it has too much circumstance or too little, because the world is too little or too much with it, because it is too near the ground or too far up among the branches. I met an old man out fishing a year ago, who said to me, 'Don Quixote and Odysseus are always near to me'; that is true for me also, for even Hamlet and Lear and Oedipus are more cloudy. No playwright ever has made or ever will make a character that will follow us out of the theatre as Don Quixote follows us out of the book,[1] for no playwright can be wholly episodical, and when one constructs, bringing one's characters into complicated relations with one another, something impersonal comes into the story. Society, fate, 'tendency,' something not quite human, begins to arrange the characters and to excite into action only so much of their humanity as they find it necessary to show to one another. The common heart will always love better the tales that have something of an old wives' tale and that look upon their hero from every side as if he alone were wonderful, as a child does with a new penny. In plays of a comedy too extravagant to photograph life, or written in verse, the construction is of a necessity woven out of naked motives and passions, but when an atmosphere of modern reality has to be built up as well, and the tendency, or fate, or society has to be shown as it is about ourselves, the characters grow fainter, and we have to read the book many times or see the play many times before we can remember them. Even then they are only possible in a certain drawing-room and among such-and-such people, and we must carry all that lumber in our heads. I thought Tolstoy's *War and Peace* the greatest story I had ever read, and yet it has gone from me; even Launcelot, ever a shadow, is more visible in my memory than all its substance.

[1] I had forgotten Falstaff, who is an episode in a chronicle play.

The Cutting of an Agate

THE PLAY OF MODERN MANNERS

Of all artistic forms that have had a large share of the world's attention, the worst is the play about modern educated people. Except where it is superficial or deliberately argumentative it fills one's soul with a sense of commonness as with dust. It has one mortal ailment. It cannot become impassioned, that is to say, vital, without making somebody gushing and sentimental. Educated and well-bred people do not wear their hearts upon their sleeves, and they have no artistic and charming language except light persiflage and no powerful language at all, and when they are deeply moved they look silently into the fireplace. Again and again I have watched some play of this sort with growing curiosity through the opening scene. The minor people argue, chaff one another, hint sometimes at some deeper stream of life just as we do in our houses, and I am content. But all the time I have been wondering why the chief character, the man who is to bear the burden of fate, is gushing, sentimental and quite without ideas. Then the great scene comes and I understand that he cannot be well-bred or self-possessed or intellectual, for if he were he would draw a chair to the fire and there would be no duologue at the end of the third act. Ibsen understood the difficulty and made all his characters a little provincial that they might not put each other out of countenance, and made a leading-article sort of poetry—phrases about vine-leaves and harps in the air —it was possible to believe them using in their moments of excitement, and if the play needed more than

274

that, they could always do something stupid. They could go out and hoist a flag as they do at the end of *Little Eyolf*. One only understands that this manner, deliberately adopted, one doubts not, had gone into his soul and filled it with dust, when one has noticed that he could no longer create a man of genius. The happiest writers are those that, knowing this form of play to be slight and passing, keep to the surface, never showing anything but the arguments and the persiflage of daily observation, or now and then, instead of the expression of passion, a stage picture, a man holding a woman's hand or sitting with his head in his hands in dim light by the red glow of a fire. It was certainly an understanding of the slightness of the form, of its incapacity for the expression of the deeper sorts of passion, that made the French invent the play with a thesis, for where there is a thesis people can grow hot in argument, almost the only kind of passion that displays itself in our daily life. The novel of contemporary educated life is upon the other hand a permanent form because, having the power of psychological description, it can follow the thought of a man who is looking into the grate.

HAS THE DRAMA OF CONTEMPORARY LIFE A ROOT OF ITS OWN?

In watching a play about modern educated people, with its meagre language and its action crushed into the narrow limits of possibility, I have found myself constantly saying: 'Maybe it has its power to move, slight as that is, from being able to suggest fundamental contrasts and passions which romantic and poetical literature have shown to be beautiful.' A man facing his enemies alone in a quarrel over the purity of the water in a Norwegian Spa and using no language but that of the newspapers can call up into our minds, let us say, the passion of Coriolanus. The lovers and fighters of old imaginative literature are more vivid experiences in the soul than anything but one's own ruling passion that is itself riddled by their thought as by lightning, and even two dumb figures on the roads can call up all that glory. Put the man who has no knowledge of literature before a play of this kind and he will say, as he has said in some form or other in every age at the first shock of naturalism, 'Why should I leave my home to hear but the words I have used there when talking of the rates?' And he will prefer to it any play where there is visible beauty or mirth, where life is exciting, at high tide as it were. It is not his fault that he will prefer in all likelihood a worse play although its kind may be greater, for we have been following the lure of science for generations and have forgotten him and his. I come always back to this thought. There is something of an old wives' tale in fine literature. The makers of it are like an old peasant telling stories of the great famine or the hangings of '98 or from his own memories. He has felt something in the depth of his mind and he wants to make it as visible and powerful to our senses as possible. He will use the most extravagant words or illustrations if they suit his purpose. Or he will invent a wild parable, and the more his mind is on fire or the more creative it is, the less will he look at the outer world or value it for its own sake. It gives him metaphors and examples, and that is all. He is even a little scornful of it, for it seems to him while the fit is on that the fire has gone out of it and left it but white ashes. I cannot explain it, but I am certain that every high thing was invented in this way, between sleeping and waking, as it were, and that peering and peeping persons are but hawkers of stolen goods. How else could their noses have grown so ravenous or their eyes so sharp?

WHY THE BLIND MAN IN ANCIENT TIMES WAS MADE A POET

A description in the *Iliad* or the *Odyssey*, unlike one in the *Aeneid* or in most modern writers, is the swift and natural observation of a man as he is shaped by life. It is a refinement of the primary hungers and has the least possible of what is merely scholarly or exceptional. It is, above all, never too observant, too professional, and when the book is closed we have had our energies enriched, for we have been in the mid-current. We have never seen anything Odysseus could not have seen while his thought was of the Cyclops, or Achilles when Briseis moved him to desire. In the art of the greatest periods there is something careless and sudden in all habitual moods, though not in their expression, because these moods are a conflagration of all the energies of active life. In primitive times the blind man became a poet, as he became a fiddler in our villages, because he had to be driven out of activities all his nature cried for, before he could be contented

277

with the praise of life. And often it is Villon or Verlaine, with impediments plain to all, who sings of life with the ancient simplicity. Poets of coming days, when once more it will be possible to write as in the great epochs, will recognise that their sacrifice shall be to refuse what blindness and evil name, or imprisonment at the outsetting, denied to men who missed thereby the sting of a deliberate refusal. The poets of the ages of silver need no refusal of life, the dome of many-coloured glass is already shattered while they live. They look at life deliberately and as if from beyond life, and the greatest of them need suffer nothing but the sadness that the saints have known. This is their aim, and their temptation is not a passionate activity, but the approval of their fellows, which comes to them in full abundance only when they delight in the general thoughts that hold together a cultivated middle-class, where irresponsibilities of position and poverty are lacking; the things that are more excellent among educated men who have political preoccupations, Augustus Caesar's affability, all that impersonal fecundity which muddies the intellectual passions. Ben Jonson says in *The Poetaster* that even the best of men without Promethean fire is but a hollow statue, and a studious man will commonly forget after some forty winters that of a certainty Promethean fire will burn somebody's fingers. It may happen that poets will be made more often by their sins than by their virtues, for general praise is unlucky, as the villages know, and not merely as I imagine—for I am superstitious about these things—because the praise of all but an equal enslaves and adds a pound to the ball at the ankle with every compliment.

All energy that comes from the whole man is as irregular as the lightning, for the communicable and forecastable and discoverable is a part only, a hungry chicken under the breast of the pelican, and the test of poetry is not in reason but in a delight not different from the delight that comes to a man at the first coming of love into the heart. I knew an old man who had spent his whole life cutting hazel and privet from the paths, and in some seventy years he had observed little but had many imaginations. He had never seen like a naturalist, never seen things as they are, for his habitual mood had been that of a man stirred in his affairs; and Shakespeare, Tintoretto, though the times were running out when Tintoretto painted, nearly all the great men of the Renaissance, looked at the world with eyes like his. Their minds were never quiescent, never, as it were, in a mood for scientific observations, always in exaltation, never—to use known words—founded upon an elimination of the personal factor; and their attention and the attention of those they worked for dwelt constantly with what is present to the mind in exaltation. I am too modern fully to enjoy Tintoretto's *Origin of the Milky Way*, I cannot fix my thoughts upon that glowing and palpitating flesh intently enough to forget, as I can the make-believe of a faery-tale, that heavy drapery hanging from a cloud, though I find my pleasure in *King Lear* heightened by the make-believe that comes upon it all when the Fool says, 'This prophecy Merlin shall make, for I live before his time';—and I always find it quite natural, so little does logic in the mere circumstance matter in the finest art, that Richard's and Richmond's tents should be side by side. I saw with delight *The Knight of the Burning Pestle* when Mr. Carr revived it, and found it none the worse because the apprentice acted a whole play upon the spur of the moment and without committing a line to heart. When *The Silent Woman* rammed a century of laughter into the two hours' traffic, I found with amazement that almost every journalist had put logic on the seat where our Lady Imagination should pronounce that unjust and favouring sentence her woman's heart is ever plotting, and had felt bound to cherish none but reasonable sympathies and to resent the baiting of that grotesque old man. I have been looking over a book of engravings made in the eighteenth century from those wall-pictures of Herculaneum and Pompeii that were, it seems, the work of journeymen copying from finer paintings, for the composition is always too good for the execution. I find in great numbers an indifference to obvious logic, to all that the eye sees at common moments. Perseus shows Andromeda the death she lived by in a pool, and though the lovers are carefully drawn the reflection is shown reversed that the forms it reflects may be seen the right side up and our eyes be the more content. There is hardly an old master who has not made known to us in some like way how little he cares for what every fool can see and every knave can praise. The men who imagined the arts were not less superstitious in religion, understanding the spiritual relations, but not the mechanical, and finding nothing that need strain the throat in those gnats the floods of Noah and Deucalion.

CONCERNING SAINTS AND ARTISTS

I took the Indian hemp with certain followers of Saint-Martin on the ground floor of a house in the Latin Quarter. I had never taken it before, and was instructed by a boisterous young poet, whose English was no better than my French. He gave me a little pellet, if I am not forgetting, an hour before dinner, and another after we had dined together at some restaurant. As we were going through the streets to the meeting-place of the Martinists, I felt suddenly that a cloud I was looking at floated in an immense space, and for an instant my being rushed out, as it seemed, into that space with ecstasy. I was myself again immediately, but the poet was wholly above himself, and presently he pointed to one of the street-lamps now brightening in the fading twilight, and cried at the top of his voice, 'Why do you look at me with your great eye?' There were perhaps a dozen people already much excited when we arrived; and after I had drunk some cups of coffee and eaten a pellet or two more, I grew very anxious to dance, but did not, as I could not remember any steps. I sat down and closed my eyes; but no, I had no visions, nothing but a sensation of some dark shadow which seemed to be telling me that some day I would go into a trance and so out of my body for a while, but not yet. I opened my eyes and looked at some red ornament on the mantel-piece, and at once the room was full of harmonies of red, but when a blue china figure caught my eye the

281

harmonies became blue upon the instant. I was puzzled, for the reds were all there, nothing had changed, but they were no longer important or harmonious; and why had the blues so unimportant but a moment ago become exciting and delightful? Thereupon it struck me that I was seeing like a painter, and that in the course of the evening every one there would change through every kind of artistic perception.

After a while a Martinist ran towards me with a piece of paper on which he had drawn a circle with a dot in it, and pointing at it with his finger he cried out, 'God, God!' Some immeasurable mystery had been revealed, and his eyes shone; and at some time or other a lean and shabby man, with rather a distinguished face, showed me his horoscope and pointed with an ecstasy of melancholy at its evil aspects. The boisterous poet, who was an old eater of the Indian hemp, had told me that it took one three months growing used to it, three months more enjoying it, and three months being cured of it. These men were in their second period; but I never forgot myself, never really rose above myself for more than a moment, and was even able to feel the absurdity of that gaiety, a Herr Nordau among the men of genius, but one that was abashed at his own sobriety. The sky outside was beginning to grey when there came a knocking at the window-shutters. Somebody opened the window, and a woman and two young girls in evening dress, who were not a little bewildered to find so many people, were helped down into the room. She and her husband's two sisters had been at a students' ball unknown to her husband, who was asleep overhead, and had thought to have crept home unobserved, but for a confederate at the window. All those talking or dancing men laughed in a dreamy way; and she, understanding that there was no judgment in the laughter of men that had no thought but of the spectacle of the world, blushed, laughed, and darted through the room and so upstairs. Alas that the hangman's rope should be own brother to that Indian happiness that keeps alone, were it not for some stray cactus, mother of as many dreams, immemorial impartiality.

THE SUBJECT-MATTER OF DRAMA

I read this sentence a few days ago, or one like it, in an obituary of Ibsen: 'Let nobody again go back to the old ballad material of Shakespeare, to murders, and ghosts, for what interests us on the stage is modern experience and the discussion of our interests'; and in another part of the article Ibsen was blamed because he had written of suicides and in other ways made use of 'the morbid terror of death.' Dramatic literature has for a long time been left to the criticism of journalists, and all these, the old stupid ones and the new clever ones, have tried to impress upon it their absorption in the life of the moment, their delight in obvious originality and in obvious logic, their shrinking from the ancient and insoluble. The writer I have quoted is much more than a journalist, but he has lived their hurried life, and instinctively turns to them for judgment. He is not thinking of the great poets and painters, of the cloud of witnesses, who are there that we may become, through our understanding of their minds, spectators of the ages, but of this age. Drama is a means of expression, not a special subject-matter, and the dramatist is as free to choose where he has a mind to, as the poet of *Endymion*, or as the painter of Mary Magdalene at the door of Simon the Pharisee. So far from the discussion of our interests and the immediate circumstance of our life being the most moving to the imagination, it is what is old and far off that stirs us the most deeply.

There is a sentence in *The Marriage of Heaven and Hell* that is meaningless until we understand Blake's system of correspondences. 'The best wine is the oldest, the best water the newest.' Water is experience, immediate sensation, and wine is emotion, and it is with the intellect, as distinguished from imagination, that we enlarge the bounds of experience and separate it from all but itself, from illusion, from memory, and create among other things science and good journalism. Emotion, on the other hand, grows intoxicating and delightful after it has been enriched with the memory of old emotions, with all the uncounted flavours of old experience; and it is necessarily some antiquity of thought, emotions that have been deepened by the experiences of many men of genius, that distinguishes the cultivated man. The subject-matter of his meditation and invention is old, and he will disdain a too conscious originality in the arts as in those matters of daily life where, is it not Balzac who says, 'we are all conservatives'? He is above all things well-bred, and whether he write or paint will not desire a technique that denies or obtrudes his long and noble descent.

Discoveries

Corneille and Racine did not deny their masters, and when Dante spoke of his master Virgil there was no crowing of the cock. In their day imitation was conscious or all but conscious, and because originality was but so much the more a part of the man himself, so much the deeper because unconscious, no quick analysis could unravel their miracle, that needed generations, it may be, for its understanding; but it is our imitation that is unconscious and that waits the certainties of time. The more religious the subject-matter of an art, the more will it be, as it were, stationary, and the more ancient will be the emotion that it arouses and the circumstance that it calls up before our eyes. When in the Middle Ages the pilgrim to Saint Patrick's Purgatory found himself on the lake-side, he found a boat made out of a hollow tree to ferry him to the cave of vision. In religious painting and poetry, crowns and swords of an ancient pattern take upon themselves new meanings, and it is impossible to separate our idea of what is noble from a mystic stair, where not men and women, but robes, jewels, incidents, ancient utilities float upward slowly over the all but sleeping mind, putting on emotional and spiritual life as they ascend until they are swallowed up by some far glory that they even were too modern and momentary to endure. All art is dream, and what the day is done with is dreaming-ripe, and what art has moulded religion accepts, and in the end all is in the wine-cup, all is in the drunken fantasy, and the grapes begin to stammer.

The Cutting of an Agate

THE TWO KINDS OF ASCETICISM

It is not possible to separate an emotion or a spiritual state from the image that calls it up and gives it expression. Michelangelo's *Moses*, Velasquez' *Philip the Second*, the colour purple, a crucifix, call into life an emotion or state that vanishes with them because they are its only possible expression, and that is why no mind is more valuable than the images it contains. The imaginative writer differs from the saint in that he identifies himself—to the neglect of his own soul, alas! —with the soul of the world, and frees himself from all that is impermanent in that soul, an ascetic not of women and wine, but of the newspapers. Those things that are permanent in the soul of the world, the great passions that trouble all and have but a brief recurring life of flower and seed in any man, are indeed renounced by the saint, who seeks not an eternal art, but his own eternity. The artist stands between the saint and the world of impermanent things, and just in so far as his mind dwells on what is impermanent in his sense, on all that 'modern experience and the discussion of our interests,' that is to say, on what never recurs, as desire and hope, terror and weariness, spring and autumn, recur, will his mind losing rhythm grow critical, as distinguished from creative, and his emotions wither. He will think less of what he sees and more of his own attitude towards it, and will express this attitude by an essentially critical selection and emphasis. I am not quite sure of my memory, but I think that Mr. Ricketts has said somewhere that he feels the critic in Velasquez

286

for the first time in painting, and we all feel the critic in Whistler and Degas, in Browning, even in Mr. Swinburne, in much great art that is not the greatest of all. The end of art is the ecstasy awakened by the presence before an ever-changing mind of what is permanent in the world, or by the arousing of that mind itself into the very delicate and fastidious mood habitual with it when it is seeking those permanent and recurring things. There is a little of both ecstasies at all times, but at this time we have a small measure of the creative impulse itself, of the divine vision, a great measure of 'the lost traveller's dream under the hill,' perhaps because all the old simple things have been painted or written, and they will only have meaning for us again when a new race or a new civilisation has made us look upon all with new eyesight.

IN THE SERPENT'S MOUTH

If it be true that God is a circle whose centre is everywhere, the saint goes to the centre, the poet and artist to the ring where everything comes round again. The poet must not seek for what is still and fixed, for that has no life for him; and if he did, his style would become cold and monotonous, and his sense of beauty faint and sickly, as are both style and beauty to my imagination in the prose and poetry of Newman, but be content to find his pleasure in all that is for ever passing away that it may come again, in the beauty of woman, in the fragile flowers of spring, in momentary heroic passion, in whatever is most fleeting, most impassioned, as it were, for its own perfection, most eager to return in its glory. Yet perhaps he must endure the impermanent a little, for these things return, but not wholly, for no two faces are alike, and, it may be, had we more learned eyes, no two flowers. Is it that all things are made by the struggle of the individual and the world, of the unchanging and the returning, and that the saint and the poet are over all, and that the poet has made his home in the serpent's mouth?

THE BLACK AND THE WHITE ARROWS

Instinct creates the recurring and the beautiful, all the winding of the serpent; but reason, the most ugly man, as Blake called it, is a drawer of the straight line, the maker of the arbitrary and the impermanent, for no recurring spring will ever bring again yesterday's clock. Sanctity has its straight line also, darting from the centre, and with these arrows the many-coloured serpent, theme of all our poetry, is maimed and hunted. He that finds the white arrow shall have wisdom older than the serpent, but what of the black arrow? How much knowledge, how heavy a quiver of the crow-feathered ebony rods, can the soul endure?

HIS MISTRESS'S EYEBROWS

The preoccupation of our art and literature with knowledge, with the surface of life, with the arbitrary, with mechanism, has arisen out of the root. A careful but not necessarily very subtle man could foretell the history of any religion if he knew its first principle, and that it would live long enough to fulfil itself. The mind can never do the same thing twice over, and having exhausted simple beauty and meaning, it passes to the strange and hidden, and at last must find its delight—having outrun its harmonies—in the emphatic and discordant. When I was a boy at the art schools I watched an older student late returned from Paris, with a wonder that had no understanding in it. He was very amorous, and every new love was the occasion of a new picture, and every new picture was uglier than its forerunner. He was excited about his mistress's eyebrows, as was fitting, but the interest of beauty had been exhausted by the logical energies of art, which destroys where it has rummaged, and can but discover, whether it will or no. We cannot discover our subject-matter by deliberate intellect, for when a subject-matter ceases to move us we must go elsewhere, and when it moves us, even though it be 'that old ballad material of Shakespeare' or even 'the morbid terror of death,' we can laugh at reason. We must not ask is the world interested in this or that, for nothing is in question but our own interest, and we can understand no other. Our place in the Hierarchy is settled for us by our choice of a subject-matter, and all good criticism is hieratic, delighting in setting things above one another, Epic and Drama above Lyric and so on, and not merely side by side. But it is our instinct and not our intellect that chooses. We can deliberately refashion our characters, but not our painting or our poetry. If our characters also were not unconsciously refashioned so completely by the unfolding of the logical energies of art, that even simple things have in the end a new aspect in our eyes, the arts would not be among those things that return for ever. The ballads that Bishop Percy gathered returned in the *Ancient Mariner*, and the delight in the world of old Greek sculptors sprang into a more delicate loveliness in that archaistic head of the young athlete down the long corridor to your left hand as you go into the British Museum. Civilisation, too, will not that also destroy where it has loved, until it shall bring the simple and natural things again, and a new Argo with all the gilding on her bows sail out to find another Fleece?

THE TRESSES OF THE HAIR

Hafiz cried to his beloved, 'I made a bargain with that brown hair before the beginning of time, and it shall not be broken through unending time,' and it may be that Mistress Nature knows that we have lived many times, and that whatsoever changes and winds into itself belongs to us. She covers her eyes away from us, but she lets us play with the tresses of her hair.

A TOWER ON THE APENNINES

The other day I was walking towards Urbino, where I was to spend the night, having crossed the Apennines from San Sepolcro, and had come to a level place on the mountain-top near the journey's end. My friends were in a carriage somewhere behind, on a road which was still ascending in great loops, and I was alone amid a visionary, fantastic, impossible scenery. It was sunset and the stormy clouds hung upon mountain after mountain, and far off on one great summit a cloud darker than the rest glimmered with lightning. Away south upon another mountain a mediaeval tower, with no building near nor any sign of life, rose into the clouds. I saw suddenly in the mind's eye an old man, erect and a little gaunt, standing in the door of the tower, while about him broke a windy light. He was the poet who had at last, because he had done so much for the word's sake, come to share in the dignity of the saint. He had hidden nothing of himself, but he had taken care of 'that dignity . . . the perfection of form . . . this lofty and severe quality . . . this virtue.' And though he had but sought it for the word's sake, or for a woman's praise, it had come at last into his body and his mind. Certainly as he stood there he knew how from behind that laborious mood, that pose, that genius, no flower of himself but all himself, looked out as from behind a mask that other Who alone of all men, the countrypeople say, is not a hair's-breadth more nor less than six feet high. He has in his ears well-instructed voices, and seeming-solid sights are before his eyes, and not, as we say of many a one, speaking in metaphor, but as this were Delphi or Eleusis, and the substance and the voice come to him among his memories which are of women's faces; for was it Columbanus or another that wrote, 'There is one among the birds that is perfect, and one perfect among the fish'?

The Cutting of an Agate

Those learned men who are a terror to children and an ignominious sight in lovers' eyes, all those butts of a traditional humour where there is something of the wisdom of peasants, are mathematicians, theologians, lawyers, men of science of various kinds. They have followed some abstract reverie, which stirs the brain only and needs that only, and have therefore stood before the looking-glass without pleasure and never known those thoughts that shape the lines of the body for beauty or animation, and wake a desire for praise or for display.

There are two pictures of Venice side by side in the house where I am writing this, a Canaletto that has little but careful drawing, and a not very emotional pleasure in clean bright air, and a Frans Francken (the younger), where the blue water, that in the other stirs one so little, can make one long to plunge into the green depth where a cloud-shadow falls. Neither painting could move us at all, if our thought did not rush out to the edges of our flesh, and it is so with all good art, whether the Victory of Samothrace which reminds the soles of our feet of swiftness, or the *Odyssey* that would send us out under the salt wind, or the young horsemen on the Parthenon, that seem happier than our boyhood ever was, and in our boyhood's way. Art bids us touch and taste and hear and see the world, and shrinks from what Blake calls mathematic form, from every abstract thing, from all that is of the brain only, from all that is not a fountain jetting from the entire hopes, memories, and sensations of the body. Its morality is personal, knows little of any general law, has no blame for Little Musgrave, no care for Lord Barnard's house, seems lighter than a breath and yet is hard and heavy, for if a man is not ready to face toil and risk, and in all gaiety of heart, his body will grow unshapely and his heart lack the wild will that stirs desire. It approved before all men those that talked or wrestled or tilted under the walls of Urbino, or sat in those great window-seats discussing all things, with love ever in their thought, when the wise Duchess ordered all, and the Lady Emilia gave the theme.

RELIGIOUS BELIEF NECESSARY TO RELIGIOUS ART

All art is sensuous, but when a man puts only his contemplative nature and his more vague desires into his art, the sensuous images through which it speaks become broken, fleeting, uncertain, or are chosen for their distance from general experience, and all grows unsubstantial and fantastic. When imagination moves in a dim world like the country of sleep in *Love's Nocturn* and 'Siren there winds her dizzy hair and sings,' we go to it for delight indeed but in our weariness. If we are to sojourn there that world must grow consistent with itself, emotion must be related to emotion by a system of ordered images, as in the *Divine Comedy*. It must grow to be symbolic, that is, for the soul can only achieve a distinct separated life where many related objects at once distinguish and arouse its energies in their fullness. All visionaries have entered into such a world in trances, and all ideal art has trance for warranty. Shelley seemed to Matthew Arnold to beat his ineffectual wings in the void, and I only made my pleasure in him contented pleasure by massing in my imagination his recurring images of towers and rivers, and caves with fountains in them, and that one Star of his, till his world had grown solid underfoot and consistent enough for the soul's habitation.

But even then I lacked something to compensate my imagination for geographical and historical reality, for the testimony of our ordinary senses, and found myself wishing for and trying to imagine, as I had also when reading Keats's *Endymion*, a crowd of believers who could put into all those strange sights the strength of their belief and the rare testimony of their visions. A little crowd had been sufficient, and I would have had Shelley a sectary that his revelation might display the only sufficient evidence of religion, miracle. All symbolic art should arise out of a real belief, and that it cannot do so in this age proves that this age is a road and not a resting-place for the imaginative arts. I can only understand others by myself, and I am certain that there are many who are not moved as they would be by that solitary light burning in the tower of Prince Athanase, because it has not entered into men's prayers nor lighted any through the sacred dark of religious contemplation.

Lyrical poems, when they but speak of emotions common to all, require not indeed a religious belief like the spiritual arts, but a life that has leisure for itself, and a society that is quickly stirred that our emotion may be strengthened by the emotion of others. All circumstance that makes emotion at once dignified and visible increases the poet's power, and I think that is why I have always longed for some stringed instrument, and a listening audience, not drawn out of the hurried streets, but from a life where it would be natural to murmur over again the singer's thought. When I heard Yvette Guilbert the other day, who has the lyre or as good, I was not content, for she sang among people whose life had nothing it could share with an exquisite art, that should rise out of life as the blade out of the spear-shaft, a song out of the mood, the fountain from its pool, all art out of the body, laughter from a happy company. I longed to make all things over again, that she might sing in some great hall, where there was no one that did not love life and speak of it continually.

THE HOLY PLACES

When all art was struck out of personality, whether as in our daily business or in the adventure of religion, there was little separation between holy and common things, and just as the arts themselves passed quickly from passion to divine contemplation, from the conversation of peasants to that of princes, the one song remembering the drunken miller and but half forgetting Cambuscan bold; so did a man feel himself near sacred presences when he turned his plough from the slope of Cruachmaa or of Olympus. The occupations and the places known to Homer or to Hesiod, those pure first artists, might, as it were, if but the fashioners' hands had loosened, have changed before the poem's end to symbols and vanished, caught up as in a golden cloud into the unchanging worlds where religion alone can discover life as well as peace. A man of that unbroken day could have all the subtlety of Shelley, and yet use no image unknown among the common people, and speak no thought that was not a deduction from the common thought. Unless the discovery of legendary knowledge and the returning belief in miracle, or what we must needs call so, can bring once more a new belief in the sanctity of common ploughland, and new wonders that reward no difficult ecclesiastical routine but the common, wayward, spirited man, we may never see again a Shelley and a Dickens in the one body, but be broken to the end. We have grown jealous of the body, and we dress it in dull unshapely clothes, that we may cherish aspiration alone. Molière being but the master of common sense lived ever in the common daylight, but Shakespeare could not, and Shakespeare seems to bring us to the very market-place, when we remember Shelley's dizzy and Landor's calm disdain of usual daily things. And at last we have Villiers de l'Isle-Adam crying in the ecstasy of a supreme culture, of a supreme refusal: 'As for living, our servants will do that for us.' One of the means of loftiness, of marmorean stillness, has been the choice of strange and far-away places for the scenery of art, but this choice has grown bitter to me, and there are moments when I cannot believe in the reality of imaginations that are not inset with the minute life of long familiar things and symbols and places. I have come to think of even Shakespeare's jour-

neys to Rome or to Verona as the outflowing of an un-
rest, a dissatisfaction with natural interests, an unstable
equilibrium of the whole European mind that would
not have come had John Palaeologus cherished, despite
that high and heady look, copied by Burne-Jones for
his Cophetua, a hearty disposition to fight the Turk. I
am orthodox and pray for a resurrection of the body,
and am certain that a man should find his Holy Land
where he first crept upon the floor, and that familiar
woods and rivers should fade into symbol with so
gradual a change that he may never discover, no, not
even in ecstasy itself, that he is beyond space, and that
time alone keeps him from Primum Mobile, Supernal
Eden, Yellow Rose over all.

1906

The Cutting of an Agate

Six years ago I was staying in a students' hotel in the Latin Quarter, and somebody, whose name I cannot recollect, introduced me to an Irishman, who, even poorer than myself, had taken a room at the top of the house. It was J. M. Synge, and I, who thought I knew the name of every Irishman who was working at literature, had never heard of him. He was a graduate of Trinity College, Dublin, too, and Trinity College does not, as a rule, produce artistic minds. He told me that he had been living in France and Germany, reading French and German literature, and that he wished to become a writer. He had, however, nothing to show but one or two poems and impressionistic essays, full of that kind of morbidity that has its root in too much brooding over methods of expression, and ways of looking upon life, which come, not out of life, but out of literature, images reflected from mirror to mirror. He had wandered among people whose life is as picturesque as the Middle Ages, playing his fiddle to Italian sailors, and listening to stories in Bavarian woods, but life had cast no light into his writings. He had learned Irish years ago, but had begun to forget it, for the only language that interested him was that conventional language of modern poetry which has begun to make us all weary. I was very weary of it, for I had finished *The Secret Rose*, and felt how it had separated my imagination from life, sending my Red Hanrahan, who should

298

have trodden the same roads with myself, into some un-
discoverable country.[1] I said: 'Give up Paris. You will
never create anything by reading Racine, and Arthur
Symons will always be a better critic of French literature. Go to the Aran Islands. Live there as if you were
one of the people themselves; express a life that has
never found expression.' I had just come from Aran,
and my imagination was full of those grey islands where
men must reap with knives because of the stones.

He went to Aran and became a part of its life, living
upon salt fish and eggs, talking Irish for the most
part, but listening also to the beautiful English which
has grown up in Irish-speaking districts, and takes its
vocabulary from the time of Malory and of the translators of the Bible, but its idiom and its vivid metaphor
from Irish. When Mr. Synge began to write in this
language, Lady Gregory had already used it finely in
her translations of Dr. Hyde's lyrics and plays, or of
old Irish literature, but she had listened with different
ears. He made his own selection of word and phrase,
choosing what would express his own personality.
Above all, he made word and phrase dance to a very
strange rhythm, which will always, till his plays have
created their own tradition, be difficult to actors who
have not learned it from his lips. It is essential, for it
perfectly fits the drifting emotion, the dreaminess, the
vague yet measureless desire, for which he would
create a dramatic form. It blurs definition, clear edges,
everything that comes from the will, it turns imagina-

[1] Since writing this I have, with Lady Gregory's help, put *Red
Hanrahan* into the common speech.—W. B. Y.

tion from all that is of the present, like a gold background in a religious picture, and it strengthens in every emotion whatever comes to it from far off, from brooding memory and dangerous hope. When he brought *The Shadow of the Glen*, his first play, to the Irish National Theatre Society, the players were puzzled by the rhythm, but gradually they became certain that his Woman of the Glen, as melancholy as a curlew, driven to distraction by her own sensitiveness, her own fineness, could not speak with any other tongue, that all his people would change their life if the rhythm changed. Perhaps no Irish countryman had ever that exact rhythm in his voice, but certainly if Mr. Synge had been born a countryman, he would have spoken like that. It makes the people of his imagination a little disembodied; it gives them a kind of innocence even in their anger and their cursing. It is part of its maker's attitude towards the world, for while it makes the clash of wills among his persons indirect and dreamy, it helps him to see the subject-matter of his art with wise, clear-seeing, unreflecting eyes; to preserve the integrity of art in an age of reasons and purposes. Whether he write of old beggars by the roadside, lamenting over the misery and ugliness of life, or of an old Aran woman mourning her drowned sons, or of a young wife married to an old husband, he has no wish to change anything, to reform anything; all these people pass by as before an open window, murmuring strange, exciting words.

If one has not fine construction, one has not drama, but if one has not beautiful or powerful and individual speech, one has not literature, or, at any rate, one has not great literature. Rabelais, Villon, Shakespeare, William Blake, would have known one another by their speech. Some of them knew how to construct a story, but all of them had abundant, resonant, beautiful, laughing, living speech. It is only the writers of our modern dramatic movement, our scientific dramatists, our naturalists of the stage, who have thought it possible to be like the greatest, and yet to cast aside even the poor persiflage of the comedians, and to write in the impersonal language that has come, not out of individual life, nor out of life at all, but out of necessities of commerce, of Parliament, of Board Schools, of hurried journeys by rail.

If there are such things as decaying art and decaying institutions, their decay must begin when the element they receive into their care from the life of every man in the world begins to rot. Literature decays when it no longer makes more beautiful, or more vivid, the language which unites it to all life, and when one finds the criticism of the student, and the purpose of the reformer, and the logic of the man of science, where there should have been the reveries of the common heart, ennobled into some raving Lear or unabashed Don Quixote. One must not forget that the death of language, the substitution of phrases as nearly impersonal as algebra for words and rhythms varying from man to man, is but a part of the tyranny of impersonal things. I have been reading through a bundle of German plays, and have found everywhere a desire, not to express hopes and alarms common to every man that ever came into the world, but politics or social passion, a veiled or open propaganda. Now it is duelling that has need of reproof; now it is the ideas of an actress, returning from the free life of the stage, that must be contrasted with the prejudice of an old-fashioned town; now it is the hostility of Christianity and Paganism in our own day that is to find an obscure symbol in a bell thrown from its tower by spirits of the wood. I compare the work of these dramatists with the greater plays of their Scandinavian master, and remember that even he, who has made so many clear-drawn characters, has made us no abundant character, no man of genius in whom we could believe, and that in him also, even when it is Emperor and Galilean that are face to face, even the most momentous figures are subordinate to some tendency, to some movement, to some inanimate energy, or to some process of thought whose very logic has changed it into mechanism—always to 'something other than human life.'

We must not measure a young talent, whether we praise or blame, with that of men who are among the greatest of our time, but we may say of any talent, following out a definition, that it takes up the tradition of great drama as it came from the hands of the Masters who are acknowledged by all time, and turns away from a dramatic movement which, though it has been served by fine talent, has been imposed upon us by science, by artificial life, by a passing order.

When the individual life no longer delights in its own energy, when the body is not made strong and beautiful by the activities of daily life, when men have no delight in decorating the body, one may be certain that one lives in a passing order, amid the inventions of a fading vitality. If Homer were alive to-day, he would only resist, after a deliberate struggle, the temptation to find his subject not in Helen's beauty, that every man has desired, nor in the wisdom and endurance of Odysseus that has been the desire of every woman that has come into the world, but in what somebody would describe, perhaps, as 'the inevitable contest,' arising out of economic causes, between the country-places and small towns on the one hand, and, upon the other, the great city of Troy, representing one knows not what 'tendency to centralisation.'

Mr. Synge has in common with the great theatre of the world, with that of Greece and that of India, with the creator of Falstaff, with Racine, a delight in language, a preoccupation with individual life. He resembles them also by a preoccupation with what is lasting and noble, that came to him, not, as I think, from books, but while he listened to old stories in the cottages, and contrasted what they remembered with reality. The only literature of the Irish countrypeople is their songs, full often of extravagant love, and their stories of kings and of kings' children. 'I will cry my fill, but not for God, but because Finn and the Fianna are not living,' says Oisin in the story. Every writer, even every small writer, who has belonged to the great tradition, has had his dream of an impossibly noble life, and the greater he is, the more does it seem to plunge him into some beautiful or bitter reverie. Some, and of these are all the earliest poets of the world, gave it direct expression; others mingle it so subtly with reality that it is a day's work to disentangle it; others bring it near by showing us whatever is most its contrary. Mr. Synge, indeed, sets before us ugly, deformed or sinful people, but his people, moved by no practical ambition, are driven by a dream of that impossible life. That we may feel how intensely his Woman of the Glen dreams of days that shall be entirely alive, she that is 'a hard woman to please' must spend her days between a sour-faced old husband, a man who goes mad upon the hills, a craven lad and a drunken tramp; and those two blind people of *The Well of the Saints* are so transformed by the dream that they choose blindness rather than reality. He tells us of realities, but he knows that art has never taken more than its symbols from anything that the eye can see or the hand measure.

It is the preoccupation of his characters with their dream that gives his plays their drifting movement, their emotional subtlety. In most of the dramatic writing of our time, and this is one of the reasons why our dramatists do not find the need for a better speech, one finds a simple motive lifted, as it were, into the full light of the stage. The ordinary student of drama will not find anywhere in *The Well of the Saints* that excitement of the will in the presence of attainable advantages, which he is accustomed to think the natural stuff of drama, and if he see it played he will wonder why act is knitted to act so loosely, why it is all like a decoration on a flat surface, why there is so much leisure in the dialogue, even in the midst of passion. If he see *The Shadow of the Glen*, he will ask, Why does this woman go out of her house? Is it because she cannot help herself, or is she content to go? Why is it not all made clearer? And yet, like everybody when caught up into great events, she does many things without being quite certain why she does them. She hardly understands at moments why her action has a certain form, more clearly than why her body is tall or short, fair or brown. She feels an emotion that she does not understand. She is driven by desires that need for their expression, not 'I admire this man,' or 'I must go, whether I will or no,' but words full of suggestion, rhythms of voice, movements that escape analysis. In addition to all this, she has something that she shares with none but the children of one man's imagination. She is intoxicated by a dream which is hardly understood by herself, but possesses her like something half remembered on a sudden wakening.

While I write, we are rehearsing *The Well of the Saints*, and are painting for it decorative scenery, mountains in one or two flat colours and without detail, ashtrees and red salleys with something of recurring pattern in their woven boughs. For though the people of the play use no phrase they could not use in daily life, we know that we are seeking to express what no eye has ever seen.

ABBEY THEATRE
January 27, 1905

The Cutting of an Agate

PREFACE TO THE FIRST EDITION OF JOHN M. SYNGE'S *POEMS AND TRANSLATIONS*

'The Lonely returns to the Lonely, the Divine to the Divinity.'
—PROCLUS.

I

WHILE THIS WORK was passing through the press Mr. J. M. Synge died. Upon the morning of his death one friend of his and mine, though away in the country, felt the burden of some heavy event, without understanding where or for whom it was to happen; but upon the same morning one of my sisters said, 'I think Mr. Synge will recover, for last night I dreamed of an ancient galley labouring in a storm and he was in the galley, and suddenly I saw it run into bright sunlight and smooth sea, and I heard the keel grate upon the sand.' The misfortune was for the living certainly, that must work on, perhaps in vain, to magnify the minds and hearts of our young men, and not for the dead that, having cast off the ailing body, is now, as I believe, all passionate and fiery, an heroical thing. Our Daimon is as dumb as was that of Socrates when they brought in the hemlock; and if we speak among ourselves, it is of the thoughts that have no savour because we cannot hear his laughter, of the work more difficult because of the strength he has taken with him, of the astringent joy and hardness that was in all he did, and of his fame in the world.

John M. Synge's Poems and Translations

II

In his Preface he speaks of these poems as having been written during the last sixteen or seventeen years, though the greater number were written very recently, and many during his last illness. *An Epitaph* and *On an Anniversary* show how early the expectation of death came to him, for they were made long ago. But the book as a whole is a farewell, written when life began to slip from him. He was a reserved man, and wished no doubt by a vague date to hide, while still living, what he felt and thought, from those about him. I asked one of the nurses in the hospital where he died if he knew he was dying, and she said, 'He may have known it for months, but he would not have spoken of it to any one.' Even the translations of poems that he has made his own by putting them into that melancholy dialect of his, seem to express his emotion at the memory of poverty and the approach of death. The whole book is of a kind almost unknown in a time when lyricism has become abstract and impersonal.

Now and then in history some man will speak a few simple sentences which never die, because his life gives them energy and meaning. They affect us as do the last words of Shakespeare's people, that gather up into themselves the energy of elaborate events, and they put strange meaning into half-forgotten things and accidents, like cries that reveal the combatants in some dim battle. Often a score of words will be enough, as when we repeat to ourselves, 'I am a servant of the Lord God of War and I understand the lovely art of the Muses,' all that remains of a once famous Greek poet and sea-rover. And is not that epitaph Swift made in Latin for his own tomb more immortal than his pamphlets, perhaps than his great allegory?—'He has gone where fierce indignation can lacerate his heart no more.' I think this book too has certain sentences, fierce or beautiful or melancholy, that will be remembered in our history, having behind their passion his quarrel with ignorance, and those passionate events, his books.

But for the violent nature that strikes brief fire in *A Question*, hidden though it was under much courtesy and silence, his genius had never borne those lion-cubs of his. He could not have loved had he not hated, nor honoured had he not scorned; though his hatred and his scorn moved him but seldom, as I think, for his whole nature was lifted up into a vision of the world, where hatred played with the grotesque and love became an ecstatic contemplation of noble life.

He once said to me, 'We must unite asceticism, stoicism, ecstasy; two of these have often come together, but not all three': and the strength that made him delight in setting the hard virtues by the soft, the bitter by the sweet, salt by mercury, the stone by the elixir, gave him a hunger for harsh facts, for ugly surprising things, for all that defies our hope. In *The Passing of the Sidhe* he is repelled by the contemplation of a beauty too far from life to appease his mood; and in his own work, benign images, ever present to his soul, must have beside them malignant reality, and the greater the brightness, the greater must the darkness be. Though like 'Oisin after the Fenians' he remembers his master and his friends, he cannot put from his mind coughing and old age and the sound of the bells. The old woman in the *Riders to the Sea,* in mourning for her six fine sons, mourns for the passing of all beauty and strength, while the drunken woman of *The Tinker's Wedding* is but the more drunken and the more thieving because she can remember great queens. And what is it but desire of ardent life, like that of Oisin for his 'golden salmon of the sea, clean hawk of the air,' that makes the young girls of *The Playboy of the Western World* prefer to any peaceful man their eyes have looked upon, a seeming murderer? Person after person in these laughing, sorrowful, heroic plays is 'the like of the little children do be listening to the stories of an old woman, and do be dreaming after in the dark night it's in grand houses of gold they are, with speckled horses to ride, and do be waking again in a short while and they destroyed with the cold, and the thatch dripping, maybe, and the starved ass braying in the yard.'

IV

It was only at the last in his unfinished *Deirdre of the Sorrows* that his mood changed. He knew some twelve months ago that he was dying, though he told no one about it but his betrothed, and he gave all his thought to this play, that he might finish it. Sometimes he would despond and say that he could not; and then his betrothed would act it for him in his sick-room, and give him heart to write again. And now by a strange chance, for he began the play before the last failing of his health, his persons awake to no disillusionment but to death only, and as if his soul already thirsted for the fiery fountains, there is nothing grotesque, but beauty only.

V

He was a solitary, undemonstrative man, never asking pity, nor complaining, nor seeking sympathy but in this book's momentary cries: all folded up in brooding intellect, knowing nothing of new books and newspapers, reading the great masters alone; and he was but the more hated because he gave his country what it needed, an unmoved mind where there is a perpetual Last Day, a trumpeting, and coming up to judgment.

April 4, 1909

J. M. SYNGE AND THE IRELAND OF HIS TIME

I

ON SATURDAY, JANUARY 26, 1907, I was lecturing in Aberdeen, and when my lecture was over I was given a telegram which said, 'Play great success.' It had been sent from Dublin after the second act of *The Playboy of the Western World*, then being performed for the first time. After one in the morning, my host brought to my bedroom this second telegram, 'Audience broke up in disorder at the word shift.' I knew no more until I got the Dublin papers on my way from Belfast to Dublin on Tuesday morning. On the Monday night no word of the play had been heard. About forty young men had sat in the front seats of the pit, and stamped and shouted and blown trumpets from the rise to the fall of the curtain. On the Tuesday night also the forty young men were there. They wished to silence what they considered a slander upon Ireland's womanhood. Irish women would never sleep under the same roof with a young man without a chaperon, nor admire a murderer, nor use a word like 'shift'; nor could any one recognise the country men and women of Davis and Kickham in these poetical, violent, grotesque persons, who used the name of God so freely, and spoke of all things that hit their fancy.

A patriotic journalism which had seen in Synge's capricious imagination the enemy of all it would have young men believe, had for years prepared for this hour, by that which is at once the greatest and most

ignoble power of journalism, the art of repeating a name
again and again with some ridiculous or evil association. The preparation had begun after the first performance of *The Shadow of the Glen*, Synge's first play,
with an assertion made in ignorance, but repeated in
dishonesty, that he had taken his fable and his characters, not from his own mind nor that profound knowledge of cot and curragh he was admitted to possess,
but 'from a writer of the Roman decadence.' Some
spontaneous dislike had been but natural, for genius
like his can but slowly, amid what it has of harsh and
strange, set forth the nobility of its beauty, and the
depth of its compassion; but the frenzy that would have
silenced his master-work was, like most violent things,
artificial, that defence of virtue by those who have but
little, which is the pomp and gallantry of journalism
and its right to govern the world.

As I stood there watching, knowing well that I saw
the dissolution of a school of patriotism that held sway
over my youth, Synge came and stood beside me, and
said, 'A young doctor has just told me that he can
hardly keep himself from jumping on to a seat, and
pointing out in that howling mob those whom he is
treating for venereal disease.'

II

Thomas Davis, whose life had the moral simplicity
which can give to actions the lasting influence that style
alone can give to words, had understood that a country
which has no national institutions must show its young

men images for the affections, although they be but diagrams of what should be or may be. He and his school imagined the Soldier, the Orator, the Patriot, the Poet, the Chieftain, and above all the Peasant; and these, as celebrated in essays and songs and stories, possessed so many virtues that no matter how England, who, as Mitchel said, 'had the ear of the world,' might slander us, Ireland, even though she could not come at the world's other ear, might go her way unabashed. But ideas and images which have to be understood and loved by large numbers of people must appeal to no rich personal experience, no patience of study, no delicacy of sense; and if at rare moments some *Memory of the Dead* can take its strength from one, at all other moments manner and matter will be rhetorical, conventional, sentimental; and language, because it is carried beyond life perpetually, will be worn and cold like the thought, with unmeaning pedantries and silences, and a dread of all that has salt and savour. After a while, in a land that has given itself to agitation overmuch, abstract thoughts are raised up between men's minds and Nature, who never does the same thing twice, or makes one man like another, till minds, whose patriotism is perhaps great enough to carry them to the scaffold, cry down natural impulse with the morbid persistence of minds unsettled by some fixed idea. They are preoccupied with the nation's future, with heroes, poets, soldiers, painters, armies, fleets, but only as these things are understood by a child in a National School, while a secret feeling that what is so unreal needs continual defence makes them bitter and restless. They are like some State which has only paper money, and seeks by punishments to make it buy whatever gold can buy. They no longer love, for only life is loved, and at last a generation is like an hysterical woman who will make unmeasured accusations and believe impossible things, because of some logical deduction from a solitary thought which has turned a portion of her mind to stone.

III

Even if what one defends be true, an attitude of defence, a continual apology, whatever the cause, makes the mind barren because it kills intellectual innocence; that delight in what is unforeseen, and in the mere spectacle of the world, the mere drifting hither and thither that must come before all true thought and emotion. A zealous Irishman, especially if he lives much out of Ireland, spends his time in a never-ending argument about Oliver Cromwell, the Danes, the penal laws, the Rebellion of 1798, the famine, the Irish peasant, and ends by substituting a traditional casuistry for a country; and if he be a Catholic, yet another casuistry, that has professors, schoolmasters, letter-writing priests and the authors of manuals to make the meshes fine, comes between him and English literature, substituting arguments and hesitations for the excitement at the first reading of the great poets which should be a sort of violent imaginative puberty. His hesitations and arguments may have been right, the Catholic philosophy may be more profound than Milton's morality, or Shelley's vehement vision; but none the less do we lose

314

life by losing that recklessness Castiglione thought necessary even in good manners, and offend our Lady Truth, who would never, had she desired a courtship so anxious and elaborate, have digged a well to be her parlour.

I admired, though we were always quarrelling, J. F. Taylor, the orator, who died just before the first controversy over these plays. It often seemed to me that when he spoke Ireland herself had spoken; one got that sense of surprise that comes when a man has said what is unforeseen because it is far from the common thought, and yet obvious because, when it has been spoken, the gate of the mind seems suddenly to roll back and reveal forgotten sights and let loose lost passions. I have never heard him speak except in some Irish literary or political society, but there at any rate, as in conversation, I found a man whose life was a ceaseless reverie over the religious and political history of Ireland. He saw himself pleading for his country before an invisible jury, perhaps of the great dead, against traitors at home and enemies abroad, and a sort of frenzy in his voice and the moral elevation of his thoughts gave him for the moment style and music. One asked oneself again and again, 'Why is not this man an artist, a man of genius, a creator of some kind?' The other day, under the influence of memory, I read through his one book, a Life of Owen Roe O'Neill, and found there no sentence detachable from its context because of wisdom or beauty. Everything was argued from a premise; and wisdom and style, whether in life or letters, come from the presence of what is self-evident, from that which requires but statement, from what Blake called 'naked beauty displayed.' The sense of what was unforeseen and obvious, the rolling backward of the gates, had gone with the living voice, with the nobility of will that made one understand what he saw and felt in what was now but argument and logic. I found myself in the presence of a mind like some noisy and powerful machine, of thought that was no part of wisdom but the apologetic of a moment, a woven thing, no intricacy of leaf and twig, of words with no more of salt and of savour than those of a Jesuit professor of literature, or of any other who does not know that there is no lasting writing which does not define the quality or carry the substance of some pleasure. How can one, if one's mind be full of abstractions and images created not for their own sake but for the sake of party, even if there were still the need, make pictures for the mind's eye and sounds that delight the ear, or discover thoughts that tighten the muscles, or quiver and tingle in the flesh, and so stand like Saint Michael with the trumpet that calls the body to resurrection?

IV

Young Ireland had taught a study of our history with the glory of Ireland for event; and this, for lack, when less than Taylor studied, of comparison with that of other countries, wrecked the historical instinct. The man who doubted, let us say, our fabulous ancient kings running up to Adam, or found but mythology in some old tale, was as hated as if he had doubted the authority of Scripture. Above all, no man was so ignorant that he had not by rote familiar arguments and statistics to drive away amid familiar applause all those that had found strange truth in the world or in their mind, and all whose knowledge had passed out of memory and become an instinct of hand or eye. There was no literature, for literature is a child of experience always, of knowledge never; and the nation itself, instead of being a dumb struggling thought seeking a mouth to utter it or hand to show it, a teeming delight that would re-create the world, had become, at best, a subject of knowledge.

V

Taylor always spoke with confidence, though he was no determined man, being easily flattered or jostled from his way; and this putting, as it were, his fiery heart into his mouth made him formidable. And I have noticed that all those who speak the thoughts of many, speak confidently, while those who speak their own thoughts are hesitating and timid, as though they spoke out of a mind and body grown sensitive to the edge of bewilderment among many impressions. They speak to us that we may give them certainty, by seeing what they have seen; and so it is that enlargement of experience does not come from those oratorical thinkers, or from those decisive rhythms that move large numbers of men, but from writers that seem by contrast as feminine as the soul when it explores in Blake's picture the recesses of the grave, carrying its faint lamp trembling and astonished; or as the Muses who are never

pictured as one-breasted Amazons, but as women needing protection. Indeed, all art which appeals to individual man and awaits the confirmation of his senses
and his reveries, seems, when arrayed against the moral
zeal, the confident logic, the ordered proof of journalism, a trifling, impertinent, vexatious thing, a tumbler
who has unrolled his carpet in the way of a marching
army.

VI

I attack things that are as dear to many as some holy
image carried hither and thither by some broken clan,
and can but say that I have felt in my body the affections I disturb, and believed that if I could raise them
into contemplation I would make possible a literature
that, finding its subject-matter all ready in men's minds,
would be, not as ours is, an interest for scholars, but
the possession of a people. I have founded societies
with this aim, and was indeed founding one in Paris
when I first met with J. M. Synge, and I have known
what it is to be changed by that I would have changed,
till I became argumentative and unmannerly, hating
men even in daily life for their opinions. And though
I was never convinced that the anatomies of last year's
leaves are a living forest, nor thought a continual
apologetic could do other than make the soul a vapour
and the body a stone, nor believed that literature can
be made by anything but by what is still blind and
dumb within ourselves, I have had to learn how hard,
in one who lives where forms of expression and habits
of thought have been born, not for the pleasure of

begetting, but for the public good, is that purification from insincerity, vanity, malignity, arrogance, which is the discovery of style. But life became sweet again when I had learnt all I had not learnt in shaping words, in defending Synge against his enemies, and knew that rich energies, fine, turbulent or gracious thoughts, whether in life or letters, are but love-children.

Synge seemed by nature unfitted to think a political thought, and with the exception of one sentence, spoken when I first met him in Paris, that implied some sort of Nationalist conviction, I cannot remember that he spoke of politics or showed any interest in men in the mass, or in any subject that is studied through abstractions and statistics. Often for months together he and I and Lady Gregory would see no one outside the Abbey Theatre, and that life, lived as it were in a ship at sea, suited him, for unlike those whose habit of mind fits them to judge of men in the mass, he was wise in judging individual men, and as wise in dealing with them as the faint energies of ill-health would permit; but of their political thoughts he long understood nothing. One night, when we were still producing plays in a little hall, certain members of the company told him that a play on the Rebellion of '98 would be a great success. After a fortnight he brought them a scenario which read like a chapter out of Rabelais. Two women, a Protestant and a Catholic, take refuge in a cave, and there quarrel about religion, abusing the Pope or Queen Elizabeth and Henry VIII, but in low voices, for the one fears to be ravished by the soldiers, the other by the rebels. At last one woman goes out because she would sooner any fate than such wicked company. Yet I doubt if he would have written at all if he did not write of Ireland, and for it, and I know that he thought creative art could only come from such preoccupation. Once when, in later years, anxious about the educational effect of our movement, I proposed adding to the Abbey Company a second company to play international drama, Synge, who had not hitherto opposed me, thought the matter so important that he did so in a formal letter.

I had spoken of a German municipal theatre as my model, and he said that the municipal theatres all over Europe gave fine performances of old classics, but did not create (he disliked modern drama for its sterility of speech, and perhaps ignored it), and that we would create nothing if we did not give all our thoughts to Ireland. Yet in Ireland he loved only what was wild in its people, and in 'the grey and wintry sides of many glens.' All the rest, all that one reasoned over, fought for, read of in leading articles, all that came from education, all that came down from Young Ireland—though for this he had not lacked a little sympathy—first wakened in him perhaps that irony which runs through all he wrote; but once awakened, he made it turn its face upon the whole of life. The women quarrelling in the cave would not have amused him if something in his nature had not looked out on most disputes, even those wherein he himself took sides, with a mischievous wisdom. He told me once that when he lived in some peasant's house, he tried to make those about him forget that he was there, and it is certain that he was silent in any crowded room. It is possible that low vitality helped him to be observant and contemplative, and made him dislike, even in solitude, those thoughts which unite us to others, much as we all dislike, when fatigue or illness has sharpened the nerves, hoardings covered with advertisements, the fronts of big theatres, big London hotels, and all architecture which has been made to impress the crowd. What blindness did for Homer, lameness for Hephaestus, asceticism for any saint you will, bad health did for him by making him ask no more of life than that it should keep him living, and above all perhaps by concentrating his imagination upon one thought, health itself. I think that all noble things are the result of warfare; great nations and classes, of warfare in the visible world, great poetry and philosophy, of invisible warfare, the division of a mind within itself, a victory, the sacrifice of a man to himself. I am certain that my friend's noble art, so full of passion and heroic beauty, is the victory of a man who in poverty and sickness created from the delight of expression, and in the contemplation that is born of the minute and delicate arrangement of images, happiness and health of mind. Some early poems have a morbid melancholy, and he himself spoke of early work he had destroyed as morbid, for as yet the craftsmanship was not fine enough to bring the artist's joy which is of one substance with that of sanctity. In one poem he waits at some street-corner for a friend, a woman perhaps, and while he waits and gradually understands that nobody is coming, he sees two funerals and shivers at the future; and in another, written on his twenty-fifth birthday, he wonders if the twenty-five years to come shall be as evil as those gone by. Later on, he can see himself as but a part of the spectacle of the world and mix into all he sees that flavour of extravagance, or of humour, or of philosophy, that makes one understand that he contemplates even his own death as if it were another's and finds in his own destiny but, as it were, a projection through a burning-glass of that general to men. There is in the creative joy an acceptance of what life brings, because we have understood the beauty of what it brings, or a hatred of death for what it takes away, which arouses within us, through some sympathy perhaps with all other men, an energy so noble, so powerful, that we laugh aloud and mock, in the terror or the sweetness of our exaltation, at death and oblivion.

In no modern writer that has written of Irish life before him, except, it may be, Miss Edgeworth in *Castle Rackrent*, was there anything to change a man's thought about the world or stir his moral nature, for they but play with pictures, persons and events, that whether well or ill observed are but an amusement for the mind where it escapes from meditation, a child's show that makes the fables of his art as significant by contrast as some procession painted on an Egyptian wall; for in these fables, an intelligence on which the tragedy of the world had been thrust in so few years that Life had no time to brew her sleepy drug has spoken of the moods that are the expression of its wisdom. All minds that have a wisdom come of tragic reality seem morbid to those that are accustomed to writers who have not faced reality at all; just as the saints, with that Obscure

Night of the Soul, which fell so certainly that they numbered it among spiritual states, one among other ascending steps, seem morbid to the rationalist and the old-fashioned Protestant controversialist. The thoughts of journalists, like the thoughts of the Irish novelists, are neither healthy nor unhealthy, not having risen to that state where either is possible, nor should we call them happy; for who, if happiness were not the supreme attainment of man, would have sought it in heroic toils, in the cell of the ascetic, or imagined it above the cheerful newspapers, above the clouds?

VII

Not that Synge brought out of the struggle with himself any definite philosophy, for philosophy in the common meaning of the word is created out of an anxiety for sympathy or obedience, and he was that rare, that distinguished, that most noble thing, which of all things still of the world is nearest to being sufficient to itself, the pure artist. Sir Philip Sidney complains of those who could hear 'sweet tunes' (by which he understands could look upon his lady) and not be stirred to 'ravishing delight.'

Or if they do delight therein, yet are so closed with wit,
As with sententious lips to set a title vain on it;
O let them hear these sacred tunes, and learn in Wonder's
    schools
To be, in things past bonds of wit, fools if they be not fools!

Ireland for three generations has been like those churlish logicians. Everything is argued over, everything has to take its trial before the dull sense and the hasty judgment, and the character of the nation has so changed that it hardly keeps but among countrypeople, or where some family tradition is still stubborn, those lineaments that made Borrow cry out as he came from among the Irish monks—his friends and entertainers for all his Spanish Bible-scattering—'O Ireland, mother of the bravest soldiers and of the most beautiful women!' It was, as I believe, to seek that old Ireland which took its mould from the duellists and scholars of the eighteenth century and from generations older still, that Synge returned again and again to Aran, to Kerry, and to the wild Blaskets.

VIII

'When I got up this morning,' he writes, after he had been a long time in Inishmaan, 'I found that the people had gone to Mass and latched the kitchen door from the outside, so that I could not open it to give myself light.

'I sat for nearly an hour beside the fire with a curious feeling that I should be quite alone in this little cottage. I am so used to sitting here with the people that I have never felt the room before as a place where any man might live and work by himself. After a while as I waited, with just light enough from the chimney to let me see the rafters and the greyness of the walls, I became indescribably mournful, for I felt that this little corner on the face of the world, and the people who live in it, have a peace and dignity from which we are shut for ever.'

324

J. M. Synge and the Ireland of his Time

This life, which he describes elsewhere as the most primitive left in Europe, satisfied some necessity of his nature. Before I met him in Paris he had wandered over much of Europe, listening to stories in the Black Forest, making friends with servants and with poor people, and this from an aesthetic interest, for he had gathered no statistics, had no money to give, and cared nothing for the wrongs of the poor, being content to pay for the pleasure of eye and ear with a tune upon the fiddle. He did not love them the better because they were poor and miserable, and it was only when he found Inishmaan and the Blaskets, where there is neither riches nor poverty, neither what he calls 'the nullity of the rich' nor 'the squalor of the poor,' that his writing lost its old morbid brooding, that he found his genius and his peace. Here were men and women who under the weight of their necessity lived, as the artist lives, in the presence of death and childhood, and the great affections and the orgiastic moment when life outleaps its limits, and who, as it is always with those who have refused or escaped the trivial and the temporary, had dignity and good manners where manners mattered. Here above all was silence from all our great orator took delight in, from formidable men, from moral indignation, from the 'sciolist' who 'is never sad,' from all in modern life that would destroy the arts; and here, to take a thought from another playwright of our school, he could love time as only women and great artists do and need never sell it.

The Cutting of an Agate

IX

As I read *The Aran Islands* right through for the first time since he showed it me in manuscript, I come to understand how much knowledge of the real life of Ireland went to the creation of a world which is yet as fantastic as the Spain of Cervantes. Here is the story of *The Playboy*, of *The Shadow of the Glen*; here is the ghost on horseback and the finding of the young man's body of *Riders to the Sea*, numberless ways of speech and vehement pictures that had seemed to owe nothing to observation, and all to some overflowing of himself, or to some mere necessity of dramatic construction. I had thought the violent quarrels of *The Well of the Saints* came from his love of bitter condiments, but here is a couple that quarrel all day long amid neighbours who gather as for a play. I had defended the burning of Christy Mahon's leg on the ground that an artist need but make his characters self-consistent, and yet that too was observation, for 'although these people are kindly towards each other and their children, they have no sympathy for the suffering of animals, and little sympathy for pain when the person who feels it is not in danger.' I had thought it was in the wantonness of fancy Martin Doul accused the smith of plucking his living ducks, but a few lines farther on, in this book where moral indignation is unknown, I read, 'Sometimes when I go into a cottage, I find all the women of the place down on their knees plucking the feathers from live ducks and geese.'

He loves all that has edge, all that is salt in the mouth,

all that is rough to the hand, all that heightens the emotions by contest, all that stings into life the sense of tragedy; and in this book, unlike the plays where nearness to his audience moves him to mischief, he shows it without thought of other taste than his. It is so constant, it is all set out so simply, so naturally, that it suggests a correspondence between a lasting mood of the soul and this life that shares the harshness of rocks and wind. The food of the spiritual-minded is sweet, an Indian scripture says, but passionate minds love bitter food. Yet he is no indifferent observer, but is certainly kind and sympathetic to all about him. When an old and ailing man, dreading the coming winter, cries at his leaving, not thinking to see him again, and he notices that the old man's mitten has a hole in it where the palm is accustomed to the stick, one knows that it is with eyes full of interested affection as befits a simple man and not in the curiosity of study. When he had left the Blaskets for the last time, he travelled with a lame pensioner who had drifted there, why Heaven knows, and one morning having missed him from the inn where they were staying, he believed he had gone back to the island, and searched everywhere and questioned everybody, till he understood of a sudden that he was jealous as though the island were a woman.

The book seems dull if you read much at a time, as the later Kerry essays do not, but nothing that he has written recalls so completely to my senses the man as he was in daily life; and as I read, there are moments when every line of his face, every inflection of his voice, grows so clear in memory that I cannot realise that he is dead. He was no nearer when we walked and talked than now while I read these unarranged, unspeculating pages, wherein the only life he loved with his whole heart reflects itself as in the still water of a pool. Thought comes to him slowly, and only after long seemingly un-meditative watching, and when it comes (and he had the same character in matters of business), it is spoken without hesitation and never changed. His conversa-tion was not an experimental thing, an instrument of research, and this made him silent; while his essays re-call events, on which one feels that he pronounces no judgment even in the depth of his own mind, because the labour of Life itself had not yet brought the philo-sophic generalisation which was almost as much his object as the emotional generalisation of beauty. A mind that generalises rapidly, continually prevents the ex-perience that would have made it feel and see deeply, just as a man whose character is too complete in youth seldom grows into any energy of moral beauty. Synge had indeed no obvious ideals, as these are understood by young men, and even, as I think, disliked them, for he once complained to me that our modern poetry was but the poetry 'of the lyrical boy,' and this lack makes his art have a strange wildness and coldness, as of a man born in some far-off spacious land and time.

x

There are artists like Byron, like Goethe, like Shelley, who have impressive personalities, active wills and all their faculties at the service of the will; but he belonged to those who, like Wordsworth, like Coleridge, like Goldsmith, like Keats, have little personality, so far as the casual eye can see, little personal will, but fiery and brooding imagination. I cannot imagine him anxious to impress or convince in any company, or saying more than was sufficient to keep the talk circling. Such men have the advantage that all they write is a part of knowledge, but they are powerless before events and have often but one visible strength, the strength to reject from life and thought all that would mar their work, or deafen them in the doing of it; and only this so long as it is a passive act. If Synge had married young or taken some profession, I doubt if he would have written books or been greatly interested in a movement like ours; but he refused various opportunities of making money in what must have been an almost unconscious preparation. He had no life outside his imagination, little interest in anything that was not its chosen subject. He hardly seemed aware of the existence of other writers. I never knew if he cared for work of mine, and do not remember that I had from him even a conventional compliment, and yet he had the most perfect modesty and simplicity in daily intercourse, self-assertion was impossible to him. On the other hand, he was useless amidst sudden events. He was much shaken by the *Playboy* riot; on the first night confused and excited, knowing not what to do, and ill before many days, but it made no difference in his work. He neither exaggerated out of defiance nor softened out of timidity. He wrote on as if nothing had happened, altering *The Tinker's Wedding* to a more unpopular form, but writing

329

a beautiful serene *Deirdre*, with, for the first time since his *Riders to the Sea*, no touch of sarcasm or defiance. Misfortune shook his physical nature while it left his intellect and his moral nature untroubled. The external self, the mask, the *persona*, was a shadow; character was all.

XI

He was a drifting silent man full of hidden passion, and loved wild islands, because there, set out in the light of day, he saw what lay hidden in himself. There is passage after passage in which he dwells upon some moment of excitement. He describes the shipping of pigs at Kilronan on the North Island for the English market:

'When the steamer was getting near, the whole drove was moved down upon the slip and the curraghs were carried out close to the sea. Then each beast was caught in its turn and thrown on its side, while its legs were hitched together in a single knot, with a tag of rope remaining, by which it could be carried.

'Probably the pain inflicted was not great, yet the animals shut their eyes and shrieked with almost human intonations, till the suggestion of the noise became so intense that the men and women who were merely looking on grew wild with excitement, and the pigs waiting their turn foamed at the mouth and tore each other with their teeth.

'After a while there was a pause. The whole slip was covered with a mass of sobbing animals, with here and there a terrified woman crouching among the bodies and patting some special favourite, to keep it quiet while the curraghs were being launched. Then the screaming began again while the pigs were carried out and laid in their places, with a waistcoat tied round their feet to keep them from damaging the canvas. They seemed to know where they were going, and looked up at me over the gunnel with an ignoble desperation that made me shudder to think that I had eaten this whimpering flesh. When the last curragh went out, I was left on the slip with a band of women and children, and one old boar who sat looking out over the sea.

'The women were over-excited, and when I tried to talk to them they crowded round me and began jeering and shrieking at me because I am not married. A dozen screamed at a time, and so rapidly that I could not understand all they were saying, yet I was able to make out that they were taking advantage of the absence of their husbands to give me the full volume of their contempt. Some little boys who were listening threw themselves down, writhing with laughter among the seaweed, and the young girls grew red and embarrassed and stared down in the surf.'

The book is full of such scenes. Now it is a crowd going by train to the Parnell celebration, now it is a woman cursing her son who made himself a spy for the police, now it is an old woman keening at a funeral. Kindred to his delight in the harsh grey stones, in the hardship of the life there, in the wind and in the mist, there is always delight in every moment of excitement, whether it is but the hysterical excitement of the women over the pigs, or some primary passion. Once, indeed, the hidden passion instead of finding expression by its choice among the passions of others shows itself in the most direct way of all, that of dream. 'Last night,' he writes, at Inishmaan, 'after walking in a dream among buildings with strangely intense light on them, I heard a faint rhythm of music beginning far away on some stringed instrument.

'It came closer to me, gradually increasing in quickness and volume with an irresistibly definite progression. When it was quite near the sound began to move in my nerves and blood, to urge me to dance with them.

'I knew that if I yielded I would be carried away into some moment of terrible agony, so I struggled to remain quiet, holding my knees together with my hands.

'The music increased continually, sounding like the strings of harps tuned to a forgotten scale, and having a resonance as searching as the strings of the 'cello.

'Then the luring excitement became more powerful than my will, and my limbs moved in spite of me.

'In a moment I swept away in a whirlwind of notes. My breath and my thoughts and every impulse of my body became a form of the dance, till I could not distinguish between the instrument or the rhythm and my own person or consciousness.

'For a while it seemed an excitement that was filled with joy; then it grew into an ecstasy where all existence was lost in the vortex of movement. I could not think that there had been a life beyond the whirling of the dance.

'Then with a shock, the ecstasy turned to agony and rage. I struggled to free myself but seemed only to increase the passion of the steps I moved to. When I shrieked I could only echo the notes of the rhythm.

'At last, with a movement of uncontrollable frenzy I broke back to consciousness and awoke.

'I dragged myself trembling to the window of the cottage and looked out. The moon was glittering across the bay and there was no sound anywhere on the island.'

XII

In all drama which would give direct expression to reverie, to the speech of the soul with itself, there is some device that checks the rapidity of dialogue. When Oedipus speaks out of the most vehement passions, he is conscious of the presence of the Chorus, men before whom he must keep up appearances, 'children latest born of Cadmus' line' who do not share his passion. Nobody is hurried or breathless. We listen to reports and discuss them, taking part as it were in a council of State. Nothing happens before our eyes. The dignity of Greek drama, and in a lesser degree of that of Corneille and Racine, depends, as contrasted with the troubled life of Shakespearian drama, on an almost even speed of dialogue, and on a so continuous exclusion of the animation of common life that thought remains lofty and language rich. Shakespeare, upon whose stage everything may happen, even the blinding of Gloucester, and who has no formal check except what is implied in the slow, elaborate structure of blank verse, obtains time for reverie by an often encumbering euphuism, and by such a loosening of his plot as will give his characters

the leisure to look at life from without. Maeterlinck—
to name the first modern of the old way who comes to
mind—reaches the same end, by choosing instead of
human beings persons who are as faint as a breath upon
a looking-glass, symbols who can speak a language
slow and heavy with dreams because their own life is
but a dream. Modern drama, on the other hand, which
accepts the tightness of the classic plot, while expressing
life directly, has been driven to make indirect its expression of the mind, which it leaves to be inferred from
some commonplace sentence or gesture as we infer it in
ordinary life; and this is, I believe, the cause of the
perpetual disappointment of the hope imagined this
hundred years that France or Spain or Germany or
Scandinavia would at last produce the master we await.

The divisions in the arts are almost all in the first
instance technical, and the great schools of drama have
been divided from one another by the form or the metal
of their mirror, by the check chosen for the rapidity of
dialogue. Synge found the check that suited his temperament in an elaboration of the dialects of Kerry and
Aran. The cadence is long and meditative, as befits the
thought of men who are much alone, and who when
they meet in one another's houses—as their way is at
the day's end—listen patiently, each man speaking in
turn and for some little time, and taking pleasure in the
vaguer meaning of the words and in their sound. Their
thought, when not merely practical, is as full of traditional wisdom and extravagant pictures as that of some
Aeschylean chorus, and no matter what the topic is, it
is as though the present were held at arm's length. It is

the reverse of rhetoric, for the speaker serves his own delight, though doubtless he would tell you that like Raftery's whiskey-drinking it was but for the company's sake. A medicinal manner of speech, too, for it could not even express, so little abstract it is and so rammed with life, those worn generalisations of National propaganda. 'I'll be telling you the finest story you'd hear any place from Dundalk to Ballinacree with great queens in it, making themselves matches from the start to the end, and they with shiny silks on them. . . . I've a grand story of the great queens of Ireland, with white necks on them the like of Sarah Casey, and fine arms would hit you a slap. . . . What good am I this night, God help me? What good are the grand stories I have when it's few would listen to an old woman, few but a girl maybe would be in great fear the time her hour was come, or little child wouldn't be sleeping with the hunger on a cold night?' That has the flavour of Homer, of the Bible, of Villon, while Cervantes would have thought it sweet in the mouth though not his food. This use of Irish dialect for noble purpose by Synge, and by Lady Gregory, who had it already in her *Cuchulain of Muirthemne*, and by Dr. Hyde in those first translations he has not equalled since, has done much for national dignity. When I was a boy I was often troubled and sorrowful because Scottish dialect was capable of noble use, but the Irish of obvious roystering humour only; and this error fixed on my imagination by so many novelists and rhymers made me listen badly. Synge wrote down words and phrases wherever he went, and with that knowledge of Irish which made all our country idioms easy to his hand, found it so rich a thing that he had begun translating into it fragments of the great literatures of the world, and had planned a complete version of *The Imitation of Christ*. It gave him imaginative richness and yet left to him the sting and tang of reality. How vivid in his translation from Villon are those 'eyes with a big gay look out of them would bring folly from a great scholar'! More vivid surely than anything in Swinburne's version, and how noble those words which are yet simple country speech, in which his Petrarch mourns that death came upon Laura just as time was making chastity easy, and the day come when 'lovers may sit together and say out all things are in their hearts,' and 'my sweet enemy was making a start, little by little, to give over her great wariness, the way she was wringing a sweet thing out of my sharp sorrow.'

XIII

I remember saying once to Synge that though it seemed to me that a conventional descriptive passage encumbered the action at the moment of crisis, I liked *The Shadow of the Glen* better than *Riders to the Sea*, that seemed for all the nobility of its end, its mood of Greek tragedy, too passive in suffering, and had quoted from Matthew Arnold's introduction to *Empedocles on Etna* to prove my point. Synge answered: 'It is a curious thing that *Riders to the Sea* succeeds with an English but not with an Irish audience, and *The Shadow of the Glen*, which is not liked by an English audience, is always liked in Ireland, though it is disliked there in theory.' Since then *Riders to the Sea* has grown into great popularity in Dublin, partly because, with the tactical instinct of an Irish mob, the demonstrators against *The Playboy* both in the Press and in the theatre, where it began the evening, selected it for applause. It is now what Shelley's *Cloud* was for many years, a comfort to those who do not like to deny altogether the genius they cannot understand. Yet I am certain that, in the long run, his grotesque plays with their lyric beauty, their violent laughter, *The Playboy of the Western World* most of all, will be loved for holding so much of the mind of Ireland. Synge has written of *The Playboy*: 'Any one who has lived in real intimacy with the Irish peasantry will know that the wildest sayings in this play are tame indeed compared with the fancies one may hear at any little hillside cottage of Geesala, or Carraroe, or Dingle Bay.' It is the strangest, the most beautiful expression in drama of that Irish fantasy which overflowing through all Irish literature that has come out of Ireland itself (compare the fantastic Irish account of the Battle of Clontarf with the sober Norse account) is the unbroken character of Irish genius. In modern days this genius has delighted in mischievous extravagance, like that of the Gaelic poet's curse upon his children: 'There are three things that I hate: the Devil that is waiting for my soul; the worms that are waiting for my body; my children, who are waiting for my wealth and care neither for my body nor my soul: O, Christ, hang all in the same noose!' I think those words were spoken with a delight in their vehemence that took out of anger half the bitterness with all the gloom. An old man on the Aran Islands told me the very tale on which *The Playboy* is founded, beginning with the words: 'If any gentleman has done a crime we'll hide him. There was a gentleman that killed his father, and I had him in my own house six months till he got away to America.' Despite the solemnity of his slow speech his eyes shone as the eyes must have shone in that Trinity College branch of the Gaelic League which began every meeting with prayers for the death of an old Fellow of College who disliked their movement, or as they certainly do when patriots are telling how short a time the prayers took to the killing of him. I have seen a crowd, when certain Dublin papers had wrought themselves into an imaginary loyalty, so possessed by what seemed the very genius of satiric fantasy that one all but looked to find some feathered heel among the cobble-stones. Part of the delight of crowd or individual is always that somebody will be angry, somebody take the sport for gloomy earnest. We are mocking at his solemnity, let us therefore so hide our malice that he may be more solemn still, and the laugh run higher yet. Why should we speak his language and so wake him from a dream of all those emotions which men feel because they should, and not because they must? Our minds, being sufficient to themselves, do not wish for victory but are content to elaborate our extravagance, if fortune aid, into wit or lyric beauty, and as for the rest, 'There are nights when a king like Conchobar would spit upon his arm-ring and queens will stick out their tongues at the rising moon.' This habit of the mind has made Oscar Wilde and Mr. Bernard Shaw the most celebrated makers of comedy to our time, and if it has sounded plainer still in the conversation of the one, and in some few speeches of the other, that is but because they have not been able to turn out of their plays an alien trick of zeal picked up in struggling youth. Yet, in Synge's plays also, fantasy gives the form and not the thought, for the core is always, as in all great art, an overpowering vision of certain virtues, and our capacity for sharing in that vision is the measure of our delight. Great art chills us at first by its coldness or its strangeness, by what seems capricious, and yet it is from these qualities it has authority, as though it had fed on locusts and wild honey. The imaginative writer shows us the world as a painter does his picture, reversed in a looking-glass, that we may see it, not as it seems to eyes habit has made dull, but as we were Adam and this the first morning; and when the new image becomes as little strange as the old we shall stay with him, because he has, besides the strangeness, not strange to him, that made us share his vision, sincerity that makes us share his feeling.

To speak of one's emotions without fear or moral ambition, to come out from under the shadow of other men's minds, to forget their needs, to be utterly oneself, that is all the Muses care for. Villon, pander, thief and man-slayer, is as immortal in their eyes, and illustrates in the cry of his ruin as great a truth, as Dante in abstract ecstasy, and touches our compassion more. All art is the disengaging of a soul from place and history, its suspension in a beautiful or terrible light to await the Judgment, though it must be, seeing that all its days were a Last Day, judged already. It may show the crimes of Italy as Dante did, or Greek mythology like Keats, or Kerry and Galway villages, and so vividly that ever after I shall look at all with like eyes, and yet I know that Cino da Pistoia thought Dante unjust, that Keats knew no Greek, that those country men and women are neither so lovable nor so lawless as 'mine author sung it me'; that I have added to my being, not my knowledge.

XIV

I wrote the most of these thoughts in my diary on the coast of Normandy, and as I finished came upon Mont-Saint-Michel, and thereupon doubted for a day the foundation of my school. Here I saw the places of assembly, those cloisters on the rock's summit, the church, the great halls where monks, or knights, or men-at-arms sat at meals, beautiful from ornament or proportion. I remembered ordinances of the Popes forbidding drinking-cups with stems of gold to these monks who had but a bare dormitory to sleep in. The individual, even in imagining, had taken more from his fellows and his fathers than he gave; one man finishing what another had begun; and all that majestic fantasy, seeming more of Egypt than of Christendom, spoke nothing to the solitary soul, but seemed to announce, whether past or yet to come, an heroic temper of social men, a bondage of adventure and of wisdom. Then I thought more patiently and I saw that what had made these but as one and given them for a thousand years the miracles of their shrine and temporal rule by land and sea, was not a condescension to knave or dolt, an impoverishment of the common thought to make it serviceable and easy, but a dead language and a communion in whatever, even to the greatest saint, is of incredible difficulty. Only by the substantiation of the soul, I thought, whether in literature or in sanctity, can we come upon those agreements, those separations from all else, that fasten men together lastingly; for while a popular and picturesque Burns and Scott can but create a province, and our Irish cries and grammars serve some passing need, Homer, Shakespeare, Dante, Goethe and all who travel in their road define races and create everlasting loyalties.

Synge, like all of the great kin, sought for the race, not through the eyes or in history, or even in the future, but where those monks found God, in the depths of the mind, and in all art like his, although it does not command—indeed because it does not—may lie the roots of far-branching events. Only that which does not teach, which does not cry out, which does not persuade, which does not condescend, which does not explain, is irresistible. It is made by men who expressed themselves to the full, and it works through the best minds; whereas the external and picturesque and declamatory writers, that they may create kilts and bagpipes and newspapers and guide-books, leave the best minds empty, and in Ireland and Scotland, England runs into the hole. It has no array of arguments and maxims, because the great and the simple (and the Muses have never known which of the two most pleases them) need their deliberate thought for the day's work, and yet will do it worse if they have not grown into or found about them, most perhaps in the minds of women, the nobleness of emotion associated with the scenery and events of their country by those great poets who have dreamed it in solitude, and who to this day in Europe are creating indestructible spiritual races, like those religion has created in the East.

September 14, 1910

John Shawe-Taylor

JOHN SHAWE-TAYLOR

THERE IS A PORTRAIT of John Shawe-Taylor by a celebrated painter in the Dublin Municipal Gallery, but, painted in the midst of a movement of the arts that exalts characteristics above the more typical qualities, it does not show us that beautiful and gracious nature. There is an exaggeration of the hollows of the cheeks and of the form of the bones which empties the face of the balance and delicacy of its lines. He was a very handsome man, as women who have imagination and tradition understand those words, and had he not been so, mind and character had been different. There are certain men, certain famous commanders of antiquity, for instance, of whose good looks the historian always speaks, and whose good looks are the image of their faculty; and these men, copying hawk or leopard, have an energy of swift decision, a power of sudden action, as if their whole body were their brain.

A few years ago he was returning from America, and the liner reached Queenstown in a storm so great that the tender that came out to it for passengers returned with only one man. It was John Shawe-Taylor, who had leaped as it was swept away from the ship.

The achievement that has made his name historic and changed the history of Ireland came from the same faculty of calculation and daring, from that instant decision of the hawk, between the movement of whose wings and the perception of whose eye no time passes capable of division. A proposal for a Land Conference

343

had been made, and cleverer men than he were but talking the life out of it. Every argument for and against had been debated over and over, and it was plain that nothing but argument would come of it. One day we found a letter in the daily papers, signed with his name, saying that a conference would be held on a certain date, and that certain leaders of the landlords and of the tenants were invited. He had made his swift calculation, probably he could not have told the reason for it: a decision had arisen out of his instinct. He was then almost an unknown man. Had the letter failed, he would have seemed a crack-brained fool to his life's end; but the calculation of his genius was justified. He had, as men of his type have often, given an expression to the hidden popular desires; and the expression of the hidden is the daring of the mind. When he had spoken, so many others spoke that the thing was taken out of the mouths of the leaders; it was as though some power deeper than our daily thought had spoken, and men recognised that common instinct, that common sense which is genius. Men like him live near this power because of something simple and impersonal within them which is, as I believe, imaged in the fire of their minds, as in the shape of their bodies and their faces.

I do not think I have known another man whose motives were so entirely pure, so entirely unmixed with any personal calculation, whether of ambition, of prudence or of vanity. He caught up into his imagination the public gain as other men their private gain. For much of his life he had seemed, though a good soldier and a good shot, and a good rider to hounds, to care

John Shawe-Taylor

deeply for nothing but religion, and this religion, so curiously lacking in denominational limits, concerned itself alone with the communion of the soul with God. Such men, before some great decision, will sometimes give to the analysis of their own motive the energy that other men give to the examination of the circumstances wherein they act, and it is often those who attain in this way to purity of motive who act most wisely at moments of great crisis. It is as though they sank a well through the soil where our habits have been built, and where our hopes take root or lie uprooted, to the lasting rock and to the living stream. They are those for whom Tennyson claimed the strength of ten, and the common and clever wonder at their simplicity and at a triumph that has always an air of miracle.

Some two years ago Ireland lost a great aesthetic genius, and it may be it should mourn, as it must mourn John Synge always, that which is gone from it in this young man's moral genius. And yet it may be that the sudden flash of his mind was of those things that come but seldom in a lifetime, and that his work is as fully accomplished as though he had lived through many laborious years.

July 1, 1911

345

The Cutting of an Agate

ART AND IDEAS

I

TWO DAYS AGO I was at the Tate Gallery to see the early Millais's, and before his *Ophelia*, as before the *Mary Magdalene* and *Mary of Galilee* of Rossetti that hung near, I recovered an old emotion. I saw these pictures as I had seen pictures in my childhood. I forgot the art criticism of friends and saw wonderful, sad, happy people, moving through the scenery of my dreams. The painting of the hair, the way it was smoothed from its central parting, something in the oval of the peaceful faces, called up memories of sketches of my father's on the margins of the first Shelley I had read, while the strong colours made me half remember studio conversations, words of Wilson, or of Potter perhaps, praise of the primary colours, heard, it may be, as I sat over my toys or a child's story-book. One picture looked familiar, and suddenly I remembered it had hung in our house for years. It was Potter's *Field Mouse*. I had learned to think in the midst of the last phase of Pre-Raphaelitism and now I had come to Pre-Raphaelitism again and rediscovered my earliest thought. I murmured to myself, 'The only painting of modern England that could give pleasure to a child, the only painting that would seem as moving as *The Pilgrim's Progress* or Hans Andersen.' 'Am I growing old,' I thought, 'like the woman in Balzac, the rich bourgeois' ambitious wife, who could not keep, when old age came upon her, from repeating the jokes of the concierge's lodge where she had been born and bred; or is it because of some change in the weather that I find beauty everywhere, even in Burne-Jones's *King Cophetua*, one of his later pictures, and find it without shame?' I have had like admiration many times in the last twenty years, for I have always loved those pictures where I meet persons associated with the poems or the religious ideas that have most moved me; but never since my boyhood have I had it without shame, without the certainty that I would hear the cock crow presently. I remembered that as a young man I had read in Schopenhauer that no man—so unworthy a thing is life seen with unbesotted eyes—would live another's life, and had thought I would be content to paint, like Burne-Jones and Morris under Rossetti's rule, the Union at Oxford, to set up there the traditional images most moving to young men while the adventure of uncommitted life can still change all to romance, even though I should know that what I painted must fade from the walls.

II

Thereon I ask myself if my conception of my own art is altering, if there, too, I praise what I once derided. When I began to write I avowed for my principles those of Arthur Hallam in his essay upon Tennyson. Tennyson, who had written but his early poems when Hallam wrote, was an example of the school of Keats and Shelley, and Keats and Shelley, unlike Wordsworth, intermixed into their poetry no elements from the general thought, but wrote out of the impression made by the world upon their delicate senses. They were of the aesthetic school—was he the inventor of the name?—and could not be popular because their readers could not understand them without attaining to a like delicacy of sensation and so must needs turn from them to Wordsworth or another, who condescended to moral maxims, or some received philosophy, a multitude of things that even common sense could understand. Wordsworth had not less genius than the others—even Hallam allowed his genius; we are not told that Mary of Galilee was more beautiful than the more popular Mary; but certainly we might consider Wordsworth a little disreputable.

I developed these principles to the rejection of all detailed description, that I might not steal the painter's business, and indeed I was always discovering some art or science that I might be rid of: and I found encouragement by noticing all round me painters[1] who were ridding their pictures, and indeed their minds, of literature. Yet those delighted senses, when I had got from them all that I could, left me discontented. Impressions that needed so elaborate a record did not seem like the handiwork of those careless old writers one imagines squabbling over a mistress, or riding on a journey, or drinking round a tavern fire, brisk and active men. Crashaw could hymn Saint Teresa in the most impersonal of ecstasies and seem no sedentary man out of reach of common sympathy, no dis-

---

[1] This thought, which seemed a discovery, was old enough. Balzac derides in a story a certain Pierre Grassou who attained an immense popularity by painting a Chouan rebel going to his death. 1924.

348

embodied mind, and yet in his day the life that appeared most rich and stirring was already half forgotten with Villon and Dante.

This difficulty was often in my mind, but I put it aside, for the new formula was a good switch while the roads were beset with geese; it set us free from politics, theology, science, all that zeal and eloquence Swinburne and Tennyson found so intoxicating after the passion of their youth had sunk, free from the conventional nobility borne hither from ancient Rome in the galley that carried academic form to vex the painters. Among the little group of poets that met at the Cheshire Cheese I alone loved criticism of Arthur Hallam's sort, with a shamefaced love—criticism founded upon general ideas was itself an impurity—and perhaps I alone knew Hallam's essay, but all silently obeyed a canon that had become powerful for all the arts since Whistler, in the confidence of his American *naïveté*, had told everybody that Japanese painting had no literary ideas. Yet all the while envious of the centuries before the Renaissance, before the coming of our intellectual class with its separate interests, I filled my imagination with the popular beliefs of Ireland, gathering them up among forgotten novelists in the British Museum or in Sligo cottages. I sought some symbolic language reaching far into the past and associated with familiar names and conspicuous hills that I might not be alone amid the obscure impressions of the senses, and I wrote essays recommending my friends to paint on chapel walls the Mother of God flying with Saint Joseph into Egypt along some Connacht road, a

Connemara shawl about her head, or mourned the richness or reality lost to Shelley's *Prometheus Unbound* because he had not discovered in England or in Ireland his Caucasus.

I notice like contradictions among my friends who are still convinced that art should not be 'complicated by ideas' while picturing Saint Brandan in stained glass for a Connemara chapel, and even among those exuberant young men who make designs for a Phallic Temple, but consider Augustus John lost amid literature.

III

But, after all, could we clear the matter up we might save some hours from sterile discussion. The arts are very conservative and have a great respect for those wanderers who still stitch into their carpets among the Mongolian plains religious symbols so old they have not even a meaning. It cannot be they would lessen an association with one another and with religion that gave them authority among ancient peoples. They are not radicals, and if they deny themselves to any it can only be to the *nouveau riche*, and if they have grown rebellious it can only be against something that is modern, something that is not simple.

I think that before the religious change that followed on the Renaissance men were greatly preoccupied with their sins, and that to-day they are troubled by other men's sins, and that this trouble has created a moral enthusiasm so full of illusion that art, knowing itself for sanctity's scapegrace brother, can-

not be of the party. We have but held to our ancient
Church, where there is an altar and no pulpit, and
founded, the guide-book tells us, upon the ruins of the
temple of Jupiter Ammon, and turned away from the
too great vigour of those who, living for mutual improvement, have a pulpit and no altar. We fear that a
novel enthusiasm might make us forget the little round
of poetical duties and imitations—humble genuflexions
and circumambulations as it were—that does not un-
seat the mind's natural impulse, and seems always but
half-conscious, almost bodily.

Painting had to free itself from a classicalism that
denied the senses, a domesticity that denied the passions, and poetry from a demagogic system of morals
which destroyed the humility, the daily dying of the
imagination in the presence of beauty. A soul shaken
by the spectacle of its sins, or discovered by the Divine
Vision in tragic delight, must offer to the love that
cannot love but to infinity, a goal unique and unshared;
while a soul busied with others' sins is soon melted to
some shape of vulgar pride. What can I offer to God
but the ghost that must return undisfeatured to the
hands that have not made the same thing twice, but
what would I have of others but that they do some
expected thing, reverence my plans, be in some way
demure and reliable? The turning of Rossetti to religious themes, his dislike of Wordsworth, were but the
one impulse, for he more than any other was in reaction against the period of philanthropy and reform
that created the pedantic composure of Wordsworth,
the rhetoric of Swinburne, the passionless sentiment of

Tennyson. The saint does not claim to be a good example, hardly even to tell men what to do, for is he not the chief of sinners, and of how little can he be certain whether in the night of the soul or lost in the sweetness coming after? Nor can that composure of the moralists be dear to one who has heard the commandment, that is for the saint and his brother the poet alike, 'Make excess ever more abundantly excessive', even were it possible to one shaken and trembling from his daily struggle.

IV

We knew that system of popular instruction was incompatible with our hopes, but we did not know how to refute it and so turned away from all ideas. We would not even permit ideas, so greatly had we come to distrust them, to leave their impressions upon our senses. Yet works of art are always begotten by previous works of art, and every masterpiece becomes the Abraham of a chosen people. When we delight in a spring day there mixes, perhaps, with our personal emotion an emotion Chaucer found in Guillaume de Lorris, who had it from the poetry of Provence; we celebrate our draughty May with an enthusiasm made ripe by more meridian suns; and all our art has its image in the Mass that would lack authority were it not descended from savage ceremonies taught amid what perils and by what spirits to naked savages. The old images, the old emotions, awakened again to overwhelming life, like the gods Heine tells of, by the belief and passion of some new soul, are the only master-

pieces. The resolution to stand alone, to owe nothing
to the past, when it is not mere sense of property, the
greed and pride of the counting-house, is the result of
that individualism of the Renaissance which had done
its work when it gave us personal freedom. The soul
which may not obscure or change its form can yet
receive those passions and symbols of antiquity, certain
they are too old to be bullies, too well-mannered not
to respect the rights of others.

Nor had we better warrant to separate one art from
another, for there has been no age before our own
wherein the arts have been other than a single authority,
a Holy Church of Romance, the might of all lying behind all, a circle of cliffs, a wilderness where every cry
has its echoes. Why should a man cease to be a scholar,
a believer, a ritualist before he begin to paint or rhyme
or to compose music, or why if he have a strong head
should he put away any means of power?

v

Yet it is plain that the casting out of ideas was the
more natural, misunderstanding though it was, because it had come to matter very little. The manner of
painting had changed, and we were interested in the
fall of drapery and the play of light without concerning
ourselves with the meaning, the emotion of the figure
itself. How many successful portrait-painters gave their
sitters the same attention, the same interest they might
have given to a ginger-beer bottle and an apple? and in
our poems an absorption in fragmentary sensuous

beauty or detachable ideas had deprived us of the power to mould vast material into a single image. What long modern poem equals the old poems in architectural unity, in symbolic importance? *The Revolt of Islam, The Excursion, Gebir, Idylls of the King,* even perhaps *The Ring and the Book,* which fills me with so much admiring astonishment that my judgment sleeps, are remembered for some occasional passage, some moment which gains little from the context. Until very lately even the short poems which contained as clearly as an Elizabethan lyric the impression of a single idea seemed accidental, so much the rule were the 'Faustines' and 'Dolores' where the verses might be arranged in any order, like shot poured out of a bag. Arnold when he withdrew his *Empedocles on Etna,* though one had been sorry to lose so much lyrical beauty for ever, showed himself a great critic by his reasons, but his *Sohrab and Rustum* proves that the unity he imagined was a classical imitation and not an organic thing, not the flow of flesh under the impulse of passionate thought.

Those poets with whom I feel myself in sympathy have tried to give to little poems the spontaneity of a gesture or of some casual emotional phrase. Meanwhile it remains for some greater time, living once more in passionate reverie, to create a *King Lear,* a *Divine Comedy,* vast worlds moulded by their own weight like drops of water.

In the visual arts, indeed, 'the fall of man into his own circumference' seems at an end, and when I look at the photograph of a picture by Gauguin, which hangs over my breakfast-table, the spectacle of tranquil Polynesian girls crowned with lilies gives me, I do not know why, religious ideas. Our appreciations of the older schools are changing too, becoming simpler, and when we take pleasure in some Chinese painting of an old man meditating upon a mountain path, we share his meditation, without forgetting the beautiful intricate pattern of the lines like those we have seen under our eyelids as we fell asleep; nor do the Bride and Bridegroom of Rajput painting, sleeping upon a house-top, or wakening when out of the still water the swans fly upward at the dawn, seem the less well painted because they remind us of many poems. We are becoming interested in expression in its first phase of energy, when all the arts play like children about the one chimney, and turbulent innocence can yet amuse those brisk and active men who have paid us so little attention of recent years. Shall we be rid of the pride of intellect, of sedentary meditation, of emotion that leaves us when the book is closed or the picture seen no more; and live amid the thoughts that can go with us by steamboat and railway as once upon horseback, or camel-back, rediscovering, by our reintegration of the mind, our more profound Pre-Raphaelitism, the old abounding, nonchalant reverie?

1913

The Cutting of an Agate

EDMUND SPENSER

I

WE KNOW LITTLE of Spenser's childhood and nothing of his parents, except that his father was
probably an Edmund Spenser of north-east Lancashire,
a man of good blood and belonging to 'a house of
ancient fame.' He was born in London in 1552, nineteen
years after the death of Ariosto, and when Tasso was
about eight years old. Full of the spirit of the Renaissance, at once passionate and artificial, looking out upon
the world now as craftsman, now as connoisseur, he
was to found his art upon theirs rather than upon the
more humane, the more noble, the less intellectual art
of Malory and the Minstrels. Deafened and blinded by
their influence, as so many of us were in boyhood by
that art of Hugo that made the old simple writers seem
but as brown bread and water, he was always to love
the journey more than its end, the landscape more than
the man, and reason more than life, and the tale less
than its telling. He entered Pembroke College, Cambridge, in 1569, and translated allegorical poems out of
Petrarch and Du Bellay. To-day a young man trans-
lates out of Verlaine and Verhaeren; but at that day
Ronsard and Du Bellay were the living poets, who
promised revolutionary and unheard-of things to a
poetry moving towards elaboration and intellect,
as ours—the serpent's tooth in his own tail again—
moves towards simplicity and instinct. At Cambridge
he met with Hobbinol of *The Shepheards Calender*,
a certain Gabriel Harvey, son of a rope-maker at

356

Edmund Spenser

Saffron Walden, but now a Fellow of Pembroke College, a notable man, some five or six years his elder. It is usual to think ill of Harvey because of his dislike of rhyme and his advocacy of classical metres, and because he complained that Spenser preferred his Faery Queen to the Nine Muses, and encouraged Hobgoblin to 'run off with the garland from Apollo.' But at that crossroad, where so many crowds mingled talking of so many lands, no one could foretell in what bed he would sleep after nightfall. Milton was in the end to dislike rhyme as much, and it is certain that rhyme is one of the secondary causes of that disintegration of the personal instincts which has given to modern poetry its deep colour for colour's sake, its overflowing pattern, its background of decorative landscape, and its insubordination of detail. At the opening of a movement we are busy with first principles, and can find out everything but the road we are to go, everything but the weight and measure of the impulse that has come to us out of life itself, for that is always in defiance of reason, always without a justification but by faith and works. Harvey set Spenser to the making of verses in classical metre, and certain lines have come down to us written in what Spenser called 'Iambicum trimetrum.' His biographers agree that they are very bad, but, though I cannot scan them,[1] I find in them the charm of what seems a sincere personal emotion. The man himself, liberated from the minute felicities of phrase and sound that are the temptation and the delight of rhyme, speaks of his mistress

[1] I could not scan them because I accentuated them unconsciously. Spoken without accent they are musical. 1924.

some thought that came to him not for the sake of poetry, but for love's sake, and the emotion instead of dissolving into detached colours, into 'the spangly gloom' that Keats saw 'froth and boil' when he put his eyes into 'the pillowy cleft,' speaks to her in poignant words as if out of a tear-stained love-letter:—

Unhappie verse, the witnesse of my unhappie state,
Make thy selfe fluttring winge for thy fast flying
Thought, and fly forth unto my love wheresoever she be.
Whether lying restlesse in heavy bedde, or else
Sitting so cheerlesse at the cheerful boorde, or else
Playing alone carelesse on her heavenlie virginals.
If in bed, tell her that my eyes can take no rest;
If at boorde, tell her that my mouth can eat no meate;
If at her virginals, tell her I can heare no mirth.

II

He left Cambridge in his twenty-fourth year, and stayed for a while in Lancashire, where he had relations, and there fell in love with one he has written of in *The Shepheards Calender* as 'Rosalind, the widdowes daughter of the Glenn,' though she was, for all her shepherding, as one learns from a College friend, 'a gentle-woman of no mean house.' She married Menalcas of the *Calender* and Spenser lamented her for years, in verses so full of disguise that one cannot say if his lamentations come out of a broken heart or are but a useful movement in the elaborate ritual of his poetry, a well-ordered incident in the mythology of his imagination. To no English poet, perhaps to no European poet before his day, had the natural expression of personal feeling been so impossible, the clear vision of the lineaments of human character so difficult; no other's head and eyes had sunk so far into 'the pillowy cleft.' After a year of this life he went to London, and by Harvey's advice and introduction entered the service of the Earl of Leicester, staying for a while in his house on the banks of the Thames; and it was there in all likelihood that he met with the Earl's nephew, Sir Philip Sidney, still little more than a boy, but with his head full of affairs of State. One can imagine that it was the great Earl or Sir Philip Sidney that gave his imagination its moral and practical turn, and one imagines him seeking from philosophical men, who distrust instinct because it disturbs contemplation, and from practical men, who distrust everything they cannot use in the routine of immediate events, that impulse and method of creation that can only be learned with surety from the technical criticism of poets, and from the excitement of some movement in the artistic life. Marlowe and Shakespeare were still at school, and Ben Jonson was but five years old. Sidney was doubtless the greatest personal influence that came into Spenser's life, and it was one that exalted moral zeal above every faculty. The great Earl impressed his imagination very deeply also, for the lamentation over the Earl of Leicester's death is more than a conventional Ode to a dead patron. Spenser's verses about men, nearly always indeed, seem to express more of personal joy and sorrow than those about women, perhaps because he was less deliberately a poet when he spoke of men. At the end of a long beautiful passage he laments that unworthy men should be in the dead Earl's place, and compares them to the fox—an unclean feeder—hiding in the lair 'the badger swept.' The imaginer of the festivals of Kenilworth was indeed the fit patron for him, and alike because of the strength and weakness of Spenser's art, one regrets that he could not have lived always in that elaborate life, a master of ceremony to the world, instead of being plunged into a life that but stirred him to bitterness, as the way is with theoretical minds in the tumults of events they cannot understand. In the winter of 1579–1580 he published *The Shepheards Calender*, a book of twelve eclogues, one for every month of the year, and dedicated it to Sir Philip Sidney. It was full of pastoral beauty and allegorical images of current events, revealing, too, that conflict between the aesthetic and moral interests that was to run through wellnigh all his works, and it became immediately famous. He was rewarded with a place as private secretary to the Lord-Lieutenant, Lord Grey de Wilton, and sent to Ireland, where he spent nearly all the rest of his life. After a few years there he bought Kilcolman Castle, which had belonged to the rebel Earl of Desmond, and the rivers and hills about this castle came much into his poetry. Our Irish Aubeg is 'Mulla mine, whose waves I taught to weep,' and the Ballyvaughan Hills it has its rise among, 'old Father Mole.' He never pictured the true countenance of Irish scenery, for his mind turned constantly to the Court of Elizabeth and to the umbrageous level lands, where his own race was already seeding like a great poppy:—

> Both heaven and heavenly graces do much more
> (Quoth he) abound in that same land then this:
> For there all happie peace and plenteous store

Conspire in one to make contented blisse.
No wayling there nor wretchednesse is heard,
No bloodie issues nor no leprosies,
No griesly famine, nor no raging sweard,
No nightly bordrags, nor no hue and cries;
The shepheards there abroad may safely lie
On hills and downes, withouten dread or daunger:
No ravenous wolves the good mans hope destroy,
Nor outlawes fell affray the forest raunger.
There learned arts do florish in great honor,
And Poets wits are had in peerlesse price.

Nor did he ever understand the people he lived among or the historical events that were changing all things about him. Lord Grey de Wilton had been recalled almost immediately, but it was his policy, brought over ready-made in his ship, that Spenser advocated throughout all his life, equally in his long prose book *The Present State of Ireland* as in the *Faerie Queene*, where Lord Grey was Artegall and the Iron Man the soldiers and executioners by whose hands he worked. Like an hysterical patient he drew a complicated web of inhuman logic out of the bowels of an insufficient premise— there was no right, no law, but that of Elizabeth, and all that opposed her opposed themselves to God, to civilisation, and to all inherited wisdom and courtesy, and should be put to death. He made two visits to England, celebrating one of them in *Colin Clouts come Home againe*, to publish the first three books and the second three books of the *Faerie Queene* respectively, and to try for some English office or pension. By the help of Raleigh, now his neighbour at Kilcolman, he had been promised a pension, but was kept out of it by Lord Burleigh, who

said, 'All that for a song!' From that day Lord Burleigh
became that 'rugged forehead' of the poems, whose cen-
sure of this or that is complained of. During the last
three or four years of his life in Ireland he married a
fair woman of his neighbourhood, and about her wrote
many intolerably artificial sonnets and that most beautiful passage in the Sixth Book of the *Faerie Queene*, which
tells of Colin Clout piping to the Graces and to her;
and he celebrated his marriage in the most beautiful of
all his poems, the *Epithalamion*. His genius was pic-
torial, and these pictures of happiness were more natural to it than any personal pride, or joy, or sorrow. His
new happiness was very brief, and just as he was rising
to something of Milton's grandeur in the fragment that
has been called *Mutabilitie*, 'the wandering companies
that keep the wood,' as he called the Irish armies, drove
him to his death. Ireland, where he saw nothing but work
for the Iron Man, was in the midst of the last struggle
of the old Celtic order with England, itself about
to turn bottom upward, of the passion of the Middle
Ages with the craft of the Renaissance. Seven years
after Spenser's arrival in Ireland a large merchant ship
had carried off from Lough Swilly, by a very crafty device common in those days, certain persons of importance. Red Hugh, a boy of fifteen, and the coming head
of Tir Conaill, and various heads of clans had been en-
ticed on board the merchant ship to drink of a fine vint-
age, and there made prisoners. All but Red Hugh were
released, on finding substitutes among the boys of their
kindred, and the captives were hurried to Dublin and
imprisoned in the Birmingham Tower. After four years

of captivity and one attempt that failed, Red Hugh and certain of his companions escaped into the Dublin mountains, one dying there of cold and privation, and from that to their own countryside. Red Hugh allied himself to Hugh O'Neill, the most powerful of the Irish leaders, an Oxford man too, a man of the Renaissance, in Camden's words 'a profound dissembling heart so as many deemed him born either for the great good or ill of his country,' and for a few years defeated English armies and shook the power of England. The Irish, stirred by these events, and with, it may be, some rumours of *The Present State of Ireland* sticking in their stomachs, drove Spenser out of doors and burnt his house, one of his children, as tradition has it, dying in the fire. He fled to England, and died some three months later in January 1599, as Ben Jonson says, 'for lack of bread.'

During the last four or five years of his life he had seen, without knowing that he saw it, the beginning of the great Elizabethan poetical movement. In 1598 he had pictured the Nine Muses lamenting each one over the evil state in England of the things that she had in charge, but, like William Blake's more beautiful *Whether on Ida's shady brow*, their lamentations should have been a cradle-song. When he died *Romeo and Juliet*, *Richard III*, and *Richard II*, and the plays of Marlowe had all been acted, and in stately houses were sung madrigals and love-songs whose like has not been in the world since. Italian influence had strengthened the old French joy that had never died out among the upper classes, and an art was being created for the last time in England which had half its beauty from continually suggesting a life hardly less beautiful than itself.

III

When Spenser was buried in Westminster Abbey many poets read verses in his praise, and then threw their verses and the pens that had written them into his tomb. Like him they belonged, for all the moral zeal that was gathering like a London fog, to that indolent, demonstrative Merry England that was about to pass away. Men still wept when they were moved, still dressed themselves in joyous colours, and spoke with many gestures. Thoughts and qualities sometimes come to their perfect expression when they are about to pass away, and Merry England was dying in plays, and in poems, and in strange adventurous men. If one of those poets who threw his copy of verses into the earth that was about to close over his master were to come alive again, he would find some shadow of the life he knew, though not the art he knew, among young men in Paris, and would think that his true country. If he came to England he would find nothing there but the triumph of the Puritan and the merchant—those enemies he had feared and hated—and he would weep perhaps, in that womanish way of his, to think that so much greatness had been, not, as he had hoped, the dawn, but the sunset of a people. He had lived in the last days of what we may call the Anglo-French nation, the old feudal nation that had been established when the Norman and the Angevin made French the language of court and market. In the time of Chaucer English poets still wrote much in French, and even English labourers lilted French songs over their work; and I cannot read any Elizabethan poem or romance without feeling the pressure of habits of emotion, and of an order of life, which were conscious, for all their Latin gaiety, of a quarrel to the death with that new Anglo-Saxon nation that was arising amid Puritan sermons and Marprelate pamphlets. This nation had driven out the language of its conquerors, and now it was to overthrow their beautiful haughty imagination and their manners, full of abandon and wilfulness, and to set in their stead earnestness and logic and the timidity and reserve of a counting-house. It had been coming for a long while, for it had made the Lollards; and when Anglo-French Chaucer was at Westminster, its poet, Langland, sang the office at Saint Paul's. Shakespeare, with his delight in great persons, with his indifference to the State, with his scorn of the crowd, with his feudal passion, was of the old nation, and Spenser, though a joyless earnestness had cast shadows upon him, and darkened his intellect wholly at times, was of the old nation too. His *Faerie Queene* was written in Merry England, but when Bunyan wrote in prison the other great English allegory, Modern England had been born. Bunyan's men would do right that they might come some day to the Delectable Mountains, and not at all that they might live happily in a world whose beauty was but an entanglement about their feet. Religion had denied the sacredness of an earth that commerce was about to corrupt and ravish, but when Spenser lived the earth had still its sheltering sacredness.

The Cutting of an Agate

His religion, where the paganism that is natural to proud and happy people had been strengthened by the Platonism of the Renaissance, cherished the beauty of the soul and the beauty of the body with, as it seemed, an equal affection. He would have had men live well, not merely that they might win eternal happiness, but that they might live splendidly among men and be celebrated in many songs. How could one live well if one had not the joy of the Creator and of the Giver of gifts? He says in his *Hymne in Honour of Beautie* that a beautiful soul, unless for some stubbornness in the ground, makes for itself a beautiful body, and he even denies that beautiful persons ever lived who had not souls as beautiful. They may have been tempted until they seemed evil, but that was the fault of others. And in his *Hymne of Heavenly Beautie* he sets a woman little known to theology, one that he names Wisdom or Beauty, above Seraphim and Cherubim and in the very bosom of God, and in the *Faerie Queene* it is pagan Venus and her lover Adonis who create the forms of all living things and send them out into the world, calling them back again to the gardens of Adonis at their lives' end to rest there, as it seems, two thousand years between life and life. He began in English poetry, despite a temperament that delighted in sensuous beauty alone with perfect delight, that worship of Intellectual Beauty which Shelley carried to a greater subtlety and applied to the whole of life.

The qualities, to each of whom he had planned to give a Knight, he had borrowed from Aristotle and partly Christianised, but not to the forgetting of their

366

heathen birth. The chief of the Knights, who would have combined in himself the qualities of all the others, had Spenser lived to finish the *Faerie Queene*, was King Arthur, the representative of an ancient quality, Magnificence. Born at the moment of change, Spenser had indeed many Puritan thoughts. It has been recorded that he cut his hair short and half regretted his hymns to Love and Beauty. But he has himself told us that the many-headed beast overthrown and bound by Calidore, Knight of Courtesy, was Puritanism itself. Puritanism, its zeal and its narrowness, and the angry suspicion that it had in common with all movements of the ill-educated, seemed no other to him than a slanderer of all fine things. One doubts, indeed, if he could have persuaded himself that there could be any virtue at all without courtesy, perhaps without something of pageant and eloquence. He was, I think, by nature altogether a man of that old Catholic feudal nation, but, like Sidney, he wanted to justify himself to his new masters. He wrote of knights and ladies, wild creatures imagined by the aristocratic poets of the twelfth century, and perhaps chiefly by English poets who had still the French tongue; but he fastened them with allegorical nails to a big barn-door of common sense, of merely practical virtue. Allegory itself had risen into general importance with the rise of the merchant class in the thirteenth and fourteenth centuries; and it was natural when that class was about for the first time to shape an age in its image, that the last epic poet of the old order should mix its art with his own long-descended, irresponsible, happy art.

IV

Allegory and, to a much greater degree, symbolism are a natural language by which the soul when entranced, or even in ordinary sleep, communes with God and with angels. They can speak of things which cannot be spoken of in any other language, but one will always, I think, feel some sense of unreality when they are used to describe things which can be described as well in ordinary words. Dante used allegory to describe visionary things, and the first maker of *The Romance of the Rose*, for all his lighter spirits, pretends that his adventures came to him in a vision one May morning; while Bunyan, by his preoccupation with Heaven and the soul, gives his simple story a visionary strangeness and intensity: he believes so little in the world that he takes us away from all ordinary standards of probability and makes us believe even in allegory for a while. Spenser, on the other hand, to whom allegory was not, as I think, natural at all, makes us feel again and again that it disappoints and interrupts our preoccupation with the beautiful and sensuous life he has called up before our eyes. It interrupts us most when he copies Langland, and writes in what he believes to be a mood of edification, and the least when he is not quite serious, when he sets before us some procession like a Court pageant made to celebrate a wedding or a crowning. One cannot think that he should have occupied himself with moral and religious questions at all. He should have been content to be, as Emerson thought Shakespeare was, a Master of the Revels to mankind.

Edmund Spenser

I am certain that he never gets that visionary air which can alone make allegory real, except when he writes out of a feeling for glory and passion. He had no deep moral or religious life. He has never a line like Dante's 'His Will is our Peace,' or like Thomas à Kempis's 'The Holy Spirit has liberated me from a multitude of opinions,' or even like Hamlet's objection to the bare bodkin. He had been made a poet by what he had almost learnt to call his sins. If he had not felt it necessary to justify his art to some serious friend, or perhaps even to 'that rugged forehead,' he would have written all his life long, one thinks, of the loves of shepherdesses and shepherds, among whom there would have been perhaps the morals of the dovecot. One is persuaded that his morality is official and impersonal—a system of life which it was his duty to support—and it is perhaps a half understanding of this that has made so many generations believe that he was the first Poet Laureate, the first salaried moralist among the poets. His processions of deadly sins, and his houses, where the very cornices are arbitrary images of virtue, are an unconscious hypocrisy, an undelighted obedience to the 'rugged forehead,' for all the while he is thinking of nothing but lovers whose bodies are quivering with the memory or the hope of long embraces. When they are not together, he will indeed embroider emblems and images much as those great ladies of the courts of love embroidered them in their castles; and when these are imagined out of a thirst for magnificence and not thought out in a mood of edification, they are beautiful enough; but they are always tapestries for corridors that lead to lovers' meetings or for the walls of marriage chambers. He was not passionate, for the passionate feed their flame in wanderings and absences, when the whole being of the beloved, every little charm of body and of soul, is always present to the mind, filling it with heroical subtleties of desire. He is a poet of the delighted senses, and his song becomes most beautiful when he writes of those islands of Phaedria and Acrasia, which angered 'that rugged forehead,' as it seems, but gave to Keats his *Belle Dame sans merci* and his 'perilous seas in faery lands forlorn,' and to William Morris his 'Water of the Wondrous Isles.'

v

The dramatists lived in a disorderly world, reproached by many, persecuted even, but following their imagination wherever it led them. Their imagination, driven hither and thither by beauty and sympathy, put on something of the nature of eternity. Their subject was always the soul, the whimsical, self-awakening, self-exciting, self-appeasing soul. They celebrated its heroical, passionate will going by its own path to immortal and invisible things. Spenser, on the other hand, except among those smooth pastoral scenes and lovely effeminate islands that have made him a great poet, tried to be of his time, or rather of the time that was all but at hand. Like Sidney, whose charm, it may be, led many into slavery, he persuaded himself that we enjoy Virgil because of the virtues of Aeneas, and so planned out his immense poem that it would set before the imagination of citizens, in whom there would soon be no great energy, innumerable blameless Aeneases. He had learned to put the State, which desires all the abundance for itself, in the place of the Church, and he found it possible to be moved by expedient emotions, merely because they were expedient, and to think serviceable thoughts with no self-contempt. He loved his Queen a little because she was the protectress of poets and an image of that old Anglo-French nation that lay a-dying, but a great deal because she was the image of the State which had taken possession of his conscience. She was over sixty years old, ugly and, historians will have it, selfish, but in his poetry she is 'fair Cynthia,' 'a crown of lilies,' 'the image of the heavens,' 'without mortal blemish', and has 'an angelic face,' where 'the red rose' has 'meddled with the white'; 'Phoebus thrusts out his golden head' but to look upon her, and blushes to find himself outshone. She is 'a fourth Grace,' 'a queen of love,' 'a sacred saint,' and 'above all her sex that ever yet has been.' In the midst of his praise of his own sweetheart he stops to re-member that Elizabeth is more beautiful, and an old man in *Daphnaïda*, although he has been brought to death's door by the death of a beautiful daughter, re-members that though his daughter 'seemed of angels' race,' she was yet but the primrose to the rose beside Elizabeth. Spenser had learned to look to the State not only as the rewarder of virtue but as the maker of right and wrong, and had begun to love and hate as it bid him. The thoughts that we find for ourselves are timid and a little secret, but those modern thoughts that we

share with large numbers are confident and very in-
solent. We have little else to-day, and when we read
our newspaper and take up its cry, above all, its cry of
hatred, we will not think very carefully, for we hear
the marching feet. When Spenser wrote of Ireland he
wrote as an official, and out of thoughts and emotions
that had been organised by the State. He was the first
of many Englishmen to see nothing but what he was
desired to see. Could he have gone there as a poet
merely, he might have found among its poets more
wonderful imaginations than even those islands of
Phaedria and Acrasia. He would have found among
wandering story-tellers, not indeed his own power of
rich, sustained description, for that belongs to lettered
ease, but certainly all the kingdom of Faery, still unfaded, of which his own poetry was often but a troubled
image. He would have found men doing by swift
strokes of the imagination much that he was doing with
painful intellect, with that imaginative reason that soon
was to drive out imagination altogether and for a long
time. He would have met with, at his own door, story-
tellers among whom the perfection of Greek art was
indeed as unknown as his own power of sustained
description, but who, none the less, imagined or remembered beautiful incidents and strange, pathetic out-
crying that made them of Homer's lineage. Flaubert
says somewhere: 'There are things in Hugo, as in
Rabelais, that I could have mended, things badly built,
but then what thrusts of power beyond the reach of
conscious art!' Is not all history but the coming of that
conscious art which first makes articulate and then

Edmund Spenser

destroys the old wild energy? Spenser, the first poet struck with remorse, the first poet who gave his heart to the State, saw nothing but disorder, where the mouths that have spoken all the fables of the poets had not yet become silent. All about him were shepherds and shepherdesses still living the life that made Theocritus and Virgil think of shepherd and poet as the one thing; but though he dreamed of Virgil's shepherds he wrote a book to advise, among many like things, the harrying of all that followed flocks upon the hills, and of all the 'wandering companies that keep the wood.' His *View of the Present State of Ireland* commends indeed the beauty of the hills and woods where they did their shepherding, in that powerful and subtle language of his which I sometimes think more full of youthful energy than even the language of the great playwrights. He is 'sure it is yet a most beautiful and sweet country as any is under heaven,' and that all would prosper but for those agitators, those 'wandering companies that keep the wood,' and he would rid it of them by a certain expeditious way. There should be four great garrisons. 'And those fowre garrisons issuing foorthe, at such convenient times as they shall have intelligence or espiall upon the enemye, will so drive him from one side to another, and tennis him amongst them, that he shall finde nowhere safe to keepe his creete, or hide himselfe, but flying from the fire shall fall into the water, and out of one daunger into another, that in short space his creete, which is his moste sustenaunce, shall be wasted in preying, or killed in driving, or starved for wante of pasture in the woodes, and he himselfe brought soe lowe, that he shall have no harte nor abilitye to indure his wretchednesse, the which will surely come to passe in very short space; for one winters well following of him will soe plucke him on his knees that he will never be able to stand up agayne.'

He could commend this expeditious way from personal knowledge, and could assure the Queen that the people of the country would soon 'consume themselves and devoure one another. The proofs whereof I saw sufficiently ensampled in these late warres in Mounster; for notwithstanding that the same was a most rich and plentifull countrey, full of corne and cattell, that you would have thought they would have bene able to stand long, yet ere one yeare and a halfe they were brought to such wretchednesse, as that any stonye harte would have rued the same. Out of every corner of the woodes and glynnes they came creeping forth upon theyr hands, for theyr legges could not beare them; they looked like anatomyes of death, they spake like ghostes crying out of theyr graves; they did eate of the dead carrions, happy were they if they could finde them, yea, and one another soone after, insoemuch as the very carcasses they spared not to scrape out of theyr graves; and if they found a plot of watercresses or shamrokes, there they flocked as to a feast for the time, yet not able long to continue therewithall; that in short space there were none allmost left, and a most populous and plentifull countrey suddaynely made voyde of man or beast; yet sure in all that warre, there perished not many by the sword, but all by the extremitye of famine.'

Edmund Spenser

VI

In a few years the Four Masters were to write the history of that time, and they were to record the goodness or the badness of Irishman and Englishman with entire impartiality. They had seen friends and relatives persecuted, but they would write of that man's poisoning and this man's charities and of the fall of great houses, and hardly with any other emotion than a thought of the pitiableness of all life. Friend and enemy would be for them a part of the spectacle of the world. They remembered indeed those Anglo-French invaders who conquered for the sake of their own strong hand, and when they had conquered became a part of the life about them, singing its songs, when they grew weary of their own Iseult and Guinevere. But famines and exterminations had not made them understand, as I think, that new invaders were among them, who fought for an alien State, for an alien religion. Such ideas were difficult to them, for they belonged to the old individual, poetical life, and spoke a language even in which it was all but impossible to think an abstract thought. They understood Spain, possibly, which persecuted in the interests of religion, but I doubt if anybody in Ireland could have understood as yet that the Anglo-Saxon nation was beginning to persecute in the service of ideas it believed to be the foundation of the State. I doubt if anybody in Ireland saw that with certainty, till the Great Demagogue had come and turned the old house of the noble into 'the house of the Poor, the lonely house, the accursed house

375

of Cromwell.' He came, another Cairbry Cat-Head, with that great rabble who had overthrown the pageantry of Church and Court, but who turned towards him faces full of the sadness and docility of their long servitude, and the old individual, poetical life went down, as it seems, for ever. He had studied Spenser's book and approved of it, as we know, finding, doubtless, his own head there, for Spenser, a king of the old race, carried a mirror which showed kings yet to come though but kings of the mob. Those Bohemian poets of the theatres were wiser, for the States that touched them nearly were the States where Helen and Dido had sorrowed, and so their mirrors showed none but beautiful heroical heads. They wandered in the places that pale passion loves, and were happy, as one thinks, and troubled little about those marching and hoarse-throated thoughts that the State has in its pay. They knew that those marchers, with the dust of so many roads upon them, are very robust and have great and well-paid generals to write expedient despatches in sound prose; and they could hear Mother Earth singing among her cornfields:—

> Weep not, my wanton! smile upon my knee;
> When thou art old there's grief enough for thee.

VII

There are moments when one can read neither Milton nor Spenser, moments when one recollects nothing but that their flesh had partly been changed to stone, but there are other moments when one recollects nothing but those habits of emotion that made the lesser poet especially a man of an older, more imaginative time. One remembers that he delighted in smooth pastoral places, because men could be busy there or gather together there, after their work, that he could love handiwork and the hum of voices. One remembers that he could still rejoice in the trees, not because they were images of loneliness and meditation, but because of their serviceableness. He could praise 'the builder oake,' 'the aspine, good for staves,' 'the cypresse funerall,' 'the eugh, obedient to the bender's will,' 'the birch for shaftes,' 'the sallow for the mill,' 'the mirrhe sweete bleeding in the bitter wound,' 'the fruitful olive,' and 'the carver holme.' He was of a time before undelighted labour had made the business of men a desecration. He carries one's memory back to Virgil's and Chaucer's praise of trees, and to the sweet-sounding song made by the old Irish poet in their praise.

I got up from reading the *Faerie Queene* the other day and wandered into another room. It was in a friend's house, and I came of a sudden to the ancient poetry and to our poetry side by side—an engraving of Claude's *Mill* hung under an engraving of Turner's *Temple of Jupiter*. Those dancing countrypeople, those cowherds, resting after the day's work, and that quiet mill-race made one think of Merry England with its glad Latin heart, of a time when men in every land found poetry and imagination in one another's company and in the day's labour. Those stately goddesses, moving in slow procession towards that marble architrave among mysterious trees, belong to Shelley's thought, and to the religion of the wilderness—the only religion possible to poetry to-day. Certainly Colin Clout, the companionable shepherd, and Calidore, the courtly man-at-arms, are gone, and Alastor is wandering from lonely river to river finding happiness in nothing but in that Star where Spenser too had imagined the fountain of perfect things. This new beauty, in losing so much, has indeed found a new loftiness, a something of religious exaltation that the old had not. It may be that those goddesses, moving with a majesty like a procession of the stars, mean something to the soul of man that those kindly women of the old poets did not mean, for all the fullness of their breasts and the joyous gravity of their eyes. Has not the wilderness been at all times a place of prophecy?

VIII

Our poetry, though it has been a deliberate bringing back of the Latin joy and the Latin love of beauty, has had to put off the old marching rhythms, that once could give delight to more than expedient hearts, in separating itself from a life where servile hands have become powerful. It has ceased to have any burden for marching shoulders, since it learned ecstasy from Smart in his mad cell, and from Blake, who made joyous little songs out of almost unintelligible visions, and from Keats, who sang of a beauty so wholly preoccupied with itself that its contemplation is a kind of lingering trance. The poet, if he would not carry burdens that are not his and obey the orders of servile lips, must sit apart in contemplative indolence playing with fragile things,

Edmund Spenser

If one chooses at hazard a Spenserian stanza out of Shelley and compares it with any stanza by Spenser, one sees the change, though it would be still more clear if one had chosen a lyrical passage. I will take a stanza out of *Laon and Cythna*, for that is story-telling and runs nearer to Spenser than the meditative *Adonais*:—

> The meteor to its far morass returned:
> The beating of our veins one interval
> Made still; and then I felt the blood that burned
> Within her frame, mingle with mine, and fall
> Around my heart like fire; and over all
> A mist was spread, the sickness of a deep
> And speechless swoon of joy, as might befall
> Two disunited spirits when they leap
> In union from this earth's obscure and fading sleep.

The rhythm is varied and troubled, and the lines, which are in Spenser like bars of gold thrown ringing one upon another, are broken capriciously. Nor is the meaning the less an inspiration of indolent Muses, for it wanders hither and thither at the beckoning of fancy. It is now busy with a meteor and now with throbbing blood that is fire, and with a mist that is a swoon and a sleep that is life. It is bound together by the vaguest suggestion, while Spenser's verse is always rushing on to some preordained thought. A 'popular poet' can still indeed write poetry of the will, just as factory girls wear the fashion of hat or dress the moneyed classes wore a year ago, but 'popular poetry' does not belong to the living imagination of the world. Old writers gave men four temperaments, and they gave the sanguineous temperament to men of active life, and it is precisely the sanguineous temperament that is fading out of poetry and most obviously out of what is most subtle and living in poetry—its pulse and breath, its rhythm. Because poetry belongs to that element in every race which is most strong, and therefore most individual, the poet is not stirred to imaginative activity by a life which is surrendering its freedom to ever new elaboration, organisation, mechanism. He has no longer a poetical will, and must be content to write out of those parts of himself which are too delicate and fiery for any deadening exercise. Every generation has more and more loosened the rhythm, more and more broken up and disorganised, for the sake of subtlety of detail, those great rhythms which move, as it were, in masses of sound. Poetry has become more spiritual, for the soul is of all things the most delicately organised, but it has lost in weight and measure and in its power of telling long stories and of dealing with great and complicated events. *Laon and Cythna*, though I think it rises sometimes into loftier air than the *Faerie Queene* and *Endymion*, though its shepherds and wandering divinities have a stranger and more intense beauty than Spenser's, has need of too watchful and minute attention for such lengthy poems. In William Morris, indeed, one finds a music smooth and unexacting like that of the old storytellers, but not their energetic pleasure, their rhythmical wills. One too often misses in his *Earthly Paradise* the minute ecstasy of modern song without finding that old happy-go-lucky tune that had kept the story marching.

Spenser's contemporaries, writing lyrics or plays full of lyrical moments, write a verse more delicately organised than his and crowd more meaning into a phrase than he, but they could not have kept one's attention through so long a poem. A friend who has a fine ear told me the other day that she had read all Spenser with delight and yet could remember only four lines. When she repeated them they were from the poem by Matthew Roydon, which is bound up with Spenser because it is a commendation of Sir Philip Sidney:—

> A sweet, attractive kind of grace,
> A full assurance given by looks,
> Continual comfort in a face,
> The lineaments of Gospel books.

Yet if one were to put even these lines beside a fine modern song one would notice that they had a stronger and rougher energy, a featherweight more, if eye and ear were fine enough to notice it, of the active will, of the happiness that comes out of life itself.

IX

I have put into this book[1] only those passages from Spenser that I want to remember and carry about with me. I have not tried to select what people call character-istic passages, for that is, I think, the way to make a dull book. One never really knows anybody's taste but one's own, and if one likes anything sincerely one may be certain that there are other people made out of the same earth to like it too. I have taken out of *The Shepheards Calender* only those parts which are about love or about

[1] *Poems of Spenser; Selected and with an Introduction by W. B. Yeats.* (T. C. and E. C. Jack, Edinburgh. N.D.)

old age, and I have taken out of the *Faerie Queene* passages about shepherds and lovers, and fauns and satyrs, and a few allegorical processions. I find that though I love symbolism, which is often the only fitting speech for some mystery of disembodied life, I am for the most part bored by allegory, which is made, as Blake says, 'by the daughters of memory,' and coldly, with no wizard frenzy. The processions I have chosen are either those, like the House of Mammon, that have enough ancient mythology, always an implicit symbolism, or, like the Cave of Despair, enough sheer passion to make one forget or forgive their allegory, or else they are, like that vision of Scudamour, so visionary, so full of a sort of ghostly midnight animation, that one is persuaded that they had some strange purpose and did truly appear in just that way to some mind worn out with war and trouble. The vision of Scudamour is, I sometimes think, the finest invention in Spenser. Until quite lately I knew nothing of Spenser but the parts I had read as a boy. I did not know that I had read so far as that vision, but year after year this thought would rise up before me coming from I knew not where. I would be alone perhaps in some old building, and I would think suddenly, 'Out of that door might come a procession of strange people doing mysterious things with tumult. They would walk over the stone floor, then suddenly vanish, and everything would become silent again.' Once I saw what is called, I think, a Board School continuation class play *Hamlet*. There was no stage, but they walked in procession into the midst of a large room full of visitors and of their friends. While they were walking in, that thought came to me again from I knew not where. I was alone in a great church watching ghostly kings and queens setting out upon their unearthly business.

It was only last summer, when I read the Fourth Book of the *Faerie Queene*, that I found I had been imagining over and over the enchanted procession of Amoret.

I give too, in a section which I call 'Gardens of Delight,' the good gardens of Adonis and the bad gardens of Phaedria and Acrasia, which are mythological and symbolical, but not allegorical, and show, more particularly those bad islands, Spenser's power of describing bodily happiness and bodily beauty at its greatest. He seemed always to feel through the eyes, imagining everything in pictures. Marlowe's *Hero and Leander* is more energetic in its sensuality, more complicated in its intellectual energy than this languid story, which pictures always a happiness that would perish if the desire to which it offers so many roses lost its indolence and its softness. There is no passion in the pleasure he has set amid perilous seas, for he would have us understand that there alone could the war-worn and the sea-worn man find dateless leisure and unrepining peace.

October 1902

THE END

W. B. YEATS

From the photograph by Howard Coster

LATER ESSAYS AND INTRODUCTIONS

Gitanjali

GITANJALI (SONG OFFERINGS) [1]

I

A FEW DAYS AGO I said to a distinguished Bengali doctor of medicine, 'I know no German, yet if a translation of a German poet had moved me, I would go to the British Museum and find books in English that would tell me something of his life, and of the history of his thought. But though these prose translations from Rabindranath Tagore have stirred my blood as nothing has for years, I shall not know anything of his life, and of the movements of thought that have made them possible, if some Indian traveller will not tell me.' It seemed to him natural that I should be moved, for he said, 'I read Rabindranath every day; to read one line of his is to forget all the troubles of the world.' I said, 'An Englishman living in London in the reign of Richard II, had he been shown translations from Petrarch or from Dante, would have found no books to answer his questions, but would have questioned some Florentine banker or Lombard merchant as I question you. For all I know, so abundant and simple is this poetry, the new Renaissance has been born in your country and I shall never know of it except by hearsay.' He answered, 'We have other poets, but none that are his equal; we call this the epoch of Rabindranath. No poet seems to me as famous in Europe as he is among us. He is as great in music as in poetry, and his songs are sung from the west of India

[1] *Gitanjali,* by Rabindranath Tagore (Macmillan & Co., 1912).

387

into Burma wherever Bengali is spoken. He was
already famous at nineteen when he wrote his first
novel; and plays written when he was but little older
are still played in Calcutta. I so much admire the
completeness of his life; when he was very young
he wrote much of natural objects, he would sit all
day in his garden; from his twenty-fifth year or so to
his thirty-fifth perhaps, when he had a great sorrow,
he wrote the most beautiful love poetry in our language'; and then he said with deep emotion, 'Words
can never express what I owed at seventeen to his love
poetry. After that his art grew deeper, it became religious and philosophical; all the aspirations of mankind are in his hymns. He is the first among our saints
who has not refused to live, but has spoken out of life
itself, and that is why we give him our love.' I may
have changed his well-chosen words in my memory
but not his thought. 'A little while ago he was to read
divine service in one of our churches—we of the
Brahma Samaj use your word "church" in English—
it was the largest in Calcutta and not only was it
crowded, people even standing in the windows, but the
streets were all but impassable because of the people.'

Other Indians came to see me and their reverence
for this man sounded strange in our world, where we
hide great and little things under the same veil of
obvious comedy and half-serious depreciation. When
we were making the cathedrals had we a like reverence
for our great men? 'Every morning at three—I know,
for I have seen it'—one said to me, 'he sits immovable
in contemplation, and for two hours does not awake

from his reverie upon the nature of God. His father, the Maha Rishi, would sometimes sit there all through the next day; once, upon a river, he fell into contemplation because of the beauty of the landscape, and the rowers waited for eight hours before they could continue their journey.' He then told me of Mr. Tagore's family and how for generations great men have come out of its cradles. 'To-day,' he said, 'there are Gogonendranath and Abanindranath Tagore, who are artists; and Dwijendranath, Rabindranath's brother, who is a great philosopher. The squirrels come from the boughs and climb on to his knees and the birds alight upon his hands.' I notice in these men's thought a sense of visible beauty and meaning as though they held that doctrine of Nietzsche that we must not believe in the moral or intellectual beauty which does not sooner or later impress itself upon physical things. I said, 'In the East you know how to keep a family illustrious. The other day the curator of a Museum pointed out to me a little dark-skinned man who was arranging their Chinese prints and said, "That is the hereditary connoisseur of the Mikado, he is the fourteenth of his family to hold the post."' He answered, 'When Rabindranath was a boy he had all round him in his home literature and music.' I thought of the abundance, of the simplicity of the poems, and said, 'In your country is there much propagandist writing, much criticism? We have to do so much, especially in my own country, that our minds gradually cease to be creative, and yet we cannot help it. If our life was not a continual warfare, we would not have taste, we would not know what is good, we would not find hearers and readers. Four-fifths of our energy is spent in the quarrel with bad taste, whether in our own minds or in the minds of others.' 'I understand,' he replied. 'We too have our propagandist writing. In the villages they recite long mythological poems adapted from the Sanskrit in the Middle Ages, and they often insert passages telling the people that they must do their duties.'

II

I have carried the manuscript of these translations about with me for days, reading it in railway trains, or on the top of omnibuses and in restaurants, and I have often had to close it lest some stranger would see how much it moved me. These lyrics—which are in the original, my Indians tell me, full of subtlety of rhythm, of untranslatable delicacies of colour, of metrical invention—display in their thought a world I have dreamed of all my life long. The work of a supreme culture, they yet appear as much the growth of the common soil as the grass and the rushes. A tradition, where poetry and religion are the same thing, has passed through the centuries, gathering from learned and unlearned metaphor and emotion, and carried back again to the multitude the thought of the scholar and of the noble. If the civilisation of Bengal remains unbroken, if that common mind which—as one divines—runs through all, is not, as with us, broken into a dozen minds that know nothing of each other, something even of what is most subtle in these verses will have come, in a few generations, to the beggar on the roads. When there was but one mind in England Chaucer wrote his *Troilus and Cressida*, and though he had written to be read, or to be read out—for our time was coming on apace—he was sung by minstrels for a while. Rabindranath Tagore, like Chaucer's forerunners, writes music for his words, and one understands at every moment that he is so abundant, so spontaneous, so daring in his passion, so full of surprise, because he is doing something which has never seemed strange, unnatural, or in need of defence. These verses will not lie in little well-printed books upon the tables of ladies who turn the pages with indolent hands that they may sigh over a life without meaning, which is yet all they can know of life, or be carried about by students at the university to be laid aside when the work of life begins, but as the generations pass, travellers will hum them on the highway and men rowing upon rivers. Lovers, while they await one another, shall find, in murmuring them, this love of God a magic gulf wherein their own more bitter passion may bathe and renew its youth. At every moment the heart of this poet flows outward to these without derogation or condescension, for it has known that they will understand; and it has filled itself with the circumstance of their lives. The traveller in the red-brown clothes that he wears that dust may not show upon him, the girl searching in her bed for the petals fallen from the wreath of her royal lover, the servant or the bride awaiting the master's home-coming in the empty house, are images of the heart turning to God. Flowers and rivers, the blowing of conch-shells, the heavy rain of the Indian July, or the parching heat, are images of the moods of that heart in union or in separation; and a man sitting in a boat upon a river playing upon a lute, like one of those figures full of mysterious meaning in a Chinese picture, is God Himself. A whole people, a whole civilisation, immeasurably strange to us, seems to have been taken up into this imagination; and yet we are not moved because of its strangeness, but because we have met our own image, as though we had walked in Rossetti's Willow Wood, or heard, perhaps for the first time in literature, our voice as in a dream.

Since the Renaissance the writing of European saints —however familiar their metaphor and the general structure of their thought—has ceased to hold our attention. We know that we must at last forsake the world, and we are accustomed in moments of weariness or exaltation to consider a voluntary forsaking; but how can we, who have read so much poetry, seen so many paintings, listened to so much music, where the cry of the flesh and the cry of the soul seem one, forsake it harshly and rudely? What have we in common with Saint Bernard covering his eyes that they may not dwell upon the beauty of the lakes of Switzerland, or with the violent rhetoric of the Book of Revelation? We would, if we might, find, as in this book, words full of courtesy. 'I have got my leave. Bid me farewell, my brothers! I bow to you all and take my departure. Here I give back the keys of my door—and I give up all claims to my house. I only ask for last kind words from you. We were neighbours for long, but I received more than I could give. Now the day has dawned and the lamp that lit my dark corner is out. A summons has come and I am ready for my journey.' And it is our own mood, when it is furthest from à Kempis or John of the Cross, that cries, 'And because I love this life, I know I shall love death as well.' Yet it is not only in our thoughts of the parting that this book fathoms all. We had not known that we loved God, hardly, it may be, that we believed in Him; yet looking backward upon our life we discover, in our exploration of the pathways of woods, in our delight in the lonely places of hills, in that mysterious claim that we have made, unavailingly, on the women that we have loved, the emotion that created this insidious sweetness. 'Entering my heart unbidden even as one of the common crowd, unknown to me, my king, thou didst press the signet of eternity upon many a fleeting moment.' This is no longer the sanctity of the cell and of the scourge; being but a lifting up, as it were, into a greater intensity of the mood of the painter, painting the dust and the sunlight, and we go for a like voice to Saint Francis and to William Blake who have seemed so alien in our violent history.

III

We write long books where no page perhaps has any quality to make writing a pleasure, being confident in some general design, just as we fight and make money and fill our heads with politics—all dull things in the doing—while Mr. Tagore, like the Indian civilisation itself, has been content to discover the soul and surrender himself to its spontaneity. He often seems to contrast his life with that of those who have lived more after our fashion, and have more seeming weight in the world, and always humbly as though he were only sure his way is best for him: 'Men going home glance at me and smile and fill me with shame. I sit like a beggar maid, drawing my skirt over my face, and when they ask me what it is I want, I drop my eyes and answer them not.' At another time, remembering how his life had once a different shape, he will say, 'Many an hour have I spent in the strife of the good and the evil, but now it is the pleasure of my playmate of the empty days to draw my heart on to him; and I know not why is this sudden call to what useless inconsequence!' An innocence, a simplicity that one does not find elsewhere in literature makes the birds and the leaves seem as near to him as they are near to children, and the changes of the seasons great events as before our thoughts had arisen between them and us. At times I wonder if he has it from the literature of Bengal or from religion, and at other times, remembering the birds alighting on his brother's hands, I find pleasure in thinking it hereditary, a mystery that was growing through the centuries like the courtesy of a Tristan or a Pelanore. Indeed, when he is speaking of children, so much a part of himself that quality seems, one is not certain that he is not also speaking of the saints: 'They build their houses with sand, and they play with empty shells. With withered leaves they weave their boats and smilingly float them on the vast deep. Children have their play on the seashore of worlds. They know

Gitanjali

not how to swim, they know not how to cast nets. Pearl-fishers dive for pearls, merchants sail in their ships, while children gather pebbles and scatter them again. They seek not for hidden treasures, they know not how to cast nets.'

September 1912

Later Essays and Introductions

BISHOP BERKELEY [1]

I

IMAGINATION, WHETHER IN LITERATURE, painting, or sculpture, sank after the death of Shakespeare; supreme intensity had passed to another faculty; it was as though Shakespeare, Dante, Michelangelo, had been reborn with all their old sublimity, their old vastness of conception, but speaking a harsh, almost unintelligible, language. Two or three generations hence, when men accept the inventions of science as a commonplace and understand that it is limited by its method to appearance, no educated man will doubt that the movement of philosophy from Spinoza to Hegel is the greatest of all works of intellect.

II

I delight in that fierce young man, whose student years passed when the battle of the Boyne, fought, as Molyneux said, to change not an English but an Irish crown, was a recent memory; who established, with Molyneux's son for secretary, a secret society to examine the philosophy of a 'neighbouring nation'; who defined that philosophy, the philosophy of Newton and Locke, in three sentences, wrote after each that Irishmen thought otherwise, and on the next page that he must publish to find if men elsewhere agreed with

[1] *Bishop Berkeley*, by J. M. Hone and H. M. Rossi. (Faber & Faber. 1931.)

396

Irishmen. What he then was, solitary, talkative, ecstatic, destructive, he showed through all his later years though but in glimpses or as something divined or inferred. It is not the fault of his biographer but of the inanimate record, or of his own inanimate pose, that he is not there in all his blood and state. But after all when we search our own experience whether of life or letters how many stand solidly? At this moment I but recall four or five intimate friends, an old woman that I never spoke to, seen at a public assembly in America, an image met ten years ago in a sudden blaze of light under my closed eyelids, William Morris, and the half symbolic image of Jonathan Swift. Yet I am indebted to Joseph Hone that Berkeley moves among those images, though not with their solidity, that when the pattern has changed, when some of its elements have gone, he will still move there. Furthermore I understand now, what I once but vaguely guessed, that these two images, standing and sounding together, Swift and Berkeley, concern all those who feel a responsibility for the thought of modern Ireland that can take away their sleep.

III

I hate what I remember of his portrait in the Fellows' Room at Trinity College; it wears a mask kept by engravers and painters from the middle of the eighteenth century for certain admired men; Phillips' Blake, contradicted by the powerful lines of the life-mask, wears it too, and the statue of the Prince Consort on Leinster

Lawn; the smooth gregarious mask of Goldsmith's *Good-Natur'd Man,* an abstraction that slipped away unexamined when Swift and Berkeley examined and mocked its kind. The portrait attributed to Vander-bank is more amusing; the painter overpowered by the admired man turns the ecclesiastical sleeves into those great sleeves worn by Titian's women, and rounds the face to a vague half-animal Venetian loveliness. One turns one's eyes from the gods or satyrs in the back-ground—the engraved figures are too small for my sight—to peer under the bowl of the fountain or behind the chair expecting to discover one of those little dogs brought into fashion by Venetian courtesans. I reject with less liking and equal incredulity the Berkeley who has come down to us in the correspondence of his day; the sage as imagined by gentlemen of fortune—a rôle accepted by Berkeley that he might not be left to starve in some garret by a generation terrified of religious scepticism and political anarchy, and loved because it hid from himself and others his own anarchy and scepticism. The *Commonplace Book* is there to show that he did not accept it without hesitation or love it with his whole heart. 'N.B. To use utmost caution not to give the least handle of offence to the Church or churchmen . . . even to speak somewhat well of the Schoolmen. . . .' 'N.B. To rein in your satirical nature.' The something unreal about his public life made him the more attractive to his contemporaries, was an essen-tial element perhaps of his incredible persuasiveness, as if he were some hieratic image; only in those specula-tions that seemed the lovable foible of a great man is he altogether real. One looks in vain for some different life lived among friends and pupils, wonders what habits of secrecy still remained. What did he say in those three sermons to undergraduates that brought so much suspicion upon him?—not perhaps what he says in the long unreadable essay upon utilitarian ethics written to save his face. Was the Bermuda project, with its learned city so carefully mapped out, a steeple in the centre, a market in each corner, more than a theme for discourse? He had left behind those earnest Fellows of Trinity College who had offered their service and might have liked converting American Indians—there is a Trinity College Mission to savage parts—and brought to America a portrait-painter and a couple of pleasant young men of fortune, and associated there with fox-hunters and immaterialist disciples. Or did he think that if he could stop all thought with his Utopian drug—what thinker has not felt the temptation?—the mask might become real? He that cannot live must dream. Did tar-water, a cure-all learnt from American Indians, suggest that though he could not quiet men's minds he might give their bodies quiet, and so bring to life that incredible benign image, the dream of a time that after the anarchy of the religious wars, the spiritual torture of Donne, of El Greco and Spinoza, longed to be protected and flattered? The first great imaginative wave had sunk, the second had not yet risen.

I think of my father, of one friend or another, even of a drunken countryman who tumbled into my carriage out of the corridor one summer night, men born

399

into our Irish solitude, of their curiosity, their rich discourse, their explosive passion, their sense of mystery as they grew old, their readiness to dress up at the suggestion of others though never quite certain what dress they wore, their occasional childish worldliness. In our eighteenth century four or five such men had genius, two or three have genius to-day.

IV

It is customary to praise English empirical genius, English sense of reality, and yet throughout the eighteenth century when her Indian Empire was founded England lived for certain great constructions that were true only in relation to the will. I spoke in the Irish Senate on the Catholic refusal of divorce and assumed that all lovers who ignored priest or registrar were immoral; upon education, and assumed that everybody who could not read the newspaper was a poor degraded creature; and had I been sent there by some religious organisation must have assumed that a child captured by a rival faith lost its soul; and had my country been at war—but who does not serve these abstractions? Without them corporate life would be impossible. They are as serviceable as those leaf-like shapes of tin that mould the ornament for the apple-pie, and we give them belief, service, devotion. How can we believe in truth that is always moth-like and fluttering and yet can terrify?—A friend and myself, both grown men, talked ourselves once into a terror of a little white moth in Burnham Beeches. And of all these the most comprehensive, the most useful, was invented by Locke when he separated the primary and secondary qualities; and from that day to this the conception of a physical world without colour, sound, taste, tangibility, though indicted by Berkeley as Burke was to indict Warren Hastings fifty years later, and proved mere abstract extension, a mere category [1] of the mind, has remained the assumption of science, the groundwork of every text-book. It worked, and the mechanical inventions of the next age, its symbols that seemed its confirmation, worked even better, and it worked best of all in England where Edmund Spenser's inscription over the gates of his magic city seemed to end 'Do not believe too much': elsewhere it is the grosser half of that dialectical materialism the Socialist Prince Mirsky calls 'the firm foundation-rock of European Socialism,' and works all the mischief Berkeley foretold.

V

The sense for what is permanent, as distinct from what is useful, for what is unique and different, for the truth that shall prevail, for what antiquity called the sphere as distinct from the gyre, comes from solitaries or from communities where the solitaries flourish, Indians with a begging-bowl, monks where their occupation is an adventure, men escaped out of

[1] This cannot, of course, be less true of time-space than of the abstract space of Newton. The Russian mathematician Vasiliev in *Space, Time and Motion* calls Berkeley 'one of the most profound thinkers of all time' and adds, 'It was Berkeley's immortal service that he decidedly rejected the external reality of space.'

machinery, improvident men that sit by the roadside and feel responsible for all that exists:—

Do not thou grieve or blush to be
As all inspired and tuneful men
And all thy great forefathers were from Homer down to Ben.

Born in such a community, Berkeley with his belief in perception, that abstract ideas are mere words, Swift with his love of perfect nature, of the Houyhnhnms, his disbelief in Newton's system and every sort of machine, Goldsmith and his delight in the particulars of common life that shocked his contemporaries, Burke with his conviction that all States not grown slowly like a forest tree are tyrannies, found in England the opposite that stung their own thought into expression and made it lucid.

VI

If J. W. Dunne's *Experiment with Time* [1] is well founded, if our nightly dreams are in part a mixture of past and future events; if with little effort we can think the like dreams awake (and my own experience supports him), I may perhaps regard the speculations of men caught in the machinery of life as mere pro-

[1] J. W. Dunne's experiments are of great value, his explanation is inconsistent. No heaping up of dimensions, what is successive in a lower dimension, simultaneous in a higher, can bring him to the Pure Act or Eternal Instant, source of simultaneity and succession alike. His Infinite Observer is not infinite. McTaggart's exposition of a somewhat similar theory in the second volume of his *Nature of Existence* is consistent with itself and with philosophical tradition.

phecy, perhaps even suggest that we honour the prophetic afflatus before every other afflatus because it is
so gregarious. Berkeley had his disciples, but they came
in twos and threes, were far apart in time and place;
no man until many years had passed lived the heartier
because he shared their theme.

VII

Berkeley thought the Seven Days not the creation
of sun and moon, beast and man, but their entrance
into time, or into human perception, or into that of
some spirit; that his study table when the room seemed
empty existed in the mind of some spirit or went back
into eternity. Though he could not describe mystery
—his age had no fitting language—his suave glittering
sentences suggest it; we feel perhaps for the first time
that eternity is always at our heels or hidden from our
eyes by the thickness of a door. Something of this
depends upon his use of common words,[1] his sparing
use of exact definitions, his conviction that he must as
far as possible accept our point of view, upon his remaining, no matter what the theme, a conversation-
alist, an easy travelled man whose attention flatters us;
upon those three dialogues of Hylas and Philonous, the
only philosophical arguments since Plotinus that are
works of art, being so well-bred, so sensible. What

---

[1] Berkeley used common words on principle. They express perception with ease, he explains in the *Commonplace Book*, but not
those abstract ideas he derided.

does it matter when we are in such good company if Michael's trumpet blares on every threshold?

VIII

I published some pages from a diary a few years back in which this passage occurs: 'A few days ago my sister Lolly dreamed that she saw three dead bodies on a bed. One had its face to the wall, one had a pink mask like a child's toy mask, and before she could look at the third somebody had put a mask on that too. While she was looking at them the body with its face to the wall suddenly moved. The same night J . . . dreamed that she saw three very long funerals and that she saw what she thought a body on a bed. She thought it the body of a brother of hers who had died lately. She lay down on the bed by it and it suddenly moved. The same night my sister Lily dreamed that she had received three telegrams.'

I draw J. W. Dunne's attention to these dreams that he may look right and left and not merely before and behind, and I assure him that if he experiments he will discover simultaneous correspondential reveries, as he did prophetic reveries, even in waking life; that there is as much warp as woof. They may be as new to psychology as his own discoveries, but that should not deter him.

The romantic movement seems related to the idealist philosophy; the naturalistic movement, Stendhal's mirror dawdling down a lane, to Locke's mechanical philosophy, as simultaneous correspondential dreams are related, not merely where there is some traceable influence but through their whole substance, and I remember that monks in the Thebaid, or was it by the Mareotic Sea, claimed 'to keep the ramparts,' meaning perhaps that all men whose thoughts skimmed the 'unconscious,' God-abetting, affected others according to their state, that what some feel others think, what some think others do. When I speak of idealist philosophy I think more of Kant than of Berkeley, who was idealist and realist alike, more of Hegel and his successors than of Kant, and when I speak of the romantic movement I think more of Manfred, more of Shelley's Prometheus, more of Jean Valjean, than of those traditional figures, Browning's Pope, the fakir-like pedlar in *The Excursion*.

IX

The romantic movement with its turbulent heroism, its self-assertion, is over, superseded by a new naturalism that leaves man helpless before the contents of his own mind. One thinks of Joyce's *Anna Livia Plurabelle*, Pound's *Cantos*, works of an heroic sincerity, the man, his active faculties in suspense, one finger beating time to a bell sounding and echoing in the depths of his own mind; of Proust who, still fascinated by Stendhal's fixed framework, seems about to close his eyes and gaze upon the pattern under his lids. This new art which has arisen in different countries simultaneously seems related, as were the three telegrams to the three bodies, to that form of the new realist philosophy which thinks that the secondary and primary qualities alike are independent of consciousness [1] ; that an object can at the same moment have contradictory qualities. This philosophy seems about to follow the analogy of an art that has more rapidly completed itself, and after deciding that a penny is bright and dark, oblong and round, hot and cold, dumb and ringing in its own right, to think of the calculations it incites, our distaste or pleasure at its sight, the decision that made us pitch it, our preference for head or tail, as independent of a consciousness that has shrunk back, grown intermittent and accidental, into the looking-glass. Some Indian Buddhists would have thought so had they pitched pennies instead of dice.

If you ask me why I do not accept a doctrine so respectable and convenient, its cruder forms so obviously resurrected to get science down from Berkeley's roast-

---

[1] This definition is taken from M. W. Catkin's 'Introduction' to her selection from Berkeley. Moore in his *Refutation of Idealism*, the manifesto of modern realism, merely affirmed the objectivity of the sense-data, the raw material from which mind fabricates the objects of sense. Of recent years he has, however, suggested that judgment may be a form of perception, and McTaggart has incorporated the suggestion in his idealistic system. Future philosophy will have to consider visions and experiences such as those recorded in *An Experiment with Time*, *An Adventure*, and in Osty's *Supernormal Faculties*. Events may be present to certain faculties, distant in time to others. Certain investigators are convinced that they obtained through the mediumship of Mrs. Crandon the fingerprints of a man dead some twenty years; and the terms idealist and realist may be about to lose their meaning. If photographs that I saw handed round in Paris thirty years ago can be repeated and mental images photographed, the distinction that Berkeley drew between what man created and what God creates will have broken down.

ing-spit, I can but answer like Zarathustra, 'Am I a barrel of memories that I should give you my reasons?' Somewhere among those memories something compels me to reject whatever—to borrow a metaphor of Coleridge's—drives mind into the quicksilver. And why should I, whose ancestors never accepted the anarchic subjectivity of the nineteenth century, accept its recoil; why should men's heads ache that never drank? I admit there are, especially in America, such signs of prophetic afflatus about this new movement in philosophy, so much consonant with the political and social movements of the time, or so readily transformable into a desire to fall back or sink in on some thing or being, that it may be the morning cock-crow of our Hellenistic Age.

x

Berkeley wrote in his *Commonplace Book*: 'The Spirit—the active thing—that which is soul, and God —is the will alone'; and then, remembering the mask that he must never lay aside, added: 'The concrete of the will and understanding I must call mind, not person, lest offence be given, there being but one volition acknowledged to be God. Mem. carefully to omit defining Person, or making much mention of it.' Then remembering that some member of his secret society had asked if our separate personalities were united in a single will, a question considered by Plotinus in the Fourth Ennead but dangerous in the eighteenth century, he wrote, 'What you ask is merely about a word, unite is no more.' Number had no existence, being like all abstract ideas a part of language. It is plain, however, from his later writings that he thought of God as a pure indivisible act, personal because at once will and understanding, which unlike the Pure Act of Italian philosophy creates passive 'ideas'—sensations—thrusts them as it were outside itself; and in this act all beings—from the hierarchy of Heaven to man and woman and doubtless to all that lives[1]—share in the measure of their worth: not the God of Protestant theology but a God that leaves room for human pride. As I enumerate these thoughts I forget that gregarious episcopal mask and remember a Berkeley that asked the Red Indian for his drugs, an angry, unscrupulous[2] solitary that I can test

[1] Berkeley has been called a utilitarian, even the first utilitarian, and the essay on Passive Obedience would support that opinion were it more than a public plea where everything must be familiar and intelligible. In the *Commonplace Book* alone is Berkeley always sincere, and there I find in paragraph 639, 'Complacency seems rather to . . . constitute the essence of volition,' which seems what an Irish poet meant who sang to some girl 'A joy within guides you,' and what I meant when I wrote 'An aimless joy is a pure joy.' Berkeley must have been familiar with Archbishop King's *De Origine Mali* which makes all joy depend 'upon the act of the agent himself, and his election'; not upon an external object. The greater the purity the greater the joy. A Sligo countryman once said to me, 'God smiles even when He condemns the lost.' Berkeley deliberately refused to define personality, and dared not say that Man in so far as he is himself, in so far as he is a personality, reflects the whole act of God; his God and Man seem cut off from one another. It was the next step, and because he did not take it Blake violently annotated *Siris*, and because he himself did take it, certain heads—'Christ Blessing'—in Mona Wilson's *Life* for instance—have an incredible still energy. It was not compatible from any point of view with Berkeley's external inanimate mask.

[2] I am thinking of his attack on Shaftesbury.

by my favourite quotations and find neither temporal nor trivial—'An old hunter talking with gods, or a high-crested chief, sailing with troops of friends to Tenedos,' and the last great oracle of Delphi commemorating the dead Plotinus, 'That wave-washed shore . . . the golden race of mighty Zeus . . . the just Aeacus, Plato, stately Pythagoras, and all the choir of immortal love.'

XI

Only where the mind partakes of a pure activity can art or life attain swiftness, volume, unity; that contemplation lost, we picture some slow-moving event, turn the mind's eye from everything else that we may experience to the full our own passivity, our personal tragedy; or like the spider in Swift's parable mistake for great possessions what we spin out of our guts and deride the bee that has nothing but its hum and its wings, its wax and its honey, its sweetness and light. 'God,' 'Heaven,' 'Immortality,' those words and their associated myths define that contemplation. Philosophy can deny them all meaning, some of the greatest human works are such denial, but we think it vulgar and jejune if it do so without despair; and history shows that it must return again and again to the problem that they set. Giambattista Vico has said that we should reject all philosophy that does not begin in myth, and it is impossible to pronounce those three words without becoming as simple as a camel-driver or a pilgrim.

409

XII

Berkeley in his youth described the *summum bonum* and the reality of Heaven as physical pleasure, and thought this conception made both more intelligible to simple men. And though he abandoned it in later life, and not merely because incompatible with the mask, one returns to it remembering Blake's talk of 'enlarged and numerous senses,' his description of Heaven as an improvement of sense, Lake Harris's denunciation of Swedenborg as a half man 'that half saw, half felt, half tasted the Kingdom of Heaven.' Berkeley was fumbling his way backward to some simple age. I think of the Zen monk's expectation, though maybe but as an inducement to passivity, of an odour of unknown flowers as contemplation reached its climax; of the Zen painter gathering into the same powerful rhythm all those things that in the work of his predecessor stood so solidly as themselves.

When Berkeley abandoned that first opinion he did not exalt in place of perception some abstract thought or law but some always undefined apprehension of spirits and their relations. Looking for a clue, I think of Coleridge's contrast between Juliet's nurse and Hamlet, remember that Shakespeare drew the nurse from observation, from passive sense-impression, but Hamlet, the Court, the whole work of art, out of himself in a pure indivisible act. There have been mystics, no doubt, who thought they knew by a knowledge as direct the creatures of their neighbourhood, partaking as it were the timeless act of their creation, and I once visited a

Cabbalist who spent the day trying to look out of the eyes of his canary; he announced at nightfall that all things had for it colour but nothing outline. His method of contemplation was probably in error.

XIII

Forty years ago intellectual young men, dissatisfied with the political poetry of Young Ireland, once the foundation of Irish politics, substituted an interest in old stories and modern peasants, and now the young men are dissatisfied again. The hereditary political aim has been accomplished; their country does not need their help; the question I have heard put again and again, 'What would he sacrifice?' is put no more, everything is upside-down; it is their aims that are unaccomplished, they that need help. They have begun to ask if their country has anything to give. Joseph Hone draws their attention to that eighteenth century when its mind became so clear that it changed the world.

July 1931

Later Essays and Introductions

MY FRIEND'S BOOK [1]

I

ONE OPENS A FRIEND'S BOOK with dread, every trick of style has its associations, we wonder perpetually—such hatred is in friendship—how a man we have buckled to our heart can have so little sense. Admiration can but feed hatred, and if we have known the man for five-and-forty years and met him once a week for the last ten, and must write about his book —and what else can be so interesting?—it may seem best to touch upon some one aspect and ignore the rest. Yet, in writing about A.E.'s *Song and its Fountains* I cannot do so; I must face all my associations, merely stating at the outset that my hatred has won the right to call itself friendship.

II

Towards the end of my Dublin schooldays an elderly servant of my mother's took an interest in a schoolboy who passed our windows daily. None of us knew his name, nor did he interest my sisters or myself or seem in any way unusual, but our servant called him 'the strayed angel.' Then I went to the art schools and found him there, turning his study of the nude into a Saint John in the Desert, with some reminiscence of da Vinci perhaps obstructing his sight. I soon discovered

[1] *Song and its Fountains*, by A.E. (George W. Russell). (Macmillan. 1932.)

412

that he possessed a faculty dormant elsewhere since the time of Swedenborg. If he sat silent for a while on the Two Rock Mountains, or any spot where man was absent, the scene would change; unknown, beautiful people would move among the rocks and trees; but this vision, unlike that of Swedenborg, remained always what seemed an unexplained, external, sensuous panorama. Another student, devout and Catholic, cried to him once in a moment of excitement, 'You will drift into a penumbra,' yet it was he himself who became unbalanced, wandering about Dublin in clothes of sackcloth stitched by his own unskilful hands, full of queer tricks to gather an audience for his moral exhortations, A.E., as George Russell names himself, becoming that influential journalist and economist Dublin knows so well. My criticism varied, sometimes calling those images a subjective intensification of such reminiscences as that which transformed his nude study, but when I had confirmed from the obscure symbolism of alchemy an explanation of the Scourging of Christ implicit in some visionary scene, I had to change my tune.

III

Three or four years later our disputes began in earnest. I insisted that these images, whether symbols projected by the subconscious, or physical facts, should be made to explain themselves; sometimes I broke off abruptly, afraid that he might never speak to me again. Sometimes I quarrelled with something said or done in the ordinary affairs of life which could not have been said or done, as I thought, had he not encountered the Magical Emblems and the Sick King and refused to ask questions that might have made the soil fruitful again.

That he should question, as Swedenborg had questioned, seemed to me of the first importance. Locke based himself upon the formula, 'Nothing in mind that has not come from sense'—sense as the seventeenth century understood it—and Leibniz commented, 'Nothing except mind.' But what if Henry More was right when he contended that men and animals drew not only universals but particulars from a supersensual source? May we not be compelled to change all our conceptions should it be proved that, in some crisis of life perhaps, we have access to the detailed circumstantial knowledge of other minds, or to the wisdom that has such knowledge for a foundation; or, as Henry More believed—unless I have forgotten his long essay on *The Immortality of the Soul*, toiled through some fifteen years ago—that the bees and birds learn to make comb and nest from that *Anima Mundi* which contains the knowledge of all dead bees and birds? What if the modern accentuation of individuality is what the Buddhists call, we are told, 'separateness,' and in intellect as in morality an error? I think of *An Adventure*, by those two Oxford ladies, heads of Colleges, who found themselves of a sudden in the Court of Marie-Antoinette; of Dunne's *Experiment with Time*, where the visions are of the future—to name but two books from a voluminous literature from which no man has as yet deduced the consequences.

'Nothing in mind that has not come from sense

except mind.' If that is the foundation even of our most profound thought, why should not contemporary schools of opinion resemble a ghastly sight of childhood: turkeys running round the yard with their heads off?

IV

In this book A.E. attempts to describe and explain some part of his experience. Swedenborg, metallurgical expert, scientific speculator, was a man of boundless curiosity, but the author of *Song and its Fountains*—landscape-painter and pastellist, when his visions were still a novelty—escapes with difficulty from mere pleasure and astonishment at the varied scene. I began by hating the book for its language. My friend, whose English at the close of the civil war was so vigorous and modern—I remember an article which found its way into the prisons and stopped a hunger strike—writes as though he were living in the 'nineties, seems convinced that spiritual truth requires a dead language. He writes 'dream' where other men write 'dreams,' a trick he and I once shared, picked up from William Sharp perhaps when the romantic movement was in its last contortions. Renaissance Platonism had ebbed out in poetic diction, isolating certain words and phrases as if they were Platonic Ideas. He has heaped up metaphors that seem to me like those wax flowers of a still older time I saw in childhood melted on the side towards the window. Yet I came to love the book for its thought.

It is almost wholly an illustration and commentary

upon Plato's doctrine of pre-natal memory. It traces back A.E.'s dominating ideas to certain impressions, the colour of a wild flower, an image from a child's story, something somebody told him about a neighbour, a vision seen under closed eyelids; always, it seems, to single images, single events, which opened, as it were, sluice-gates into the will. A poet, he contends, does not transmute into song what he has learned in experience. He reverses the order and says that the poet first imagines and that later the imagination attracts its affinities. The more we study those affinities as distinct from the first impulse the more realistic is our art, which explains why a certain novelist of my acquaintance, who can describe with the most convincing detail the clothes, houses, tricks of speech of his characters, is yet the most unobservant of men. The author of *Song and its Fountains* shows the origin of certain of his poems and believes that we can all trace back our lives as a whole from event to event to those first acts of the mind, and those acts through vision to the pre-natal life. While so engaged he came upon a moral idea which seems to me both beautiful and terrible. He had an intuition that in some pre-natal life there had been 'downfall and tragic defeat'; he had begun a 'concentration upon that intuition' and almost at once became terrified. He seemed to be warned away from some knowledge he could not have endured, a warning which may have preserved his sanity while confining vision to a seemingly sensuous and external panorama, and substituting an emotional apprehension for analysis. He thinks that when a man is to attain great wisdom he first learns all the evil of his past, assumes responsibility for his share in that evil, follows out with a complete knowledge the consequence of every act, repents the sin of twenty thousand years, unified at last in thought, and only when this agony has been exhausted can he recall what was 'lovely and beloved.' We do not re-live the past, for our life is always our own, always novel, but dream back or think back to that first purity. Is not all spiritual knowledge perhaps a reversal, a return? Or, as he sums up in one of those quotations from his own verse which give the book its chief beauty:—

I know, when I come to my own immortal, I will find there
In a myriad instant all that the wandering soul found fair:
Empires that never crumbled, and thrones all glorious yet,
And hearts ere they were broken, and eyes ere they were wet.

Plotinus had not this thought; the Cambridge Platonists, the more exhaustive ethical logic of Christianity spurring them on, might have discovered it had not the soul's re-birth, though it fascinated Glanvil, been a dangerous theme. Now, however, that McTaggart has made that doctrine the foundation of the first English systematic philosophy, one can invite attention to what may bring all past ages into the circle of conscience.

v

I turn the pages once more and find that my friend has excused his lack of questioning curiosity better than I had thought. 'The Spirit,' as he calls the ultimate reality, gave to some 'the infinite vision,' but he had

417

been content 'to know that it was there,' and through that knowledge was 'often happy'; had he stirred 'it would have vanished'; and then he cries out in an unrhymed poem that seems to me new:—

> If I would stay thee
> Thou art gone inward, and thy light as lost
> As the flying fish is, a pearly shadow that leaps
> From the dark blue to slide in the dark blue.

He cannot follow, he adds, the stern passage of sanctity ascending from anguish to delight, nor worship spirit under some majestic form:—

> My secret was thy gentleness. I know
> No nurse had ever crooned a lullaby
> So softly as thou the music that guides the loud
> Tempest in its going forth.

April 1932

Prometheus Unbound

PROMETHEUS UNBOUND

I

WHEN I WAS A YOUNG MAN I wrote two essays calling Shelley's dominant symbol the Morning Star, his poetry the poetry of desire.[1] I had meant to explain *Prometheus Unbound*, but some passing difficulty turned me from a task that began to seem impossible. What does Shelley mean by Demogorgon? It lives in the centre of the earth, the sphere of Parmenides, perhaps, in a darkness that sends forth 'rays of gloom' as 'light from the meridian sun'; it names itself 'eternity.' When it has succeeded Jupiter, 'the supreme of living things,' as he did Saturn, when it and Jupiter have gone to lie 'henceforth in darkness,' Prometheus is set free, Nature purified. Shelley the political revolutionary expected miracle, the Kingdom of God in the twinkling of an eye, like some Christian of the first century. He had accepted Berkeley's philosophy as expounded in Sir William Drummond's *Academical Questions*. The ultimate reality is not thought, for thought cannot create but 'can only perceive,' the created world is a stream of images in the human mind, the stream and cavern of his symbolism; this stream is Time. Eternity is the abyss which receives and creates. Sometimes the soul is a boat, and in this boat Asia sails against the current from age to youth, from youth to infancy, and so to the pre-natal condition 'peopled by shapes too bright to see.' In the fourth

[1] See p. 65 above, 'The Philosophy of Shelley's Poetry.'

act this condition, man's first happiness and his last, sings its ecstatic song; and yet although the first and last it is always near at hand, 'Tir ná nOg is not far from any of us,' as a countrywoman said to me.

> That garden sweet, that lady fair,
> And all sweet shapes and odours there,
> In truth have never passed away;
> 'Tis we, 'tis ours, are changed; not they.

Why, then, does Demogorgon, whose task is beneficent, who lies in wait behind 'the mighty portal . . . whence the oracular vapour is hurled up Which lonely men drink wandering in their youth,' bear so terrible a shape, and not to the eyes of Jupiter, external necessity, alone, but to those of Asia, who is identical with the Venus-Urania of the *Athanase?* Why is Shelley terrified of the Last Day like a Victorian child? It was not terrible to Blake: 'For the cherub with the flaming sword is hereby commanded to leave his guard at the Tree of Life; and when he does the whole creation will be consumed and appear infinite and holy, whereas it now appears finite and corrupt.'

II

Demogorgon made his plot incoherent, its interpretation impossible; it was thrust there by that something which again and again forced him to balance the object of desire conceived as miraculous and superhuman, with nightmare. Shelley told his friends of attempts upon his life or his liberty, elaborating details between delusion and deceit, believed himself infected with elephantiasis because he had sat opposite a fat woman in an omnibus, encountered terrifying apparitions, one a woman with eyes in her breasts; nor did his friendships escape obsession, his admired Elizabeth Hitchener became 'the brown demon . . . an artful, superficial, ugly, hermaphroditical beast of a woman'; nor was *Prometheus* the only nightmare-ridden work; there is nothing in *Swellfoot the Tyrant* but the cold rhetoric of obsession; *The Cenci*, for all its magnificent construction, is made unendurable upon the stage by an artificial character, the scapegoat of his unconscious hatred. When somebody asked Aubrey Beardsley towards the end of his life why he secreted indecencies in odd corners of his designs, more than once necessitating the destruction of a plate, he answered, 'Something compels me to sacrifice to Priapus.' Shelley, whose art is allied to that of the Salome drawings where sex is sublimated to an unearthly receptivity, though more ardent and positive, imagined under a like compulsion whatever seemed dark, destructive, indefinite. Blake, though he had his brown demons, kept his freedom in essentials; he had encountered with what seemed his physical eyes but one nightmare, 'scaly, speckled, very awful,' and thought such could visit but seldom imaginative men.

III

Shelley was not a mystic, his system of thought was constructed by his logical faculty to satisfy desire, not a symbolical revelation received after the suspension of all desire. He could neither say with Dante, 'His will is our peace,' nor with Finn in the Irish story, 'The best music is what happens.'

There is a form of meditation which permits an image or symbol to generate itself, and the images and symbols so generated build themselves up into coherent structures often beautiful and startling. When a young man I made an exhaustive study of this condition in myself and in others, choosing as a rule for the initiatory symbol a name or form associated with the cabbalistic Sephiroth, or with one of the five traditional elements. Sometimes, though not in my own case, trance intervened and the structure attained a seeming physical solidity; this, however, seldom happened and was considered undesirable. Almost always, after some days or weeks of meditation, a form emerged in sleep or amid the ordinary affairs of life to show or speak some significant message, or at some moment a strange hidden will controlled the unconscious movements of the body. If the experimentalist had an impassioned purpose, a propaganda, let us say, and no critical sense, he might become obsessed by images, voices, that had, it seemed, for their sole object to guard his purpose or to express its contrary and threaten it. The mystic, on the other hand, is in no such danger; he so lives whether in East or West, whether he be Ramakrishna or Boehme, as to dedicate his initiatory image, and its generated images, not to his own but to the Divine Purpose, and after certain years attains the saint's miraculous life. There have been others unfitted for such a life by nature or station, who could yet dedicate their actions and acquire what William Morris has called lucky eyes: 'all that he does unwitting he does well.' There is much curious evidence to show that the Divine Purpose so invoked descends into the mind at moments of inspiration, not as spiritual life alone but as what seems a physical brightness. Perhaps everybody that pursues that life, for however short a time, even, as it were, but touches it, experiences now and again during sleep bright coherent dreams where something is shown or spoken that grows in meaning with the passage of time. Blake spoke of this 'stronger and better light,' called its source 'the human form divine,' Shelley's 'harmonious soul of many a soul,' or, as we might say, the Divine Purpose. The stationary, joyous energy of certain among his figures, 'Christ Blessing', for instance, or of his own life when we regard it as a whole as contrasted with the sadness and disquiet of Shelley's, suggests radiating light. We understand why the first Christian painters encircled certain heads with light. Because this source or purpose is always an action, never a system of thought, its man can attend, as Shelley would not, to the whole drama of life, simplicities, banalities, intoxications, even lie upon his left side and eat dung, set free 'from a multitude of opinions.'

It was as a mystic that Blake wrote 'Sweet joy befall thee,' 'Soft deceit and idleness,' 'The Holy Word walks among the ancient trees.' Shelley's art shows that he was an unconverted man though certainly a visionary, what people call 'psychic'; his landscapes are vaporised and generalised by his purpose, his spirits have not

423

the separated existence even of those that in *Manfred*
curse and yet have 'sweet and melancholy' voices.
He was the tyrant of his own being, nor was it in all
likelihood a part of the plan that it should find freedom,
seeing that he worked as did Keats and Marlowe, un-
correcting and unhesitating, as though he knew the
shortness of his life. That life, and all lives, would be
unintelligible to me did I not think of them as an
exfoliation prolonged from life to life; he sang of
something beginning.

IV

When I was in my early twenties Shelley was much
talked about. London had its important 'Shelley
Society,' *The Cenci* had been performed and forbidden,
provincial sketching clubs displayed pictures by young
women of the burning of Shelley's body. The orthodox
religion, as our mothers had taught it, was no longer
credible; those who could not substitute connoisseur-
ship, or some humanitarian or scientific pursuit, found
a substitute in Shelley. He had shared our curiosities,
our political problems, our conviction that, despite all
experience to the contrary, love is enough; and unlike
Blake, isolated by an arbitrary symbolism, he seemed
to sum up all that was metaphysical in English poetry.
When in middle life I looked back I found that he and
not Blake, whom I had studied more and with more
approval, had shaped my life, and when I thought of
the tumultuous and often tragic lives of friends or

acquaintance, I attributed to his direct or indirect influence their Jacobin frenzies, their brown demons.

v

Another study of that time, less general, more confined to exceptional men, was that of Balzac as a social philosopher. When I was thirteen or fourteen I heard somebody say that he changed men's lives, nor can I think it a coincidence that an epoch founded in such thought as Shelley's ended with an art of solidity and complexity. Me at any rate he saved from the pursuit of a beauty that, seeming at once absolute and external, requires, to strike a balance, hatred as absolute. Yet Balzac is no complete solution, for that can be found in religion alone. One of the sensations of my childhood was a description of a now lost design of Nettleship's, *God creating Evil*, a vast, terrifying face, a woman and a tiger rising from the forehead. Why did it seem so blasphemous and so profound? It was many years before I understood that we must not demand even the welfare of the human race, nor traffic with divinity in our prayers. It moves outside our antinomies, it may be our lot to worship in terror: 'Did He who made the lamb make thee?'

July 30, 1932

Later Essays and Introductions

AN INDIAN MONK [1]

I

I WROTE AN INTRODUCTION to the beautiful *Gitanjali* of Tagore, and now, twenty years afterwards, draw attention to a book that may prove of comparable importance, *An Indian Monk*, by Shri Purohit Swāmi. A little more than a year ago I met its author, but lately arrived in Europe, at Mr. Sturge Moore's house. He had been sent by his Master, or spiritual director, that he might interpret the religious life of India, but had no fixed plan. Perhaps he should publish his poems, perhaps, like Vivekānanda, go to America. He had gone to Rome, thinking it was but courteous to pay his respects to the Holy Father, but though the Abbots of the most orthodox Hindu shrines had given him their blessing, and 'the organiser of the Bhārat-Dharma Mahāmandal . . . a general letter of introduction,' he was not received. Then he had come to England and called upon the Poet Laureate, who entertained him. He is a man of fifty, broken in health by the austerities of his religious life; he must have been a stalwart man and he is still handsome. He makes one think of some Catholic theologian who has lived in the best society, confessed people out of Henry James's novels, had some position at Court where he could engage the most absorbed attention without raising his voice, but that is only at first sight. He is something

[1] *An Indian Monk: His Life and Adventures*, by Shri Purohit Swāmi. (Macmillan. 1932.)

426

much simpler, more childlike and ancient. During lunch he and I, Sturge Moore, and an attaché from the Egyptian Legation, exceedingly well read in European literature, discussed his plans and ideas. The attaché, born into a Jewish family that had lived among Mohammedans for generations, seemed more Christian in his point of view than Moore or myself. Presently the attaché said: 'Well, I suppose what matters is to do all the good one can.' 'By no means,' said the monk. 'If you have that object you may help some few people, but you will have a bankrupt soul. I must do what my Master bids, the responsibility is His.' That sentence, spoken without any desire to startle, interested me the more because I had heard the like from other Indians. Once when I stayed at Wilfrid Blunt's I talked to an exceedingly religious Mohammedan, kept there that he might not run himself into political trouble in India. He spoke of the coming independence of India, but declared that India would never organise. 'There are only three eternal nations,' he said, 'India, Persia, China; Greece organised and Greece is dead.' I remembered too that an able Indian doctor I met when questioning London Indians about Tagore said of a certain Indian leader, 'We do not think him sincere; he taught virtues merely because he thought them necessary to India.' This care for the spontaneity of the soul seems to me Asia at its finest and where it is most different from Europe, the explanation perhaps why it has confronted our moral earnestness and our control of Nature with its asceticism and its courtesy.

We sat on for a couple of hours after lunch while

427

the monk, in answer to my questions, told of his child-hood, his life at the University, of spiritual forms that he had seen, of seven years' meditation in his house, of nine years' wandering with his begging-bowl. Presently I said: 'The ideas of India have been expounded again and again, nor do we lack ideas of our own; discussion has been exhausted, but we lack experience. Write what you have just told us; keep out all philosophy, unless it interprets something seen or done.'

I found afterwards that I had startled and shocked him, for an Indian monk who speaks of himself contradicts all tradition, but that after much examination of his conscience he came to the conclusion that those traditions were no longer binding, and that besides, as he explained to Sturge Moore, a monk, a certain stage of initiation reached, is bound by nothing but the will of his Master. He took my advice and brought his book, chapter by chapter, to Sturge Moore for correction. Sturge Moore, one of our finest critics, would say: 'You have told us too much of this, or too little of that; you must make us see that temple more clearly,' or he would cross something out, or alter a word, helping him to master our European sense of form.

II

The book lies before me complete; it seems to me something I have waited for since I was seventeen years old. About that age, bored by an Irish Protestant point of view that suggested by its blank abstraction chloride of lime, I began to question the countrypeople about apparitions. Some dozen years later Lady Gregory collected with my help the stories in her *Visions and Beliefs*. Again and again, she and I felt that we had got down, as it were, into some fibrous darkness, into some matrix out of which everything has come, some condition that brought together as though into a single scheme 'exultations, agonies,' and the apparitions seen by dogs and horses; but there was always something lacking. We came upon visionaries of whom it was impossible to say whether they were Christian or Pagan, found memories of jugglers like those of India, found fragments of a belief that associated Eternity with field and road, not with buildings; but these visionaries, memories, fragments, were eccentric, alien, shut off, as it were, under the plate glass of a museum; I had found something of what I wanted but not all, the explanatory intellect had disappeared. When Shri Purohit Swāmi described his journey up those seven thousand steps at Mount Girnār, that creaking bed, that sound of pattens in the little old half-forgotten temple, and fitted everything into an ancient discipline, a philosophy that satisfied the intellect, I found all I wanted.

III

Byzantine mystical theologians, Simeon, Callistus, Ignatius, and many others, taught a form of prayer or mental discipline resembling his. The devotee must say continually, even though his thought be elsewhere, 'Lord Jesus Christ, have mercy upon us'; a modern

Russian pilgrim [1] of their school repeated those words daily twelve thousand times, 'Lord Jesus Christ' as he drew in his breath, 'have mercy upon us' as he breathed it out, until they had grown automatic and were repeated in his sleep; he became, as he said, not speaker but listener.[2] Shri Purohit Swāmi writes: 'I repeated the Gāyitri, the most sacred Mantram, and became so habituated that even in my dreams I continued. When talking with others my mind went on unconsciously muttering, "We meditate on the supreme splendour of that Divine Being. May it illuminate our intellects."' The Russian pilgrim begged dry bread from door to door; a monk of Mount Athos is at this moment travelling through the world and living upon 'fifty acorns a day.' My Indian monk's habitual diet is milk and fruit, but his austerity at times has been greater; he writes of a certain pilgrimage: 'I refused to take either milk or fruit by the way and only drank water from time to time; my friend sang the glory of the Master' (their divine Lord Dattātreya) 'whenever I sat for rest under the shade of a tree, and would try to find and bring water to me.'

[1] The Rev. R. M. French has translated his autobiography into English and calls it *The Way of a Pilgrim*. 'Of the pilgrim's identity nothing is known,' he writes; 'in some way his manuscript, or a copy of it, came into the hands of a monk on Mount Athos, in whose possession it was found by the Abbot of Saint Michael's Monastery at Kazan.'

[2] The Swāmi comments, 'Some of the Yogis of India practise Ajapā-japa Mantram. Ajapā-japa is very short and easy. They repeat "Soham" as they draw in the breath and "Hamsah" as they breathe it out. "Soham Hamsah" means, "I am that Hamsa"—the eternal self, or soul.'

An Indian Monk

IV

The prayers, however, are unlike, for the Russian's prayer implies original sin, that of the Indian asks for an inspired intellect; and this unlikeness is fundamental, the source perhaps of all other differences. The Russian, like most European mystics, distrusts visions though he admits their reality, seems indifferent to Nature, may perhaps dread it like Saint Bernard, who passed the Swiss Lakes with averted eyes. The Indian, upon the other hand, approaches God through vision, speaks continually of the beauty and terror of the great mountains, interrupts his prayer to listen to the song of birds, remembers with delight the nightingale that disturbed his meditation by alighting upon his head and singing there, recalls after many years the whiteness of a sheet, the softness of a pillow, the gold embroidery upon a shoe. These things are indeed part of the 'splendour of that Divine Being.' The first four Christian centuries shared his thought; Byzantine theologians that named their great church 'The Holy Wisdom' sang it; so, too, did those Irish monks who made innumerable poems about bird and beast, and spread the doctrine that Christ was the most beautiful of men. Some Irish saint, whose name I have forgotten, sang, 'There is one among the birds that is perfect, one among the fish, one perfect among men.'

v

'And there are also many other things which Jesus did, the which, if they should be written every one, I suppose that even the world itself could not contain the books that should be written,' but Christendom has based itself upon four short books and for long insisted that all must interpret them in the same way. It was at times dangerous for a painter to vary, however slightly, the position of the Nails upon the Cross. The greatest saints have had their books examined by the Holy Office, for East and West seem each other's contraries—the East so independent spiritually, so ready to submit to the conqueror; the West so independent politically, so ready to submit to its Church. The West impregnated an East full of spiritual turbulence, and that turbulence brought forth a child Western in complexion and in feature. Since the Renaissance, literature, science, and the fine arts have left the Church and sought elsewhere the variety necessary to their existence; perhaps the converse impregnation has begun, the East as male. Being most impressed by arts that I have myself practised, I remember our selection for admiration of old masterpieces where 'tonal values,' or the sense of weight and bulk that is the particular discovery of Europe, are the least apparent: some flower of Botticelli's, perhaps, that seems a separate intellectual existence. Then I think of the sensuous deliberation Spenser brought into English literature, of the magic of *Christabel* or *Kubla Khan*, of the wise pedlar in the *Excursion*, of Ahasuerus in *Hellas*, and wisdom, magic, sensation, seem Asiatic. We have borrowed directly from the East and selected for admiration or repetition everything in our own past that is least European, as though groping backward towards our common mother.

VI

Perhaps dogmatism was the necessary check upon European violence, asceticism upon the Asiatic fecundity. When Christ said, 'I and my Father are One,' it is possible to interpret Him as Shri Purohit Swāmi interprets his Master's 'I am Brahma.' The One is present in all numbers, Brahma in all men though self-conscious in the ascetic alone; and the plain man admits the evidence, for beat the pupil and the ascetic's back is scored, and the ascetic, if he please, can exhaust in his own body an epidemic that might have swept away the village. Nor can a single image, that of Christ, Krishna, or Buddha, represent God to the exclusion of other images. Shri Purohit Swāmi worshipped God at first as represented in a certain religious picture with an exciting history and no artistic merit, come to him through some accident of his personal history; but before the ascent of Mount Girnār, his Master, though he has forgotten to record the incident in this book, transferred to him by a glance 'the vision of the formless'; after that he could still worship God under any image but an image chosen by himself. That initiation with its final freedom is itself an epitome of the soul's

433

gradual escape, in its passage through many incarnations, from all that is external and predestined.

The Swāmi is a minstrel and story-teller where all popular literature is religious; yet all his poems are love-songs, lullabies, or songs of loyalty to friend or master, for in his belief and in that of his hearers he can but offer to God the service learnt in service of man or woman; nor can any single service symbolise man's relation to God. He must be sung as the soul's husband, bride, child, and friend. I asked for translations of these songs, which he sings in a sweet, not very strong voice, to a music which seems to employ intervals smaller than those of European music, especially for translations of those in Marāthi, his native tongue; for what poet is at his best out of his native tongue? He has, however, sent me translations of his poems in Urdu and Hindi as well, for his pilgrimage as it encircles India expends but two months in his native State, and everywhere he must sing. The English hymn-writer, writing not as himself but as the congregation, is a rhetorician; but the Indian convention, founded upon the most poignant personal emotion, should make poets. The Swāmi has beautiful dramatic ideas, but only somebody born into one of those three tongues can say whether he has added that irrational element which has made 'Sing a Song of Sixpence' immortal. This is from Marāthi:—

> Sweet are His eyes, sweet His looks,
> The love they look exceeding sweet,
> Sweet are His lips, sweet His kiss,
> The love displayed exceeding sweet,

An Indian Monk

Sweet His words, His promise sweet,
Presence and absence both are sweet,
The pangs of love exceeding sweet.

This is from Hindi:—

I know that I am a great sinner,
That there is no remedy,
But let Thy will be done.
If my Lord wishes He need not speak to me.
All I ask is that of His bounty
He walk by my side through my life.
I will behave well
Though He never embrace me—
O Lord, Thou art my Master
And I Thy slave.

This is from Urdu:—

Shall I do this?
Shall I do that?
My hands are empty,
All that talk amounts to nothing.
Never will I do anything,
Never, never will I do anything;
Having been commanded to woo Thee
I should keep myself wide awake
Or else sleep away my life.
I am unfit to do the first,
But I can sleep with open eyes,
And I can always pretend to laugh,
And I can weep for the state I am in;
But my laugh has gone for good,
And gone the charm of tears.

And this too is from Urdu:—

A miracle indeed!
Thou art Lord of All Power.
I asked a little power,
Thou gavest me a begging-bowl.

VII

Our moral indignation, our uniform law, perhaps even our public spirit, may come from the Christian conviction that the soul has but one life to find or lose salvation in: the Asiatic courtesy from the conviction that there are many lives. There are Indian courtesans that meditate many hours a day awaiting without sense of sin their moment, perhaps many lives hence, to leave man for God. For the present they are efficient courtesans. Ascetics, as this book tells, have lived in their houses and received pilgrims there. Kings, princes, beggars, soldiers, courtesans, and the fool by the wayside are equal to the eye of sanctity, for everybody's road is different, everybody awaits his moment.

VIII

The reader of the lives of European devotees may at first be disappointed in this book; the author's life is modelled upon no sacred example, ordered by no well-tried conventual discipline. He is pleased to remember that he learnt his book quickly at the college, that he overcame the wrestler, that he showed courage before the assassin's knife; and yet, though he display our foibles and vanities, he has what we have not, though we once had it—heroic ecstatic passion prolonged through years, through many vicissitudes. Certain Indian, Chinese, and Japanese representations of the Buddha, and of other Divine beings, have a little round lump on the centre of the forehead; ecstatics have sometimes received, as it were from the seal of the God, a similar mark. It corresponds to the wounds made as though by nails upon the hands and feet of some Christian saint, but the symbolism differs. The wounds signify God's sacrifice for man—'Jesus Christ, have mercy upon us'—that round mark the third eye, no physical organ, but the mind's direct apprehension of the truth, above all antinomies, as the mark itself is above eyes, ears, nostrils, in their duality—'splendour of that Divine Being.' During our first meetings, whether within doors or without, Shri Purohit Swāmi's orange turban hid his forehead to the eyes, but he took it off one hot day during lunch, and I saw the little round lump. Marks somewhat resembling those made by nails have been produced upon the hands and feet of patients in a French hospital by hypnotic suggestion, and it is usual, although the wounds of the Saints seen by credible witnesses were deeper, more painful, more disfiguring, to attribute those wounds to auto-suggestion. My own studies, which have not been brief or superficial, compel me to admit suggestion, but to deny with a fervour like that of some humble ignorant Catholic that it can come out of the mind of the ecstatic. Some day I shall ask Shri Purohit Swāmi if the mark first appeared upon his forehead when he lay unconscious upon the top of Mount Girnār.

September 5, 1932

Later Essays and Introductions

LOUIS LAMBERT

I

SOMETIMES I MEET SOMEBODY who read *Louis Lambert* in his 'teens and find that he and I have put it among our sacred books, those books that expound destiny with such a mysterious authority that they furnish texts for pious meditation. Yet *Louis Lambert* is more or less materialistic; all things originate in a substance which is the common element of electricity, heat, and light. In the brain the animal transforms it, in proportion to the strength of the brain, into will. This will creates out of itself thought and sense and by their means absorbs more and more of the parent substance. Though we speak of five senses there is only one, light, for tasting, hearing, smelling are light or sight transformed by different mutations of the substance. Balzac, who describes his own schooldays when he describes Louis Lambert's, may have found in that library at the Vendôme College, founded by learned Oratorians, the works of Bonaventura and of his contemporary Grosseteste, for to Bonaventura hearing, tasting, smelling are forms of light, while to Grosseteste light confers form upon the First Matter. Light is corporeality, he declares, or that of which corporeality is made, a point from which spheral space or corporeality flows as from nothing; a miracle repeated whenever our candle is lit. *Louis Lambert* gives, as it seems, this ancient doctrine, Greek in origin, a materialistic turn by substituting for that

438

first formless matter something that is less the ether of science which began to take its place at the close of the seventeenth century than the common element without attributes described by Crookes: that material Absolute sought by Balthazar Claes in crucible and retort. Berkeley, Balzac's opposite physically and mentally, substituted God, and in *Siris*, like Grosseteste, made light or visibility (our principal perception or sensation) the common form of all particular objects.

II

There is no evidence that Balzac knew that things exist in being perceived, or, to adopt the formula of a later idealism, that they exist in being thought; his powerful body, his imagination which saw everywhere weight and magnitude, the science of his day, made him, like Descartes, consider matter as independent of mind. What then drove him half-way back to the mediaeval hypothesis? At some time of life, probably while still at college, before or during the composition of that *Treatise upon the Will* which he attributes to Louis Lambert, he must have had, or met in others, supernormal experiences resembling those that occur again and again in the *Comédie humaine*. Passages in *Séraphita* suggest familiarity with a state known to me in youth, a state transcending sleep when forms, often of great beauty, appear minutely articulated in brilliant light, forms that express by word or action some spiritual idea and are so moulded or tinted that they make all human flesh seem unhealthy. Then he must have known of, or had some vision of, objects distant in time or place, perhaps in the remote past like that vision seen by Lucien de Rubempré before his death. Something more profound, more rooted in the blood than mere speculation, drove him to Swedenborg, perhaps to Bonaventura and Grosseteste; constrained him to think of the human mind as capable, during some emotional crisis, or, as in the case of Louis Lambert by an accident of genius, of containing within itself all that is significant in human history and of relating that history to timeless reality. He was able to do this by considering light, or fire, not as the child but as the parent or grandparent of the physical senses,[1] by reviving the old doctrine of the animal spirits. 'In the *Timaeus* of Plato,' writes Berkeley, 'there is something like a net of fire, and rays of fire in the human body. Doth this not seem to mean the animal spirit flowing, or rather darting, through the nerves?' This fire is certainly that energy which in *Séraphita* is distinguished from will, and it is doubtless through its agency that will can rise above the human lot, or act beyond the range of the normal senses. 'If we believe Diogenes Laertius,' writes Berkeley, 'the Pythagorean philosophers thought there was a certain pure heat or fire which had something divine in it, by the participation whereof man becomes allied to the Gods. And according to the Platonists, Heaven is not defined

[1] I think it probable that Éliphas Lévi found his 'Astral Light' not, as he said, in Saint-Martin, where the one deep student of that eighteenth-century mystic known to me has searched for it in vain, but in *Louis Lambert*.

so much by its local situation as by its purity. The purest and most excellent fire, that is Heaven, saith Facinus.'

III

Louis Lambert's withdrawal into a state of dumb helpless wisdom on the day before what should have been his happy marriage, or into that madness which was an escape from the conflict between his desire of eternity and his sexual desire, suggests certain experiments of Balzac's day. As the mesmeric trance deepened the subject attained, not merely that vision of distant scenes described in *Ursule Mirouët*, but wisdom. Perhaps, too, a Desplein or a Bianchon had pointed out that at times during such experiments the body became icy cold as though its heat had come not from itself but from the now absent soul; an ancient doctrine Mr. Carrington has supported by a curious book. The body, he contends, does not draw its heat from the combustion of food but during sleep from an unknown source. Balzac, could he have known our modern psychical research, would have noticed that the medium passing into trance is cold, that the thermometer may register a chill in the air, that now and again some 'spirit' describes those brilliant lights that flit so silently about the room as the source of the energy used in the levitation of objects or in the production of voices, nor would he have failed to interest himself in Ochorowicz's suggestion that certain luminous egg-shaped objects, appearing and disappearing suddenly in the darkness, were the irreducible physical minimum of personality.

IV

Louis Lambert, having attributed to man two natures, one that of an angel, hesitates; perhaps, he says, man has not two natures, perhaps, though merely men, we are capable of incomprehensible acts which we, in our admiration for the incomprehensible, attribute to spiritual beings. Here are the two doctrines which dominate our psychical research—spiritualism and animism—the first in Anglo-Saxon countries, where the Fox Sisters had so great an effect, the second upon the Continent, where the Mesmerists, perhaps more through Balzac, George Sand, Dumas, than by direct influence, have accustomed students to think that a personal illumination or state of power can be aroused by experimental means. When Balzac speaks through Séraphita or describes the Duchesse de Langeais playing upon the organ, he thinks of the choir of Heaven, when he creates a Desplein or a Bianchon he is, as I think, both animist and materialist.

Will, having drawn to itself, one of Louis Lambert's aphorisms explains, a sufficient quantity of the substance (light or matter), becomes a most powerful mechanism, for it is like some great stream drawing to itself lesser streams, it may even acquire the qualities of the substance, 'the swiftness of light, the penetrating power of electricity,' or it becomes aware of an 'X', an unknown something which consumes and burns, the Word which is for ever generating the substance. Here, though but for a moment, Balzac's thought and that of Berkeley coincide. The Word is that which turns number into movement, but number (division, magnitude, enumeration) is described by Séraphita as unreal and as involving in unreality all our science. Two and two cannot be four, for nature has no two things alike. Every part is a separate thing and therefore itself a whole and so on. Is movement reality or does it share the unreality of number, its source? Balzac but touches and passes on, absorbed in drama. One could fill the gaps in his thought, substitute definition for his vague suggestion, were not that to lose the bull-necked man, the great eater, whose work resembles his body, the mechanist and materialist who wrote upon the darkness with a burnt stick such sacred and exciting symbols.

A modern painter, who thinks, like Whistler, that a picture must be perfect from the first sketch, growing in richness of detail but not in unity, knows that a work of art must remain fluid to the finish, that an alteration in some minor character or in some detail of colour compels alteration elsewhere. He knows, too, having learnt in disappointment and fatigue, that if his first sketch lacks unity he will not know how to finish. But what is true of the work of art is true of the painter's or dramatist's own life, and if the work is not to be a closed circuit that first sketch has been shaped by desires and alarms arising from another sketch, made not for art but for life. The specialist may add fact to fact, postponing synthesis till greater knowledge, but the man cannot, for, lacking it, he can neither understand nor see correctly. Jane Austen, Scott, Fielding, inherited that other sketch in its clearest and simplest form, but Balzac had to find it in his own mind. His sketch is *Louis Lambert*, the demonstration of its truth is that it made possible the *Comédie humaine*.

In the *Comédie humaine* society is seen as a struggle for survival, each character an expression of will, the struggle Darwin was to describe a few years later, without what our instinct repudiates, Darwin's exaltation of accidental variations. Privilege, pride, the rights of property, are seen preserving the family against individual man armed with Liberty, Equality, Fraternity; and because the French Revolution was recent, he seems to prefer that wing of the Historical Antinomy that best fosters fine manners, minds set too high for intrigue and fear. He could be just to Catherine de'Medici who preserved the State, personification of the family, to Napoleon who created the State; but, dreading, as I think, that hatred might infect his thought, brought into the action no great figure of the Revolution; personifying in the distant figure of Calvin what he called the war of ideas with the State. Will, or passion which is but blind will, is always at crisis, or approaching crisis; everything else seems eliminated, or is made fantastic or violent that the will, without seeming to do so, may exceed nature. Charles Grandet when the story is near its climax slips away to the Indies, earns a large fortune, is back again before we have turned the page; Balzac, who invents detail with so much ease, knows that here it would slacken the pulse. Then, too, always somewhere in the background must lurk Vautrin, Séraphita, the Thirteen. He creates the impossible that all may seem possible. He is like

444

those painters who set patches of pure colour side by side, knowing that they will combine in the eye into the glitter of a wave, into the sober brown of a grass seed. And this world of his, where everything happens in a blaze of light, and not the France of the historians, is early nineteenth-century France to thousands all over Europe.

V

Twenty years ago I read Tolstoy, Dostoievsky, Flaubert with delight, but never opened them again. I belong to a generation that returns to Balzac alone. The Russians make us debate some point of view peculiar to the author, Flaubert etherialises all with his conviction that life is no better than a smell of cooking through a grating. But Balzac leaves us when the book is closed amid the crowd that fills the boxes and the galleries of grand opera; even after hearing Séraphita amid her snows, we return to that crowd which is always right because there is so much history in its veins, to those kings, generals, diplomats, beautiful ladies, to that young Bianchon, to that young Desplein, to all those shabby students of the arts sitting in the galleries. Tolstoy, Dostoievsky, Flaubert draw to their support scholars and sectaries, their readers stand above the theme or beside it, they judge and they reject; but there in the crowded theatre are Balzac's readers and his theme, seen with his eyes they have become philosophy without ceasing to be history. They do not make this impression upon us because of their multitude, there is almost a comparable multitude in *War and Peace*, but because that first sketch that gives unity is an adaptation to his need and time of all that moulded Europe. Stendhal created a modern art; the seminary in *Le Rouge et le noir*, unlike that described by Balzac in *Louis Lambert*, is of his own time and is judged according to its standards, is wholly reflected in the dawdling mirror that was to empty modern literature; but something compelled Balzac while still at school to travel backward, as did the mind of Louis Lambert, to accept all that lay hidden in his blood and in his nerves. Here and there in Blake, in Keats, in Blunt, in Browning, for I cannot judge the rhythm of words in any language but my own, there is a deep masculine resonance, that comes, I think, from a perfect accord between intellect and blood, lacking elsewhere since the death of Cowley. These men, whose rhythm seems to combine the bull and the nightingale, were not modern one had rejected us, two had ignored us, one had surpassed us. I find what seems their match in those passages in the *Comédie humaine* that suddenly startle us with a wisdom deeper than intellect and seem to demand an audience of the daring and the powerful. I have lived from boyhood in the shadow, as it were, of that enumeration of famous women in *La Recherche de l'absolu* ending with the sentence, 'Blessed are the imperfect, for theirs is the Kingdom of Love.' Dante might have made it or some great mediaeval monk, preaching in Rheims.

Louis Lambert

VI

When I lectured in America the other day, I always invited questions and was constantly asked about books I had never heard of, books everybody was reading. Once I said, 'Lionel Johnson held that a man should have read through all good books before he was forty and after that be satisfied with six.' Then somebody asked what would be my six books, and I said I wanted six authors not six books, and I named four authors, choosing not from those that I should, but from those that did most move me, and said I had forgotten the names of the other two. 'First comes Shakespeare,' I said. 'Then the *Arabian Nights* in its latest English version, then William Morris, who gives me all the great stories, Homer and the Sagas included, then Balzac, who saved me from Jacobin and Jacobite.'

July 1934

Later Essays and Introductions

THE HOLY MOUNTAIN [1]

I

'I KNOW NOTHING but the novels of Balzac, and the Aphorisms of Patanjali. I once knew other things, but I am an old man with a poor memory.' There must be some reason why I wanted to write that lying sentence, for it has been in my head for weeks. Is it that whenever I have been tempted to go to Japan, China, or India for my philosophy, Balzac has brought me back, reminded me of my preoccupation with national, social, personal problems, convinced me that I cannot escape from our *Comédie humaine?* We philosophise that we may reduce our minds to a single energy, and thereby save our souls and feed our bodies. We prove what we must and assume the rest upon hearsay. No two civilisations prove or assume the same things, but behind both hides the unchanging experience of simple men and women. When I read the travels of Purohit Swāmi, or of his Master, Bhagwān Shri Hamsa, I am among familiar things. *Séraphita* has prepared me for those adventures, those apparitions, and I remember that the knights and hermits who prepared the ground for our *Comédie humaine* preferred, it may be, such adventures to philosophy, such apparitions to dogma:—

> One wise friend, or one
> Better than wise, being fair.

[1] *The Holy Mountain*, being the Story of a Pilgrimage to Lake Mānas and of Initiation on Mount Kailās in Tibet, by Bhagwān Shri Hamsa. Translated from the Marāthi by Shri Purohit Swāmi. (Faber & Faber. 1934.)

448

The Holy Mountain

II

Shri Purohit Swāmi at the beginning of this century was a Mr. Purohit, student of the University of Bombay. He had inherited from his Marāthā fathers the worship of Dattātreya, the first Yogi, spiritual Father of all Yogis since, or, as we would say, their patron saint. He had seen him in his dreams, but such knowledge is insufficient; dream words are few and hard to understand; he needed for guide some man who could point out from personal experience what meditations enrich the waking mind. For a time he ceased to read. When he fixed his attention upon the Lord Dattātreya even the *Bhagavad-Gitā* distracted him.

The students had come to associate scholarship with a weak body and shabby clothes, and there was a reaction towards athletics; he had prided himself on being scholar, athlete, dandy, but because women, notorious disturbers of meditation, attracted him, and were attracted, he ate little, grew a beard and dressed out of the fashion. Finding that among holy people his mind grew quiet, he frequented temples and places of pilgrimage; because contact with a supernatural being is never attained through the waking mind, but through the act of what is called the 'unconscious mind,' he repeated thousands of times every day: 'We meditate upon the supreme splendour of that Divine Being. May it illuminate our intellects,' until he spoke those words in his sleep, or silently while engaged in conversation. At a temple in Narsobā Wādi he met a beautiful courtesan who had come seeking a cure for

449

some ailment, found the cure, but whenever she attempted to return to her lover, fell sick at the border of the territory, and now sat there, and would while life lasted, dressed in a white robe, praising her Divine Master to the notes of her lute. She had prayed, not foreseeing its consequence, not only for physical, but for spiritual health, and the 'unconscious mind' had heard her prayer.

III

But because he could not persuade those Masters he found acceptable to accept him, he sank into despair. He sat weeping in his room; a friend knocked at the door, asked him to meet a certain Shri Nātēkār Swāmi, now known as Bhagwān Shri Hamsa, who had just arrived. 'We ascended the stairs of Keertikar building,' he writes, 'and were admitted into a small room at the top floor. As I entered, the Swāmi, who was sitting upon a tiger's skin, rose. Our eyes met.' And Shri Nātēkār Swāmi, though so far as Mr. Purohit knew they had never seen each other, said: 'We meet again after a long time.' He was the elder by four years. He came of a wealthy family, and his father, dreading that his son would become a wandering monk, as had uncles and ancestors, had made him marry at the age of sixteen; but one day while he sat reading upon a river bank, his soul awoke, and throwing book and European clothes into the river, he began a life of austerity. The countrypeople account for his sanctity with a story as incredible to modern ears as any told of the childhood of some European saint, but symbolising an alliance between body and soul our theology rejects. A certain beautiful married woman at the age of twenty had, with her husband's consent, become a pilgrim. After wandering from Himālayān shrine to shrine for many years, she had found a home in a ruined temple at Brahmāvarta. Some called her the mad woman, and some, because of the cotton mat that covered her loins, 'the Lady of the Mat.' She had but two possessions, that cotton mat and her lute. Shri Nātēkār Swāmi's father went on pilgrimage to Brahmāvarta with his son, then but a child. Father and son visited the Lady of the Mat. The child climbed on to her knees. She said: 'Leave him with me; I will take care of him.' The father did not dare to disobey, but was alarmed because she had no food but a daily piece of bread brought her by a water-carrier. When he returned next day with food, the child would not touch it, because the Saint had fed him from her breast. She fed him for a fortnight, then gave him back to his father, saying: 'He will know when a grown man what I have done for him.' One day the Saint called the water-carrier, told him that she was about to leave the world. Because he wept, she gave him her mat as a relic, told him that he must bring her lute to the boy she had fed. Then as she played and sang, the waters of the Ganges became disturbed, first little waves, then great waves; the more she sang, the greater grew the waves. When they touched her feet, she handed the lute to the water-carrier. A moment later they had swept her away; then, upon the instant, all was still.

Mr. Purohit took up once more the life of a student. When he had passed, to please his father, his final law examination, he was summoned by Dattātreya in a dream. He and his Master set out for Mount Girnār, where the footprints of Dattātreya are shown upon a rock. He repeated all day: 'We meditate upon the supreme splendour of that Divine Being.' At the foot of the Mountain, he vowed to throw himself from the cliff if his Divine Master remained hidden. As they climbed the seven thousand steps, he neither ate nor drank, though he had starved himself for weeks, and he had constantly to lie down to rest. At the full moon of 25th December 1907, the birthday of Dattātreya, they reached the summit. He fell asleep upon the sacred footprints as the sun set, and did not awake till the moon was in the sky. As he awoke he knew that Dattātreya had in his sleep accepted him, and when he felt his forehead, he found in the centre the first trace of that small mound that is the Indian equivalent to the Christian stigmata. He had attained *Sushupti* or unconscious *Samādhi*, a dreamless sleep that differs from that of every sleeper in some part of the night, every insect in the chrysalis, every hibernating animal, every soul between death and birth, because attained through the sacrifice of the physical senses, and through meditation upon a divine personality, a personality at once historical and yet his own spiritual Self. Henceforth that personality, that Self, would be able, though always without his knowledge, to employ his senses and, as in the East the bodily movements are classified as senses, to direct his life. He was not isolated, however, as are men of genius or intellect, for henceforth all those in whom that Self had awakened were his neighbours.

Already while his attainment was incomplete, when he had not even reached the top of the steps, he had seen a beautiful slender woman, with dark bright eyes and red lips, leaning against a tree, and as she vanished, received her benediction, and now as he descended, another of the Masters of Wisdom, a bright-eyed man, appeared.

Although accepted, although henceforth not Mr. Purohit but Shri Purohit Swāmi, he refused to accompany his friend, who had in a meditation known as *Savikalpa-Samādhi* been ordered to seek *Turiyā*, the greater or conscious *Samādhi*, at Mount Kailās, the legendary Meru; he thought himself unworthy, that he had not freed himself from the world, and could but carry it upon the journey.

IV

Sometimes they came in contact with that Europeanised India England has created with a higher education which is always conducted in the English language. Shri Purohit Swāmi saw to his Master's comforts, left him stretched out for sleep in a first-class carriage, went to find a third-class carriage for himself, but there was not even standing room. He decided to return to his Master, but found an empty carriage. His Master had left the train and was sitting upon a bench, naked but for a loin-cloth. A Europeanised Indian had denounced him for wearing silk and travelling first-class, and all monks and pilgrims for bringing discredit upon India by their superstitions and idleness. So he stripped off his silk clothes, saying that though they seemed to have come with his destiny, they were of no importance. Then, because the stranger was still unsatisfied, had given him his luggage and his ticket. They were able, however, to continue their journey, for just when the train was about to start, the Europeanised Indian returned and threw clothes, luggage, and ticket into the carriage. He had been attacked by remorse. When they reached their destination, Shri Nātēkār Swāmi sat down in the prescribed attitude, passed into *Samādhi*, and Shri Purohit Swāmi, openly rejoicing, sang his praises—Divine and Human Master, one in that dark or bright meditation:—

> 'Lead me to that Kingdom of Thine
> Where there is no pleasure of union
> Nor displeasure of separation,
> Where the self is in eternal happiness.
> Thou alone canst thither lead the ailing soul'

—verse after verse, until his Master came out of meditation with a cry: 'Victory, victory to the Lord Dattātreya.'

v

Much Chinese and Japanese painting is a celebration of mountains, and so sacred were those mountains that Japanese artists, down to the invention of the colour-print, constantly recomposed the characters of Chinese mountain scenery, as though they were the letters of an alphabet, into great masterpieces, traditional and spontaneous. I think of the face of the Virgin in

The Holy Mountain

Siennese painting, preserving, after the supporting saints had lost it, a Byzantine character. To Indians, Chinese, and Mongols, mountains from the earliest times have been the dwelling-places of the Gods. Their kings before any great decision have climbed some mountain, and of all these mountains Kailās, or Mount Meru, as it is called in the *Mahabharata*, was the most famous. Sven Hedin calls it the most famous of all mountains, pointing out that Mont Blanc is unknown to the crowded nations of the East. Thousands of Hindu, Tibetan and Chinese pilgrims, Vedāntic, or Buddhist, or of some older faith have encircled it, some bowing at every step, some falling prostrate, measuring the ground with their bodies; an outer ring for all, an inner and more perilous for those called by the priests to its greater penance. On another ring, higher yet, inaccessible to human feet, the Gods move in adoration. Still greater numbers have known it from the *Mahabharata* or from the poetry of Kalidās, known that a tree covered with miraculous fruit rises from the lake at its foot, that sacred swans sing there, that the four great rivers of India rise there, with sands of gold, silver, emerald, and ruby, that at certain seasons from the lake—here Dattātreya is himself the speaker—springs a golden phallus. Mānas Sarowar, the lake's full name, means 'The great intellectual Lake,' and in this Mountain, this Lake, a dozen races find the birthplace of their Gods and of themselves. We too have learnt from Dante to imagine our Eden, or Earthly Paradise, upon a mountain, penitential rings upon the slope.

VI

Shri Nātēkār Swāmi visited other sacred places in the Himālayās before starting for Mount Kailās, travelling sometimes alone and almost always by unfrequented routes. He recalls the narrow escape of himself and his Nepālese guide in the Dehrādun forest from an infuriated elephant, by dropping from a precipice to lie stunned at its foot; but once he had started, his travels record local customs, his pleasure in scenery, some occasional hardship—for a time little that one does not find in Ekai Kawaguchi's *Three Years in Tibet*. Sometimes he and his three coolies sleep on the ground, sometimes in a temple or cave; sometimes there is difficulty about food, or about a mule or ass to carry it; sometimes he notices that the guest-house is full of fleas; once he is so cold he has to surround himself with lambs, two at his head, two at his back, and six or seven about the rest of his body. Sometimes he forms a brief friendship with a Tibetan official or fellow-pilgrim. Pilgrims for untold years doubtless have had such adventures. Now and then something reminds us that we accompany a holy man. Once he and his coolies were caught by a score of mounted robbers. For a moment he was dumb with terror, then he became suddenly calm, closed his eyes, turned towards Mount Kailās, bowed in adoration of his Master, sat down in the Yogi posture that is called *Padmasan* and waited in silence. The robbers fell silent also. Then one, the strongest and fiercest, asked his name and business, and what money he carried. He explained, or tried to explain by signs, that he was a pilgrim and had no money. The robber called four of the other robbers, said he would kill him and his coolies and take their clothes. Whereat Shri Nātēkār Swāmi called upon the name of his Master, thrust his neck forward to await the blow of the sword, and went into meditation. When he awoke, his eyes wet with tears of adoration, the robber was kneeling before him, his head upon his thumbs; the other robbers, their swords sheathed, were fanning the swooning coolies.

At Lake Mānas Sarowar the supernatural begins to stir the pot. He had, according to his vow, to spend two weeks upon its bank, bathing twice a day in its icy water, taking but one meal a day, and at that nothing but the tea Tibetans mix with butter, and speaking not a word. At five in the morning of the last day of penance he heard a voice towards the west, the direction of Mount Kailās, a woman's voice as it seemed, singing the Mandukya Upanishad's description of the four states of the soul: the waking state corresponding to the letter '*A*', where physical objects are present; the dreaming state corresponding to the letter '*U*', where mental objects are present; the state of dreamless sleep corresponding to the letter '*M*', where all seems darkness to the soul, because all there is lost in Brahma, creator of mental and physical objects; the final state corresponding to the whole sacred word '*Aum*', consciousness bound to no object, bliss bound to no aim, *Turiyā*, pure personality. He searched the shore but could find no one; even his binoculars showed it empty. He sent his coolies to inquire at the neighbouring monastery, but nobody could tell them of the singer. Then he paced the sands, thinking of the voice, but when he had gone a hundred yards, was startled to see before him the print of a human foot. He told his coolies that they must gather up the baggage and follow, that he had set out for Mount Kailās. He followed the footprints for two or three miles along the south shore, but near the rocky western shore they grew indistinct and disappeared. He went on in the direction they had taken till stopped by an ascent too steep for his exhausted body.

After two days' travelling, one day through storm and hail, spending the nights in a cave and in a foul hut made out of loose stones piled up on four sides, a great single slab for roof, he began his penitential circuit. At the eastern side the guide, pointing to a cave a thousand feet above his head, said that a great Hindu saint lived there, but that he knew no way to reach it. Shri Nātēkār Swāmi and the guide began to climb, but before they had gone a quarter of the way the guide was taken ill. The Swāmi told him to return to the coolies, that he and they must remain a week in a Buddhist guest-house, then if they heard nothing of their master, return to India.

The ice began fifty yards below the cave; that past, came a perpendicular cliff with notches for hand and foot cut in the rock, and seven feet from the bottom the mouth of the cave. He climbed, and crawling through darkness, found a dim lamp and an oldish naked man, sitting upon a tiger's skin. He prostrated himself in reverence and said: 'Lord, it is your grace that has brought this servant to your hallowed feet.' The naked man laughed and said: '*Acha, Vatsa, Uthake baitho,*' which means—'My darling, get up!' He was told that he might ask anything except for age, name, and parentage. He asked in Hindi, Marāthi, in English, and the answer came always in the same language, perfect in grammar and accent. He noticed that whatever the language, that language alone was used, no foreign word admitted, and became convinced that his host knew all languages. It was he who had sung the Mandukya Upanishad and made those foot-prints on the sand, and it was because of that old acquaintance that he had called him darling. Shri Nātēkār Swāmi stayed there for three days, eating nothing, but drinking water, and during those three days his host neither ate nor drank. Then he returned to his coolies, and having told them to wait for a week, set out alone for Gaurikund, a little lake high up upon Mount Kailās, wherein he was to cast sand from the southernmost point of India and so complete his pilgrimage. Pilgrims such as he perpetually encircle that religious India which keeps Mount Kailās within its borders, that all the land may be blessed by their passing feet.

After two nights spent in hollows of the ice, his overcoat about his head, his feet drawn up to his ribs, he came back defeated, but set out again the next day, and after a climb of five thousand feet, reached the lake, and there, twenty feet from the shore, broke through five feet of ice, cast in the sand, sat down, passed into meditation awaiting the object of his pilgrimage, the physical presence of his Divine Master, Dattātreya. He has described his uncertainty as to whether he would live or die, recorded the exact placing of his staff, what points of the compass he had first looked at, what words he spoke, his different postures, a tiger's skin that he had brought for his seat; details all settled by tradition. For three days he remained in meditation, gradually the mental image of his Master grew dim, voices spoke. Three times he heard the words: 'O my child, O my dear,' but he knew that if he opened his eyes while the mental image remained he would fail. What were voices to him if he could not see the physical form? At last the mental image suddenly vanished. He opened his eyes, and Dattātreya stood before him, made him perform certain further ceremonies, admitted him to the Giri order of Sanyāsins, promised to keep his heart from straying to physical things, and named him Hamsa, which means 'soul,' but is also the name of those emblems of the soul, the white-winged, red-beaked, red-legged water-birds of Lake Mānas Sarowar.

VII

Shri Purohit Swāmi claims that his Master gained, at that mountain lake, *Turiyā*, whereas he himself had but gained upon Mount Girnār a dreamless sleep, *Sushupti*. The philosophy and technique of both of these states are described in the *Yoga-Sutras* or Aphorisms of Patanjali, written somewhere between the third and fifth centuries of our era, but containing

a far older tradition, or in the voluminous comment-
aries, written between the middle of the seventh and
the ninth centuries. The Spirit, the Self that is in all
selves, the pure mirror, is the source of intelligence,
but Matter is the source of all energy, all creative
power, all that separates one thing from another, not
Matter as understood by Hobbes and his Mechanists,
Matter as understood in Russia, where the Government has silenced the Mechanist, but interpreted with
profound logic almost what Schopenhauer understood
by Will. If I think of the table on which I am writing,
my mental image is as much Matter as the table itself,
though of 'a subtler kind,'[1] and I am able to think
correctly, because the Matter I call Mind takes the
shape of this or that physical object, and this Matter,
physical and mental, has three aspects—'*Tamas*, darkness, frustration; *Rajas*, activity, passion; *Satva*,
brightness, wisdom.' In one of the Patanjali comment-
aries there is a detailed analysis of the stages of concentration that would be Hegelian did they include the
Self in their dialectic. The first is the fixing of attention
upon some place or object, the navel, the tip of the
tongue. Any object will serve so long as it belongs to
oneself and is an immediate perception, not something
inferred or heard of; or one may fix attention upon
the form of some God, for a God is but the Self.
But one cannot fix attention without some stream of
thought, so if the object be the tongue, one thinks of
the tongue as symbol or function. As I write the word,

[1] 'Subtler', 'finer', because it penetrates all things. Ordinary
matter cannot go through the wall, mind can.

I think at once of Blake's 'False Tongue' which is the 'vegetative' sense, then I remember that according to Patanjali meditation upon the tongue awakens the perception of taste or colour or sound. The taste, colour, and sound so perceived attain supernormal perfection as fact and idea draw together. Should one choose a God as the theme of meditation, the majesty of his face, or the beauty of his ear-rings, may, as trance deepens, express all majesty, all beauty. The second stage is this identity between idea and fact, between thought and sense; an identity that recalls the description of dreams in the Upanishads. The third stage is *Sushupti*, a complete disappearance of all but this identity. Nothing exists but that ravening tongue,[1] or that majesty, that beauty; the man has disappeared as the sculptor in his statue, the musician in his music. One remembers the Japanese philosopher's saying, 'What the artist perceives through a medium, the saint perceives immediately.'

In the fourth stage the ascetic enters one or more of these stages at will and retains his complete memory when he returns; this is *Turiyā*, but as yet only in the form called *Savikalpa*; full *Turiyā* or 'seedless' *Samādhi* comes when all these states are as a single timeless act, and that act is pure or unimpeded personality, all existence brought into the words: 'I am.' It resembles that last Greek number, a multiple of all numbers because there is nothing outside it, nothing to make a new beginning. It is not only seedless but objectless

[1] The tongue represents colour and sound, perhaps because the ascetic can see the point of nose or tongue, but not his eyes or ears.

because objects are lost in complete light. Darkness is the causal body of existence. Objects are its serrates and dentures. One remembers those lines of Coleridge:

> Resembles life what once was deemed of light,
> Too ample in itself for human sight?
> An absolute self—an element ungrounded—
> All that we see, all colours of all shade,
> By encroach of darkness made?

VIII

If *Turiyā* be attained, the ascetic may remain in Life until the results of past lives are exhausted or because he would serve his fellows. While such binding to the past remains, or duty to the living, it must, one would think, be incomplete, something less than absolute Self. Probably such an ascetic regards complete 'seed-less' *Samādhi* as an ideal form, an all but unattainable ideal that he must approach through life after life: a central experience, touched or it may be but symbolised at some moment when some quality of life flowers.

The life of an ascetic is a preparation for meditation. He repeats the name of some God thousands of times a day, frequents a shrine, is convinced that he must offer there all the devotion, all the passion aroused in his present life, or in his past lives, by friend, master, child, and wife. If he finds it impossible at once to transform sexual into spiritual desire, he may beseech the God to come as a woman. The God may send some strange woman as his emblem, but should he come himself, the ascetic wakes at dawn to find his empty bed fragrant with some temple incense, or patches of saffron paste upon his breast; but, whether the God send or come, every need soon fades, except that for unity with God. Nor is supernormal sense confined to the moments of concentration; he will suddenly smell amid the ordinary occupations of life, perhaps in the middle of winter, an odour of spring flowers, or have an unimaginable sense of physical well-being that is described as a transformation of the sense of touch, or meet in empty places melodious sound, or a fine sight. I have been told that somewhere in India sits a musician into whose mouth pupils put food and drink. He was accustomed to listen to such sounds and imitate them, but one day the hand he had thrust out towards the string stopped in mid-air and became rigid; from that day he has remained drunk and lost in *Sushupti*.

The ascetic who has not freed his mind of ambition and passion may pass, not into *Sushupti*, but into a distortion of the second stage of concentration, analogous to that of dreaming-sleep; sense and thought are one, but the bond between that unity and his ego remains unbroken. He is in the condition of the witches who project afar their passion-driven souls in some animal shape, while their bodies lie at home, or of that woman in Murasaki's book who killed, without knowing it, her enemy in a dream. On the other hand, the ascetic who has attained *Turiyā* enters this second stage wide awake, and as there is nothing outside his will, he can shape a new body to his need, or use the body of another. The old ascetic of the cavern was in this stage when he sang and left his footprints on the sand. Those who have attained 'seedless' *Samādhi* are said to be physically immortal; they do not die, but make themselves invisible. The story-tellers describe them dissolving their bodies while they seem to bathe, or leaving, like Christ, an empty tomb: at will, they pass into the Source.

An ascetic who has rid himself of passion may, though unfitted for *Turiyā*, seek, like many Greeks, wisdom through those self-luminous and coherent dreams that seem to surround, like a ring of foam, the dark pool of dreamless sleep. If devoted to some God, or to some other image of the Universal Self, he may pass that ring, obtain *Sushupti* in its highest form, the dreamless sleep of the soul in God. When he returns to waking life, he is still an instrument of that other Will; those upon whom his attention falls may grow more fortunate, but his own fortune will be no better; a miracle may happen under his eyes, but, because it must be as though waking he still slept, he neither knows nor may inquire whether his sacrifice has played a part. He may even, as I imagine, be ignorant of common things, be somewhat childish as though he cannot see by daylight, resemble in all things the pure fool of European tradition. After death indeed he attains liberation, becoming one of those spirits that have no life but to obey that Self who creates all things in dreamless sleep:—

> There is in God, some say,
> A deep but dazzling darkness: as men here
> Say it is late and dusky, because they
> See not all clear.
> O for that Night, where I in Him
> Might live invisible and dim!

The ascetic seeking *Savikalpa-Samādhi* identifies it with *Satva*, but calls *Sushupti*, which he identifies with *Tamas*, the *Samādhi* of a fool, because in that state he is ignorant, and because he is liable to fall back upon it, as though sinking into lethargy, but he who thinks *Sushupti* the supreme self-surrender, must, I am persuaded, identify *Sushupti* with *Satva*, the waking life of sense with *Tamas*. *Savikalpa-Samādhi* is, as it were, ringed with the activities of life, *Sushupti* ringed with dreams, and both rings are *Rajas*, while *Savikalpa-Samādhi* and *Sushupti* are alternatively light and darkness. Neither is in itself the final deliverance or return into the Source, for *Rajas*, *Tamas*, *Satva* constitute 'matter,' or 'nature' without beginning, without reality. The Vedāntic philosophers, unlike Buddha, direct our attention to bright or intelligible perfection, but seek timeless perfection, seedless *Samādhi*, beyond it in the isolated Soul, that is yet in all souls.

IX

In 1818 Hegel, his head full of the intellectual pride of the eighteenth century, was expounding history. Indifferent, as always, to the individual soul, he had taken for his theme the rise and fall of nations. Greece, he explained, first delivered mankind from nature; the Egyptian Sphinx, for all its human face, was Asiatic and animal; but when Oedipus answered the riddle, that Sphinx was compelled to leap into the abyss; the riddle, 'What goes first on four legs, then upon two, then upon three?' called up man. Nature is bondage, its virtue no more than the custom of clan or race, a plant rooted outside man, a law blindly obeyed. From that moment on, intellect or Spirit, that which has value in itself, began to prevail, and now in Hegel's own day the climax had come, not crippled age but wisdom; there had been many rehearsals, for every civilisation, no matter where its birth, began with Asia, but the play itself had been saved up for our patronage. A few years more and religion would be absorbed in the State, art in philosophy, God's Will proved to be man's will.

I can imagine Balzac, that great eater, his mediaeval humility greater than his pride, answering: 'Man's intellect or Spirit can do nothing but bear witness; Nature alone is active—I have heard the clergy talk of Grace, but that is beyond my knowledge—I refuse to confine Nature to claw, paw, and hoof. It is the irrational glory that reaches perfection at the mid-moment, at the Renaissance of every civilisation. Raphael and Michelangelo closed our sixth century, for our civilisation began when Romanesque displaced Byzantine architecture. Great empires are founded by lovers of women and of money; they are destroyed by men of ideas. There is a continual conflict—I too have my dialectic—the perfection of Nature is the decline of Spirit, the perfection of Spirit is the decline of Nature. In the Spiritual dawn when Raphael painted the Camera della Segnatura, and the Medician Popes dreamed of uniting Christianity and Paganism, all that was sacred with all that was secular, Europe might have made its plan, begun the solution of its problems, but individualism came instead; the egg, instead of hatching, burst. The *Peau de chagrin*[1] and *Catherine de Médicis* contain my philosophy of History. Genius and talent have torn Europe to pieces. The *Divina Commedia* summed up and closed the Europe that created Mont Saint-Michel, Chartres Cathedral, the Europe that went upon its knees or upon all fours. The *Comédie humaine* has closed the counter-movement, that kept her upon two legs. In my open letter to the Duchesse de Castries I foretell the future. What was, before man stood up, an impulse in our blood, returns as an external necessity. We shall become one through violence or imitation; and, because we can no longer create, gather, as Rome did, the treasures of the world in some one place. As we grow old we accumulate abstract substitutes for experience, commodities of all kinds, but an old pensioner that taps upon the ground where he once crawled is no wit the wiser for all his proverbs. You should have gone to Hugo with that romantic dream. When I was young I wanted to take opium—Paris had just discovered it—but I could not, because I would not surrender my will. My *Comédie humaine* will cure the world of all Utopias, but you were born too soon.'

That last sentence would have been untrue. Balzac's influence has reached some exceptional men and women. Hegel's Philosophy of History dominates the masses, though they have not heard his name, as

---

[1] Hegel's lectures were not published until 1837, seven years after the publication of the *Peau de chagrin*. Balzac probably derived his thought from classical sources. It is more like Vico's than Hegel's.

The Holy Mountain

Rousseau's philosophy did in the nineteenth and later eighteenth centuries, and has shed more blood.

X

Here and there in the Upanishads mention is made of the moon's bright fortnight, the nights from the new to the full moon, and of the dark fortnight of the moon's decline. He that lives in the first becomes fire or an eater; he that lives in the second becomes fuel and food to the living (Schopenhauer's essay upon Love reversed). He that moves towards the full moon may, if wise, go to the Gods (expressed or symbolised in the senses) and share their long lives, or if to Brahma's question 'Who are you?' he can answer 'Yourself,' pass out of those three penitential circles, that of common men, that of gifted men, that of the Gods, and find some cavern upon Meru, and so pass out of all life. Upon the other hand, those that move towards the dark of the moon, if they are pious, as the crowd is pious, if they can offer the right sacrifices, pray at the right temples, can go to the blessed Ghosts, to the Heaven of their fathers, find what peace can be found between death and birth. The Upanishads denied any escape for these. The new thinkers arrayed their asceticism, their complete individuality against the tribal dancers, spirit mediums, ritual poetry, orgiastic ceremonies, soma-drinking priests of the popular religion: 'As for living, our servants will do that for us.'

The bright fortnight's escape is *Turiyā*, and in the dark fortnight, the ascetic who, unlike the common people, asks nothing of God or Ghost, may, though unworthy of *Turiyā*, find *Sushupti* an absorption in God, as if the Soul were His food or fuel.

Man is born into 'a mortal birth of twelve months or thirteen months,' into the lunar year that sometimes requires an extra month that it may keep the proper seasons, from which it is plain that every incarnation is divided into twelve or thirteen cycles. As the first and last crescents are nearest the Sun, the visionary must have seen in those cycles a conflict between Moon and Sun, or when Greek astronomy had reached India, between a Moon that has taken the Sun's light into itself, 'I am yourself,' and the Moon lost in the Sun's light, between Sun in Moon and Moon in Sun. The Eastern poet saw the Moon as the Sun's bride; now in solitude; now offered to her Bridegroom in a self-abandonment unknown to our poetry. A European would think perhaps of the moonlit and moonless nights alone, call the increasing moon man's personality, as it fills into the round and becomes perfect, overthrowing the black night of oblivion. Am I not justified in discovering there the conflict between subjectivity and objectivity, between Self and Not-Self, between waking life and dreamless sleep?

The year of twelve or thirteen months that constitutes a single lifetime was thought of as a day or night in a still greater year, and that year divided in its turn into months, and so on until we reach some greatest year. One must imagine everywhere enclosed one within another, circles of Sun in Moon, Moon in Sun. Mixed with these mythological or symbolic periods were others founded upon the astronomical fantasy of Greece. Certain cycles must have begun when all the planets stood toeing a line like young athletes. If the equinoctial Sun encircles the Zodiac in thirty-six thousand years, as Alexandrian Greece imagined, why not consider that but one month in a still greater year? Indifferent to history, India delighted in vast periods, which solemnised the mind, seeming to unite it to the ageless heavens. The Indian would have understood the dialectic of Balzac, but not that of Hegel—what could he have made of Hegel's optimism?—but never cared to discover in those great periods a conflict of civilisations and of nations. Even the Great Year of Proclus, though that is cold and abstract compared with the conception that has begun to flit before modern minds, was impossible to the Indian's imagination. Preoccupied with the seeds of action, discoverable by those who have rejected all that is not themselves, he left to Europe the study and creation of civilisation. This he could do, perhaps, because the villages that nurtured his childhood were subject to no change but that of the seasons—their life, as it were, the symbolical syntax wherein we may write the History of the World.

XI

Greek and Roman speculation generally made the Great Year solar, but the symbolism is little different. The two extremes correspond to the Sun's passage through Capricorn and Cancer. In the first the world was nourished by water—Philaeus called it 'the lunar water'; in the second by the 'Fire of Heaven.'

471

Later Essays and Introductions

I find my imagination setting in one line *Turiyā*—full moon, mirror-like bright water, Mount Meru; and in the other *Sushupti*, moonless night, 'dazzling darkness'—Mount Girnār.

Does not every civilisation as it approaches or recedes from its full moon seem as it were to shiver into the premonition of some perfection born out of itself, perhaps even of some return to its first Source? Does not one discover in the faces of Madonnas and holy women painted by Raphael or da Vinci, if never before or since, a condition of soul where all is still and finished, all experience wound up upon a bobbin? Does one not hear those lips murmur that, despite whatever illusion we cherish, we came from no immaturity, but out of our own perfection like ships that 'all their swelling canvas wear'? Does not every new civilisation, upon the other hand, imagine that it was born in revelation, or that it comes from dependence upon dark or unknown powers, that it can but open its eyes with difficulty after some long night's sleep or winter's hibernation?

'For this one thing above all I would be praised as a man,
That in my words and my deeds I have kept those laws in
    mind
Olympian Zeus, and that high clear Empyrean,
Fashioned, and not some man or people of mankind,
Even those sacred laws nor age nor sleep can blind.

              . . . should a man forget
The holy images, the Delphian Sybil's trance,
And the world's navel-stone, and not be punished for it
And seem most fortunate, or even blesséd perchance,
Why should we honour the Gods, or join the sacred dance?'

The Holy Mountain

P.S.—I have made much use during the writing of this essay of Shri Purohit Swāmi's *An Indian Monk* (Macmillan), of his unpublished translation of the *Yoga-Sutras* of Patanjali, and of the standard translation of the same work published by Harvard University. I thank Shri Purohit Swāmi for answering many questions.

Bhagwān Shri Hamsa was born at Dhuliā on the 15th of June 1878. He was the younger son of Pāndu Tātyā Nātēkār, a well-known pleader. As he lost his mother at the age of four, his father and elder brother took care of him. When Pāndu Tātyā learned from an astrologer that his son would become a Yogi, he forbade him to read the *Gitā* and found him a wife. He was married in his sixteenth year. But one day, sitting on the banks of the Indrāyani at Dehu, he decided to renounce the world. He threw his European clothes into the river. He began to practise austerities; he read the *Guru-Charitra*, the Life of Dattātreya—repeated the *Gāyatri Mantram*, took milk for his sole food. After three and a half years of this life, he went on pilgrimage encircling the whole of India, and visited once every year Mount Girnār, where the footprints of Dattātreya are shown to pilgrims. Then in 1908 he made the pilgrimage to Mount Kailās described in the following pages.

1934

Later Essays and Introductions

THE MANDUKYA UPANISHAD [1]

I

WHEN I WROTE my introduction to *The Holy Mountain*, I did not analyse Bhagwān Shri Hamsa's vision by the frozen lake, and that has been heavy on my conscience. The culmination of the pilgrimage, it should have been the culmination of my argument, but I shied away from it. Then after the publication of the book I asked Shri Purohit Swāmi if a passer-by, were one possible amid such desolation, could have seen the God. He said 'No,' and now that I was not compelled to assume a materialisation like that which showed the medium and itself side by side and permitted Sir William Crookes to feel its beating heart, my intellect could begin its analysis. Analysis seemed important because of the connection, still vague in my imagination, between pilgrimage and vision, scenery and the pilgrim's salvation. Forty years ago my closest friend planned a walk through Ireland, a long stick with a head like the letter 'T' in his hand, that he might preach the return of those ancient gods that seemed a part of the soil and the blood. Alarmed for his life—Irish Christianity is not gentle—I brought him to Sir Horace Plunkett, who made him a successful organiser of co-operative banks. I have since regretted an action that entangled in practical discussion a mind ripe for spiritual theory. Judea had, he said, robbed all

[1] Published in the *Criterion*, July 1935, under the title *Māndookya Upanishad*, with an Introduction by William Butler Yeats.

474

countries; men once thought their own neighbourhood holy, but had now to discover their Holy Land in an atlas. Yet all might be changed could he but discover three old men who lived somewhere in Ireland in a white thatched cottage, beside a telegraph post; or could he but lie upon certain mountains until his soul sank down into the great lakes of spiritual fire under his feet. Was he a German Christian born too soon or a Swedenborg I had turned from the road before his vision clarified? He was not as strange as he seems in memory; such ideas were in other Irish minds; I had made a map of ancient Ireland with the sacred places marked upon it in red ink, and Standish O'Grady had announced in his weekly Review that Slieve-namon would yet be more famous than Olympus. An old Tory uncle used to say, 'Everything that comes to Ireland becomes a reality'; the modern interest in folk-lore, a scientific curiosity elsewhere, had transformed our thought. And now, compelled by that transfiguration, I must ask why Bhagwān Shri Hamsa had to go that pilgrimage and no other, and to meet his God amid such desolation upon Kailās.

II

Bhagwān Shri Hamsa, almost at the end of his journey, heard a spiritual voice:—

'At 5 A.M. I heard strains of melodious music sung by a human voice coming from the west. In rapt attention I listened and thought it the voice of a woman. I decided, a little later, that the chant of Shri

Mandukya Upanishad was being sung. Through the binoculars I searched in the direction from whence came the melodious sound, but saw no human figure on that beach of sand. I strained my eyes and gazed all round, but there was no trace of any human figure. The music lasted half an hour, then it ceased, and the incident began to trouble me. What could have been the meaning of this sweet chant of the Mandukya Upanishad in this solitary region?' Two days later a naked ascetic in a cavern claimed to have been present, singing, in his spiritual body. That shortest and the most comprehensive of the Upanishads examines the sacred syllables: 'the word *Aum* is the imperishable Spirit. This universe is the manifestation. The past, the present, the future, everything, is *Aum*, and whatever transcends this division of time, that too is *Aum*.' Then the short paragraphs describe the letters: '*A*' is the physical or waking state; '*U*' the dream state, where only mental substances appear; '*M*' is deep sleep, where man 'feels no desire, creates no dream,' yet is this sleep called 'conscious' because he is now united to sleepless Self, creator of all, source of all, unknowable, unthinkable, ungraspable, a union with it sole proof of its existence. The Self, whereto man is now united, expressed by our articulation of the whole word, is the fourth state.

I have already compared these four states with the four stages of concentration described by a commentator upon Patanjali: the first with the selection of some place, object or image, as the theme of meditation; the second with the mutual transformation, the drawing, as it were, together, of theme and thought, fact and idea; the dreamer creating his dream, the sculptor toiling to set free the imprisoned image; the third with the union of theme and thought, fact and idea, so complete that there is nothing more to do, nothing left but statue and dream; the sculptor has gone, the dreamer has gone, there is nobody even to remember that statue and dream are there; the mind is plunged in *Sushupti*, unconscious *Samādhi*. In its fourth state, symbolical of or relevant to the Self, the mind can enter all or any of the previous states at will; joyous, unobstructed, it can transform itself, dissolve itself, create itself. It has found conscious *Samādhi*, passed beyond generation that is rooted always in the unconscious, found seedless *Samādhi*. It is the old theme of philosophy, the union of Self and Not-Self, but in the conflagration of that union there is, as in the biblical vision, 'the form of the fourth.'

III

At last, after a climb of five thousand feet Bhagwān Shri Hamsa sat by the frozen lake, awaiting initiation:

'My ideal was to have a sight of the physical form of the Lord Dattātreya Himself, and to get myself initiated into the realisation of the Self. I was determined either to realise this or to die in meditation while sitting in Yogic posture.

'I began by looking in all four directions and then spread my tiger's skin on the icy floor of the lake, planting my staff on the right. I again looked at the sky and at Mount Kailās, crying "Victory, Victory to the Lord, my Master!" I stood for a few minutes facing the north. After this I sat on the tiger's skin in the Siddhāsana posture, with my face towards the north. In short, I began to face the final ordeal. It was sunset. I closed my eyes and passed into meditation, all along trying to fix the mind steadily on a mental image of the Lord Dattātreya in the centre between my eyebrows.

'The first night I experienced terrible hardships. Bitter cold, piercing winds, incessant snow, inordinate hunger, and deadly solitude combined to harass the mind; the body became numb and unable to bear the pangs. Snow covered me up to my breast and, till after midnight, I was fighting desperately with my mind. . . .

'Every moment increased the intensity of my yearning to see my Master, and it was while I was in this state that I thought I heard a voice. I did not leave my meditation. Later on I found that the image which formed the subject of my meditation grew more and more dim. Yet I refused to allow my mind to leave its point of concentration; instead I fixed it there with added determination.

'"O my child! O my dear!" I heard these words thrice, but did not open my eyes, for the mental image of my Master was still there between the eyebrows. I wanted to see the Lord Dattātreya in physical form, and naturally it was impossible for me to be satisfied with His voice alone. Moreover, no sight of a physical form was possible until the mental one had disappeared. As I was so keen about the physical sight, I did not leave my meditation, though I heard the call three times.

'At last, all of a sudden, the mental form disappeared. Automatically my eyes were opened and I saw, standing before me, the Lord Dattātreya, my Master, in his physical form. At once I prostrated myself on the icy ground like a staff and placed my head on His lotus feet.

'Three days had passed like three moments for me! My Master lifted me up like the Divine Mother and hugged me to His breast and caressed me all over the body. Thereafter He gave me the Mantra (sacred words) and initiated me into the realisation of the Self. What a great bliss it was! I cannot describe that joy, as it is beyond any description through words.'

IV

This final vision is that form completed in the third state, the third stage, not as it appears in dreamless sleep but as it appears in the fourth state, the fourth stage, or to conscious man. When the ascetic meditates upon the tip of his tongue, let us say, he begins with an object, and this object slowly transforms and is transformed by his thought until they are one. When he meditates upon an image of God, he begins with thought, God subjectively conceived, and this thought is slowly transformed by, and transforms its object, divine reality, until suddenly superseded by the unity of thought and fact. Yet he is not aware of all this, there is a voice that would persuade him to open his eyes too soon, the event is unforeseen, has taken place in what we call, because we sit in the stalls and watch the play, the unconscious. The Indian, upon the other hand, calls it the conscious, because, whereas we are fragmentary, forgetting, remembering, sleeping, waking, spread out into past, present, future, permitting to our leg, to our finger, to our intestines, partly or completely separate consciousness, it is the 'unbroken consciousness of the Self,' the Self that never sleeps, that is never divided, but even when our thought transforms it, is still the same. It is the Universal Self but also that of a civilisation; to Bhagwān Shri Hamsa, Dattātreya is the object, or goal, not of his pilgrimage only, but of his whole life. But we must not think of it as a target, as something struck or seized when subject or object unite, but as the sole being that is completely alive, completely active; our approach is revelation. The pilgrim has meditated, prayed, fasted, almost met his death in snow and ice, strained his heroic will to the utmost, fragments of his consciousness have lived in suffering for months, perhaps for years, but the Self has brought the event, the supreme drama, out of its freedom, and this revelation, because the work of unlimited power, has been sudden. The Mantra, the sacred fire that he must presently light, the caress given to all parts of his body, are from the memory of the race, the immemorial ritual; but 'the initiation into the realisation of the Self' is wordless, unique, an act of the unbroken consciousness alone. For this initiation Bhagwān Shri Hamsa finds only technical language:—

'*Manas* (mind) merged into *Antahkarana* (heart); the *Antahkarana* with the *Manas* merged into the

The Mandukya Upanishad

Chitta (mind-stuff); the *Chitta* along with *Antahkarana* and *Manas* merged into *Buddhi* (intellect); the *Buddhi* with *Chitta*, *Antahkarana*, and *Manas* merged into *Ahankar* (egoism); and the *Ahankar* along with *Buddhi*, *Chitta*, *Antahkarana*, and *Manas*—all merged into the Absolute Brahma! I found myself reflected everywhere in the whole Universe!'

V

The Heart is unity, harmony. The Mind is no more to be occupied with external events, it must, as it seems, turn upon itself, be occupied with itself, but that is impossible, for the Discursive Mind must by its nature pursue something, find something. It seems as if its separation from external things, its union with itself, must be accompanied rather than followed by its union with *Chitta*. It is *Chitta*, perhaps, which most separates Indian from European thought. We think of man, his ideas and concepts facing external nature, or as fashioning that nature according to those ideas and concepts from unknown material or from nothing. *Chitta* is mental substance—mind-stuff is the more usual translation—and this substance must always take its shape from something; it is, as we would say, suggestible, it must copy some external object or symbolise the universal Self. If I shut my eyes and try to recall table and chair, I see them as transformations of the *Chitta*. Indeed, the actual table and chair are but the *Chitta* posited by the mind, the personality, in space, where, because two things cannot occupy the

481

same place, there is discord and suffering. By with-
drawing into our own mind we discover the *Chitta*
united to Heart and therefore pure. It is divided into
Tamas, or heaviness, exhaustion; *Rajas*, or passion,
violence, movement; *Satva*, or wisdom, peace, beauty.
Or we can sum up all as darkness, lightning, light,
Boehme's three. Because *Satva* reflects the Self, from
it, or from it united to *Rajas* come all works of wisdom
and beauty. When those dreams created by recent or
present physical events are absent from our dreams,
Discursive Mind is united to *Chitta*, and this *Chitta* is
not isolated, as we think subjective mind is isolated; in
so far as *Satva* reflects the Self, it is common to all
whose minds contain the same reflection: the images
of the Gods can pass from mind to mind, our closed
eyes may look upon a world shared, as the physical
world is shared, though difference in the degree of
purity has been substituted for difference of place.

Buddhi is described as that which 'distinguishes'
between *Tamas*, *Rajas*, *Satva*, that it may cling to
Satva, but 'distinguishes' suggests Discursive Mind;
perhaps it instantly recognises and clings. But it is confined to form, for even when most transparent, *Chitta*
is form, the third state, the third concentration, are
still in form. Then *Manas*, Heart, *Chitta*, *Buddhi*, are
united to egoism, or personality, as it should be called.
Personality is first of all the man as he has been made
by his Karma; he is set in the external world because
that, too, has been made by his Karma. Even though
initiation be complete, his nature so gathered up into
itself that he can create no new Karma, he must await

the exhaustion of the old. In pure personality, seedless *Samādhi*, there is nothing but that bare 'I am' which is Brahma. The initiate, all old Karma exhausted, is 'the Human Form Divine' of Blake, that Unity of Being Dante compared to a perfectly proportioned human body; henceforth he is self-creating. But the Universal Self is a fountain, not a cistern, the Supreme Good must perpetually give itself. The world is necessary to the Self, must receive 'the excess of its delights,' and in this Self all delivered selves are present, ordering all things, from the Pole Star to the passing wind. They are indeed those spirits Shelley imagined in his *Adonais* as visiting the inspired and the innocent.

VI

Bhagwān Shri Hamsa knew that he must not open his eyes while 'the mental image' of his Master 'was still there between the eyebrows,' though that Master himself, trying him to the utmost, spoke endearing words. Had he opened his eyes too soon, he would have seen nothing. Before we can see objective truth we must exhaust subjective. This exhaustion, expressed in the drama of Master and disciple, had been going on all his life, the perilous pilgrimage but a climax. To seek God too soon is not less sinful than to seek God too late; we must love, man, woman, or child, we must exhaust ambition, intellect, desire, dedicating all things as they pass, or we come to God with empty hands.

VII

An Indian devotee may recognise that he approaches the Self through a transfiguration of sexual desire; he repeats thousands of times a day words of adoration, calls before his eyes a thousand times the divine image. He is not always solitary, there is another method, that of the Tantric philosophy, where a man and woman, when in sexual union, transfigure each other's images into the masculine and feminine characters of God, but the man must not finish, vitality must not pass beyond his body, beyond his being. There are married people who, though they do not forbid the passage of the seed, practise, not necessarily at the moment of union, a meditation, wherein the man seeks the divine Self as present in his wife, the wife the divine Self as present in the man. There may be trance, and the presence of one with another though a great distance separates. If one alone meditates, the other knows; one may call for, and receive through the other, divine protection. Did this worship, this meditation, establish among us romantic love, was it prevalent in Northern Europe during the twelfth century? In the German epic *Parsifal* Gawain drives a dagger through his hand without knowing it during his love-trance, Parsifal falls into such a trance when a drop of blood upon snow recalls to his mind a tear upon his wife's cheek, and before he awakes overthrows many knights. When riding into battle he prays not to God but to his wife, and she, falling into trance, protects him. One thinks, too, of that mysterious poem by Chrétien de Troyes, wherein Vivien, having laid

484

The Mandukya Upanishad

Merlin, personification of wisdom, by the side of dead lovers, closes their tomb.

VIII

I think it certain that Europeans, travelling the same way, enduring the same fasts, saying the same prayers, would have received nothing but perhaps a few broken dreams. Bhagwān Shri Hamsa's evocation of 'the conscious,' of 'the unconscious,' depended in part upon innumerable associations from childhood on, in part upon race-memory. I have read somewhere that the Aryan race, afterwards the creator of the Vedas and the Upanishads, lingered long, perhaps for many generations, in the country about Kailās, or Mount Meru as it is called in the Vedas, certainly longer than the Children of Israel about Sinai. Who knows what beginning, what act of creation, is commemorated in that legend of a golden phallus rising once in every year from the waters of Mānas Sarowar, or to what source Bhagwān Shri Hamsa, like many before, like many that will come after, made his perilous journey, not what his dreams or his undreaming sleep recalled?

Though I have to thank Shri Purohit Swāmi for answering many questions, he must not be held responsible for my conclusions.

1935

PARNELL

IN THE LATE 'EIGHTIES I read in the newspapers that an Oxford undergraduate, Henry Harrison, had been tried, and whether condemned or acquitted I do not remember, for some gallant reckless action at an eviction in Donegal. Years afterwards I came to know him slightly, met him perhaps half a dozen times. Two or three weeks ago he walked into my garden, a man broken by time, and sat by my wheeled chair. He had, I knew, a life-long devotion to Parnell's memory, had helped his widow and children with legal and financial advice, had been asked to write an official 'Life' which was never written. He brought me his book *Parnell Vindicated* and asked my help to make it known in Dublin; Ensor, in his book *England, 1870-1914,* had spoken of it as 'the main, final source of information,' but Irish newspapers had ignored it, seemed to prefer the story told in the undefended divorce case of a seduced wife and a deceived husband. I asked what I could do, for who listened to a poet until he was dead, but he insisted that words of mine would reach somebody or other he could not. A couple of days ago the verses at the end of this note came into my head, and I thought that they might suggest to somebody that there was nothing discreditable in Parnell's love for his mistress and his wife.

Parnell Vindicated proves beyond controversy that when Parnell met her, Mrs. O'Shea was 'a free woman'; that while a rich old woman lived she could not seek divorce; that Captain O'Shea knew of their liaison from the first; that he sold his wife for money and for other substantial advantages; that for £20,000, could Parnell have raised that sum, he was ready to let the divorce proceedings go, not against Parnell, but himself; that he extracted money from Parnell and Parnell's widow; that a well-known book signed by her, but only here and there her work, whenever it put him in a better light was 'forgery . . . no less hurtful to Parnell's honour' than the Piggot Letters; that the Irish leaders knew all about the liaison after a certain election in the middle 'eighties if not sooner; that the Liberal leaders knew from May 1882, when Sir William Harcourt told the Cabinet, apparently upon the evidence of his detectives.

I was once enough of a politician to contemplate politics ever since with amusement. The leading articles, the speeches, the resolutions of the shocked Irish and English politicians, the sudden reversal of all the barrel-organs, the alphabets running back from Z to A, sycophantic fiction become libel, eulogy vituperation, what could be more amusing? Henry Harrison does not ask if Gladstone knew and his biographers deny it. I have no doubt that he did; he used Mrs. O'Shea as an intermediary while negotiating with Parnell. Leveson-Gower, after consultation with Lord Granville, drew his attention to the rumours, but Gladstone, who, in Mr. Ensor's words, 'shared with many Victorians a dislike to hearing or repeating scandal, treated this as idle gossip.' But he must have heard more than rumours from the mouth of his own

Home Secretary in 1882. A great Victorian once said to me, 'There are things that may be done but never spoken of.' Gladstone was in his private life, what he could not be in his public, a tolerant man of the world. Wilfrid Blunt brought him to see a well-known courtesan, the 'Esther' of the sonnets, and Gladstone, charmed by a charming woman, returned alone some days later with no profligate intention but to present forty pounds of tea. They were all tolerant men of the world except the peasant-born Irish members; toleration is most often found beside ornamental waters, upon smooth lawns, amid conversations that have no object but pleasure. But all were caught in that public insincerity which was about to bring such discredit upon democracy. All over the world men are turning to Dictators, Communist or Fascist. Who can keep company with the Goddess Astrea if both his eyes are upon the brindled cat?

I cannot, however, look upon Captain O'Shea as merely amusing. I am not sufficiently unselfish. He has endangered the future of Irish dramatic literature by making melodrama too easy, and I am a theatre director; for drama one must imagine, and I cannot imagine what Captain O'Shea thought of himself when he looked into the mirror. The complacent husband may have charm and dignity like the old French painter who called upon some friends of mine to say that he was taking his wife into the country for a change: 'I always knew that Persian lover would turn out badly, I do hope she will choose better next time,' and then two or three years later to say he had falsified her age upon her tombstone: 'She never liked people to know her age.' But what of the complacent husband who is 'in effect a blackmailer' (Ensor, page 565) and yet is such a dashing figure that a Cabinet Minister considering a duel consults him upon the point of honour? There is something interesting there, but too much is left to the imagination. Those who knew him in his vigorous years are underground or over ninety.

COME GATHER ROUND ME, PARNELLITES

Come gather round me, Parnellites,
And praise our chosen man;
Stand upright on your legs awhile,
Stand upright while you can,
For soon we lie where he is laid,
And he is underground;
Come fill up all those glasses
And pass the bottle round.

And here's a cogent reason,
And I have many more,
He fought the might of England
And saved the Irish poor,
Whatever good a farmer's got
He brought it all to pass;
And here's another reason,
That Parnell loved a lass.

And here's a final reason,
He was of such a kind
Every man that sings a song
Keeps Parnell in his mind,

For Parnell was a proud man,
No prouder trod the ground,
And a proud man's a lovely man,
So pass the bottle round.

The Bishops and the Party
That tragic story made,
A husband that had sold his wife
And after that betrayed;
But stories that live longest
Are sung above the glass,
And Parnell loved his country,
And Parnell loved his lass.

1936

Modern Poetry

MODERN POETRY: A BROADCAST

THE PERIOD from the death of Tennyson until the present moment has, it seems, more good lyric poets than any similar period since the seventeenth century—no great overpowering figures, but many poets who have written some three or four lyrics apiece which may be permanent in our literature. It did not always seem so; even two years ago I should have said the opposite; I should have named three or four poets and said there was nobody else who mattered. Then I gave all my time to the study of that poetry. There was a club of poets—you may know its name, 'The Rhymers' Club'—which first met, I think, a few months before the death of Tennyson and lasted seven or eight years. It met in a Fleet Street tavern called 'The Cheshire Cheese.' Two members of the Club are vivid in my memory: Ernest Dowson, timid, silent, a little melancholy, lax in body, vague in attitude; Lionel Johnson, determined, erect, his few words dogmatic, almost a dwarf but beautifully made, his features cut in ivory. His thought dominated the scene and gave the Club its character. Nothing of importance could be discovered, he would say, science must be confined to the kitchen or the workshop; only philosophy and religion could solve the great secret, and they said all their say years ago; a gentleman was a man who understood Greek. I was full of crude speculation that made me ashamed. I remember praying that I might get my imagination fixed upon life itself, like the imagination of Chaucer. In those days I was a convinced ascetic, yet I envied Dowson his dissipated life. I thought it must be easy to think like Chaucer when you lived among those morbid, elegant, tragic women suggested by Dowson's poetry, painted and drawn by his friends Conder and Beardsley. You must all know those famous lines that are in so many anthologies:—

> Unto us they belong,
> Us the bitter and gay,
> Wine and woman and song.

When I repeated those beautiful lines it never occurred to me to wonder why the Dowson I knew seemed neither gay nor bitter. A provincial, conscious of clumsiness and lack of self-possession, I still more envied Lionel Johnson, who had met, as I believed, everybody of importance. If one spoke of some famous ecclesiastic or statesman he would say: 'I know him intimately,' and quote some conversation that laid bare that man's soul. He was never a satirist, being too courteous, too just, for that distortion. One felt that these conversations had happened exactly as he said. Years were to pass before I discovered that Dowson's life, except when he came to the Rhymers' or called upon some friend selected for an extreme respectability, was a sordid round of drink and cheap harlots; that Lionel Johnson had never met those famous men, that he never met anybody, because he got up at nightfall, got drunk at a public-house or worked half the night, sat the other half, a glass of whisky at his elbow, staring at the brown corduroy curtains that protected from dust the books that lined his walls, imagining the puppets that were the true companions of his mind. He met Dowson, but then Dowson was nobody and he was convinced that he did Dowson good. He had no interest in women, and on that subject was perhaps eloquent. Some friends of mine saw them one moonlight night returning from the 'Crown' public-house which had just closed, their zig-zagging feet requiring the whole width of Oxford Street, Lionel Johnson talking. My friend stood still eavesdropping; Lionel Johnson was expounding a Father of the Church. Their piety, in Dowson a penitential sadness, in Lionel Johnson more often a noble ecstasy, was, as I think, illuminated and intensified by their contrasting puppet-shows, those elegant, tragic penitents, those great men in their triumph. You may know Lionel Johnson's poem on the statue of King Charles, or that characteristic poem that begins: 'Ah, see the fair chivalry come, the Companions of Christ.' In my present mood, remembering his scholarship, remembering that his religious sense was never divided from his sense of the past, I recall most vividly his 'Church of a Dream':—

Sadly the dead leaves rustle in the whistling wind,
Around the weather-worn, grey church, low down the vale:
The Saints in golden vesture shake before the gale;
The glorious windows shake, where still they dwell enshrined;
Old Saints by long-dead, shrivelled hands, long since designed:
There still, although the world autumnal be, and pale,
Still in their golden vesture the old Saints prevail;
Alone with Christ, desolate else, left by mankind.

Only one ancient priest offers the Sacrifice,
Murmuring holy Latin immemorial:

Swaying with tremulous hands the old- censer full of spice,
In grey, sweet incense clouds; blue, sweet clouds mystical:
To him, in place of men, for he is old, suffice
Melancholy remembrances and vesperal.

There were other poets, generally a few years
younger, who having escaped that first wave of excitement lived tame and orderly lives. But they, too, were
in reaction against everything Victorian.

A church in the style of Inigo Jones opens on to a
grass lawn a few hundred yards from the Marble Arch.
It was designed by a member of the Rhymers' Club,
whose architecture, like his poetry, seemed to exist less
for his own sake than to illustrate his genius as a connoisseur. I have sometimes thought that masterpiece,
perhaps the smallest church in London, the most
appropriate symbol of all that was most characteristic
in the art of my friends. Their poems seemed to say:
'You will remember us the longer because we are very
small, very unambitious.' Yet my friends were most
ambitious men; they wished to express life at its intense
moments, those moments that are brief because of their
intensity, and at those moments alone. In the Victorian
era the most famous poetry was often a passage in a
poem of some length, perhaps of great length, a poem
full of thoughts that might have been expressed in
prose. A short lyric seemed an accident, an inter-
ruption amid more serious work. Somebody has quoted
Browning as saying that he could have written many
lyrics had he thought them worth the trouble. The aim
of my friends, my own aim, if it sometimes made us
prefer the acorn to the oak, the small to the great, freed

us from many things that we thought an impurity. Swinburne, Tennyson, Arnold, Browning, had admitted so much psychology, science, moral fervour. Had not Verlaine said of *In Memoriam*, 'When he should have been broken-hearted he had many reminiscences'? We tried to write like the poets of the Greek Anthology, or like Catullus, or like the Jacobean lyrists, men who wrote while poetry was still pure. We did not look forward or look outward, we left that to the prose writers; we looked back. We thought it was in the very nature of poetry to look back, to resemble those Swedenborgian angels who are described as moving for ever towards the dayspring of their youth. In this we were all, orderly and disorderly alike, in full agreement.

When I think of the Rhymers' Club and grow weary of those luckless men, I think of another circle that was in full agreement. It gathered round Charles Ricketts, one of the greatest connoisseurs of any age, an artist whose woodcuts prolonged the inspiration of Rossetti, whose paintings mirrored the rich colouring of Delacroix. When we studied his art we studied our double. We, too, thought always that style should be proud of its ancestry, of its traditional high breeding, that an ostentatious originality was out of place whether in the arts or in good manners. When the Rhymers' Club was breaking up I read enthusiastic reviews of the first book of Sturge Moore and grew jealous. He did not belong to the Rhymers' Club and I wanted to believe that we had all the good poets; but one evening Charles Ricketts brought me to a riverside house at Richmond and introduced me to Edith Cooper. She put into my unwilling hands Sturge Moore's book and made me read out and discuss certain poems. I surrendered. I took back all I had said against him. I was most moved by his poem called *The Dying Swan*:—

> O silver-throated Swan
> Struck, struck! a golden dart
> Clean through thy breast has gone
> Home to thy heart.
> Thrill, thrill, O silver throat!
> O silver trumpet, pour
> Love for defiance back
> On him who smote!
> And brim, brim o'er
> With love; and ruby-dye thy track
> Down thy last living reach
> Of river, sail the golden light . . .
> Enter the sun's heart . . . even teach,
> O wondrous-gifted Pain, teach thou
> The god to love, let him learn how.

Edith Cooper herself seemed a dry, precise, precious, pious, finicking old maid; with an aunt, a Miss Bradley, she had written under the name of 'Michael Field' tragedies in the Elizabethan manner, which I seem to remember after forty or fifty years as occasionally powerful but spoilt by strained emotion and laboured metaphor; they had already fallen into oblivion, but under the influence of Charles Ricketts she had studied Greek and found a new character, a second youth. She had begun, though I did not know it for many years, a series of little poems, masterpieces of simplicity, which resemble certain of Landor's lyrics, though her voice is not so deep, but high, thin, and sweet.

> Thine elder that I am, thou must not cling
> To me, nor mournful for my love entreat:
> And yet, Alcaeus, as the sudden spring
> Is love, yea, and to veiled Demeter sweet.
> Sweeter than tone of harp, more gold than gold
> Is thy young voice to me; yet, ah, the pain
> To learn I am beloved now I am old,
> Who, in my youth, loved, as thou must, in vain.

And here is another, which because it hints at so much more than it says, is very moving.

> They bring me gifts, they honour me,
> Now I am growing old;
> And wondering youth crowds round my knee,
> As if I had a mystery
> And worship to unfold.
>
> To me the tender, blushing bride
> Doth come with lips that fail;
> I feel her heart beat at my side
> And cry: 'Like Ares in his pride,
> Hail, noble bridegroom, hail!'

My generation, because it disliked Victorian rhetorical moral fervour, came to dislike all rhetoric. In France, where there was a similar movement, a poet had written, 'Take rhetoric and wring its neck.' People began to imitate old ballads because an old ballad is never rhetorical. I think of *A Shropshire Lad*, of certain poems by Hardy, of Kipling's *Saint Helena Lullaby*, and his *The Looking-Glass*. I will not read any of that famous poetry but a poem nobody ever heard of. When I was a young man, York Powell, an Oxford Don, was renowned for his miraculous learning, but only his few intimates, perhaps only those much younger than himself, knew that he was not the dry man he seemed. From the top of a bus, somewhere between Victoria and Walham Green, he pointed out to me a pawnshop he had once found very useful; I was in his rooms at Oxford when he replied to somebody who had asked him to become Proctor that the older he grew the less and less difference could he see between right and wrong. He used to frequent prize-fights with my brother, a lad in his twenties, and it was in a Broadside, a mixture of hand-coloured prints and poetry published by my brother, and now long out of print, that I discovered the poem I am now about to read. It is a translation from the French of Paul Fort.

> The pretty maid she died, she died, in love-bed as she lay;
> They took her to the church-yard; all at the break of day;
> They laid her all alone there: all in her white array;
> They laid her all alone there: a-coffin'd in the clay:
> And they came back so merrily: all at the dawn of day;
> A-singing all so merrily: '*The dog must have his day!*'
> The pretty maid is dead, is dead; in love-bed as she lay;
> And they are off afield to work: as they do every day.

The poems I have read resemble in certain characteristics all modern poetry up to the Great War. The centaurs and amazons of Sturge Moore, the Tristram and Isoult of Binyon's noble poem—there were always some long poems; my Deirdre, my Cuchulain had been written about for centuries and our public wished for nothing else. Here and there some young revolutionist would boast that his eyes were on the present or the future, or even denounce all poetry back to Dante, but we were content; we wrote as men had always written. Then established things were shaken by the Great War. All civilised men had believed in progress, in a warless future, in always-increasing wealth, but now influential young men began to wonder if anything could last or if anything were worth fighting for. In the third year of the War came the most revolutionary man in poetry during my lifetime, though his revolution was stylistic alone—T. S. Eliot published his first book. No romantic word or sound, nothing reminiscent, nothing in the least like the painting of Ricketts could be permitted henceforth. Poetry must resemble prose, and both must accept the vocabulary of their time; nor must there be any special subject-matter. Tristram and Isoult were not a more suitable theme than Paddington Railway Station. The past had deceived us: let us accept the worthless present.

> The morning comes to consciousness
> Of faint stale smells of beer
> From the sawdust-trampled street
> With all its muddy feet that press
> To early coffee-stands. . . .
> One thinks of all the hands
> That are raising dingy shades
> In a thousand furnished rooms.

We older writers disliked this new poetry, but were forced to admit its satiric intensity. It was in Eliot that certain revolutionary War poets, young men who felt they had been dragged away from their studies, from their pleasant life, by the blundering frenzy of old men, found the greater part of their style. They were too near their subject-matter to do, as I think, work of permanent importance, but their social passion, their sense of tragedy, their modernity, have passed into young influential poets of to-day: Auden, Spender, MacNeice, Day Lewis, and others. Some of these poets are Communists, but even in those who are not, there is an overwhelming social bitterness. Some speak of the War in which none were old enough to have served:—

> I've heard them lilting at loom and belting,
> Lasses lilting before dawn of day;
> But now they are silent, not gamesome and gallant—
> The flowers of the town are rotting away.
>
> There was laughing and loving in the lanes at evening;
> Handsome were the boys then, and girls were gay.
> But lost in Flanders by medalled commanders
> The lads of the village are melted away.

This poetry is supported by critics who think it the poetry of the future—in my youth I heard much of the music of the future—and attack all not of their school. A poet of an older school has named them 'the racketeers.' Sometimes they attack Miss Edith Sitwell, who seems to me an important poet, shaped as they are by the disillusionment that followed the Great War. Among her fauns, cats, columbines, clowns, wicked fairies, into that phantasmagoria which reminds me of a ballet called *The Sleeping Beauty*, loved by the last of the Tsars, she interjects a nightmare horror of death and decay. I commend to you *The Hambone and the Heart*, and *The Lament of Edward Blastock*, as among the most tragic poems of our time. Her language is the traditional language of literature, but twisted, torn, complicated, jerked here and there by strained resemblances, unnatural contacts, forced upon it by terror or by some violence beating in her blood, some primitive obsession that civilisation can no longer exorcise. I find her obscure, exasperating, delightful. I think I like her best when she seems a child, terrified and delighted by the story it is inventing. I will read you a little poem she has called *Ass-Face*, but first I must explain its imagery which has taken me a couple of minutes to puzzle out, not because it is obscure, but because image follows image too quickly to be understood at a first hearing. I prefer to think of Ass-Face as a personality invented by some child at a nursery window after dark. The starry heavens are the lighted bars and saloons of public-houses, and the descending light is asses' milk which makes Ass-Face drunk. But this light is thought of the next moment as bright threads floating down in spirals to make a dress for Columbine, and the next moment after that as milk spirting on the sands of the sea—one thinks of the glittering foam—a sea which brays like an ass, and is covered because it is a rough sea by an ass's hide. Along the shore there are trees, and under these trees beavers are building Babel, and these beavers think that the noise Ass-Face makes in his drunkenness is Cain and Abel fighting. Then somehow as the vision ends the starlight has turned into the houses that the beavers are building. But their Babel and their houses are like white lace, and we are told that Ass-Face will spoil them all.

When you listen to this poem, you should become two people, one a sage who thinks perhaps that Ass-Face is the stupefying frenzy of nature, one a child listening to a poem as irrational as a 'Sing a Song of Sixpence':—

> Ass-Face drank
> The asses' milk of the stars . . .
> The milky spirals as they sank
> From heaven's saloons and golden bars,
> Made a gown
> For Columbine,
> Spirting down
> On sands divine
> By the asses' hide of the sea
> (With each tide braying free).
> And the beavers building Babel
> Beneath each tree's thin beard,
> Said, 'Is it Cain and Abel
> Fighting again we heard?'
> It is Ass-Face, Ass-Face,
> Drunk on the milk of the stars,
> Who will spoil their houses of white lace—
> Expelled from the golden bars!

I think profound philosophy must come from terror. An abyss opens under our feet; inherited convictions, the pre-suppositions of our thoughts, those Fathers of the Church Lionel Johnson expounded, drop into the abyss. Whether we will or no we must ask the ancient questions: Is there reality anywhere? Is there a God?

Is there a Soul? We cry with the Indian Sacred Book: 'They have put a golden stopper into the neck of the bottle; pull it! Let out reality!'

Some seven years after the close of the War, seven years of meditation, came Turner's *Seven Days of the Sun*, Dorothy Wellesley's *Matrix*, Herbert Read's *Mutations of the Phoenix*, T. S. Eliot's *Waste Land*; long philosophical poems; and even now the young Communist poets complicate their short lyrics with difficult metaphysics.

If you are lovers of poetry, and it is for such that I speak, you know *The Waste Land*, but perhaps not the other poems that I have named, though you will certainly know Dorothy Wellesley's poem in praise of horses, and probably Turner's praise of a mountain in Mexico with a romantic name. To three, perhaps to all four of these writers, what we call the solid earth was manufactured by the human mind from unknown raw material. They do not think this because of Kant and Berkeley, who are an old story, but because of something that has got into the air since a famous French mathematician wrote 'Space is a creation of our ancestors.' Eliot's historical and scholarly mind seems to have added this further thought, probably from Nicholas of Cusa: reality is expressed in a series of contradictions, or is that unknowable something that supports the centre of the see-saw.

At the still point of the turning world. Neither flesh nor
    fleshless;
Neither from nor towards; at the still point, there the dance
    is,

But neither arrest nor movement. And do not call it fixity.
Where past and future are gathered. Neither movement from
    nor towards,
Neither ascent nor decline. Except for the point, the still
    point,
There would be no dance, and there is only the dance.

All are pessimists; Dorothy Wellesley thinks that the 'unconceived,' as she calls those that have not yet been melted into that subjective creation we call the world, are alone happy. They are a part of the unknown raw material which the manufacturer has neglected. They have escaped the torture of the senses, the boredom of that automatic return of the same sensation Eliot has described. I will read you a passage from her poem *Matrix:*—

    Where, then, are the unborn ones?
    Do they eternally go,
    Cloud-wracks of souls tormented,
    Through ether for ever?

    No such ventures theirs, no.
    They crowd in the core of the earth;
    They lie in the loam,
    Laid backward by slice of the plough;
    They sit in the rock:
    In a matrix of amethyst crouches a man,
    Pigmy, a part of the womb,
    Of the stone,
    For ever, for all time, now.

    All things there are his own:
    The light on water, the leaves,
    The spray of the wild yellow rose;

Modern Poetry

Beautiful as to the born
Are the stars to the unconceived;
The twilight, the morn, of their sight,
Are lovelier than to the born.

Turner, the poet, mathematician, musician, thinks that the horror of the world is in its beauty. Beautiful forms deceive us, because if we grasp them, they dissolve into what he calls 'confused sensation'; and destroy us because they drag us under the machinery of nature; if it were possible he would, like a Buddhist, or a connoisseur, kill or suspend desire. He does not see men and women as the puppets of Eliot's poetry, repeating over and over the same trivial movements, but as the reflections of a terrible Olympus. I will read you his poem upon the procession of the mannequins.

I have seen mannequins,
As white and gold as lilies,
Swaying their tall bodies across the burnished floor
Of *Reville* or *Paquin*;
Writhing in colour and line,
Curved tropical flowers
As bright as thunderbolts,
Or hooded in dark furs
The sun's pale splash
In English autumn woods.

And I have watched these soft explosions of life
As astronomers watch the combustion of stars.
The violence of supernatural power
Upon their faces,
White orbits
Of incalculable forces.

And I have had no desire for their bodies
But have felt the whiteness of a lily
Upon my palate;
And the solidity of their slender curves
Like a beautiful mathematical proposition
In my brain.

But in the expression of their faces
Terror.

Cruelty in the eyes, nostrils, and lips—
Pain
thou passion-flower, thou wreath, thou orbit,
thou spiritual rotation,
thou smile upon a pedestal,
Peony of the garden of Paradise!

Many Irish men and women must be listening, and they may wonder why I have said nothing of modern Irish poetry. I have not done so because it moves in a different direction and belongs to a different story. Modern Irish poetry began in the midst of that rediscovery of folk thought I described when quoting York Powell's translation from Paul Fort. The English movement, checked by the realism of Eliot, the social passion of the War poets, gave way to an impersonal philosophical poetry. Because Ireland has a still living folk tradition, her poets cannot get it out of their heads that they themselves, good-tempered or bad-tempered, tall or short, will be remembered by the common people. Instead of turning to impersonal philosophy, they have hardened and deepened their personalities. I could have taken as examples Synge or James Stephens, men I have never ceased to delight in. But I prefer to quote poetry of which you have probably never heard, though it is among the greatest lyric poetry of our time.

Some twelve years ago political enemies came to Senator Gogarty's house while they knew he would be in his bath and so unable to reach his revolver, made him dress, brought him to an empty house on the edge of the Liffey. They told him nothing, but he felt certain he was to be kept as hostage and shot after the inevitable execution of a certain man then in prison. Self-possessed and daring, he escaped, and while swimming the cold December river, vowed two swans to it if it would land him safely. I was present some weeks later when, in the presence of the Head of the State and other notables, the two swans were launched. That story shows the man—scholar, wit, poet, gay adventurer. In one poem, written years afterwards, the man who dedicated the swans dedicates the poems, and the mood has not changed:—

> Tall unpopular men,
> Slim proud women who move
> As women walked in the islands when
> Temples were built to Love,
> I sing to you. With you
> Beauty at best can live,
> Beauty that dwells with the rare and few,
> Cold and imperative.
> He who had Caesar's ear
> Sang to the lonely and strong.
> Virgil made an austere
> Venus Muse of his song.

Here is another poem characteristic of those poems which have restored the emotion of heroism to lyric poetry:—

Our friends go with us as we go
  Down the long path where Beauty wends,
Where all we love forgathers, so
  Why should we fear to join our friends?

Who would survive them to outlast
  His children; to outwear his fame—
Left when the Triumph has gone past—
  To win from Age, not Time, a name?

Then do not shudder at the knife
  That Death's indifferent hand drives home,
But with the Strivers leave the Strife,
  Nor, after Caesar, skulk in Rome.

When I have read you a poem I have tried to read it rhythmically; I may be a bad reader; or read badly because I am out of sorts, or self-conscious; but there is no other method. A poem is an elaboration of the rhythms of common speech and their association with profound feeling. To read a poem like prose, that hearers unaccustomed to poetry may find it easy to understand, is to turn it into bad, florid prose. If anybody reads or recites poetry as if it were prose from some public platform, I ask you, speaking for poets, living, dead, or unborn, to protest in whatever way occurs to your perhaps youthful minds; if they recite or read by wireless, I ask you to express your indignation by letter. William Morris, coming out of a hall where somebody had read or recited his *Sigurd the Volsung*, said: 'It cost me a lot of damned hard work to get that thing into verse.'

1936

A GENERAL INTRODUCTION FOR MY WORK [1]

I. THE FIRST PRINCIPLE

A POET WRITES always of his personal life, in his finest work out of its tragedy, whatever it be, remorse, lost love, or mere loneliness; he never speaks directly as to someone at the breakfast table, there is always a phantasmagoria. Dante and Milton had mythologies, Shakespeare the characters of English history or of traditional romance; even when the poet seems most himself, when he is Raleigh and gives potentates the lie, or Shelley 'a nerve o'er which do creep the else unfelt oppressions of this earth,' or Byron when 'the soul wears out the breast' as 'the sword outwears its sheath,' he is never the bundle of accident and incoherence that sits down to breakfast; he has been reborn as an idea, something intended, complete. A novelist might describe his accidence, his incoherence, he must not; he is more type than man, more passion than type. He is Lear, Romeo, Oedipus, Tiresias; he has stepped out of a play, and even the woman he loves is Rosalind, Cleopatra, never The Dark Lady. He is part of his own phantasmagoria and we adore him because nature has grown intelligible, and by so doing a part of our creative power. 'When mind is lost in the light of the Self,' says the Prashna Upanishad, 'it dreams no more; still in the body it is lost in happiness.' 'A wise man seeks in Self,' says the Chandogya Upanishad, 'those

[1] Written for a complete edition of Yeats's works which was never produced.

that are alive and those that are dead and gets what the world cannot give.' The world knows nothing because it has made nothing, we know everything because we have made everything.

II. SUBJECT-MATTER

It was through the old Fenian leader John O'Leary I found my theme. His long imprisonment, his longer banishment, his magnificent head, his scholarship, his pride, his integrity, all that aristocratic dream nourished amid little shops and little farms, had drawn around him a group of young men; I was but eighteen or nineteen and had already, under the influence of *The Faerie Queene* and *The Sad Shepherd*, written a pastoral play, and under that of Shelley's *Prometheus Unbound* two plays, one staged somewhere in the Caucasus, the other in a crater of the moon; and I knew myself to be vague and incoherent. He gave me the poems of Thomas Davis, said they were not good poetry but had changed his life when a young man, spoke of other poets associated with Davis and *The Nation* newspaper, probably lent me their books. I saw even more clearly than O'Leary that they were not good poetry. I read nothing but romantic literature; hated that dry eighteenth-century rhetoric; but they had one quality I admired and admire: they were not separated individual men; they spoke or tried to speak out of a people to a people; behind them stretched the generations. I knew, though but now and then as young men know things, that I must turn from that modern literature Jonathan Swift compared to the web a spider draws out of its bowels; I hated and still hate with an ever growing hatred the literature of the point of view. I wanted, if my ignorance permitted, to get back to Homer, to those that fed at his table. I wanted to cry as all men cried, to laugh as all men laughed, and the Young Ireland poets when not writing mere politics had the same want, but they did not know that the common and its befitting language is the research of a lifetime and when found may lack popular recognition. Then somebody, not O'Leary, told me of Standish O'Grady and his interpretation of Irish legends. O'Leary had sent me to O'Curry, but his unarranged and uninterpreted history defeated my boyish indolence.

A generation before *The Nation* newspaper was founded the Royal Irish Academy had begun the study of ancient Irish literature. That study was as much a gift from the Protestant aristocracy which had created the Parliament as *The Nation* and its school, though Davis and Mitchel were Protestants; was a gift from the Catholic middle classes who were to create the Irish Free State. The Academy persuaded the English Government to finance an ordnance survey on a large scale; scholars, including that great scholar O'Donovan, were sent from village to village recording names and their legends. Perhaps it was the last moment when such work could be well done, the memory of the people was still intact, the collectors themselves had perhaps heard or seen the banshee; the Royal Irish Academy and its public with equal enthusiasm

511

welcomed Pagan and Christian; thought the Round Towers a commemoration of Persian fire-worship. There was little orthodoxy to take alarm; the Catholics were crushed and cowed; an honoured great-uncle of mine—his portrait by some forgotten master hangs upon my bedroom wall—a Church of Ireland rector, would upon occasion boast that you could not ask a question he could not answer with a perfectly appropriate blasphemy or indecency. When several counties had been surveyed but nothing published, the Government, afraid of rousing dangerous patriotic emotion, withdrew support; large manuscript volumes remain containing much picturesque correspondence between scholars.

When modern Irish literature began, O'Grady's influence predominated. He could delight us with an extravagance we were too critical to share; a day will come, he said, when Slieve-na-mon will be more famous than Olympus; yet he was no Nationalist as we understood the word, but in rebellion, as he was fond of explaining, against the House of Commons, not against the King. His cousin, that great scholar Hayes O'Grady, would not join our non-political Irish Literary Society because he considered it a Fenian body, but boasted that although he had lived in England for forty years he had never made an English friend. He worked at the British Museum compiling their Gaelic catalogue and translating our heroic tales in an eighteenth-century frenzy; his heroine 'fractured her heart,' his hero 'ascended to the apex of the eminence' and there 'vibrated his javelin,' and afterwards took ship upon 'colossal ocean's superficies.' Both O'Gradys considered themselves as representing the old Irish land-owning aristocracy; both probably, Standish O'Grady certainly, thought that England, because decadent and democratic, had betrayed their order. It was another member of that order, Lady Gregory, who was to do for the heroic legends in *Gods and Fighting Men* and in *Cuchulain of Muirthemne* what Lady Charlotte Guest's *Mabinogion* had done with less beauty and style for those of Wales. Standish O'Grady had much modern sentiment, his style, like that of John Mitchel forty years before, shaped by Carlyle; she formed her style upon the Anglo-Irish dialect of her neighbourhood, an old vivid speech with a partly Tudor vocabulary, a syntax partly moulded by men who still thought in Gaelic.

I had heard in Sligo cottages or from pilots at Rosses Point endless stories of apparitions, whether of the recent dead or of the people of history and legend, of that Queen Maeve whose reputed cairn stands on the mountain over the bay. Then at the British Museum I read stories Irish writers of the 'forties and 'fifties had written of such apparitions, but they enraged me more than pleased because they turned the country visions into a joke. But when I went from cottage to cottage with Lady Gregory and watched her hand recording that great collection she has called *Visions and Beliefs* I escaped disfiguring humour.

Behind all Irish history hangs a great tapestry, even Christianity had to accept it and be itself pictured there. Nobody looking at its dim folds can say where

Christianity begins and Druidism ends; 'There is one perfect among the birds, one perfect among the fish, and one among men that is perfect.' I can only explain by that suggestion of recent scholars—Professor Burkitt of Cambridge commended it to my attention—that St. Patrick came to Ireland not in the fifth century but towards the end of the second. The great controversies had not begun; Easter was still the first full moon after the Equinox. Upon that day the world had been created, the Ark rested upon Ararat, Moses led the Israelites out of Egypt; the umbilical cord which united Christianity to the ancient world had not yet been cut, Christ was still the half-brother of Dionysus. A man just tonsured by the Druids could learn from the nearest Christian neighbour to sign himself with the Cross without sense of incongruity, nor would his children acquire that sense. The organised clans weakened Church organisation, they could accept the monk but not the bishop.

A modern man, *The Golden Bough* and *Human Personality* in his head, finds much that is congenial in St. Patrick's Creed as recorded in his Confessions, and nothing to reject except the word 'soon' in the statement that Christ will soon judge the quick and the dead. He can repeat it, believe it even, without a thought of the historic Christ, or ancient Judea, or of anything subject to historical conjecture and shifting evidence; I repeat it and think of 'the Self' in the Upanishads. Into this tradition, oral and written, went in later years fragments of Neo-Platonism, cabbalistic words—I have heard the words 'tetragrammaton agla' in Doneraile—the floating debris of mediaeval thought, but nothing that did not please the solitary mind. Even the religious equivalent for Baroque and Rococo could not come to us as thought, perhaps because Gaelic is incapable of abstraction. It came as cruelty. That tapestry filled the scene at the birth of modern Irish literature, it is there in the Synge of *The Well of the Saints*, in James Stephens, and in Lady Gregory throughout, in all of George Russell that did not come from the Upanishads, and in all but my later poetry.

Sometimes I am told in commendation, if the newspaper is Irish, in condemnation if English, that my movement perished under the firing squads of 1916; sometimes that those firing squads made our realistic movement possible. If that statement is true, and it is only so in part, for romance was everywhere receding, it is because in the imagination of Pearse and his fellow soldiers the Sacrifice of the Mass had found the Red Branch in the tapestry; they went out to die calling upon Cuchulain:—

> Fall, Hercules, from Heaven in tempests hurled
> To cleanse the beastly stable of this world.

In one sense the poets of 1916 were not of what the newspapers call my school. The Gaelic League, made timid by a modern popularisation of Catholicism sprung from the aspidistra and not from the root of Jesse, dreaded intellectual daring and stuck to dictionary and grammar. Pearse and MacDonagh and others among the executed men would have done, or attempted, in Gaelic what we did or attempted in English.

Our mythology, our legends, differ from those of other European countries because down to the end of the seventeenth century they had the attention, perhaps the unquestioned belief, of peasant and noble alike; Homer belongs to sedentary men, even to-day our ancient queens, our mediaeval soldiers and lovers, can make a pedlar shudder. I can put my own thought, despair perhaps from the study of present circumstance in the light of ancient philosophy, into the mouth of rambling poets of the seventeenth century, or even of some imagined ballad singer of to-day, and the deeper my thought the more credible, the more peasant-like, are ballad singer and rambling poet. Some modern poets contend that jazz and music-hall songs are the folk art of our time, that we should mould our art upon them; we Irish poets, modern men also, reject every folk art that does not go back to Olympus. Give me time and a little youth and I will prove that even 'Johnny, I hardly knew ye' goes back.

Mr. Arnold Toynbee in an annex to the second volume of *The Study of History* describes the birth and decay of what he calls the Far Western Christian culture; it lost at the Synod of Whitby its chance of mastering Europe, suffered final ecclesiastical defeat in the twelfth century with 'the thoroughgoing incorporation of the Irish Christendom into the Roman Church. In the political and literary spheres' it lasted unbroken till the seventeenth century. He then insists that if 'Jewish Zionism and Irish Nationalism succeed in achieving their aims, then Jewry and Irishry will each fit into its own tiny niche . . . among sixty or seventy national communities', find life somewhat easier, but cease to be 'the relic of an independent society . . . the romance of Ancient Ireland has at last come to an end . . . Modern Ireland has made up her mind, in our generation, to find her level as a willing inmate in our workaday Western world.'

If Irish literature goes on as my generation planned it, it may do something to keep the 'Irishry' living, nor will the work of the realists hinder, nor the figures they imagine, nor those described in memoirs of the revolution. These last especially, like certain great political predecessors, Parnell, Swift, Lord Edward, have stepped back into the tapestry. It may be indeed that certain characteristics of the 'Irishry' must grow in importance. When Lady Gregory asked me to annotate her *Visions and Beliefs* I began, that I might understand what she had taken down in Galway, an investigation of contemporary spiritualism. For several years I frequented those mediums who in various poor parts of London instruct artisans or their wives for a few pence upon their relations to their dead, to their employers, and to their children; then I compared what she had heard in Galway, or I in London, with the visions of Swedenborg, and, after my inadequate notes had been published, with Indian belief. If Lady Gregory had not said when we passed an old man in the woods, 'That man may know the secret of the ages,' I might never have talked with Shri Purohit Swāmi nor made him translate his Master's travels in Tibet, nor helped him translate the Upanishads. I think I now know why the gamekeeper at Coole heard the footsteps of a deer on the edge of the lake where no deer had passed for a hundred years, and why a certain cracked old priest said that nobody had been to hell or heaven in his time, meaning thereby that the Rath had got them all; that the dead stayed where they had lived, or near it, sought no abstract region of blessing or punishment but retreated, as it were, into the hidden character of their neighbourhood. I am convinced that in two or three generations it will become generally known that the mechanical theory has no reality, that the natural and supernatural are knit together, that to escape a dangerous fanaticism we must study a new science; at that moment Europeans may find something attractive in a Christ posed against a background not of Judaism but of Druidism, not shut off in dead history, but flowing, concrete, phenomenal.

I was born into this faith, have lived in it, and shall die in it; my Christ, a legitimate deduction from the Creed of St. Patrick as I think, is that Unity of Being Dante compared to a perfectly proportioned human body, Blake's 'Imagination,' what the Upanishads have named 'Self': nor is this unity distant and therefore intellectually understandable, but imminent, differing from man to man and age to age, taking upon itself pain and ugliness, 'eye of newt, and toe of frog.'

Subconscious preoccupation with this theme brought me *A Vision*, its harsh geometry an incomplete interpretation. The 'Irishry' have preserved their ancient 'deposit' through wars which, during the sixteenth and seventeenth centuries, became wars of extermination; no people, Lecky said at the opening of his *Ireland in the Eighteenth Century*, have undergone greater persecution, nor did that persecution altogether cease up to our own day. No people hate as we do in whom that past is always alive, there are moments when hatred poisons my life and I accuse myself of effeminacy because I have not given it adequate expression. It is not enough to have put it into the mouth of a rambling peasant poet. Then I remind myself that though mine is the first English marriage I know of in the direct line, all my family names are English, and that I owe my soul to Shakespeare, to Spenser and to Blake, perhaps to William Morris, and to the English language in which I think, speak, and write, that everything I love has come to me through English; my hatred tortures me with love, my love with hate. I am like the Tibetan monk who dreams at his initiation that he is eaten by a wild beast and learns on waking that he himself is eater and eaten. This is Irish hatred and solitude, the hatred of human life that made Swift write *Gulliver* and the epitaph upon his tomb, that can still make us wag between extremes and doubt our sanity.

Again and again I am asked why I do not write in Gaelic. Some four or five years ago I was invited to dinner by a London society and found myself among London journalists, Indian students, and foreign political refugees. An Indian paper says it was a dinner in my honour; I hope not; I have forgotten, though I have a clear memory of my own angry mind. I should have spoken as men are expected to speak at public dinners; I should have paid and been paid conventional compliments; then they would speak of the refugees; from that on all would be lively and topical, foreign tyranny would be arraigned, England seem even to those confused Indians the protector of liberty; I grew angrier and angrier; Wordsworth, that typical Englishman, had published his famous sonnet to François Dominique Toussaint, a Santo Domingo Negro:—

> There's not a breathing of the common wind
> That will forget thee

in the year when Emmet conspired and died, and he remembered that rebellion as little as the half hanging and the pitch cap that preceded it by half a dozen years. That there might be no topical speeches I denounced the oppression of the people of India; being a man of letters, not a politician, I told how they had been forced to learn everything, even their own Sanskrit, through the vehicle of English till the first discoverer of wisdom had become bywords for vague abstract facility. I begged the Indian writers present to remember that no man can think or write with music and vigour except in his mother tongue. I turned a friendly audience hostile, yet when I think of that scene I am unrepentant and angry.

I could no more have written in Gaelic than can those Indians write in English; Gaelic is my national language, but it is not my mother tongue.

A General Introduction for my Work

III. STYLE AND ATTITUDE

Style is almost unconscious. I know what I have tried to do, little what I have done. Contemporary lyric poems, even those that moved me—*The Stream's Secret, Dolores*—seemed too long, but an Irish preference for a swift current might be mere indolence, yet Burns may have felt the same when he read Thomson and Cowper. The English mind is meditative, rich, deliberate; it may remember the Thames valley. I planned to write short lyrics or poetic drama where every speech would be short and concentrated, knit by dramatic tension, and I did so with more confidence because young English poets were at that time writing out of emotion at the moment of crisis, though their old slow-moving meditation returned almost at once. Then, and in this English poetry has followed my lead, I tried to make the language of poetry coincide with that of passionate, normal speech. I wanted to write in whatever language comes most naturally when we soliloquise, as I do all day long, upon the events of our own lives or of any life where we can see ourselves for the moment. I sometimes compare myself with the mad old slum women I hear denouncing and remembering; 'How dare you,' I heard one say of some imaginary suitor, 'and you without health or a home!' If I spoke my thoughts aloud they might be as angry and as wild. It was a long time before I had made a language to my liking; I began to make it when I discovered some twenty years ago that I must seek, not as Wordsworth thought, words in common use, but a

powerful and passionate syntax, and a complete coincidence between period and stanza. Because I need a
passionate syntax for passionate subject-matter I compel myself to accept those traditional metres that have
developed with the language. Ezra Pound, Turner,
Lawrence wrote admirable free verse, I could not. I
would lose myself, become joyless like those mad old
women. The translators of the Bible, Sir Thomas
Browne, certain translators from the Greek when translators still bothered about rhythm, created a form
midway between prose and verse that seems natural to
impersonal meditation; but all that is personal soon
rots; it must be packed in ice or salt. Once when I was
in delirium from pneumonia I dictated a letter to
George Moore telling him to eat salt because it was
a symbol of eternity; the delirium passed, I had no
memory of that letter, but I must have meant what I
now mean. If I wrote of personal love or sorrow in
free verse, or in any rhythm that left it unchanged,
amid all its accidence, I would be full of self-contempt
because of my egotism and indiscretion, and foresee
the boredom of my reader. I must choose a traditional
stanza, even what I alter must seem traditional. I
commit my emotion to shepherds, herdsmen, camel-
drivers, learned men, Milton's or Shelley's Platonist,
that tower Palmer drew. Talk to me of originality and
I will turn on you with rage. I am a crowd, I am a
lonely man, I am nothing. Ancient salt is best packing.
The heroes of Shakespeare convey to us through their
looks, or through the metaphorical patterns of their
speech, the sudden enlargement of their vision, their

ecstasy at the approach of death: 'She should have died hereafter,' 'Of many thousand kisses, the poor last,' 'Absent thee from felicity awhile.' They have become God or Mother Goddess, the pelican, 'My baby at my breast,' but all must be cold; no actress has ever sobbed when she played Cleopatra, even the shallow brain of a producer has never thought of such a thing. The supernatural is present, cold winds blow across our hands, upon our faces, the thermometer falls, and because of that cold we are hated by journalists and groundlings. There may be in this or that detail painful tragedy, but in the whole work none. I have heard Lady Gregory say, rejecting some play in the modern manner sent to the Abbey Theatre, 'Tragedy must be a joy to the man who dies.' Nor is it any different with lyrics, songs, narrative poems; neither scholars nor the populace have sung or read anything generation after generation because of its pain. The maid of honour whose tragedy they sing must be lifted out of history with timeless pattern, she is one of the four Maries, the rhythm is old and familiar, imagination must dance, must be carried beyond feeling into the aboriginal ice. Is ice the correct word? I once boasted, copying the phrase from a letter of my father's, that I would write a poem 'cold and passionate as the dawn.'

When I wrote in blank verse I was dissatisfied; my vaguely mediaeval *Countess Cathleen* fitted the measure, but our Heroic Age went better, or so I fancied, in the ballad metre of *The Green Helmet*. There was something in what I felt about Deirdre, about Cuchulain, that rejected the Renaissance and its characteristic metres, and this was a principal reason why I created in dance plays the form that varies blank verse with lyric metres. When I speak blank verse and analyse my feelings, I stand at a moment of history when instinct, its traditional songs and dances, its general agreement, is of the past. I have been cast up out of the whale's belly though I still remember the sound and sway that came from beyond its ribs, and, like the Queen in Paul Fort's ballad, I smell of the fish of the sea. The contrapuntal structure of the verse, to employ a term adopted by Robert Bridges, combines the past and present. If I repeat the first line of *Paradise Lost* so as to emphasise its five feet I am among the folk singers—'Of mán's first dísobédience ánd the frúit,' but speak it as I should I cross it with another emphasis, that of passionate prose—'Of mán's fírst disobédience and the frúit,' or 'Of mán's fírst dísobedience and the frúit'; the folk song is still there, but a ghostly voice, an unvariable possibility, an unconscious norm. What moves me and my hearer is a vivid speech that has no laws except that it must not exorcise the ghostly voice. I am awake and asleep, at my moment of revelation, self-possessed in self-surrender; there is no rhyme, no echo of the beaten drum, the dancing foot, that would overset my balance. When I was a boy I wrote a poem upon dancing that had one good line: 'They snatch with their hands at the sleep of the skies.' If I sat down and thought for a year I would discover that but for certain syllabic limitations, a rejection or acceptance of certain elisions, I must wake or sleep.

The Countess Cathleen could speak a blank verse

which I had loosened, almost put out of joint, for her
need, because I thought of her as mediaeval and thereby
connected her with the general European movement.
For Deirdre and Cuchulain and all the other figures of
Irish legend are still in the whale's belly.

IV. WHITHER?

The young English poets reject dream and personal
emotion; they have thought out opinions that join
them to this or that political party; they employ an
intricate psychology, action in character, not as in the
ballads character in action, and all consider that they
have a right to the same close attention that men pay
to the mathematician and the metaphysician. One of
the more distinguished has just explained that man has
hitherto slept but must now awake. They are determined to express the factory, the metropolis, that they
may be modern. Young men teaching school in some
picturesque cathedral town, or settled for life in Capri
or in Sicily, defend their type of metaphor by saying
that it comes naturally to a man who travels to his
work by Tube. I am indebted to a man of this school
who went through my work at my request, crossing
out all conventional metaphors, but they seem to me
to have rejected also those dream associations which
were the whole art of Mallarmé. He had topped a
previous wave. As they express not what the Upanishads call 'that ancient Self' but individual intellect,
they have the right to choose the man in the Tube
because of his objective importance. They attempt to

kill the whale, push the Renaissance higher yet, out-think Leonardo; their verse kills the folk ghost and yet would remain verse. I am joined to the 'Irishry' and I expect a counter-Renaissance. No doubt it is part of the game to push that Renaissance; I make no complaint; I am accustomed to the geometrical arrangement of history in *A Vision*, but I go deeper than 'custom' for my convictions. When I stand upon O'Connell Bridge in the half-light and notice that discordant architecture, all those electric signs, where modern heterogeneity has taken physical form, a vague hatred comes up out of my own dark and I am certain that wherever in Europe there are minds strong enough to lead others the same vague hatred rises; in four or five or in less generations this hatred will have issued in violence and imposed some kind of rule of kindred. I cannot know the nature of that rule, for its opposite fills the light; all I can do to bring it nearer is to intensify my hatred. I am no Nationalist, except in Ireland for passing reasons; State and Nation are the work of intellect, and when you consider what comes before and after them they are, as Victor Hugo said of something or other, not worth the blade of grass God gives for the nest of the linnet.

1937

An Introduction for my Plays

AN INTRODUCTION FOR MY PLAYS [1]

I

THE THEATRE for which these plays were written was the creation of seven people: four players, Sara Allgood, her sister Maire O'Neill, girls in a blind factory who joined a patriotic society; William Fay, Frank Fay, an electric light fitter and an accountant's clerk who got up plays at a coffee-house; three writers, Lady Gregory, John Synge, and I. If we all told the story we would all tell it differently. Somewhere among my printed diaries is a note describing how on the same night my two sisters and their servant dreamt the same dream in three different grotesque forms. Once I was in meditation with three students of the supernormal faculties; our instructor had given us the same theme, what, I have forgotten; one saw a ripe fruit, one an unripe, one a lit torch, one an unlit. Science has never thought about the subject and so has no explanation of those parallel streams that make up a great part of history. When I follow back my stream to its source I find two dominant desires: I wanted to get rid of irrelevant movement—the stage must become still that words might keep all their vividness— and I wanted vivid words. When I saw a London play, I saw actors crossing the stage not because the play compelled them, but because a producer said they must do so to keep the attention of the audience; and I heard

[1] Written for a complete edition of Yeats's works which was never produced.

527

words that had no vividness except what they borrowed from the situation. It seems that I was confirmed in this idea or I found it when I first saw Sarah Bernhardt play in *Phèdre*, and that it was I who converted the players, but I am old, I must have many false memories; perhaps I was Synge's convert. It was certainly a day of triumph when the first act of *The Well of the Saints* held its audience, though the two chief persons sat side by side under a stone cross from start to finish. This rejection of all needless movement first drew the attention of critics. The players still try to preserve it, though audiences accustomed to the cinema expect constant change; perhaps it was most necessary in that first period when the comedies of Lady Gregory, the tragi-comedies of Synge, my own blank-verse plays, made up our repertory, all needing whether in verse or prose an ear attentive to every rhythm.

I hated the existing conventions of the theatre, not because conventions are wrong but because soliloquies and players who must always face the audience and stand far apart when they speak—'dressing the stage' it was called—had been mixed up with too many bad plays to be endurable. Frank Fay agreed, yet he knew the history of all the conventions and sometimes loved them. I would put into his hands a spear instead of a sword because I knew that he would flourish a sword in imitation of an actor in an eighteenth-century engraving. He knew everything, even that Racine at rehearsal made his leading lady speak on musical notes and that Ireland had preserved longer than England the rhythmical utterance of the Shakespearean stage.

An Introduction for my Plays

He was openly, dogmatically, of that school of Talma
which permits an actor, as Gordon Craig has said, to
throw up an arm calling down the thunderbolts of
Heaven, instead of seeming to pick up pins from the
floor. Were he living now and both of us young, I
would ask his help to elaborate new conventions in
writing and representation; for Synge, Lady Gregory,
and I were all instinctively of the school of Talma.
Do not those tragic sentences, 'shivering into seventy
winters,' 'a starved ass braying in the yard,' require
convention as much as a blank-verse line? And there
are scenes in *The Well of the Saints* which seem to me
over-rich in words because the realistic action does
not permit that stilling and slowing which turns the
imagination in upon itself.

II

I wanted all my poetry to be spoken on a stage or
sung and, because I did not understand my own instincts, gave half a dozen wrong or secondary reasons;
but a month ago I understood my reasons. I have spent
my life in clearing out of poetry every phrase written
for the eye, and bringing all back to syntax that is
for ear alone. Let the eye take delight in the form of
the singer and in the panorama of the stage and be content with that. Charles Ricketts once designed for me
a black jester costume for the singer, and both he
and Craig helped with the panorama, but my audience
was for comedy—for Synge, for Lady Gregory, for

O'Casey—not for me. I was content, for I knew that comedy was the modern art.

As I altered my syntax I altered my intellect. Browning said that he could not write a successful play because interested not in character in action but in action in character. I had begun to get rid of everything that is not, whether in lyric or dramatic poetry, in some sense character in action; a pause in the midst of action perhaps, but action always its end and theme. 'Write for the ear,' I thought, so that you may be instantly understood as when actor or folk singer stands before an audience. I delight in active men, taking the same delight in soldier and craftsman; I would have poetry turn its back upon all that modish curiosity, psychology—the poetic theme has always been present. I recall an Indian tale: certain men said to the greatest of the sages, 'Who are your Masters?' And he replied, 'The wind and the harlot, the virgin and the child, the lion and the eagle.'

1937

THE END

530